S

The Satellite Sex:
The Media and Women's Issues
in English Canada, 1966-1971

The Satellite Sex:
The Media and Women's Issues
in English Canada, 1966-1971

Barbara M. Freeman

Wilfrid Laurier University Press

This book has been published with the help of a grant from the Humanities and Social Sciences Federation of Canada, using funds provided by the Social Sciences and Humanities Research Council of Canada. We acknowledge the support of the Canada Council for the Arts for our publishing program. We acknowledge the financial support of the Government of Canada through the Book Publishing Industry Development Program for our publishing activities.

National Library of Canada Cataloguing in Publication Data

Freeman, Barbara M., 1947–

The satellite sex: the media and women's issues in English Canada, 1966–1971

Includes bibliographical references and index.
ISBN 0-88920-370-9

1. Royal Commission on the Status of Women in Canada—Press coverage.
2. Women—Press coverage—Canada—History—20th century. 3. Feminism in mass media. I. Title

PN4914.W58F73 2001   070.4′4930542′0971   C2001-930459-5

© 2001 Wilfrid Laurier University Press
Waterloo, Ontario, Canada   N2L 3C5

Cover design by Leslie Macredie.
Back cover: top and middle photographs by Brian Kent,
The Vancouver Sun, bottom photograph from *The Ottawa Citizen.*

∞

Printed in Canada

To Gabriella

Contents

Illustrations

Preface

$\mathcal{T}$his study is the first book-length discussion about the ways in which the print and broadcast news media have covered women's issues in Canada. It is a feminist cultural studies analysis of an important period in the history of Canadian women, 1966-1971. During this time issues of concern to women across the country were aired before a federal inquiry, the Royal Commission on the Status of Women, which issued its recommendations 30 years ago. Using the media coverage of the concerns women raised at the time, *The Satellite Sex* demonstrates the strengths and weakness of journalism practice, and questions in particular the notion of professional objectivity. It finds that in the Canadian case, the ways in which the media covered women's issues were much more complex than previous, mostly American, studies of the same era have revealed.

Specifically, this book addresses the relationship between the Commission and the media, the reporters' understandings of professional practice, and the ways in which they covered the issues as they came up at the hearings and were discussed in the Commission's *Report*. The issues included cultural understandings of both femininity and feminism; the meaning of equality for women in education, the workforce and public life; new definitions of marital status, "working mothers" and reproductive freedom; and the specific goals and needs of aboriginal women. It also raises questions about the marginalization and loss of strong feminist voices in today's news media.

Acknowledgments

I owe a great deal of thanks to several key people who have guided and supported my efforts, although, of course, as the writer of this book, I acknowledge all responsibility for its contents.

I was fortunate to have one of Canada's most accomplished media historians, Mary Vipond of Concordia University in Montreal, as my principal advisor on the dissertation upon which this book is based. Dr. Vipond unfailingly provided valuable insight and guidance, and her ongoing support over the years is much appreciated. I chose to study at Concordia because she was there, and I was right.

I also owe a great deal to Diana Pedersen and Graham Carr, also of Concordia's History Department, who were very supportive as well. My thanks also to others who have contributed to this work at its various stages, including Mary Kinnear, Professor of History at St. John's College, University of Winnipeg; and, at Concordia, Rosemarie Schade of the History Department, Enn Raudsepp of the Journalism Department, and various fellow members of the Simone de Beauvoir Institute for Women's Studies, especially my good friend Martha Saunders, who opened her home to me while I was in Montreal. Special thanks as well to fellow researcher Jane Arscott of Athabasca University, Alberta, for sharing her ideas on women, citizenship and the Royal Commission on the Status of Women.

Personal interviews with the people involved in the work of the Commission are an important component of this study, as are archival holdings of the media record. For their generous cooperation, I am grateful to the late Florence Bird, to the surviving commissioners and their staff, to the journalists, producers and cartoonists who covered their efforts, and to the family of the late Ed Reid of the CBC. Ernie Dick, the former Chief Archivist of the CBC, made my way through its broadcast records a lot smoother, and I am very grateful to him. My thanks also to the CBC for the use of its news and current affairs programming, including *CBC Matinee* and *Take 30*, and the staff at the CBC Radio and Television Archives in Toronto, the National Archives of Canada, the Public Archives of Nova Scotia, the City of Vancouver Archives, the City of Ottawa Archives, and the Carleton University Library, who were invariably, courteous, professional and helpful.

I wish I could have included all the photographs and editorial cartoons that I came across during the course of my research, but availability and cost limited my choice, although the ones you will see are among the very best. For copyright permissions, I thank the cartoonist Sid Barron, Yardley Jones, Rusins Kaufmanis, Dow Nieuwenhuis, the late Len Norris, James Reidford, Merle Tingley (Ting) and Edd Uluschak, and the families, estates and employers of Robert Chambers, Duncan Macpherson and Ed Reid, as well as Kathryn Keate Hazel, *Chatelaine*, Pacific Press, the *Toronto Star*, and the National Archives of Canada.

I am very grateful to Sandra Woolfrey, formerly of Wilfrid Laurier University Press, for her prompt and encouraging response to the original manuscript and her help with revisions, and to the present director, Brian Henderson, managing editor, Carroll Klein, my copy editor, Maura Brown, and the staff for seeing it through. In Ottawa, Claire Gigantes generously read an earlier version and provided encouraging editorial feedback.

Behind the scenes, there have been several colleagues who have provided me with their ideas, expertise or moral support, which is very much appreciated. They include Carman Cumming, Chris Dornan, Deborah Gorham, Peter Johansen, Michèle Martin, Catherine McKercher, Vincent Mosco, Ross Eaman, Eileen Saunders, Lynne van Luven, Jill Vickers, and the late Wilf Kesterton.

My student research assistants, Janice Hendrick, Rhonda Noyce, Michelle Murphy, Jennifer Tribe, Cameron Kennedy and Mary Zingarelli, transcribed and checked over the interviews, and the students in my "Gender and the Journalist" courses over the years listened to my ideas and made some interesting suggestions of their own.

As always, I am grateful to those good people who compose my personal support system, especially my "study buddy" and good friend, Leona Crabb, who shared many coffees and ideas as we both plowed our way through our respective dissertations. Fellow doctoral candidates Maryann Farkas and the late Keith Lowther were there for me at critical moments.

At home, my long-time companion, Gabriella Goliger, did more than her share of the dishwashing, laundry and dog walking, not to speak of ego propping and chapter editing. As she has also been engaged in writing and publishing her own work, an anthology of short stories, she deserves extra credit for her loving generosity of spirit.

As always, I am grateful to my late parents, Tom and Marie Freeman, and to my sisters and brother, Carole Heffernan, Valerie Miller and Sterry Freeman, for being so proud of my efforts.

Introduction

*L*ately, a spate of revisionist articles and books, both popular and academic, have suggested that the baby boom generation of feminists and their younger acolytes have gone "too far" in their continuing demands for equality. The argument goes something like this: we have won all the major battles and it is time to "Junk the Feminist Slogans: The War's Over." Some of this assessment has come from a few younger journalists who have recently produced critiques of the women's movement. Other writers are more seasoned opponents of feminism. While they are writing from different political perspectives, they are all essentially grappling with the argument that "old-style" feminism is just not working and may even be backfiring.[1]

Just as telling as the critiques from the young, however, has been a creeping backlash against the advances women and minorities have made in the last three decades, which has taken the form of shunning and disdaining anything declared to be "politically correct," an unfortunate term that has the effect of throwing the baby out with the bath water. Generally, these writers tend to blame "radical feminists" of the leftist variety for just about any social ill or perceived government meddling that they oppose.

Terence Corcoran, writing in *The Globe and Mail*, hotly declared that the federal Human Rights Tribunal's pay equity decision of July 1998 which favoured the lowest-paid and mostly female civil servants—a decision based on the legal precept of equal pay for work of equal value—was a "radical feminist monster" steeped in Marxism that could cost the federal government five billion dollars in back pay. What Corcoran omitted in his tirade, which essentially stereotyped feminists, was the fact that it was Canadian women from all walks of life and political persuasions who demanded an end to unequal pay thirty years ago. They had many other grievances, too, including discriminatory labour and marriage laws, inadequate pensions, unfair taxation rules, limited educational and career opportunities, severe restrictions on reproductive freedom, and the absence of government-sponsored childcare. Most of them would never have considered themselves feminists, let alone Marxists. They were acting on the humanist, liberal democratic impulse of the post-World War II years, which, while influenced to some degree by socialist thinking, was essentially capitalist and individualistic in nature. Although many regulations and practices have changed in women's favour since then—often with the help of progressive men—fair remuneration is still an issue for many women, especially when even the federal government prevaricates over enforcing its own laws.[2]

Other injustices close to many women's hearts also remain outstanding, such as the sexual double standard that still emphasizes a woman's physical appearance over her abilities, unequal representation in politics and public life despite the gains women politicians have made,[3] the lack of adequate childcare and governments' unwillingness to provide it, and difficulty obtaining abortions in some cities even though the procedure is now legal.[4] Too many minority women, including aboriginals, still struggle with poverty and the other indignities that are a direct result of racial and sexual discrimination.[5] Lesbians, women who were barely mentioned in polite company 30 years ago, have gained a great deal in basic rights and freedoms since then, but many still feel that it's not safe to come out to their employers and close associates.[6]

Missing from much media commentary on women's issues, aside from a strong dose of reality, is a sense of history that would put the current debates about gender into perspective as the most recent phase of an ongoing grassroots movement for change. This book is my way of trying to set the historical record straight, both as an account of women's attempts to attain equality in Canadian society and as a study of how the English Canadian media covered those issues 30 years ago, using news-gathering techniques that are still common today. It explores how the Canadian news media, print and broadcast, covered women's issues in the late 1960s, using the Royal Commission on the Status of Women as the vehicle that gave these issues concentrated exposure. Using this evidence as a case study,[7] it also challenges the current thinking on the women's movement of that era as well as the journalistic conventions of objectivity, fairness and balance. It questions whether these values really allow reporters to get to the heart of the matter when they cover women's issues.

The Royal Commission and Women's Issues as a Media Case Study

In February 1967, Prime Minister Lester B. Pearson, responding to determined lobbying from women's groups, appointed the Royal Commission on the Status of Women in Canada (RCSW) to listen to complaints and suggestions regarding the systemic legal, economic and social inequities that were making the lives of Canadian women difficult. Pearson named seven commissioners, five women and two men, representing various areas of the country. They were the Chair, Florence Bird, Elsie Gregory MacGill, Jeanne Lapointe, Doris Ogilvie, Lola Lange, Jacques Henripin and John Humphrey, who replaced Donald Gordon, Jr. after he left during the first year. From April to October 1968, the commissioners held hearings across the country, receiving briefs from many women's groups and other organizations, and from individual women and men. The Commission released its *Report* with its recommendations in early December 1970.

As a federal public inquiry conducted in the glare of the media spotlight, it was a watershed for Canadian women, a historical first that allowed issues previously deemed part of the private or domestic sphere to become the focus of intense discussion in the public sphere. This is not to say that all women conducted their lives in the home, as many were working for pay, were involved in politics and public life, and were leading organizations dedicated to improving the lot of women. But social convention superficially separated the sexes into "private" and "public," with men taking the lead roles in world affairs. While theorists examining the intersection of gender issues with public sphere debates today question whether the media really allow full airing of women's concerns,[8] the coverage of the issues brought before the Commission 30 years ago gave women the opportunity to engage in public debate about their seemingly private lives, and helped shaped the political, legal, economic and social changes that would result.

In retrospect, the Chair of the Commission, Florence Bird, remarked that "The Satellite Sex" would have been a good title for its final report, because it illustrated just how profoundly women played a supporting role to men rather than contributing to society as their equals.[9] The actual title, *Report of the Royal Commission on the Status of Women in Canada*, was staid and understated, given the circumstances it described. The *Report's* stylized aqua and blue cover opened to reveal close to 500 pages with 167 recommendations, clearly documenting Canadian women's undeniable concerns about the implications of inequality between the sexes. As the economy continued to expand, and women became better educated, they were chafing at the social mores of the immediate post-war era, which valued safe middle-class domesticity partly as an antidote to the upheavals of the Depression and war. Their everyday activities had fallen well behind their own experiences of what they could achieve, especially now that they could control the size of their families using the birth control pill and other methods. Although more and more married women were either rejoining the workforce or remaining in jobs they had taken during the war, they were still devalued in relation to men in the eyes of the law and the state, and this had a serious impact on their economic status and freedom.[10] Native women had many of the same concerns, but their complaints related mainly to their living conditions, and the real barriers systemic racism presented to their aspirations for freedom, progress, and recognition and respect for their cultural differences from white women.

All this evidence was well documented at the Commission hearings, as indicated in its *Report* and in the existing academic studies about this federal inquiry as representative of liberal feminism and its effects on public policy.[11] While some of these studies declared that media coverage was a positive factor in the Commission's bid for public and political attention, the original analysis behind this contention was both limited and generated by Commission officials themselves; in fact, the extent and subtleties of the media's role have not been examined in any great detail.[12] Since the media are often the main transmitters of information about political, economic and social issues to both our leaders and the public, it is just as important to examine those messages in their historical and cultural context as it is to evaluate other aspects of the political process.

The journalists who covered the Commission saw it mainly as an opportunity to examine and report on women's concerns about the inequalities in Canadian society that had a negative impact on their lives. These issues surfaced as matters of public debate mainly through media coverage that deserves a separate analysis of its own, especially because the Canadian experience was very different from the American one on which so many media studies of this period are based. Essentially, I argue that women and their issues were not "symbolically annihilated" by the media of the day, as one early American study suggested, even though, at the time, most news of interest to women on both sides of the border appeared on the women's pages of the newspaper, in women's magazines, or on daytime radio and television programs specifically targeted at housewives.[13] On the contrary, I have found that in Canada, this segregation of women's interests[14] could work to the advantage of the liberal women's movement, reflecting a pattern of reciprocity between feminists and the media that other scholars note was discernible in the United States at the time.[15] It meant that several journalists became specialists on issues relating to women, that the women they interviewed, rather than men, more often became the quotable authorities or "experts,"[16] and that there was usually some coverage of even the most routine Commission hearing. Yet, this study is not an open and shut demonstration of the success of female advocacy, as editors and journalists could be dismissive and critical of the Commission, of the women who presented briefs, and of feminist leaders. Regardless of their sympathy for underprivileged women, including many native women, the journalists were not above using stereotypes in presenting their problems.

While the gender-segregated environment in which Canadian journalists operated thus allowed progressive, liberal coverage of women's concerns, the reporters' somewhat fluid loyalty to the professional ideals of objectivity, fairness and balance still limited their analysis of the issues, reflecting an unease with radicalism and an overriding concern that female "equality" should be contained within certain acceptable limits. The mainstream news media are not, given their capitalist nature, revolutionary, and feminist messages tend to be eventually subsumed within the status quo.[17] Moreover, because the media generally focus on people and events in the news but are rarely concerned with in-depth analysis of the issues,[18] the day-to-day coverage of the Commission's hearings, and of its final recommendations tended to be superficial. The resulting messages about women and their issues were thus very complex. They were neither as negative nor as positive as various North American studies of the media and the women's movement of that period have suggested. In fact, my research suggests a model recently put forward by Marian Meyers in her discussion of popular media and women in the United States at the turn of the twenty-first century, in which she argues that media coverage of women's issues has progressed since the days of Tuchman's "symbolic annihilation" thesis. She describes today's media representations as "fractured…the images and messages inconsistent and contradictory, torn between traditional, misogynistic notions of women and their roles on the one hand, and feminist ideals of equality for women on the other."[19] Actually, that was how the Canadian media covered women's issues in the 1960s. Certainly, they did not promote radical political solutions to gender inequalities, or for that matter, initiate new ways to report on them.

Feminist Cultural Analysis and Journalism Practice

The challenge for this study was to find a theoretical framework that would help to explain the connections among social attitudes towards gender roles, the specific issues aired before the Commission, and how the media covered them at this particular stage in the political, economic and social history of Canadian women. Given the complexity of the problem, I have applied a feminist cultural analysis, making gender the central component of the study. With the aid of archival records, I examine how the media covered women's issues in a specifically Canadian historical context, using cultural and sociological theories about the production of news, and discourse analysis of the written, spoken and visual language of journalism as it was used in the 1960s, including some photographs and cartoons. More specifically, I have applied this theoretical and methodological approach to a case study—the media coverage of Canadian women's issues as they were debated during an important moment in the evolution of the women's movement, the tenure of the Royal Commission on the Status of Women in Canada.

An interdisciplinary project which attempts to marry media analysis with women's social history presents considerable challenges. Recent review literature written by media historians points out that the relatively modern field of mass communication research tends to be ahistorical, and does not often take gender into account. This is true of the development of theory within the field, and of the research that has evolved from it, as Hanno Hardt and Bonnie Brennan point out.[20] These writers encourage researchers to evaluate the values that historically informed the events and issues under study, including consideration of gender, class, race, and other variables. Rather than the linear, "objective" approach adopted by many American journalism historians, their "cultural materialist" approach "assumes a different understanding of media history...as an expression of a collective process involving various class interests under specific political, economic and cultural circumstances."[21] Sue Curry Jansen further points out that gender shapes much of our experience of the world, and should be a definitive consideration, rather than a variable, for mass communication historians if we are to understand "the multiple and multifaceted ways that gendered patterns of communication and gendered distributions of power are variously constructed and replicated by different social institutions and structures of knowledge."[22]

To date, historians of the Canadian media, operating as they are in a relatively new academic area, have understandably concentrated on the evolution of the early press, and on government regulation and its effects on the development of radio and television, rather than cultural issues,[23] although there are some biographies and other studies available that examine the role gender has played in journalism over the last century.[24] The field of mass communication studies, on the other hand, deals mostly with today's issues and trends, and too few of these studies take gender into account.[25] Those that do, tend to deal with deficiencies in the ways in which the media cover women's issues today, rather than analyze how they did so in the past,[26] although there are some exceptions.[27] Yet, while the workings of the Canadian news media and the ways in which they approached women's issues must be examined in their own historical and cultural context, contemporary media theory and its applications can also be helpful in establishing the links between cultural analysis and journalism practice.

A feminist cultural studies approach allows for both a discussion of the language, methods and rituals of newsgathering in a sex-segregated news environment and an exploration of social attitudes towards Canadian women that were reflected and reinforced by the media of 30 years ago. As Dutch mass communication scholar Liesbet van Zoonen writes:

> An acknowledgement of the historical specificity of current dominant beliefs about women and men opens up new ways of conceptualizing gender, not as universally given, but as socially constructed. The issue, then, is...to analyze how and why particular constructions of masculinity and femininity arise in historical contexts, how and why certain constructions gain dominance over others and how dominant constructions relate to the lived realities of women and men.

She also points out that the medium, format and genre in which a story narrative about women appears have an important bearing on how it is presented: one must distinguish among commercial and public media, print and broadcast, newscasts and soap operas, and take into account the importance of the various media products to their audiences.[28] Van Zoonen has since built on these earlier theories of social construction to present the concept of gender as discourse, which she describes as "a set of overlapping and sometimes contradictory cultural descriptions and prescriptions," with the media being among the sites where these negotiations take place.[29]

The very language that the reporters and their editors used in presenting the perspectives of the women who testified before the Commission had a bearing on how the news stories were published and aired. Here I borrow from Teun A. van Dijk, who also studies the contemporary Dutch media and elaborates on the idea of news as "discourse," one which stems from studies in several disciplines, including linguistics, literary studies, anthropology, cognitive psychology, semiotics and speech communication. Van Dijk's idea of "discourse" embraces not just the language of news and how it is used, but theories that have to do with newsroom procedures, as well as cultural understandings of the issues in the news which are shared by journalists, editors and the public alike. He argues, "a considerable amount of generally shared knowledge, beliefs, norms, and values must be presupposed. Without such taken-for-granted information, the news would not be intelligible."[30] Similarly, I have found that the editors and journalists examined in this study assumed that their audiences would share essentially the same attitudes and beliefs about Canadian women's social roles as they did, and that certain words used in women's testimony to the Commission and transferred to news stories and headlines—words such as "democracy," "equality" and "choice"—resonated with everyone in much the same way.

According to van Dijk, the elements that go into constructing news as discourse also involve what other theorists have identified as newsroom rituals. These rituals include the ways in which events, often second-hand to the journalist, are originally interpreted in news releases, press conferences and other journalists' stories, among other sources; the reporter's assigning of authority and credibility to some "experts" or witnesses and not to others; how the headline, lead or first paragraph, and the rest of the details are structured in a hierarchical, top-down "pyramid" style; assumed reader expectations; and news-gathering routines compromising the quality of the final product.[31]

The work of Ericson, Baranek and Chan, which focuses mainly on how the contemporary Canadian media cover the legal system, is useful when applied to the interplay between sources and journalists; in this case, the Royal Commission and the reporters who covered it.[32] The reporters relied a great deal on news releases, press conferences and summaries of briefs provided by the Commission, while editorial writers, columnists and cartoonists relied on information provided by other journalists in their accounts of the hearings. In their in-person interviews, the reporters were invariably respectful of the commissioners, and chose to quote women whose briefs they covered according to what they thought would strike a chord with the public. The "angles" they chose for these stories were reflected in their leads, or first paragraphs, and picked up by editors who wrote headlines to match. The journalists' task, then, was to present stories about women's concerns according to accepted news values, and in deference to the most immediate constraint reporters have, their deadlines.

The Objectivity Debates

News values are the variables which help journalists decide how a story should be structured, values that are embedded in our culture. In North America, where newspapers supposedly eschew party politics, Canadian and American scholars are particularly critical of one of the most cherished values of journalism practice, namely "objectivity, a tool that ideally helps the journalist ascertain the truth."[33] Schudson has defined the original intent of this ideal as "the separation of facts from values," but its meaning and impact have been hotly debated among media historians, especially in the United States, as well as in the journalism field at large. But these analyses are based on the American experience.[34]

Using both Canadian and American examples, Robert A. Hackett, Yuezhi Zhao and Satu Repo write that "objectivity" as an ideal evolved later in Canada than it did in the United States for various historical, political and commercial reasons. In both countries, there was a strong cultural connection between "objectivity" and Enlightenment ideals of liberal democracy, especially as they were expressed in the labour and commercial presses of late nineteenth-century Canada, which eventually replaced the partisan press built on strong political affiliations. Slowly, the nineteenth-century concept of "objectivity" evolved from a format that allowed for both advocacy and reliance on observable facts, to the "just the facts" model of the World War II years, to the interpretative reporting of the 1960s and beyond, which relied on experts of various kinds, and even the ordinary "man in the street," as sources of information. Still, as the authors note, this model did not allow Canadian reporters and editors, even on the most liberal papers, to challenge the liberal-democratic notion of "objectivity" embraced by the commercial press and to adopt, for example, social democratic views in their everyday reporting.[35]

Whatever its historical origins and political biases, by the late 1960s even American journalism textbooks used on both sides of the US/Canada border acknowledged that true "objectivity" was probably impossible, but it was important to present "fair and balanced" coverage, another related paradigm with a long history, mainly by covering "both" sides of a story.[36] Since a story can have many sides to it, this is a very limited approach which has much to do with the lack of space and time the print and broadcast media give to most events. Still, this general ideal was accepted in newsrooms in both the United States and Canada in the 1960s.[37] Certainly, interpretative "objectivity" was an ideal that was understood by the journalists who covered women's issues at the time of the Royal Commission. Some of them acknowledged in retrospect that it is a slippery concept, but an important goal all the same, designed to provide the public with the context of news stories, in other words, the "truth" of the matter.[38]

Modern scholars are also grappling with the meanings behind journalistic ideals and how they enhance or distort cultural understandings of gender issues. Michèle Martin presents the notion of "objectivity" as male subjectivity in disguise and which actually serves to support the status quo. That is one reason for news editors' resistance to feminist perspectives in news stories. "Moreover, for women, there are ways of looking at reality other than that based on the objectivity/subjectivity dichotomy, for these notions are too narrowly defined to reflect the pluralism of society and the diversity of human experiences adequately."[39] Perhaps this gendered outlook contributed to the difference in attitudes between most of the women and the few men who produced stories and columns about women's concerns in the 1960s. Even today, as van Zoonen points out, there is still a common cultural perception that women journalists, regardless of their professional training, are more engaged and interested than men in human interest and consumer news, social policy and women's issues. The work they produce is regarded as less "objective" than that of male reporters.[40]

Media analysts have argued for years that presumptions of "truth," "objectivity" and "fairness and balance" are essentially undermined by the ways in which news is gathered, produced and distributed, and by an undue emphasis on several crucial elements that make a story newsworthy—elements that are embedded as values in our culture. They include: conflict, often between two oppositional sides in a dispute; unusualness, which introduces a person, an argument or an event appearing to clash with the usual social expectations or norms; timeliness, which suggests a connection with other events or issues happening at the same time; proximity, that is, a geographical or philosophical connection with the audience; an emphasis on elites or hierarchies, that is, prominent men or women who represent expertise or authority, or otherwise pique audience interest; a focus on "personalities" or ordinary people to whom audiences can presumably relate; and a story's relevance or familiarity to editors, journalists and audiences, a familiarity founded in the storytelling conventions of our culture. The more it includes these elements, the "harder" and more saleable the story.[41] This journalistic approach has changed very little over the years, and was the model used by most of the journalists whose work is examined in this study, regardless of the specific women's issue they were covering.

Understanding these newsroom rituals can help us make the connections between the general cultural environment and journalism practice,[42] including the personal perspectives of the reporters concerned, the nature of their beats, and their gender as well.[43] Certainly, there were discernible differences in the ways in which Canadian newspapers, *Chatelaine* magazine, and CBC radio and television covered women's issues during the time of the Royal Commission, differences that can be attributed to the culture, rituals and procedures of each newsgathering unit, and even the personal perspectives of the individuals who worked there, both women and men.

The Visual Record

Another aspect of news discourse in this case is the images the media used in covering the Commission hearings, and in their final analyses of the recommendations. The TV footage from the 1960s, which was black-and-white film rather than colour videotape, and the photographs that appeared in the newspapers and magazines, had much in common in the ways they were used to represent "reality" to the viewer. Stuart Hall writes that a photo is chosen for its immediate news value, but also for the way in which it fits into the political-moral discourse of society and the particular editorial biases of the newspaper concerned,[44] including, by extension, certain biases about how women should behave. In the moving and still images, ideology and photographic style combined to produce visual stereotypes, even when very different issues were being covered. As John Langer comments of TV news film: "A repertoire of visual stereotypes emerges which become self-perpetuating and continuous so that selected and rehearsed symbols from past stories control the pattern for visual representation in subsequent stories."[45] Editorial respect or disdain for any of the principals involved in the Commission's proceedings were mirrored in news photos that were accordingly complimentary or unflattering, while TV footage, especially film shot and edited in montage style, played up feminine stereotypes that contrasted sharply with the serious intent behind the hundreds of briefs Canadian women presented during the hearings.

Similarly, scholars who have examined editorial cartoons emphasize their role as satiric commentary on society's mores, and as a statement of what the artist considers should be its norms. They are thus an important measure of cultural attitudes towards women as expressed in the news media, including myths and stereotypes, and are worthy of some consideration here. Most studies of Canadian editorial cartooning do not explicitly examine gender. Those that do consider it focus on social and labour reform in the nineteenth century, not feminist cultural analysis in the twentieth century. While these studies are valuable and appreciated, it is more useful for my purposes to turn to cultural theories about myth, allegory and gender.[46]

Forty years ago, Roland Barthes argued "myth is a type of speech" which can be transmitted in pictures, including caricatures, as well as in written language. In other words, cartoons can be a kind of language, or discourse. Further, he wrote, myth takes on a distorted significance or "truth" of its own; otherwise it is not effective. It "transforms history into Nature."[47] The clever cartoonist strikes a chord, whether the viewer's reaction is one of laughter or disdain, because he or she is drawing on cultural myths to present a social commentary on a given situation. Often, the "myth" embedded in the cartoon is based on a cultural stereotype, or label.[48]

Barthes writes of the petit bourgeois man who is unable to imagine the Other, in this case, a racial minority person. "If he comes face to face with him, he blinds himself, ignores or denies him, or else transforms him into himself."[49] The response to woman as "Other"[50] is similar, and leads, in the case of cartooning, into sex-role stereotypes which often present any woman who threatens the gender status quo as intellectually, emotionally, physically or sexually "masculine" and, therefore, laughable.

The origins of engendered images in political cartoons can be found in representations of women in antiquity,[51] but one of the most useful allegories that connects the manifestations of womanhood I have encountered in cartoons about women's issues in the 1960s is that of the disorderly or unruly woman, a darker manifestation of the classic, idealized allegory of womanhood. Many of the threatening female figures in western culture are disorderly: older, ugly, bossy and not deferential to men, or alternatively, befuddled, eccentric old ladies who have little power. Sometimes they are young women with intellectual or professional ambitions who, the illustrator suggests, really ought to be devoting themselves to domestic duties.[52]

There is room for a great deal of interpretation about the role of the disorderly woman, however. Indeed, as Natalie Zemon Davis suggested in her classic essay on women in early modern France, "Women on Top," the unruly woman could also be a champion against evil forces, depending on how she was represented and what the issues concerned.[53] Nevertheless, most editorial cartoonists have traditionally depicted women's rights advocates as aggressive buffoons, man-hating blue-stockings[54] and strident suffragettes who dominated wimpy men.[55]

During the Commission's tenure, the cartoonists had a field day, often representing the women who appeared at the hearings as either overbearing bullies or simpering idiots. Very few of the cartoons appeared sympathetic to the women's complaints, yet it is possible to read more than one meaning into their work. This is especially true when they also caricatured male politicians or other leaders who abuse their authority over women. In addition, cartoonists tend to see themselves as the observers and recorders of political or social events and attitudes, much as journalists do, and rarely admit any personal involvement.[56] Still, they often have a way of inserting their own perspectives; for example, Robert W. Chambers drew a caricature of his own head for his "Little Man" character, the ordinary male citizen who so often appeared in his cartoons in *The Chronicle-Herald* of Halifax, Nova Scotia, and other newspapers.[57]

The Media Record and Women's History

While feminist cultural theories of media history and analysis provide an overriding framework for this examination, an understanding of the history of Canadian women is central. Most of this history will be discussed in the context of the following chapters, but there are some points which will be made here, including historian Joan Sangster's argument that it is important to focus on women's experiences as separate from men's where appropriate.[58] Further, as Susan Henry emphasizes, if we want to understand women journalists' roles in publicizing women's issues, we must place media history within the context of women's history as well as within that of communication studies which focus on gender.[59]

The media coverage of women's issues examined in this book is, in a sense, both a record of women's social and cultural history and an aspect of it. In journalistic terms it was primarily a "women's story" because, by and large, men inside and outside the media paid very little attention to what was going on. Although the Commission proceedings were dominated by business, professional and volunteer women's groups and clubs, women from many walks of life, including union leaders, factory workers, farm women, high school and university students, poor women, single mothers, socialist activists, and aboriginal women, presented briefs. Even journalists engaged in a struggle for equality within their own profession personally appeared before the Commission or gave their opinions from the floor.[60] Few men testified at the hearings, were present in the audience, or, with one exception, even covered the Commission on an ongoing basis. Although male journalists did write about the Commission or about some aspects of women's rights on occasion, it was generally their female colleagues who kept tabs on the issues. The women were the real experts, not the men, even though there were ongoing attempts by the Commission and by journalists of both sexes to involve more men in the discussions. In this sense, then, the media coverage of the Royal Commission falls foremost within the context of women's history, and, consequently, I will highlight the "women's" story rather than that of the men.

The broader issues of "gender" also represent an important category of this analysis, however.[61] Simply put, gender history is about power relations in society in a given time period,[62] and the media are among the main transmitters of information about what is allowable behaviour for women. In the case of the Commission, the hearings were the result of female pressure on a gendered political system that was dominated by male politicians and civil servants. The witnesses to that struggle were journalists, who operated within a media culture which was also gendered. That is, male journalists and their views predominated in most newspapers, magazines and broadcast media, and tussled for dominance even within the "women's" programs of the Canadian Broadcasting Corporation (CBC). Only the "female ghettos" of the women's newspaper pages and *Chatelaine* magazine allowed women's voices to dominate. Many female journalists who wanted to be accepted on an "equal" professional basis with their male colleagues were beginning to doubt the value of this segregation. The background context of their media coverage and the Commission itself, then, is part of our "gender" history.

The News Media of the 1960s and the Archival Record

The historical context of media operations during the 1960s is an important factor in this investigation. At that time Canada's 116 daily newspapers were increasingly coming under the control of a few chains. Then, as now, our news stands were dominated by American magazines, which far outnumbered Canadian publications. Most of our radio and television stations were privately owned and a few were still independent, as they were in the US, but here the CBC had a strong presence as a public broadcaster, much more than it does in today's fragmented market. American television programming, which could be tuned in using both over-the-air signals and a new system, cable TV, was popular with Canadians living in the larger urban centres and along the border. In fact, all these factors were issues during the time of the Royal Commission, as its tenure overlapped with that of the Special Senate (Davey) Committee on Mass Media, which the government appointed in 1969 to explore concentration of ownership and journalistic practice, but not inequality between the sexes in the newsroom.[63]

All cultural analysis involving the historical media record rests on archival evidence which, in the case I present here, is extensive. There are about 1,500 newspaper and magazine clippings and a handful of broadcast scripts in the papers of the Royal Commission on the Status of Women in the National Archives, and some media material in other collections as well.[64] Much of the same material can also be found in the copies of the general circulation magazines and daily and weekly newspapers that are available on microfilm at the National Library of Canada.

Although the CBC covered royal commissions as a matter of course, this was the first time the hearings of such a federal inquiry received regular, ongoing broadcast coverage. It is my good fortune that some unknown, prescient soul in the CBC kept almost all the coverage of the Commission produced for the two national women's programs on daily radio and TV, respectively *Matinee* and *Take 30*. These programs are available either in the CBC Broadcast Archives in Toronto or the National Archives of Canada in Ottawa, along with the coverage of the Commission by reporters working for CBC radio news. Unfortunately, there was little radio current affairs coverage, outside of *Matinee*, and few TV news and current affairs programs, outside of *Take 30*. The TV news coverage that survives is mainly in the form of some audio copies of *The National* which, of course, reveal little pictorially, or as brief film clips, with no continuity script. Segments about the Commission from three current affairs TV programs also survived. I decided that this material was inadequate for proper analysis, but I noted that the content of this fragmented material suggests that CBC TV news and current affairs tended to treat the Commission hearings as entertainment more than as a serious inquiry into the status of women. Altogether, I analyzed about 16 hours of radio and TV programming.[65]

Most of the other documentation about the Commission is in its own administrative records, and in the papers of two of its members, Florence Bird and Elsie Gregory MacGill. These collections contain important details about the inner workings of this federal inquiry, including its ongoing public relations campaign directed at the media and the public. There were very detailed minutes of the commissioners' first meetings, which I found in the papers of Commissioner MacGill.[66] Researchers can be grateful to her for keeping these papers, as the commissioners all initially agreed to destroy them.[67] Those minutes became less revealing as time went on, however, so it was very difficult to reconstruct exactly what happened at each meeting, especially when the commissioners began to discuss their recommendations after the hearings were over and closed their deliberations to the media. It was much easier to follow what went on at the actual hearings, because the Commission had them recorded on audio tape, rather than prepare transcripts, and researcher copies of those tapes are now available at the National Archives as well. These tapes were very useful for checking the media coverage against what the delegations presenting briefs to the Commission actually said.[68]

For this project I relied not only on the articles about the Commission and its own documents and audio tapes, but on my own interviews with the surviving commissioners and the media workers involved, both women and men. As Linda Steiner has argued, autobiography, when placed in the context of newsgathering practices, can be a useful tool in understanding how stories are covered in gendered spaces such as newsrooms.[69] The National Archives also holds the records of the Canadian Women's Press Club, which I found useful for my discussion of gender relations between men and women in the journalism profession, and issues such as equal pay and sex-segregated press clubs.[70]

While I tried to analyze several aspects of the media coverage of Canadian women's issues in the late 1960s and early 1970s, this study is limited in two ways. It focuses on English Canada because the impetus for a royal commission came primarily from anglophone women, and because the history of women's issues in Quebec, which is so centred on their national identity, deserves a full and separate media study of its own, as do those of Acadiennes and other francophone women in Canada. Moreover, relatively little of the francophone print coverage was original but consisted of direct translations of Canadian Press stories.[71]

The question of how the Canadian public responded to the media coverage of women's issues cannot be adequately answered here either. While contemporary analysts emphasize the importance of reader and audience response to media coverage,[72] the impact of media content on an audience and how it might influence subsequent news stories is still contentious theoretically, partly because it is difficult to measure in contemporary terms without a controlled study. It is virtually impossible to do this in historical context, especially in light of the less than adequate measuring procedures available at the time.[73] To my knowledge, there were no questions about the impact of media coverage in public opinion polls on women's issues in the 1960s.[74]

Nevertheless, I have included here some letters to the editor, comments from formal and informal media surveys and feedback from radio listeners to give an indication of what the public was thinking about women's issues. I do so with reservations. Letters from readers, survey comments and audio tapes of broadcast call-in shows, while they can provide some evidence of audience attitude and interpretation, are subject to a great deal of "gate-keeping" from editors and are not a reliable measure, especially when social activists and their opponents organize letter or phone-in campaigns to get their messages across.[75] Gate-keeping is the practice of editors or radio production assistants randomly picking and choosing material for publication or broadcast, including comments from readers, listeners and viewers. Ericson et al. note that letters to the editor undergo the same process of news evaluation as other copy and that those from "authorized knowers," that is, sources already known to the editors, tend to get the most space.[76] We do know that the media coverage inspired a group of white women from Rosemere, Quebec, and a native woman from a reserve outside of Regina, to present briefs to the Commission, because they said so on television during the hearings.[77] We also know that, initially at least, the media's coverage of women's issues in this particular venue appeared to have little impact on the Liberal government of the day when it came to dealing with the Commission's recommendations.[78]

Overview of *The Satellite Sex*

Taking media theory and historical context into account, as well as extensive archival evidence, this book attempts to show how the Canadian news media covered the issues brought before an important federal inquiry into the status of women, and what academic researchers and journalists can learn from that experience as one significant women's rights century ends, and we march, more or less bravely, into the next. Chapter 1 discusses the systemic inequities Canadian women were living under in the 1960s, how the federal inquiry came about, and the Commission's media strategy, which was an important element of its mandate and influenced the news coverage of women's concerns to a significant degree. The second chapter focuses on the journalists, mainly women, who made women's issues their priority during this time. These reporters were struggling to make inroads into their own profession and so this particular federal inquiry touched a chord with many of them, as it did, for different reasons, with their male colleagues. It includes a discussion of the working lives of several of the key journalists, how they regarded the issue of "objectivity" and other norms, especially in relation to women's issues, and explores contemporary tensions between men and women in the field. The historical tradition of separate media for both sexes was just then coming under attack from both inside and outside the profession, which also had a bearing on the coverage of the Commission in particular and women's issues in general.

The subsequent chapters highlight the specific conditions under which Canadian women lived, as presented in the complaints they brought to the inquiry, the ways in which these news stories were played, and the feminist discourse the media used, or avoided, in presenting them. These themes concern images of women, particularly the perceived tensions between femininity and feminism; what the word "equal" meant, especially in the context of education, paid work and political life; traditional and new perceptions of "marital status"; the debates about "working mothers"; the various slogans used in discussions about reproductive rights, such as "abortion on demand"; and the media's treatment of "equality" and "difference" issues as they surfaced in the testimony from aboriginal women. The final chapter will deal with the ways in which the media constructed women's issues in relation to both the Commission's *Report*, which was tabled two years after the hearings ended, and to the women's liberation groups that gained momentum during that period.

As this study will show, there were good reasons why women went to battle for their rights in the 1960s. Most of them considered themselves not "feminists," but ordinary people who wanted to make life better for themselves and other women. Though certainly not "radicals," they were often labelled as such simply for daring to speak out. The few who did regard themselves as radicals and/or feminists said so bravely and proudly.

There is no denying that Canadian women have made much progress in the last three decades, but that does not mean that nothing else needs to be done, or that all the issues have been resolved. Since then, our economic and political system has changed. The governments of today are far more right-wing and corporate-minded than they were in the 1960s, and so are most of the media,[79] a situation that progressive women and men experience as a "backlash."[80] Yet the level of conservative resistance, even three decades ago, among some of the powerful male editorial writers, columnists and cartoonists raises questions about the media's complicity in making sure that if women were to get ahead, it would not be by much. Today's anti-political correctness rhetoric is just another spin on the bombast Mackenzie Porter and Dennis Braithwaite, among others, produced in the 1960s.

It seems naive to suggest, as liberal feminists once believed, that an increase in the number of women in the newsroom would necessarily translate into better coverage of women and their issues.[81] Today, the numbers of women journalists are frozen at 28 percent in print and 37 percent in television, a rough average of one woman to every two men, which is the reverse of the gender proportions in most journalism schools. While the same study has found that female journalists tend to be more socially conscious than their male colleagues, relatively few of those women are in senior positions.[82]

The "women's movement" was, and still is, a grassroots struggle, regardless of the conservative media's present attempts to demonize "feminists." Perhaps a look back at what women went through in the 1960s will help Canadians of all generations reclaim our courage and relive the pride we felt at the significant changes women accomplished, whether we choose to call ourselves feminists or not. Maybe it will prompt my media and academic colleagues, younger and older, to reassess their own professional attitudes towards social movements in general, and women's issues in particular. This is also a book for my students, women and men both, so that they will understand media coverage of gender issues in the past and so do a thoughtful and clear-headed job of analyzing them in the future.

Chapter 1

"Democracy," "Equal Opportunities" and "Merit": Selling Women's Issues to the Media

We may be able, not only to give women equal opportunity in every aspect of life, which is what the government has asked us to do, but maybe help to create a society in which people will be judged on MERIT, not by the colour of their skin, or their religion or their sex.

—Florence Bird, on CBC TV's *Take 30.*

*W*ith these words, Florence Bird summed up the reasons for having a federal inquiry into the status of women, a message she, as its Chair, worked hard to get out to the media and the public. The setting for this television interview, the garden room of the decidedly upscale Empress Hotel in Victoria, BC, was, ironically, not exactly a gathering place for "ordinary" women. Nevertheless, Bird and her colleagues on the Royal Commission decided, in the spirit of the time, that they must emphasize women's concerns as matters of liberal "democracy," "equal opportunities" and "merit."[1]

As Ericson et al. have pointed out, "news discourse" often involves the continued and repetitive use of "signs" or words, such as

Notes to Chapter 1 are on pp. 255–61.

19

"democracy," which invoke an easily understood rationale for the stance of official bodies. In this case, it could suggest the Commission's open-mindedness and fairness in the minds of reporters and the public.[2] But first we must look at the context of this federal public inquiry, and its attempts to control the media's coverage of its own mandate, of women's issues as they were discussed at the hearings, and of the Commission's subsequent *Report*.

Canadian Women, the Public Sphere and the 1960s

The Royal Commission on the Status of Women in Canada (RCSW) allowed Canadian women to publicly raise issues that they were concerned about, issues that were commonly considered to belong to the domestic or private side of life. In recent years, feminist theorists in the fields of political philosophy and communications, among others, have been questioning theoretical and cultural understandings of the "public sphere" in the democratic context. Briefly, they argue that, historically, it was more than an environment which allowed educated, propertied, bourgeois male citizens to engage in open debate, in speech and in print, about civic and other issues during the eighteenth century, while the women stayed away. There were oppositional publics, such as women and other disenfranchised groups, who also had an impact on the body politic, and still do.[3] As a Canadian communications theorist, Barbara L. Marshall points out, a feminist public sphere serves a dual function: "internally, it seeks to confirm the specificity of and create solidarity among women, and externally, it seeks to disseminate feminist redefinitions of society, press claims on behalf of women, and challenge existing authority structures. That is, it is committed to both solidarity and plurality."[4]

The hearings of the Royal Commission in late 1960s Canada represented a women's public sphere that could be broadly interpreted as feminist in the liberal sense, given its mandate of investigating equal opportunities for women. Moreover, just as Marshall argues that Canada's English radical feminist print media reflected an oppositional, public sphere for women from about 1972 onwards,[5] I suggest that the mainstream media coverage of women's issues during the Royal Commission a few years earlier was a manifestation of a mainly liberal feminist public sphere. Most of the news stories appeared in media that were sex-segregated at the time—the women's pages, a woman's magazine, and on the CBC "women's programming"—and relayed to the public the previously "private" concerns of Canada's female citizens, and their desire that our democratic political system be changed to accommodate their needs. While this coverage was limited to voices that were mainly white and middle-class, it still represented a public discussion of women's concerns that was considered revolutionary at the time.

The economic, political and social climate of Canada in the 1960s had lent itself to such an investigation into women's lives. Business investments and exports were growing, and the Liberal government of Lester B. Pearson, believing that spending money would strengthen the economy, freely distributed loans and grants for rural development, national health programs, Canada and Quebec pension plans, mothers' allowances, and a number of federal inquiries on housing, poverty and other social issues. In addition, Pearson's last years in Parliament were marked by events that were designed to promote pride of citizenship among all Canadians: the adoption of a new national flag and the hosting of the World Exposition, Expo '67, in Montreal.[6] The Royal Commission on the Status of Women was, purportedly, another exercise to ensure that Canada was a democratic country for all its citizens, but was also a minority government's response to pressure brought on it by experienced women's groups utilizing an impeccable sense of political timing.

What had been a Cold War obsession with conservative "democracy" as the only bulwark against communism, especially in the United States, had shifted during the '60s to more liberal concerns about the dispossessed within western society, especially as economic times improved after the war.[7] As political economist Sue Findlay has pointed out, there was an essential contradiction between affluence on the one hand and powerlessness on the other which made liberal democratic states vulnerable to the demands of the various "rights" movements of the time.[8]

In Canada, the main issue of contention was the split between English Canada and Quebec over the meaning of nationalism which, with the birth of the radical separatist group, the Front de Libération du Québec (FLQ), was to become more violent.[9] There was also a movement toward a pro-Canada nationalism, on the right and the left, and a resistance to what was seen as increasing American power over Canadian political and cultural life,[10] including its media,[11] which lasted well into the next decade. Nevertheless, students influenced by their peers south of the border protested against Canadian support of America's involvement in Vietnam,[12] demanded an end to racial injustice, and fought for more autonomy on their own campuses. Many adopted Marxist approaches to challenging the ideological status quo.[13] Other groups, including the aboriginal peoples, also began demanding recognition.[14]

Another trend in Canada and elsewhere was the perception that women's power was growing, a perception based partly on the impact they had already made as members of an expanding labour force and partly on the feeling that there was already a "sex war" going on in society as middle-class women chafed at restrictive laws that curtailed their private and public activities. After World War II, women had been encouraged to remain at home, but as the economy expanded, they were attracted into the paid labour force.[15] In 1961, about one-third of the labour force was female. By 1971, that figure had risen to almost 40 percent, or about three million women, half of whom were married. Most of them were employed in the growing services industries. What women did at work did not change all that much from the early post-war years, however; they still tended to be clustered in administration and support services partly because some of the old restrictions against their full involvement in the labour force had not been lifted.[16] Even though more women than ever before were receiving a college education, most of them were still trained to expect that once they were married and had children, they would not be going out to work or pursuing independent careers.[17]

At the same time, there was a "sexual revolution" going on through challenges to the restrictive mores of the 1950s, most obviously a growing acceptance of sex outside of marriage. The Pearson government updated laws that limited individual rights in areas which, after the advent of the birth control pill, were increasingly accepted as matters of conscience and personal sexual freedom. Parliament removed some of the severe restrictions on access to birth control, abortion and divorce, issues which fundamentally affected women's lives. Most of the discussion was not about whether there should be more freedom, but how much, and the new laws still curtailed women's choices quite a bit.[18]

Considering their circumstances, it was not surprising that Betty Friedan's groundbreaking book, *The Feminine Mystique,* touched a nerve with those women in North America who found life in the home, particularly the suburbs, isolating, lonely and boring, especially after their children were in school all day. Friedan pointed her finger at, among other institutions, the media, particularly women's magazines, for upholding domesticated ideals of women's function in society. White women who were college educated seemed particularly taken by her message: that they were unhappy because they had been letting their best skills and talents go to waste in the name of outdated gender expectations that placed motherhood above all else.[19]

Daughters witnessed their mothers' unhappiness and became angry when they realized that there were still few options for women who wanted to go beyond the goals to which the older generation had aspired.[20] Friedan's book added ammunition to Simone de Beauvoir's *The Second Sex,* written a decade before, in which de Beauvoir had emphasized that women must be economically independent to have power and influence.[21]

In Canada, discontent with women's lot was primarily focused within the women's clubs and organizations that had been founded over 50 years earlier. As historian Terry Crowley has pointed out,

Canadian feminist leaders were equating women's rights with human rights as early as the 1890s, but even then, "there was an irreconcilable contradiction between those who aspired to gender equality and those who believed in the need for gender-specific laws to account for sexual differences."[22] Older English Canadian feminists held strong cultural memories of the legal battles that had been won for women's rights in this country, specifically the vote for women outside Quebec during World War I and the subsequent "Persons case" in which five feminists successfully proved that women were legally "persons" eligible to sit in the Senate. Middle-aged and older women remembered the new volunteer and paid job opportunities they had enjoyed during World War II which, although limited in many respects, expanded their perceptions of their own abilities. Ever since the end of the war, groups such as the Business and Professional Women had fought for more rights for women and had won modest victories along the way, including limited equal pay laws in the federal sphere and in several provinces. During the 1960s, women's activism still belonged, by and large, to these mainstream, older women's organizations.[23] Although there were concerns that their numbers were dwindling and that younger women were not interested in joining, they still formed a strong constituency of varying political hues.[24] Aside from the Federation of Business and Professional Women, they included the National Council of Women of Canada and its local groups, as well as the Women's Institutes, the Canadian Federation of University Women, and similar organizations with particular constituencies, such as teachers, nurses and social workers. There were also groups which were not so easily identified as feminist, such as the women's auxiliaries of the main political parties, church organizations and men's service groups, including the Liberal Women, the Catholic Women's League and the Jaycettes.[25] There were other groups with a particular focus, like the Elizabeth Fry Society, whose members worked with women in prison, and the Voice of Women (VoW), which started in 1961 as a mothers' protest group against nuclear testing and had evolved into an activist peace group by the end of the decade.[26] Many women, most of them housewives, were involved in the consumer boycotts of the late 1960s. Some observers considered the boycotts to be another manifestation of the growing impetus towards protests of all kinds.[27]

Other women were involved with left-wing political parties and groups. These women would eventually break off from the so-called New Left groups dominated by men to form their own organizations, modelled after American ones such as the Women's Liberation Movement. In 1967, the transition in leadership between women's club feminism and radical feminism had barely begun in Canada, however, and was not taken much into account by the Royal Commission on the

Status of Women, even after the younger movement began gaining momentum.[28]

In order to persuade the federal government that Canada needed such an inquiry, the leaders of the established women's groups had to marshall their arguments. They pointed to the similar experiences of women in other countries, particularly the United States. In 1961, President John F. Kennedy had appointed a commission to look into the status of women, even though it was an essentially conservative body, set up to counter political pressure for an Equal Rights Amendment, and dealt mainly with women in the workforce. The report of the Commission, *American Women*, nevertheless added to the mounting evidence that women were not treated equally and that their talents were being wasted. When liberal American feminists became unhappy with the slow pace of change they formed the National Organization of Women (NOW) to pressure the federal and state governments on women's equality rights. Later, federal legislation outlawing racial discrimination was amended to include protection for women as well. By 1968, more radical women who had been involved in civil rights and left-wing campus groups challenged the sexism of their male leaders and broke away to fight for women's rights on their own.[29]

While it is apparent that Canadian feminist leaders of all stripes were influenced by events in the United States, there were many differences between them and their American counterparts. Political scientist Jill Vickers writes that English-Canadian feminists operated in a context she calls "radical liberalism." They were more tolerant of diversity in the ranks than American feminists were at the same stage, encouraged dialogue and, unlike the Americans, were firm believers in the advantages the welfare state held for women.[30] From their perspective, it was only common sense to ask for a federal inquiry into their status, their only reservation being the possibility that once it was over, its report might be "pigeon-holed and forgotten" as had been similar suggestions from the women's subcommittee on post-war reconstruction 25 years previously.[31]

The United Nations (UN), greatly under the influence of the United States at the time, was in 1967 preparing to enact the Declaration on the Elimination of Discrimination against Women, which was passed unanimously by the General Assembly on November 7 of that year. The following year, 1968, was to be the UN's International Year of Human Rights. The Canadian government had already appointed several Royal Commissions and other inquiries through the 1960s, a practice which helped it decide on its policies but was not without its critics, especially as the bills mounted. They included the Carter Commission on Taxation, appointed by Conservative Prime Minister John Diefenbaker in 1962, and the Royal

Commission on Bilingualism and Biculturalism, appointed by Pearson in 1963.[32]

Canadian Women Lobby for a Public Inquiry

These factors, and the election that the Liberal minority government was facing in 1968, added up to a climate in which women's demands for equality were likely to be heard, given a concerted and well-timed push from women's groups. This occurred in 1966, when Laura Sabia, the head of the Canadian Federation of University Women, decided that they had better work together if they wanted anything done. She formed the Committee for the Equality of Women in Canada (CEWC), an umbrella organization of 32 anglophone women's groups which had the backing of the Quebec Federation of Women.

The minutes of the CEWC meetings, and some of the media coverage, make it clear that the members adopted the rhetoric of the United Nations in asking for a federal inquiry as a matter of women's human rights. Sabia told the women at their first meeting that Canada was ignoring existing international conventions on equality for women, such as the UN Universal Declaration of Human Rights and the Convention on the Political Rights of Women, which came from the UN's Commission on the Status of Women, established in 1946. "We should go to the government and demand action now. Why? Because 1968 is the United Nations Year of Human Rights and women's rights are part of human rights."[33]

Since a minority government was in power, Sabia and her colleagues saw the advantage of pressing their point. Canadian Press quoted her as saying, "If we can say we represent 50 percent of the population—oh, those votes."[34] Even though the women were aware that many of their demands had to do with provincial jurisdiction, they also knew that the Commission on Bilingualism and Biculturalism had crossed federal/provincial lines, and a federal Royal Commission had several advantages. These advantages included adequate government funding, the ability to hire experts to conduct studies, the duty to make recommendations, and the expected media coverage.[35] The Quebec Federation of Women and Liberal Party women would later demand additional inquiries be held at the provincial level.[36] The CEWC also let the prime minister know they had found it particularly ironic that the Canadian government was planning a high-profile conference to mark the UN's International Year of Human Rights in 1968, but not one woman had been appointed to the planning committee. They considered holding their own conference.[37]

In November 1966, the CEWC committee, with over 70 women attending in support, presented its brief to the federal government. The brief emphasized the need for Canada to recognize, among other factors, "the equality of men and women as persons" and the need to reform laws and employment practices "to ensure their [women's] equality of opportunity" and allow women "full participation" in Canadian life. It hoped that such a commission would report in time for the UN's International Year of Human Rights.[38]

> *. . . pinch of patience,*
> *root of reason, leg of leaven,*
> *tongue of dove.*

Figure 1.1. Reidford, *The Globe and Mail*, 10 Jan. 1967. Courtesy of James Reidford and *The Globe and Mail*.

When the government did not respond immediately, Laura Sabia impulsively told a reporter that the two million women represented by the member groups of the CEWC would plan marches on Ottawa, "and if we have to use violence, damn it, we will." It was a threat that the media misinterpreted to mean that she would organize one large march of that many furious women on Parliament Hill, a threat that was highly unlikely, even logistically, but had a certain credence in an era of boycotts, protests and demonstrations.[39] Pearson was also being pressured by the only woman in the federal Cabinet, and one of the few in the House of Commons, Secretary of State Judy LaMarsh. Cartoonist James Reidford of *The Globe and Mail* depicted LaMarsh trying to exert a calming influence on a group of strident women's rights activists creating a feminist potion in a witches' cauldron[40] (see fig. 1.1). In the end, they got their federal inquiry, a story that also made the front pages of several newspapers and the CBC network news.[41] A combination of the right political and economic climate, "determination and thoroughness"[42] on the part of feminist leaders, LaMarsh's influence, and a little media excitement had worked wonders.

The Royal Commission, Its Mandate and the Media

The Prime Minister appointed Florence Bird, as the first female chair of a royal commission in Canadian history. She was an American-born liberal democrat from an upper-class Philadelphia family and was well known in Canada as "Anne Francis," a veteran journalist and broadcaster with expertise in Canadian politics, international affairs and women's issues. Like many women of her generation, her early career stemmed from her volunteer work during World War II, when she had been press relations officer for the Winnipeg Voluntary Bureau. She had also acted as radio and television chair of the National Council of Women, and chair of both the Winnipeg and Ottawa branches of the Canadian Institute for International Affairs. For 15 years before her appointment to the Commission, she had written a weekly newsletter on the status of women in Canada for the International Service of the CBC. Bird not only had strong connections to the media, she had demonstrated through her work a strong sympathy with UN principles and women's issues. At the time of her appointment to the Commission, she saw herself essentially as a humanist, and approached the equality of women and men within that framework.[43]

As the Chair, Bird had to reconcile her own liberal democratic principles about press freedom and women's rights with her duty, as she saw it, to protect this sensitive government inquiry from negative publicity. Although a journalist by profession, in her new position she was answerable to the Prime Minister, who was also a personal friend, and had to rely on the advice of senior politicians and civil servants who had overseen other federal inquiries. She recognized that reporters' intrusions into the everyday workings of the Commission staff, and especially the private deliberations of the commissioners, could wreak havoc. At the same time, she was experienced enough to know that she needed the media on her side.[44]

Consequently, as archival evidence reveals, she and the media battled to control the news about the Commission. In other words, the commissioners, and especially Bird, took the UN's human rights model and translated it into media strategy. This was particularly evident after John Humphrey replaced Donald Gordon, Jr., who resigned. Humphrey was a law professor from McGill University in Montreal who had served as the Director of the Human Rights Commission at the UN and had helped draft its Universal Declaration of Human Rights. His appointment just before the hearings began strengthened the philosophical connections between the Commission and the UN.[45]

Given that the western media has always prided itself as essential to the maintenance of a free and democratic society,[46] the Commission's message should have been an easy sell. But that was not always the case. The Commission and reporters engaged in what mass communication scholars Ericson et al. refer to as "an eternal dance of secrecy and revelation"; that is, the common struggle for information control between official sources and journalists. These authors argue that official bodies are usually "more concerned about news that is influential and helpful than about news that is impartial, accurate and balanced. Objectivity is less an issue than political objectives."[47]

Several instances of potential or real confusion had a bearing on how the Commission carried out its business and how journalists reported on it. One was the Commission's terms of reference. According to Canadian Press, the Prime Minister's Office had initially announced that it would be asked to recommend the steps the federal government should take *"to ensure their (women's) equality with men in all aspects of Canadian society."* According to the Commission records, it would be asked to recommend the steps the federal government should take *"to ensure for women equal opportunities with men in all aspects of Canadian society."* "Equal opportunities with men" is very different from "equality with men," and is in line with liberal thinking which equated "equality" with sameness.[48] As political philosopher Jane Arscott has pointed out, the new nomenclature was a departure from the original understanding of the CEWC, which envisioned full participation, or citizenship, for Canadian women in all areas of life. Arscott writes that the RCSW's "equal opportunities" approach "implicitly adopts a sameness standard of treatment and makes male norms the preferred standard of achievement."[49] It was, in essence, a liberal feminist argument, which, as philosopher

Lorraine Code explains, "leaves (narrowly defined) masculine values intact and does not address the systemic injustices fostered by the patriarchal relations that sustain women's sexual and economic dependence." Liberalism equated "equality" with sameness; "difference" between women and men, including biological differences, or differences among women, such as racial background, was something that liberal thinkers regarded simply as individualism which must be respected. It was cause for neither "special treatment" nor celebration. It was simply assumed that the conditions under which women operated were essentially the same as those for men, and all they needed were "equal opportunities" to succeed as men did. More critical views of relations between the sexes came from socialist feminists, who blamed capitalism, and later, from radical feminists, who blamed "patriarchy" or a gendered social system in which men were often privileged over women.[50]

The members of the Commission formalized their new approach with a vote, possibly because *equality* was too broad and contentious and had already attracted strong criticism in the media. An earlier Commission news release had referred to the terms of reference as "a list of the things we have been asked to do to make sure that women have full equality in our country." On her copy Commissioner Elsie Gregory MacGill had scrawled a comment to the effect that Commissioner Donald Gordon, Jr., had suggested that this wording was used "to savage us." The minutes of their meeting note that he suggested that the term "equal opportunities" be used henceforth in all official documents.[51]

The Media and Criticism of the Commission

The initial media response to the appointment of the Commission was more negative than positive. There were a number of complaints that the Commission was not only opportunistic, it was going to be a waste of taxpayers' money. These points were underlined either directly through editorials and columns, or indirectly, via coverage of comments made by high-profile women and men who opposed having another federal inquiry, or were concerned about the cost.[52] Ordinary citizens became involved in the media discourse as well, through newspaper surveys and letters to the editor. *The Ottawa Journal* declared that 70 percent of the men and women its reporter spoke to reacted negatively to the news that there would be a federal inquiry into the status of women. It extrapolated that result to general disapproval, declaring "Most in Ottawa Think Probe Will Accomplish Little." Since the newspaper never said exactly how many people it polled in what appeared to be a street survey, the headline could well have been misleading.[53] Other people who did not really welcome an inquiry into women's status wrote cranky letters to newspaper editors saying that they thought the Commission was a waste of money and time. M.M. Brown of Burlington, Ontario, wrote to the Toronto *Telegram*, "I'm sick and tired of these women telling other women how they should live. Nothing fazes them. Why should it? Travelling the country at my expense must sure be nice....I would blush to take such money."[54] But there were others who appreciated what the Commission was trying to achieve. Using a pen name, "United Standard" told the Dundas, Ontario, *Star*'s readers that it would not do for women to be too complacent, because when they encounter problems, they "will be glad that the Commission is working to help them as in union there is strength for women to have the status they have worked so hard to attain."[55] Even the media coverage of the Commission story garnered public response in newspapers large and small. One reader scolded *The Ottawa Journal* on its sneering editorial about the Commission, while a traditionalist challenged a column in the *Uxbridge Times Journal*, Ontario, for suggesting that changes were needed in the status of homemakers.[56]

The debates in the media continued through the Commission's tenure and were often linked to the delays and expense dogging the Royal Commission on Bilingualism and Biculturalism.[57] In March 1970, when it was revealed that the women's commission was still not ready to submit its *Report*, the criticism was renewed. The argument that the RCSW had been in business a shorter time and was expected to cost 1.7 million dollars compared with nine million seemed to make no difference to its detractors. Nor did the fact that half of Canada's population—the women—were being denied the same citizenship rights as the men, and were still not welcome in many all-male bastions.[58] A rare cartoon in support of the Commission was rendered by Len Norris of *The Vancouver Sun*, who depicted one of the upper-crust, elderly denizens of the opulent but outmoded Anathema Club grumbling over the inquiry. "I trust the membership committee is keeping a wary eye on this tomfoolery"[59] (see fig. 1.2).

The media also carried criticism from various interest groups, including organized labour, that the Commission was not truly representative of the Canadian people. It was not unusual for commissions of inquiry to be dominated by well-educated, middle- or upper-class professionals and academics as members, researchers and consultants; moreover, the makeup of this and other commissions gives credence to the observations of sociologists who commented on the strong connections between the government and business and media "elites."[60] Donald Gordon, Jr., for example, was a former journalist and broadcaster and, at the time of his appointment to the Commission, a university professor. He is the son of Donald Gordon, a prominent Liberal and a family friend of the Prime Minister.[61]

The traditional practice was to try to involve groups not directly represented on the Commission as advisors, or as writers of briefs, but it didn't always work out that way. For example, the Canadian Labour Congress complained to the media that there was no qualified female trade unionist among the commissioners to provide "a much needed balance."[62] During its tenure, the Commission would also be criticized for not having poor people or anyone under 30 among its members.[63] It was rarely mentioned that Commissioner Elsie MacGill, a survivor of polio, used two canes, and that Humphrey had lost an arm, as disability was not considered a category for official representation at that time.[64]

Figure 1.2. "I trust the membership committee is keeping a wary eye on this tomfoolery." Norris, *The Vancouver Sun*, 26 Feb. 1969. Courtesy of Len Norris. National Archives of Canada C-107230.

Underlying much of the sniping at the Commission was the fact that official concern about women's issues was considered laughable in many quarters, so a great deal was riding on its public image as a women's inquiry dominated by female commissioners. This problem greatly concerned Florence Bird. Although she was generally respected by her media colleagues, this did not protect her from some criticism and ridicule. At 59, the tall, white-haired and well-bred Bird, with her well-modulated Bryn Mawr accent and a sharp intelligence, was an imposing figure. Her position as a member of the country's elite, and her status as a career woman with no children of her own was played up in one cartoon. It depicted Bird as "Anne Francis," clipboard in hand, leaning out of a helicopter meant to represent the Commission. She hovered above a woman, who was weighed down by her five children but nonetheless was running pell-mell down the road after a man with a briefcase. The caption had Bird asking her, in interview style: "Madam, in the long race down the Road Through Life do you feel that you are competing on an equal footing with men?"[65]

Figure 1.3. "Madam, in the long race down the Road Through Life do you feel that you are competing on an equal footing with Men?" Chambers, *The Windsor Star,* 14 Feb. 1967. Courtesy of Mrs. Anita Chambers. Public Archives of Nova Scotia.

The message was that Bird was a career journalist, not your typical wife and mother, and might not be able to understand the real pressures most women were under.

Bird later recalled being "terribly depressed" and "horrified" by the negative media coverage that greeted the establishment of the Commission and her own appointment, but she felt that as Chair she had to keep up the morale of the other commissioners and the staff, especially in the first few months. She initially took control of the Commission's public relations campaign, and, with the executive secretary and the press officers, was the only one allowed to answer media queries.[66] Aside from news releases and other strategies aimed at journalists, there were other methods of getting public attention. One of the priorities of the Commission was to reach Canadian women in every way possible to get them to write letters or submit briefs. The

Commission distributed brochures to supermarkets, libraries and women's groups, put ads in the newspapers, sponsored several surveys and in various ways tried to target women from all walks of life.[67] The complaints they received in return covered several areas including media images of women; equality in education, at work and within their marriages; reproductive rights; the problems of working mothers; and issues affecting aboriginal women. Even from these initial responses, it was quite evident that Canadian women had a long way to go before achieving equality with men.[68]

The Commission's Media Strategy

Despite Bird's best efforts, the Commission ran into image problems at various times during its tenure. They stemmed from tensions among the commissioners and staff, some of which led to more expense and delays in getting the *Report* published. Barred from the commissioners' private deliberations, reporters only found out the half of it, but it was enough to cause Bird and her staff some uneasy moments. They quickly did as much damage control as they could, including trying to screen out the media and otherwise influence their coverage. Another major task was to make sure nothing untoward happened at the hearings that might reflect badly on the Commission, which, after all, was both representative of the federal government and could validate women's concerns.

Initially, all journalists were regarded as a necessary evil. Unattributed notes from the commissioners' first meeting mention the importance of the Chair giving out just enough of their plans "to keep press happy and out of the way. There is no use fighting the press or entering into controversy through them."[69] But soon, under Bird's direction, the Commission was courting the reporters who might support it and saw the removal of at least one it did not like.

This particular incident involved destructive personality clashes behind the Commission's doors. In November of 1967, Commissioner Donald Gordon, Jr. quit, followed closely by the Commission's research director, David Kirk, and two of the junior staff, including its first press officer, Sandra Came. Kirk later sued the government for breach of contract.[70] Journalist Susan Becker of the Canadian Press (CP) news agency wrote about the resignations in a story that hit the newspapers across the country. Many of the headlines stressed the division within the Commission, and that it was one of the men who quit.[71] Shortly afterwards, she was removed from the Commission assignment altogether. It is not clear exactly how or why this happened, but the minutes of the commissioners' meeting indicate that it might have had something to do with her story. Bird explained to her fellow commissioners that Becker, "who wrote the derogatory and harmful article about the

Commission," had been scheduled to accompany them on its hearings. "The Director of the Canadian Press has now removed her from this assignment." Becker's replacement was to be Rosemary Speirs, who visited Bird two days before she broke this news to the other commissioners. Bird told them that she hoped that "all of us will do everything possible to make her (Speirs) feel that she is important and that we rely on her to give us objective and friendly coverage."[72]

Neither Becker nor her bureau chief at the time understood the order, which came from their superiors in Toronto, and Bird did not remember the incident when I quizzed her about it.[73] Speirs recalls that she thought that no one was covering the hearings in the first place, as was the usual practice regarding royal commissions at CP, and that she volunteered to go because she was a feminist herself, had fought sexism in the newsroom, and knew it would be a good story.[74] Speirs was not easily led, however. Her stories about the hearings and the Commission, which were read across the country, often played up conflict, unusualness and controversy in the best journalistic tradition.

Bird's biggest challenge was to persuade the Canadian public that this inquiry was an unbiased and apolitical exercise in "democracy," in which the views of women from all walks of life were more than welcome, the better for the Commission to help the government come up with policies that would allow "equal opportunities" to those who merited them. The other commissioners took the same line.[75] This model of liberal democracy, because it equated human rights with sameness, did not embrace differences among Canadian women and their needs. Bird almost always insisted to reporters that Canadian women right across the country were experiencing the same problems and wanted the same "equality of opportunity," notwithstanding some of the obvious regional, rural/urban and racial variations. This was her approach in her first interviews and news conferences and those she held later, before and after each hearing.[76] The hearings themselves were a trickier exercise in media management. Journalist Margaret Weiers of the *Toronto Daily Star* recalled later that Bird ruled the proceedings with "steel fingers in peau de soie gloves,"[77] that is, with an adept firmness expressed with ladylike diplomacy. At the beginning of each session, Bird explained to her audience that it was a democratic, apolitical process, and that the commissioners were there to listen and ask questions but not put forward views of their own.[78]

Behind the scenes, however, the staff had been instructed to control anyone who might be disruptive and to try to divert the media's attention from the most contentious presentations. The Commission records show that its first press officer, Sandra Came, had been encouraged to quietly find out who was presenting briefs "and perhaps forestall in this way some embarrassing episodes with so-called 'crackpots.'" Bird even had John Stewart, a staff member with training in psychology, warn her if he thought that some odd character might cause a disturbance so that she would not be caught off guard. In one case, a man in the audience stood up and declared loudly that women who smoked should be shot, a probable reference to Commissioner Lola Lange's penchant for cigarettes. Bird's usual way of dealing with such people was to assure them that their views were important and promise to meet with them privately after the hearing.[79]

Bird was afraid, with good reason, that the media would focus on unforeseen disruptions, argumentative or unusual presentations, or critical comments from the floor mike. On one occasion the Commission strayed into the highly volatile territory of English-French relations. In Calgary, a member of the staff had covered up portraits of the Queen and Prince Philip in the room in which the hearings were being held at the Palliser Hotel. The media reported that this was done to mollify the French Canadian Commissioners, Jeanne Lapointe and Jacques Henripin, which Bird later declared was ridiculous since both were loyal federalists. She explained that it was a "junior member of staff" who covered them because she was afraid they would be damaged as the TV lights were being erected close by; the staff forgot to undrape the portraits after the equipment was set up. But the local papers played up the incident, CP carried the story, and the leader of the opposition, Robert Stanfield, asked a question about it in the House of Commons. Bird wrote an explanation for the Prime Minister and apologized to the manager of the hotel and others who objected.[80] Overall, it was an embarrassing incident.

The media also looked for conflict in the briefs presented to the inquiry, which was something else Bird wanted to downplay. After several outspoken women in British Columbia and on the Prairies, whom the reporters painted as radicals, came to the hearings, the Commission proceeded with even more caution. According to Angela Burke, the next press officer, "some aspects which would have been detrimental to the Commission were kept out of print, off radio and television, due partially to my good relationships with the media generally." She did not specify what these "aspects" were.[81]

In order to avert more publicity that could be damaging to its reputation, the Commission actually tried to control which briefs would get journalists' attention. Burke suggested that the most questionable ones that might result in "sensational publicity" be scheduled for the lunch hour, when most reporters were away filing their stories. At her instigation, it was also decided not to give the press advance copies of potentially troublesome briefs and, starting with the central hearings in late May, to hire other journalists to write more acceptable thematic summaries for their colleagues at the press table.[82]

Knowing that the media and the public tended to blur the lines between the briefs and the Commission, Bird and her colleagues used the news conferences that preceded and ended the hearings in every city to play down any perceived "militancy," "man-hating," or "revolutionary" agenda which might have been suggested by any of the participants. This was partly in response to the advice of a public relations firm, which emphasized that Bird should stress what the hearings revealed about women's needs, but should not comment directly on specific briefs.[83] As part of its democratic strategy, the Commission had also been careful to court the opinions of men, although few showed up at the hearings. Some journalists picked up on the Commission's defensiveness about their absence. The lead in one story read: "There's no discrimination against men on the Royal Commission on the Status of Women," while another, quoting Bird, said she personally liked men very much and was sure they would want the same things women did once they understood the truth of their situation.[84]

The Media and the Commissioners' Struggle for Internal Consensus

The next phase of the commissioners' deliberations occurred after the hearings were over, when they gathered to discuss the various submissions and their recommendations. They decided among themselves not to speak to journalists about these matters, but Bird repeatedly reneged in an apparent attempt to handle media speculation, thus alienating some of her fellow commissioners. She met with several writers, including Rosemary Speirs, who later interviewed her again for an article for *Chatelaine*, which strongly supported the inquiry, and had her photographed amid stacks of briefs (see fig. 1.4). This photograph relayed in no uncertain terms that Canadian women were concerned about their status, regardless of what the critics were saying about the Commission.[85] Bird explained to her fellow commissioners, "I did not feel I could refuse to be photographed because *Chatelaine* has done so much to help the Commission." She generally felt that she could not turn down requests from reputable journalists, and that "it is important to do what we can to educate the mass media." On the one hand, she wanted reporters to stress that the women who presented briefs were "real human beings," with real problems. On the other, she did not want to be drawn into any discussions about legislation the Commission might propose, and she personally waylaid at least one journalist who came to the office looking for more information about the research.[86] When the only female cabinet minister, Judy LaMarsh, said in her memoirs that the Commission's research program was inadequate, Bird defended it on CBC radio's national open-line program, *Cross Country Checkup*, because it was a live program which could not be edited, and she had more control over the content.[87]

Figure 1.4. Florence Bird (Anne Francis), *Chatelaine*, July 1969. Courtesy of *Chatelaine* Magazine©Rogers Publishing Ltd. National Archives of Canada PA-135131.

In another instance either Bird or one of her staff used the media to put pressure on the two male commissioners, John Humphrey and Jacques Henripin, who were balking at some of the recommendations. In the fall of 1969, Speirs wrote an article about the deadline for the "sure to be controversial report" being pushed back again until the spring of 1970. She explained that "an observer close to the Commission" had revealed that its members were having trouble agreeing, and that the more conservative ones, particularly the two men, were apparently being difficult. According to the article, Bird diplomatically blamed the delays on the all-encompassing nature of the RCSW mandate to look into every aspect of the status of women, "the difficulties of separating specific women's problems from the problems of society as a whole" in areas such as poverty, and deciding what came under federal as opposed to provincial jurisdiction. She was quoted as saying the commissioners "'came through very united'" from the hearings, were reaching unanimous agreement on their recommendations to the federal government and that she did not expect there would be any minority reports. Speirs also noted that Bird, who later recalled that she was terrified of leaks to the media, had "bound all other members of the commission and its staff of 30 researchers and secretaries at the Ottawa headquarters to strict secrecy" and ordered that research reports, already completed, were not to be released until after the main *Report*.[88]

Speirs' story irritated Commissioner John Humphrey who demanded an explanation from Bird at the commissioners' next meeting, saying that they had agreed they would not speak to the media and that the story put unfair pressure on the two men, which could compromise the *Report*. The minutes paraphrased him as asking, "Why give an interview to someone who had already shown her bias?" Bird admitted that she had taken Speirs out to lunch, but that she had not given her an interview as such, and had only repeated the kinds of general statements she had made when the hearings had ended. She insisted that she did not know who the "observer close to the Commission" was, that she had not even mentioned delays in getting the *Report* out, or cited any deadline for the following spring. Jacques Henripin did discuss the difficulties the commissioners were having regarding the abortion issue, but it is not clear if this was before or after Speirs' article appeared. Monique Bégin, the executive secretary, denied speaking to any reporters at all. Humphrey suggested a joint news conference, or a statement from the Chair which would be vetted by the others, to rectify the damage. Bird insisted that an official response would do more harm than good, and she ignored the commissioners' vote to have a press statement prepared because "silence is golden" and she did not want any questions in the House of Commons.[89]

The Mixed Success of the Commission's Media Strategy

The Commission's media strategy was only partly successful in deflecting criticism from an inquiry which was considered controversial from the start. It began with a set goal in mind, although it was mitigated by certain constraints having to do with the political climate in which it was conceived. There was little doubt that the laws affecting women needed changing, especially as women demanded more freedom to plan their lives around work outside the home. Still, their concerns were marginalized in society to such a degree that it was considered necessary to be circumspect about fostering change. It could come, but within the rhetorical and philosophical limits set by a liberal democratic government, a predominantly liberal women's lobby group, and the Commission itself, all of which looked to the United

Nations' model of individual rights for guidance. Therefore, the Commission adopted a rhetoric of "democracy" and "equal opportunities" which might resonate better with the Canadian public and the media than "equality with men" or women's "rights," which could conceivably sound radical. When mounting expenses, unforeseen incidents, or internal problems and delays threatened the Commission's carefully controlled public image, it adopted what Ericson et al. have noted are standard public relations strategies to contain the damage, strategies which did not always coincide with its purported "democratic" outlook. Still, they write, "There is considerable variation in who controls the process, depending on the context, the type of sources involved, the type of news organizations involved and what is at issue."[90]

Much of the critical media coverage came from the "news" side, that is, the largely masculine world of political reporting and editorial commentary. Despite these skirmishes, there is no doubt that there was large support for the Royal Commission on the Status of Women in the segment of the media that was still, by and large, a world unto itself, the women's pages of the newspapers, *Chatelaine* magazine and women's programs on the CBC. As the next chapter will illustrate, the Commission's mandate resonated with journalists, one way or the other, partly because of the gender divisions within their own profession.

Chapter 2

"Top Perch Out for Newshens": Journalistic "Objectivity" On Trial

---

A room crowded with delegations of women waiting to present briefs, knots of middle-aged housewives waiting to hear what was wrong with them, batteries of girl reporters trying to look disengaged (I mean, baby, this has nothing to do with me)…and eight assorted uncomfortable men, three of them photographers….In Ottawa, none of the parliamentary press gallery's big-name newspapermen bothered to attend.

—Christina McCall Newman, in *Saturday Night*

*C*hristina McCall Newman's description of a public hearing in Ottawa in October 1968, the last stop on the Commission's tour of the country, reflected the deep gender division apparent among the public and the media over women's rights in Canada. Her article in *Saturday Night* magazine was entitled, somewhat defensively, "What's So Funny about the Royal Commission on the Status of Women?" and juxtaposed the touching reality of some of the testimony at the hearings with the dismissive attitude taken by English-language newspapers in particular. It also recorded her own changing response, from amused scepticism to "anger, pride, pity and fear" as she read briefs and listened to audio tapes of the hearings that had been held in other parts of the country. She concluded that this Commission was "one of the most important public inquiries since the war," examining, as it did, "the quality of Canadian life."[1]

McCall Newman was a latecomer to the Commission inquiry. Other women working in the media had been covering the story for close to two years, counting the CEWC's intervention, and had long staked out their various positions. There were reasons why most of them supported it, and women's rights, to varying degrees. It had to do with the history of women media workers, their place in the profession in the 1960s, how they regarded issues of journalistic practices such as "objectivity" in relation to women's issues, and how their own personal and work experiences and those of other women affected their approach to the Commission compared to that of their male colleagues. These factors suggest that it would have been virtually impossible for them to be disengaged from the Commission proceedings.

Journalists, Sex-Segregation and the Commission

The women who worked in broadcasting and the press in English Canada in the 1960s were a minority operating mainly in a segregated environment, producing programs and articles for "women's" radio and television shows, *Chatelaine* magazine or the women's pages of the daily newspapers. Only a few of these media workers had managed to find their way into CBC news and current affairs during prime time, worked beside men on the "hard news" beats in newsrooms or, like McCall Newman, were published in the country's newsmagazines.[2] In journalism, as in most other fields, the work women did reflected long-held cultural attitudes, based on biological determinism, that, as females who were destined to be wives and mothers, they were fit only for certain kinds of segregated work. Or, as Armstrong and Armstrong succinctly explain this attitude, "Women's biological equipment seals their fate, determines their social place."[3] With a few notable exceptions, such as Cora Hind of the *Winnipeg Free Press*,[4] women had been shut out of the "hard news" beats in journalism and broadcasting from the beginning.

The women's pages of the newspapers were invented in the late nineteenth century in response to a higher education level for urban women, new technological advances such as faster presses, and the demands of advertisers, who wanted to attract larger audiences. Although these women were expected to focus mainly on fashions, recipes and household hints, from these early days they were constantly dealing with women's issues, broadly defined: equal pay, acceptable roles for women, temperance and the vote. When male colleagues shut them out of their news organizations, they formed their own, the Canadian Women's Press Club, in 1904. Until the 1960s, they operated in what was effectly a domestic sphere, one which was also reflected in the women's magazines, including *Chatelaine* which began in 1928. During World War II, new opportunities opened up, and many women became active in the government's war effort or worked as general news reporters or editors, but for most, this reprieve was short lived. Like many of their contemporaries, there were women journalists who were happy to quit work after the war, but there was also resentment at the idea that the ones who had temporarily left the women's pages had to return to them or be out of a job.[5]

In keeping with the post-war atmosphere, the women's pages of the 1950s to the mid-1960s were a compendium of romantic and domestic concerns, dotted with engagement and wedding announcements, recipes and household hints. The "women's department" had little stature in the world of journalism and was literally segregated in a separate enclosure within the general newsroom area, even in the late 1960s. The pattern was similar in broadcasting, where programs designed for women in both radio and television also concentrated mainly on domestic concerns. Most women did not work in general newsrooms or specialize in news and current affairs commentary on either radio or television, but, again, there were exceptions to the rule, such as Florence Bird.[6]

As the 1960s advanced, liberal thinkers who questioned biological determinism argued that what held women back was not "nature" but nurture, that is socialization. Like other women professionals, female newspaper reporters grew restless at their confinement and at the outdated social mores behind it, and began to cover the hard-edged stories that fell more within the category of "social issues" than "women's news," a trend reflected in the gradual switch from the "women's pages" to "lifestyle" sections by the early 1970s. Still other journalists were determined to break into the general newsrooms from the start. Like other women, journalists' economic futures depended on how successful the women's movement would be in changing not just laws, but attitudes about what they were capable of doing. It is no surprise, really, that women journalists and broadcasters could hardly be "objective" about the Royal Commission on the Status of Women.[7] Neither could their male colleagues, because major social changes would mean that they, like other men, would have to make room for, and compete with, women in their own profession, and accommodate new demands from wives and lovers in their private lives.

There is no evidence to suggest that Canadian newsmen were different from most North American men. A recent US study addresses some of the turmoil about gender identity American men were feeling at the time, including unhappiness with bureaucratic straitjackets in the business world and the "hippie" rebellion against male authoritative icons, such as the soldier and the statesman. But many men, especially older ones, resisted substantial changes in sex roles longer than women did, partly out of fear of losing their masculinity.[8]

Male and female journalists were not only segregated according to gender, but also divided in their approach to the Commission. There were exceptions to the norm on both sides, but, generally, male columnists and editorial writers criticized or ridiculed the very idea of a commission on women, and were quite sceptical about the whole process. Women at the CBC and *Chatelaine* magazine, and those writing or editing for the newspapers, were sympathetic. Florence Bird was a familiar and generally respected colleague; the journalists saw it as their duty to their predominantly female audiences to cover the Commission; the nature of their previous assignments had made them familiar with issues affecting women; and several of them had also experienced discrimination and conflicts with men in their own professional and personal lives.

During the Commission's tenure, there were highly symbolic fights to integrate first the Parliamentary Press Gallery annual dinners and then the membership of the National Press Club, moves which were parallelled by efforts to spread "women's news" throughout the newspaper and turn the women's pages into "lifestyle" pages which would interest both sexes. For example, in a letter to the *Toronto Daily Star*, Marjaleena Repo of Toronto suggested that it was time, given the status of women inquiry, to abolish the women's page. "In printing a women's section you perpetuate an effective form of discrimination.... This can only thwart the development of the female journalist on your staff."[9] Harold J. Levy of Toronto scolded the *The Globe and Mail* for continuing with its women's section. He argued that the range of articles on social issues found in those pages were of interest to all readers. "By preserving an artificial and socially outmoded division of subject matter, *The Globe* is discouraging a significant portion of its readers from reading articles of vital social concern."[10] Barbara M. Coutts of Toronto, responding to Levy's letter, criticized *The Globe* for aiming all the medical stories at women. "The next time you write about rising costs of housing and consumer goods on the financial pages I suggest that you write an article to go beside it about vasectomies. The men might get the message."[11]

The "Objectivity" Factor

Regardless of whether they wrote for general news or the women's pages, journalists of both sexes generally adhered to the same professional standards, and to be "objective" was still one of the main principles of news and current affairs reporting in the 1960s. Even in 1974,

98 percent of journalists and editors cited in one study said they believed strongly in objectivity.[12] American journalism historians tend to link the "objectivity" ideal to the Enlightenment era, during which it was argued that the presentation of conflicting opinions would lead to the truth about a given situation. In journalism, "objectivity" was considered the key to determining the truth, which could only be done if the reporter presented others' conflicting viewpoints but kept "his" own feelings and biases to himself. It was also a way of protecting the journalist from criticism.[13]

Hackett and Zhao see objectivity as a ritual which is supposed to guarantee credibility. It is understood as such, not just by journalists, but also by political leaders, advertisers, interest groups and the public at large.[14] Ericson et al. have found, however, that contrary to most of the academic literature on news reporting, journalists do not operate by consensus but often disagree among themselves and with their editors.[15] In the case of the Commission coverage, tensions over gender surfaced according to the culture of each medium, each genre and each format in which journalists and broadcasters carried out their assignments, as well as among individual reporters.

The Canadian Press news agency was considered one model of journalistic standards, partly because most of the daily newspapers belonged to it. CP was a cooperative which operated a large central bureau in Toronto and several smaller ones across the country. The news agency would either cover major events with its own reporting staff, or have its editors send edited versions of stories that appeared in the local press to its member newspapers in other cities. Stories in English would be translated for the French-language papers. CP used teletype machines to send out fast-breaking news and the regular mail for features with no specific deadline. It picked up foreign news from other agencies such as United Press International (UPI) and the Associated Press (AP). Copies of photographs, with captions, were transmitted electronically and were large enough to be cropped at the receiving end.

The *CP Style Book*, used by CP and many of the 100 newspapers it served, declared that the news agency had "no interest except to fulfil its purpose—unbiased, fearless recording of fact. Conflicting sides of a dispute are given balanced, objective treatment. Accuracy is fundamental." These instructions, which were taken seriously by CP staff, did not mean that reporters could not be creative. "Stories can be bright, touching, inspiring or humorous without encroaching on the standards of impartiality, accuracy and good taste." How to produce these emotionally touching stories without jeopardizing the objective standards of rational impartiality was left to the reporters, "rewrite men" and filing editors at CP, and to the legions of copy editors who would handle the story at the agency's member newspapers. Some of them, such as *The Globe and Mail*, had their own guides as well, which also expected reporters to keep their stories "free of bias or partisanship." Opinion belonged on the editorial page.[16]

This is not to say that bias went unacknowledged, however. As one journalism textbook explained at length, "objectivity" was always complicated by a reporter's "unconscious bias" about a subject, and there was still some debate in the profession over whether even seasoned journalists should write interpretative or analytical articles.[17] At the same time, these texts, which historically relegated female journalists to the sidelines, did not interrogate the still prevalent masculine approach that posed "objectivity" as a rational ideal.[18]

Although there was some division in the profession over whether journalists should be neutral recorders of events or take a more participatory role as investigative reporters, most of them, both men and women, subscribed to some elements of both views and interpreted professional strictures broadly and individually.[19] Magazine writers were freer to interpret events and even editorialize in their articles than were newspaper journalists. There was a general understanding, however, that while one could bring the agenda of a specific group or government body to the attention of one's readers if they could benefit from that knowledge, the journalist concerned could not join any organization, including a women's group, and report on its activities at the same time. That would be a conflict of interest. But, as the women themselves have acknowledged, there were other ways of getting the message out.

The Journalists' Career Stories

Much of the information about the working lives of women journalists in this book comes from interviews with them. Oral history is not an exact science, but it does help the researcher put the lives and work of the people being interviewed into perspective. Historian Joan Sangster regards the theory and methodology of oral history in feminist research as contested territory, revealing the tensions between "poststructuralists" and "materialists." Sangster warns that a postmodern emphasis on "de-construction" of women's memories to the point where they are rendered valueless is not only politically suspect, but denies the links between their experiences and documented events in social and material history, especially instances of oppression and inequality. It is more important, she argues, to take the interviewees' subjectivity and lived experience into account, as well as other major factors that will affect their memories, such as their gender, race, class and political outlook. Sangster writes: "Asking why and how women explain, rationalize and make sense of their past offers insight into the social and material framework within which they operated, the perceived choices and cultural patterns they faced, and the complex relationship between individual consciousness and culture."[20]

With the exception of Florence Bird and Angela Burke, the public relations officer, none of the former commissioners or staff could remember much about the media coverage of the Commission, although some recalled certain details about its internal difficulties.[21] When asked about covering the hearings and the *Report* 30 years ago, most of the journalists had trouble remembering specific incidents and stories. This is hardly surprising, since each one has been active in the profession from 30-40 years, and all would normally produce more than one story a day, and sometimes several. Neither the women nor the men could remember why a certain story was handled the way it was or what they were feeling at the time, let alone how much editorial supervision they experienced. What the journalists remembered about the Commission often had more to do with the edited versions of what they wrote or broadcast, rather than what actually happened. In other words, they will remember the briefs or recommendations that struck them as interesting, not the hearings or the Commission *Report* in detail.

In most media analysis, this examination of the people who produced the stories is not done, unless it is a sociological study of newsrooms and how they work.[22] In this case, it is important to get a sense of how the reporters and editors who covered the Commission dealt with the conflict between the professional need to be "objective" and their own pro-feminist feelings. Most of the women and men interviewed said they were trained to present both sides of the story and not to become involved politically themselves, but the women especially privately favoured at least a liberal, equality model of women's rights, which was the dominant theme during the time of the Commission hearings, and part of the Commission's own public relations strategy.

The interviews for this book focused mainly on the women journalists who were the most engaged in the coverage of women's issues generally and the Commission in particular, attended hearings in more than one city or venue, and/or covered or commented on its initial appointment or its *Report*. There were also interviews with two journalists who presented their own briefs at the hearings, as well as two others whose connections with the Commission were minimal but who were able to provide important information about the history of women journalists in Canada and gender relations within the media. It is particularly important to understand their working conditions and personal outlooks on women's issues because they affected the coverage they produced. Although their personal experiences varied, most of the women remember a great deal about the general inequities women suffered at the time, particularly in their own profession.

Male journalists were interviewed on slightly different grounds than the women, since men did not cover the Commission hearings on a regular basis. Some did, however, cover or comment on the *Report* and well remember a time when they worked almost entirely in all-male environments, or the mixed gender environment of the CBC's women's programs. The main difficulty was getting them all to be open about their feelings concerning gender relations at the time, even though it was 30 years ago. Some were more guarded than others, possibly because the thrust of this research is clearly feminist, and they were being asked why certain attitudes about women prevailed in the journalism profession and in society at large in the 1960s, which could imply their own complicity. There were several important self-revelations all the same, and all the men contributed clear memories of the technical aspects of their daily routines, which helped put their work into context.

The women had both professional and personal reasons for being interested in the Royal Commission inquiry, but the degree of enthusiasm and commitment to women's rights varied. The journalists who paid the most attention to the Commission worked at CP and the major newspapers, but, certainly, many others from smaller publications took notice as well. Most of the women interviewed for this study saw themselves as feminists in spirit, and were largely sympathetic. Because they were reporters, and not editorial writers or columnists, they were expected to keep their overt opinions to themselves, however.

Their degree of independence from editorial control varied from newsroom to newsroom, but tended to be consistent with their professional experience. "Cubs" or newcomers were usually supervised closely, while more seasoned reporters were left more to their own devices but were still subject to their news editors' assignment priorities and "blue pencil" copy editing. Veteran journalists with specialized beats or who were off on assignment "on the road" were the ones most likely to be trusted with analytical or interpretative articles. The women who covered women's issues, and the Commission, were not all new to the field, as earlier research suggested; a number of them had several years of experience. Those who were women's page editors assigned local stories and chose others from wire service copy, and often did the editing, page layout and headlines.[23]

In 1960, Jean Sharp left her job on the women's page of the *Hamilton Spectator* to join CP as its women's editor in Toronto. Sharp wrote a regular column called "Tea Time Topics" in which she covered, among other things, the doings of women's groups, including Laura Sabia's CEWC. She did not get directly involved in women's activism herself, but saw those organizations as being very influential and felt they should be covered. "I was their mouthpiece, if you will." She also wrote background articles, including one about women's rights under various provincial laws. Sharp liked her independent niche at CP, since she was pretty much her own boss, but she was well aware that she did not have a very high status in the media world. "Even now, if someone asks me what I did at CP, and I say I was the women's editor, I can see this kind of, 'oh,' look come across their faces. I wasn't a real reporter, I wasn't a real news person. And a lot of the women's editors would have felt that way." She recalls that when she got together for regional meetings with the women's page editors served by CP, they would swap stories about being snubbed.[24]

Some of the women who were hired at CP in the mid-to-late 1960s went to the agency's various bureaus across Canada where they did general or specialized news. Rosemary Speirs was interested in organized labour, including issues affecting women, and did not want to be compartmentalized away from mainstream, meaning general, news. "I'd rather women's issues were mainstream news." Even a woman with her credentials had some persuading to do if she wanted to work in the newsroom. Speirs had written a column for the Toronto *Telegram* when she was 17, and then went on to the University of Toronto, where she was deputy editor of *The Varsity*. She was among the women who protested the fact that two of the university's institutions, Massey College and Hart House, were all-male. Around 1964, as she was starting a PhD in history on organized labour, she applied for a summer job at CP in Toronto. During her interview with the bureau chief, John Dauphinee, she tried to impress him with her experience to date. When he told her, "'We don't hire little girls,'" she rose in her seat and responded indignantly, "'I am not a little girl!'" He laughed and gave her the job, apparently confident that she could handle her male colleagues in the large Toronto bureau. Speirs also finished her PhD in labour history, a rare accomplishment for a working journalist even today.

She did not have an easy time of it during her first couple of years at CP and had to confront outright male bias and resistance when she first joined the men. Upon her arrival at the Toronto bureau, some of them immediately started a petition in protest, declaring that they would not be able to relax and be themselves in her presence. Some time later, she was assigned to the copy desk in CP's Montreal newsroom. As she was about to take her place on "the rim," as it was called, the men all stood up and walked out. Speirs, who knew she had her bosses' support, found blatant prejudice much easier to deal with than discrimination that is systemic and hidden. "You can yell and scream and fight back about it and have it out....I was alone, feeling sort of like a pioneer. It was kind of exciting." It was Speirs who replaced Susan Becker on the Commission assignment, which she was glad to have. "I was a feminist, I was a woman, I was working in an all-male world, and well aware of the difficulties I was having in it, so I was interested in the issues that were before the Royal Commission. I also thought it was going to be an excellent story. And it was."[25]

Speirs' experience was not uniform across the CP system, however, and much seemed to depend on the location and size of the bureau as to how well the women got along. Elinor Reading's initial experiences were not as difficult as those Speirs encountered. Reading, an American, held a Master's degree in English Literature and had been a teacher before she moved to Alberta in the 1960s, a move precipitated by her desire to eventually see the far north. Although she was paid at the same rate, initially, as a copy boy, Reading remembers the CP bureau in Edmonton as a small, friendly place where she learned duties a beginner did not ordinarily get to do in the larger bureaus, including copy editing and rewriting as well as reporting. She had difficulties only with a man her own age who did not like receiving instructions from a woman, but was able to handle him with the help of an older male colleague. At the time, "I was one of those tiresome young women who are inclined to say that they hadn't ever encountered any prejudice or difficulty in their lives, and at that time I certainly hadn't." She was mainly interested in the Commission because she wanted to cover the visit that Florence Bird and another commissioner, Lola Lange, made to the Yukon and the Northwest Territories in August of 1968. It was Reading's first trip to the North.[26]

On the newspapers, women as a group were slow to get away from the women's pages and into the general newsrooms. Some of them started out as secretaries, even on liberal papers like *The Montreal Star*. Sheila Arnopoulos was first hired there in the mid-sixties as a secretary to the literary editor in the entertainment section. Arnopoulos, who was college educated and a bilingual anglophone, recalls that she did much more than type and file. At her own request, her boss allowed her to interview authors, write book and music reviews, and do page makeup, as well. But, "I was still getting a secretary's salary." Her way out was the women's page, a move that she and its editor, Zoe Bieler, had to negotiate with her reluctant boss, who, unknown to Arnopoulos, had earlier turned down the same request. When she confronted him about it, "His response was, 'but you're only going to get married.'...He was really angry, and he said 'you will never write for this section again.'" Once on the women's page, she was considered a "reporter" rather than a "secretary," and got more money and respect. "You could not compare the way I was treated." At the time, the paper was not unionized. Bieler ran her women's page with eight full-time staff and several part-timers, and encouraged her reporters to do "hard news" stories and features on politics, medicine and other general interest areas. It was *Star* policy that if the premier of Quebec spoke to a women's group, then one of her reporters would cover his speech.

Arnopoulos was interested in social issues of various kinds, including poverty, immigration, and reproductive rights, which she covered for the women's page and later, for the "city side" in the general newsroom. She wrote stories concerning the Commission's appeals for briefs and reported on the hearings in Montreal, Toronto and Ottawa during the spring and fall of 1968.[27]

The Toronto newspapers paid the most attention to the Commission, especially the *Toronto Daily Star*, which originally planned to assign a reporter to follow the hearings across the country, a decision that was rescinded because of budget considerations. But Margaret Weiers, who was supposed to go, kept tabs on the hearings, often writing up stories from the briefs sent to her by the organizations that presented them. Weiers had cut her journalistic teeth on weekly and daily newspapers in Saskatchewan in the 1950s, and was delighted to land a job on the *Star* because it had a reputation as a liberal and progressive newspaper, unlike the more prestigious but business-oriented *Globe and Mail*. "If you're growing up in Saskatchewan, you don't have much truck nor trade with the business establishment of the wicked East."

Just as she started working on the women's pages, the *Star* was unionized under the Newspaper Guild, and the women were given equal pay with the reporters in general news, most of whom were men. Before that, "the reporters who worked on the women's pages were not (considered) real reporters and therefore didn't deserve to be paid as much as the men." Weiers was the test case. She was required to work six weeks on general news to prove that women's page reporters were as good as general news reporters, which she did. It meant that no other woman who came after her had to prove the same point. As late as 1970, as a member of the Guild executive, she criticized some unionized newspapers, including one in southern Ontario, which still paid their "society" reporters less than general news reporters. She urged women who were union members to become more active and start demanding an end to those kinds of practices.

The *Star* newsroom, as liberal as it was, had a fair number of what would now be called "sexist" men, but Weiers does not think it was worse there than anywhere else. How the women reacted to them depended on "temperament and personality.... I never had much problem with it myself. But I think that was because of the kind of person I was. I don't brook fools gladly to start with." Weiers, who later wrote editorials for the *Star*, also feels she had room to advance as a reporter, but she did not want to take on anything that might have had a detrimental effect on her family life. For most of her career, she worked full time and hired a housekeeper to help with childcare. Weiers, who considered herself a feminist but would not have joined a women's club, saw the value of the Commission, not only in the political sphere, but as an educational tool as well. She regards her newspapers' decision to survey male readers about women's rights and pass the results on to the Commission as a good marketing strategy for the paper rather than an editorial conflict of interest.[28]

The *Star's* rival was *The Telegram*, a conservative newspaper with popular appeal, which was eventually killed off in the tough circulation battle that was going on in Toronto at the time. Two of the women who worked there have very different perceptions of how women journalists were treated, which had to do with their personal outlooks and circumstances at the time. Yvonne Crittenden saw journalism as a line of work which allowed a married woman with children, like herself, to balance her domestic life and career. After a few years at home raising her children, she was able to return to the profession feeling more mature and even better at her job. Crittenden, who was, and is, a feminist but not of the "card-carrying" variety, felt that the Commission story was the biggest event for Canadian women "since suffrage." But she also felt that it was a venue mainly for professional women, and that had she been a full-time homemaker, like many of her readers, she might not have been as interested in what was going on.

Crittenden did not feel discriminated against at the *Telegram* and recalls that women were treated and paid equally because it was also unionized under the Guild. "Now male reporters were pretty chauvinist, but then men all were in those days.... I was lucky. I had good, good male colleagues," as well as a supportive husband. "There never seemed to be any barriers to what I wanted to do." As for reporting, the idea that one had to present a balanced view was not restricted to North America, as Crittenden had learned the same principle in Australia, where she was born and spent her early adult years. "I was, you know, trained very strictly.... You had to give both sides of the question, you never inserted your own personal views into the story...so I was a very fair-minded, objective reporter." To join a woman's group would have been out of the question for her, too.[29]

Maggie Siggins, who started her journalism career as a *Telegram* reporter in 1965 on the day she graduated from the journalism program at Ryerson Polytechnic in Toronto, remembers the newspaper differently. Siggins specialized in interpretative feature articles on subjects such as poverty, birth control and abortion and, later, the Women's Liberation Movement, whose ideas attracted her. She remembers being sent to the women's department as "punishment" when she did something to displease her editors, such as coming back from an assignment late. From Siggins' perspective, and that of other women journalists, some of the more conservative men resented the bright, better educated young women who were entering the field, especially those like herself who were considered sympathetic to "radical" ideas, and would use any excuse to try to rein them in.

Unlike Crittenden, Siggins recalls gender tension in the newsroom which sometimes took the form of "terrible, fearful screaming matches" about what work women journalists were capable of doing and other issues to do with women's rights. There were also debates about whether the *Telegram* was devoting too much space to the Commission, which one male reporter dismissed as "crap." At a later point, male resentment took the form of "days" of so-called playful bra-strap snapping to the comment, "I guess *you're* not a bra-burner," which ended when the women objected to management. Siggins also recalls that some of the younger men supported the more liberal view of women's rights, "even more than they would be now, because it was part of the whole radical kind of thing," that is, the rebellious atmosphere of the 1960s and early '70s.[30]

Siggins, who covered the Commission hearings in Toronto and, later, local reaction to the *Report*, saw the inquiry as somewhat passé in the light of the women's liberation movement. She thinks that management would have trusted Crittenden, who was a "super reporter" and more inclined to include the "establishment" line in her stories, to cover the hearings rather than herself. Siggins, hypothetically using the example of working mothers, said her colleague would cover the comments of a woman who did not want to stay home and care for her children, and balance them with comments from one who did. Siggins would be more interested in pursuing the ideas of the career woman. But even Siggins toed the line of non-involvement in women's groups, as taken as she was with radical feminism. As the women's liberation movement gathered strength between 1968 and 1970, she covered protests and consciousness-raising groups but felt ambivalent about getting involved herself. She recognized that the term "women's libber" carried "a lot of baggage" and she also admits that as a single woman she did not want to alienate men she found attractive. Her professional position as a journalist "was kind of a shield for me....I was not supposed to march up and down Yonge Street....I was not supposed to go and sit-in at an office, but...in another way, I was totally committed."[31]

While all these women gave varying degrees of support to women's issues and the Commission through their work, they stopped short of presenting briefs themselves. But several journalists did speak out. One of them, who originally sent in a brief as a private citizen, found herself publicly criticizing the Newspaper Guild by the time she appeared before the commissioners.

She is Eleanor Dunn, who took journalism courses at Carleton University in the mid-1950s, and later became a partner in a company which ran weekly newspapers in two Ottawa neighbourhoods. It was a full-time but not particularly lucrative occupation for Dunn, who, together with her husband, also a journalist, had five children to support. She had the same complaints as many other mothers who worked outside the home. She was very unhappy about the difficulty of getting good child care; she could not claim household help as a tax deduction; and pensions did not provide adequate survivor benefits. Dunn was also a member of a Conservative riding association and had a few things to say as well about the way political parties treated women. "I did what I normally do when I get mad, I put pencil to paper"; this time, firing off a brief to the Commission, as did hundreds of other women. She also wrote an opinion piece in favour of the inquiry on the front page of *The Ottawa Times Weekly*: "Royal Commission Welcome."[32]

Soon afterwards, Dunn accepted a job as the assistant women's editor on *The Ottawa Citizen* because the pay was better, the hours were more regular, and it could eventually lead to a job in general news. When the national hearings were held in Ottawa in October of 1968, Dunn greeted the Commission with an enthusiastic article, leading with, "They're here at last."[33] She covered the hearings for the *Citizen*, and, under a pen name, her old weeklies, and one evening left the press table to address the Commissioners. She complained about the way women in politics were treated but, rather than talk about the problems of working mothers, she accused some newspapers and the Guild of unfair labour practices. She said that at the *Citizen* and other unionized papers, management and the union circumvented equal pay laws by shunting female journalists into the women's departments, and then maintaining they did not do substantially the same work as the men.[34] During her testimony to the Commission, she mentioned that the *Citizen* contract was up for renewal in a few months, which suggests that her intervention was a pressure tactic. The Guild denied her accusations.[35] Later, she presented a brief to the Special Senate Committee on Mass Media.[36]

Generally, Dunn recalls, she avoided direct conflicts of interest throughout her career in that she never actually reported on areas in which she was personally involved. Nevertheless, she apparently felt strongly enough to break that rule when she thought that women in her own profession were being treated badly by the union which was supposed to help them. Her superiors did not try to punish her for appearing at the status of women hearing, possibly, Dunn said, because she was a Guild member and could have grieved. She laughs ironically when she adds, "On the other hand, they may not have felt this was too important anyway." She does think that women's anger against unfair laws, apparent at the Commission hearings, helped change attitudes and "caused some of our male co-workers to think twice." She also feels the Commission and the attention it received resulted in improved working conditions for women journalists. "The main thing it did was give an awful lot of us confidence to stand up for our rights."[37]

These press women, then, approached the Commission inquiry as an interesting, newsworthy event which would have repercussions for their readers and, invariably, for themselves as women. Their level of commitment and personal involvement in the hearings and the women's rights movement varied but, with the exception of Dunn and a few others, stopped at direct intervention.

The Canadian Women's Press Club and the Commission

Their reasons for supporting women's rights differed, but it is clear that professional and personal considerations played a role. Some of these reasons surfaced, indirectly, in two briefs to the Commission from the Canadian Women's Press Club (CWPC), one of which demanded changes in laws and practices that hurt all women, including its members, and another that pinpointed discrimination against women within the media.

Florence Bird had asked the CWPC for a brief when she met with its members in June of 1967, and the executive was happy to comply, as were other journalists. The CWPC had earlier sent the results of a 1964 internal survey to the Commission for its research. The membership, about 700 strong, was more or less evenly divided between public relations specialists, and journalists and broadcasters. The survey showed that they generally fit the profile of many women in the workforce.

Their average age was 43 and their salaries ranged from less than $4,000 to $10,000 a year. A substantial number of them were mothers who worked outside the home. Of the 296 survey respondents who worked full-time, 112 had children and 122 were the sole support for their families. Seventeen part-timers were supporting their families as well. Even if many of these women were not themselves in dire economic circumstances, they certainly had colleagues who were.[38]

The brief from the national executive of the CWPC outlined laws and practices they felt should be changed, noting, for example, that several of the club's self-supporting members had been refused bank loans "simply because they are women," a common financial barrier at the time. Their submission included a copy of the UN Declaration on the Elimination of Discrimination against Women, which indicates that the CWPC wanted to demonstrate that it was on the same liberal wavelength as the Commission when it came to women's rights. Certainly, they were not a particularly radical group. Under questioning from the commissioners, their spokeswomen said that women in journalism were not paid equally, but the CWPC did not take a stand one way or the other on unionism as a solution. The CP story on their brief mentioned that exchange, but quoted a CWPC spokeswoman as saying only that women who wanted a union were drowned out by male colleagues who did not. In the Toronto *Telegram* and *Toronto Daily Star* versions of the CP story, editors had also defensively inserted the information, in parentheses, that their male and female reporters received the same wage.[39]

The other brief was from the Toronto branch of the CWPC and complained about its members' working conditions. It was presented by Marjorie McEnaney, a freelance journalist and broadcaster who had worked for years for CBC Talks and Public Affairs. During the time she was regularly employed, she had fought, unsuccessfully, to win back the federal civil service pension she had lost when she married. McEnaney presented the results of surveys conducted among the club's members and some of their employers, which indicated that changes were overdue at the CBC, the major newspapers in Toronto and an unnamed news agency, which was likely CP. The CWPC was disappointed at the low response rate from its members (20%) and their employers (11%), but also felt that their answers were representative. About 73 percent of the women said they made less than $4,000 a year, and about one-third of them worked freelance. About three-quarters of them said that they were not given the same opportunities as men to get ahead and would welcome promotions. The survey did not include data on working mothers, but some members said that, contrary to what employers thought, they would be less likely to quit work when they married or had children if they had better-paying jobs. The survey also indicated that media executives saw the women as being suited only for the low-paying positions, and assumed that the reporters among them were simply not interested in covering news, politics or sports.

It is difficult to make exact comparisons with the salaries male journalists were getting, as that kind of documentation is hard to come by. Reporters' salaries depended on the area of the country, the size of the media outlet, and whether or not they were working in a union shop. Only a dozen newspapers, the CBC and two private broadcasters were affiliated with the American Newspaper Guild, and most were concentrated in Toronto and Vancouver. According to the *Report of the Special Senate Committee on Mass Media*, in 1967-71, unionized reporters with five years experience made $9,724 at the *Toronto Daily Star* for a 35-hour work week. Those with six years experience who worked at the *Oshawa Times*, a smaller Ontario newspaper, made about two thousand dollars a year less for a 40-hour work week. The Senate committee could not find statistics for most journalists, however, because they were not members of the American Newspaper Guild.

Broadcast program staff, including reporters working for private radio and television, which was not ordinarily unionized, made an average of about $6,000–$6,400. The *Report* does not differentiate between men and women's salaries, but anecdotal evidence suggests that women made the same as men in unionized shops as long as they were given the same job descriptions. Otherwise, they made less.[40]

From their briefs it is clear that the press club women wanted change and saw themselves in the vanguard. According to the Toronto CWPC, "It will be difficult for women to take their place and contribute their full potential, unless the mass media point the way, by word as well as by deed."[41] CP's Rosemary Speirs covered the story, which the Vancouver *Province*, using common slang for female reporters, headlined, "Top Perch out for Newshens."[42]

The Role of *Chatelaine* Magazine

While newspaper women could be said to support equality for women generally, no publication championed this caused more directly than *Chatelaine*. It led the stable of Maclean Hunter magazines with a circulation of over 950,000, a respectable number in a market swamped by American imports such as *Ladies Home Journal, Good Housekeeping, McCall's* and *Redbook*. The editor was Doris Anderson, who was raised in a matriarchal home environment in Calgary, was a graduate of the University of Alberta and saw no reason why she couldn't have both a career and a family life. She recalls experiencing discrimination herself at Maclean Hunter, where she was not paid equally with male editors and had to fight for the title of editor, even though she was already doing the job. Because she was about to marry, her bosses thought she was not going to stay on.

Under Anderson's leadership, *Chatelaine* increasingly reflected a balance between traditional domestic content and a progressive editorial outlook on women's concerns. She believes that her magazine was covering issues Betty Friedan talked about long before *The Feminine Mystique* was published, and her own editorials became more feminist as time went on. She saw it as part of her job to keep women informed and educated about the issues touching their lives. "I think the secret was to always be ahead of the reader, but not too far ahead so that you lost her trust." Maclean Hunter did not interfere with her editorial line, Anderson explains, because *Chatelaine* was its biggest money-maker at the time. Her brand of liberal feminism actually sold very well because her readers, many of them homemakers, "were way ahead of where religious leaders and the media thought they were."

Chatelaine took a pro-Commission stance from the moment that Laura Sabia began to push for the inquiry. Maclean Hunter had very clear guidelines forbidding its editors to endorse political parties or become overtly involved in specific organizations, which Anderson obeyed. It meant that, while she covered the initial CEWC meetings, she could not have lobbied herself for a Royal Commission the way Laura Sabia did. She saw her job as persuading Canadian women that a Commission was an important way to air the issues; "publicizing it, and getting support for it."[43]

Even so, it could be argued that *Chatelaine* pushed the ethical understanding of "objectivity," even for a magazine, to the limit. Her staff worked with the Commission to coordinate the publicity for a readership survey asking women what changes they would like to see in discriminatory laws and practices, the results of which it both published and presented to the Commission as a brief. Florence Bird, who also asked Anderson's advice as a resource person who was knowledgeable about Canadian women, told her that she thought her approach was the right one and paid her "a personal tribute to what you are doing to help women grow up."[44]

It was not Anderson but a staff writer, Mollie Gillen, who was responsible for the survey and the articles about it. Gillen, then in her fifties, spent her early child-rearing years writing short stories for magazines before going back to work as an information officer in the federal civil service. After a move to Toronto from Ottawa in 1961 and a brief stint as copy editor for the women's page on *The Globe and Mail*, she went to *Chatelaine*. Gillen was married twice, and had firsthand knowledge of the ways in which laws governing marriage, divorce and marital property could affect women. It also annoyed her that the predominantly female staff at *Chatelaine* were paid less than the men who worked for *Maclean's*. She wrote accompanying articles for the survey in which she supported changing the laws and practices governing marriage and divorce, equal pay, childcare and reproductive freedom, among others. The rest of the staff helped formulate the questions and she was delighted at the readers' responses, 11,000 of them, which were mostly "slanted the way we hoped they would be."[45]

Gender Relations at CBC Current Affairs

At the CBC, there was a complicating factor: as a crown corporation, it came under the purview of the Royal Commission, and Florence Bird was well aware that the women she once worked with had complained over the years about management practices that curtailed their ambitions.[46] As the CWPC brief from Marjorie McEnaney noted, management was dragging its feet at hiring women for prime-time news and current affairs, and seemed content to leave them in the safe harbour of daytime programming.[47] Generally, there appeared to be vast differences in the working relationships between men and women, depending on whether they worked in current affairs or news, in TV or radio. In prime time television, current affairs shows were virtually all-male venues which took an aggressively investigative and adversarial stance to most stories, especially to anything that smacked of "authority." The men delighted in putting politicians and others on the hot seat and demanding answers to tough questions. Female regulars on programs such as *This Hour Has Seven Days* and *Weekend* were attractive singers and entertainers, not journalists.[48]

The few surviving programs suggest that some of these men did not look very kindly upon the Commission or women's rights. For example, before he himself was appointed to the Commission, Donald Gordon, Jr., in his capacity as co-host of a program called *Twenty Million Questions*, interviewed Laura Sabia in her home about the CEWC's campaign for a federal inquiry into the status of women. The transcript shows that Gordon's questions matched the confrontational style of public affairs journalism at the time. At the end of the program, he told his co-host, Charles Lynch, that as long as bright young women kept quiet in class, and wives deferred to their husbands, "until the physicians heal themselves, they're not going to get much action." Lynch, an *Ottawa Citizen* columnist who tended to be flippant in his avowed support for women's rights, said that of the couples he knew, the wives tended to be smarter than the husbands. Responded Gordon, "I find the women are prettier."[49]

In contrast, the women who were concentrated in daytime programming took a much more serious view of the Commission and women's rights—and with good reason. Traditionally, there was a strong commitment to women's issues among CBC women. Individual exceptions notwithstanding, they tended to be progressive and well-educated and had been embroiled in their own occasional battles with management on equality issues over the preceding 30 years. Just before the Commission was appointed, four senior women, including Helen James, the former head of women's programming, quit in disgust when they were blocked from advancing in the corporation. Because the CBC fell under its mandate, the Commission planned a study of promotion opportunities for women in the corporation, and it appears that Bird met with James and the other women who had left. In the mid-1970s, Bird was a consultant on a task force looking into the status of women at the CBC, and recalls that even then senior executives played down suggestions there was problem. The task force, however, discovered that the CBC was badly in need of an equal opportunity policy.[50]

Within the women's programs, such as *CBC Matinee* and *Take 30*, men and women worked together on a more or less equal basis, barring the occupational division between male technical crew and female production assistants. An executive producer of *Matinee*, Lynn Higgins, recalls that the CBC was an exciting place where intellectual inquiry was welcome. There were senior male producers who mentored and supported women and, with her youthful optimism, Higgins had no idea that there might be a "glass ceiling." By the late 1960s, both programs carried, as a matter of course, items about politics, international affairs, science and the arts that were not restricted to the so-called woman's point of view, although consumer and domestic affairs were certainly included in the mix.[51]

The supervisor of daytime programming for radio and television, Dodi Robb, believed that there were thousands of women trapped with children in the suburbs who hungered to know what was going on in the world. She also felt that it was important to have men and women working together on her programs because it produced a more balanced perspective. Robb and the women under her charge were quite committed to seeing the Royal Commission covered on both *Matinee* and on the national TV program for women, *Take 30*. It was a stand that Robb admits was "absolutely biased," but she "did not care" because she believed that the Commission, and the possibilities for change that it represented, was so important for Canadian women. When it came to what went over the air, however, Robb felt that the coverage must be based on fairness and balance, the two cousins of "objectivity," a concept that she agrees is hard to pin down. "I think the whole idea of objectivity shifts all the time. Everyone's their own bundle of contradictions and beliefs, starting at the cradle.... Unless you're a robot...you cannot go in and do a story...without having a lot of feeling about it. So you have to always try to present the two sides of a story, especially if it's a particularly controversial one."[52]

The CBC's policy was that it was not acceptable for a reporter, on-air host, or a program to adopt a point of view, regardless of personal feelings, or to support "one side or another" on controversial issues. It also said a "range" of opinions should be presented.[53] At *Take 30*, there were no hard and fast rules, however. The executive producer of the program, Glenn Sarty, remembers that the unit operated more or less by group consensus. Stories should be "right...plausible...the decent thing."

Sarty came to *Take 30* wanting to make his mark in current affairs. He hired men, including Ed Reid, to correct what he felt was a predominance of women in the unit and sent Reid on the road with the Commission because he could spare him, but not Adrienne Clarkson, who was a regular co-host with Paul Soles. Sarty declares that he would have "thrown a fit" if anyone had suggested that he choose a woman for the assignment because of her sex; he felt the decision was up to him.[54]

Soles was a veteran broadcaster and a dramatic and comic actor who, Robb recalls, was a warm, affable presence on the air, quite funny sometimes, and popular with the show's audience. Soles had worked with women at CFPL in London, Ontario, and recalls that he took the mixed gender environment of CBC Toronto for granted. He does not recall that the on-air gender balance was ever discussed. "It was simply a given that if you had an interest and you could help the show, you were there."[55] Nevertheless, *The Globe and Mail* mentioned after one Commission hearing in Toronto that of the six-person *Take 30* crew covering it, only one was a woman and she was an assistant to the producer.[56]

Ed Reid, who did the reporting, was experienced in film production, television and radio, which, for Robb, made him the ideal person for the Commission story, and he was the only male who covered all of the hearings and the *Report* as well. According to Robb and his colleagues, he was a modest man of quiet integrity, unfailingly courteous, and very professional. Reid was also a kind-hearted man who strongly believed in human rights. Soles remembers: "He could be touched, truly touched, properly touched by the plight and vulnerability of others. Thus he was ideally placed to be in this forum (the hearings) where sensitivity was required. You don't want a bull in this shop."[57]

Figure 2.1. Reid, *Take 30*, Apr.-June 1968. Courtesy of the Estate of Edmund Reid by its Executor, Anthony F. Reid.

Reid usually kept his true thoughts and feelings to himself, but it was possible to discern what he was thinking through his wry, funny cartoons of birds with human characteristics, which he would pass around to his co-workers. The women who worked with him felt he essentially supported equality between the sexes but was certainly not comfortable with "radical" expressions of feminist sentiments.[58] This became abundantly clear after the Commission hearings in British Columbia. He drew a worried looking male bird wearing eyeglasses like Reid's own, standing with his back to a TV camera. He was staring in dismay at a group of angry bird women rushing towards him, two with placards reading "Go Girls Go" and "Stamp Out Men." The female birds were drawn to fit different stereotypes of the feminist: the large overbearing woman, the bluestocking, the suffragette and others. Bringing up the rear was a mother bird staring balefully at the large egg in her baby carriage (see fig. 2.1). The cartoon ran under the credits of the first *Take 30* program from the west coast where, Reid told the show's co-hosts, women seemed to take "more extreme positions" and show "more open hostility towards men" than they did on the Prairies.[59]

Reid occasionally expressed his opinions on the air, but was also fairly careful about what he said. When a colleague once asked him during a radio program whether he generally separated his "point of view as broadcaster from [his] point of view as an individual or a person," Reid replied, carefully: "I'm not a highbrow, and I'm not a lowbrow, so that puts me in the middle. And in many ways I'm in the middle as far as my own tastes and my own interests go. I know from past experience that to a certain extent it matches the opinions of a fair number of people in the audience. Now, you can go too far that way, but frankly, you have to rely a fair amount on your own instincts."[60]

Whenever he was asked how he felt about covering the Commission, or what he was finding out about women, Reid would quip, "They sure can talk!"[61] At one point, he said on *Matinee* that he had to be very careful about his facial expression during the hearings because he was often the only man in the audience and the women would look at him to see how he was reacting to critical comments from those presenting briefs.[62] On this assignment, it might also have been difficult for him to keep his professional distance from Florence Bird because he had been her producer on several of her radio commentaries and her neighbour in Ottawa. Bird, who had also contributed to *Matinee*, felt, however, that both of them understood their professional functions well in relation to the Commission.[63]

On most of the *Take 30* programs about the Commission hearings, Reid and Soles dominated the studio discussion, as the female host, Adrienne Clarkson, was absent about half the time, possibly on other assignments or a day off. Clarkson, who came to Canada with her parents from Hong Kong when she was a child, was teaching English literature at the University of Toronto and working on her PhD when she started on *Take 30* as a book reviewer. Highly regarded for her intelligence and her natural broadcasting ability, she was a rarity in Canadian television at the time because she was both a woman and of Chinese descent.

Clarkson does not believe that she was ever discriminated against at the CBC, but certainly knew women who were and has been known to give her female colleagues a boost behind the scenes. When she was on *Take 30* programs about the federal inquiry, Clarkson appeared with both men, or with Reid on his own. She and Florence Bird discussed the Commission at length in early 1967 and, outside of the Commission story, Clarkson interviewed several women's movement leaders, including Betty Friedan. When she was in the studio, she made her pro-Commission views known and even said on the air that she was tempted to present a brief herself. She does not remember making that comment, but remarks: "Well, I'm glad to think that I would have been as enlightened to say that." She likely would have told the Commission that women weren't prepared for the reality of the double load. Work outside the home is based on a masculine model of careerism, "completely in a male image...,I think I thought that then. I don't think I've ever really changed that point of view."[64]

On *Matinee*, Reid worked with his female co-host, Pat Patterson, while a male announcer, usually Rex Loring, opened and closed the program. For *Matinee*, Reid often phoned in reports from the road. One day a week he joined her in the Toronto studio to discuss taped excerpts from the hearings, having first met her for lunch, as was their usual practice, to prepare for the show. She and Reid discussed the outlines of their script but ad-libbed much of their on-air conversations.

Patterson believes CBC management considered that each host had different talents. Her background and strengths were in music, hosting and interviewing personalities, while Reid had a better grasp of political stories, a perception which she considered a fair assessment. Like most producers, hosts, and other on-air contributors in current affairs, Patterson has worked on contract or freelanced for most of her career. She recalls times when she felt that she was not paid or treated well, but also recalls getting along well with colleagues like Reid.

Patterson found it exciting that a Royal Commission on women had been announced but, as an on-air host of *Matinee*, always felt she must be "objective," not expressing an opinion, or even indicating it in her tone of voice. "By and large we had to present things for what they were. And I think that's fair enough. I think it's a different kind of broadcasting if the on-air person is also the opinion person."[65]

As one of the few males present at most of the hearings, Reid was guaranteed some status as a representative of the "male" point of view on the air, which allowed him more leeway than Patterson in expressing an opinion on the issues aired at the hearings. On *Matinee*, he was the educated, roving reporter and Patterson was the self-effacing stay-at-home host and entertainment interviewer, a split that reflected gender roles in society at the time but, interestingly, cast him in a less "objective" role, in the traditional sense, than it did her.

Regardless of what was said on the air, because the CBC was a crown corporation there was a fair amount of discussion behind the scenes between Bird and her former colleagues, which further complicated the whole issue of "objectivity." The Commission records show that around June of 1967 Bird, Robb, five women producers, including Wendy Blair from *Matinee*, and 16 of the CBC's local women commentators from cities across the country attended a meeting in Toronto. Patterson's name did not appear on that list. Some of the commentators discussed conditions for women in general in their own locales, and Bird did not specify exactly what, if anything, they suggested concerning their own working conditions. She referred to it as a "valuable" meeting, however, during which the women exchanged ideas that would interest the Commission's Control Group in charge of research. It was at that meeting that Robb promised national and local coverage, on both radio and television, for which she had speedily to prepare a budget. The coverage would be "expensive," according to Bird, and require extra funding, but Robb somehow managed to get it. Wendy Blair of *Matinee* "cheered" her with the comment, paraphrased in Bird's report, that the Commission's public relations strategy was paying off: "She [Blair] said that the commentators all felt there was more understanding of what the Commission was about and more sympathy with it." Three of the commentators at the meeting taped interviews with Bird there and others lined up interviews with her or other Commissioners later. Robb was among six career women who met with Lola Lange to discuss women in the workforce, and another senior executive, Betty Zimmerman, took part in a similar gathering. Today Robb recalls that, as the only woman in the boardroom she often had to remind senior management, when they were looking for people to do important jobs, that there were talented women available as well as men.[66]

CBC women were not the only ones to speak to Bird in private or to present briefs. Several journalists spoke to the Commission informally, including Ed Reid. Shortly after the hearings started, Reid told Patterson on the air on *Matinee* that he and his *Take 30* camera crew had arranged to meet with Bird privately and informally. The crew, Reid reported, had become emotionally involved in the Commission story; in fact, the sound man was so touched by something that was said at one of the hearings that he broke into applause. Reid, speaking hesitantly, as if unsure of his ground, seemed to be saying that the impetus for the meeting with Bird came from the crew, but he was involved as well. He said that the commissioners "know that *we* do have some views," and were interested in "the observations of people who have been watching them all along....I think there may be some useful things that, ah...they may be interested in some of the points that the fellows want to make."[67]

At the time, the Commission had been anxious to hear from men, as not many had been showing up at the hearings. Bird, who was already sure of Reid's loyalty, later remembered how the flippant attitude of the crew had been changing as they witnessed woman after woman coming forward with her testimony. The men discussed their views with her after cooking her supper in their rented accommodations. "And they, the chief cameraman, not Ed, whom I knew of course was devoted, became sort of very admiring of us and of me, too. It was very interesting, you see." She would not reveal the contents of any confidential letters, briefs or opinions, such as the one presented by Reid and the *Take 30* crew, so it is not clear whether they discussed gender relations within the CBC itself.[68]

Reid did not shy away from the topic when it actually came up on the air, although he chose to treat it lightly, as entertainment, probably out of self-defence. On *Matinee,* he kidded with Marjorie McEnaney when she presented the CWPC brief, asking her if she wanted only women on the air on *Matinee* and if his job was going to be safe. She explained that she wanted the CBC to have more women in prime time and reporting the news. The program ended with Patterson and Loring assuring audiences that their unit was 50-50 male/female, that their executive producer was a woman and that they were "all working together on '*CBC Matinee.'"*[69]

That it was Reid, and not Patterson, covering the Commission did not entirely escape public notice, either. When a woman at the Charlottetown hearing, who admitted she was being facetious, complained about it at the floor mike, Reid playfully aired the tape without warning his co-host. Patterson, caught off-guard, chuckled and quickly changed the subject. A briefer segment from the woman in Charlottetown was aired and joked about on *Take 30* as well. No explanation was given on either program, so listeners and viewers never did find out who was behind the decision to use Reid and not Patterson for the Commission assignment. They also did not catch Bird, who, after insisting that the woman at the floor mike "not discuss personalities," laughed heartily but quietly, and commented to a colleague, "Poor Ed! And he's doing such a good job." Today, Patterson recalls that, aside from any executive decision that was taken, she had a young son and would not have wanted to be away from him for too long.[70]

The CBC current affairs approach to "journalistic objectivity" obviously allowed a lot of leeway. Male commentators felt free to criticize the idea of having a Commission for women, while Dodi Robb and her units made it their mandate to support it. But it was also expected that a women's program commit its staff to coverage of the inquiry because it was regarded as important to its audience. Since the CBC itself, and gender relations within it, fell under the Commission's mandate, they felt strongly enough about the issues to give Bird herself some suggestions behind the scenes. Reid and his crew, as representative of masculine opinion, also made suggestions off the air, but he did make that clear in his coverage. Reid was allowed to interview his friend, former neighbour and colleague; in fact, he had to, since she was chairing the Commission. He could interview former and present colleagues presenting briefs, and tease his seemingly straightlaced co-host about why she was not doing his job, because it had come up at a hearing.

Gender Relations at CBC *News*

The men and the very few women who worked in CBC radio news generally took a more straightforward approach to the Commission story in line with what two of its reporters, Tom Earle and Gail Scott, both recall as fairly strict rules about "objectivity" on the air, regardless of one's personal biases. In those days, they went by the *CBC News Style Guide*, which insisted on "balance" and "impartiality." Earle covered the Commission's appointment and the *Report* from the Parliamentary Press Gallery, where he was CBC Radio's bureau chief. For him, the appointment of the Commission and, later, the filing of its recommendations, were "just another story," one of several he would file in the space of a week.

Earle had joined CBC Montreal in 1953 and worked almost entirely in an all-male environment until the late 1960s. The CBC News model of objectivity became second nature to him. It was not just a matter of presenting "both" sides of the story, he recalls. "You just knew instinctively that you had to be very, very careful and back up what you said." One could also do informed analysis in which the reporter would cite often unnamed authorities, as in: "'But the general view on Parliament Hill is that the government's bill...will cause a great deal of trouble.' That would be fair enough. There wasn't a fine line. There was a fine line about making outright statements," at least if you were a CBC newsman. According to Earle, there was great rivalry between the CBC radio's news and current affairs units, specifically the prime-time programs, where the understanding of objectivity was a little different. Producers and on-air staff prided themselves on taking a "broad" and "analytical view" of the news, and, he thought, tended to "look down" at the general news reporters.

It is also apparent from some of the surviving scripts and broadcasts that some of the men also tended to look down on women. In order to guard its reputation for being "unbiased," CBC News often used newspaper writers as commentators to present what were essentially broadcast versions of columns and editorials. Even when men declared that there was some basis for complaint about the inequities women suffered, they tended to qualify their statements and deliver them in patronizing tones. As a *Telegram* columnist, Frank Tumpane pointed out in his own somewhat supercilious commentary on *The World At Six*, "The militant female can detect the dreadful simpering tones of male condescension a mile away and there's nothing a militant female despises more than male loftiness."[71]

At CBC News, as in many newspapers, an atmosphere of male camaraderie, fed by heavy workloads and intense deadline pressures, encouraged a masculine "mystique" about being a journalist that included, in some individual cases, heavy drinking on and off the job. Gail Scott, hired by the CBC in 1967 as one of its first female news reporters, remembers CBOT in Ottawa, where she covered news for both radio and TV, and the national radio newsroom in Toronto as "systemically dysfunctional.... Alcohol abuse was rampant, overt and covert sexual harassment was rampant and there were no indications that anyone thought that this ought not to be happening. This was just the norm, you know." Scott was another of the young, talented, and very well-educated women coming into the profession at the time. She had studied languages, literature and theatre as a university undergraduate and went on to the Sorbonne and a theatre school in Paris for a while, but eventually abandoned her early ambitions to become an actor. Back in Canada, she graduated from the journalism program at Carleton University and interned for a time at CBOT. She applied for a job there at the insistence of a CBC newsman, John Drewery, who felt that it was high time women were hired as news reporters. Scott, who covered the Commission's national hearings in Ottawa as a single woman in her twenties, made $6,000 a year as a junior editor at the CBC in Ottawa in 1968, and $10,000 only two years later when she took on the senior editorial role of coordinating news coverage from Parliament Hill. But her case was rare.

Although she emphasizes that she means no disrespect to her former colleagues or the CBC, Scott laughs as she recalls that the newsroom atmosphere she experienced was like "a bad war movie. I mean we're in the trenches and the deadline is the enemy, and by God, we made that so have another drink. And as the sole female you were a cross between (not that I ever had the body for that)...a Florence Nightingale and Marilyn Monroe. You're there with the bandaids...Mother Earth, sex symbol, girlfriend, whatever. It was strange, quite strange."

Leers and snide remarks, when they did occur, came from some male peers, not from men she interviewed. Scott coped by ignoring most of it, or sending it up; one year, she hosted the annual Press Gallery dinner wearing a bikini; another year, a diaphanous "genie" costume, "which was all *deliberately* geared to be nothing other than deserving of cat calls and hoots and whatever. I loved every minute of it." Much of the time she pretended that everything was fine when it wasn't; that she was a mature and sophisticated woman of the world and she could handle anything that was going on and perform well professionally, too. It was a coping strategy she believes other newswomen used as well. "We put up with an awful lot of garbage... afraid of being perceived as...whining or just being a woman, or letting down the side, or ratting, or vulnerable or whatever. I mean, you spent a lot of time pretending to be someone you weren't to fit in." Scott covered the Commission's national hearings in Ottawa and other stories relating to women, as part of her general news beat.[72]

Male Media Workers and the Question of Women's Rights

While editorial reaction to the establishment of the Commission was mixed, and there were individual men who supported the equality of women, evidence suggests that, as a group, senior male journalists and editors had reservations about the demands Canadian women were starting to make. A 1970 Canada-wide survey by the Vanier Institute of the Family suggested that newspaper editors, station managers and program directors were generally conservative, especially on two issues, sex outside of marriage and mothers working outside the home. Their personal circumstances varied, but it appears that most were married to women who stayed home with their young children, the usual pattern at the time. It is interesting to note that this survey was conducted after the Commission hearings and suggests a great deal of resistance on the part of senior men in the media, regardless of the messages Canadian women were sending them.[73] Angela Burke, the Commission's public relations officer, found that the editors and news directors she visited in the line of duty were suspicious and fearful of the federal inquiry because they weren't sure how all that talk about women's equality would affect their own domestic lives. She tried to mollify them by implying that their spouses were not among the disadvantaged women who needed the Commission's help. "The way I thought to stem [their fears] was by being non-controversial and saying 'Well, you know, there are some women who haven't been as fortunate as some others such as your wives and myself'...and that was the tone I took mostly." In several letters to editors, she made it clear that the Commission valued their "male viewpoints."[74]

Burke's efforts followed initial commentaries in the newspapers and on the air in which some of the men either played the Commission for laughs or worked themselves into a fury over it. Both negative tendencies were considered part of their repertoire as iconoclasts, columnists, commentators and cartoonists, and were not taken too seriously inside the profession.[75] What they had to say, however, suggests that media women had good reasons to back the Commission, privately and publicly, since some of these men had high public profiles and could certainly fuel public resentment and disdain.

Aside from their concerns about the costs of the inquiry, the male commentators made joking parallels between English and French and men and women, ridiculed the women who wanted an inquiry, or just made fun of women in general. George Bain of *The Globe and Mail* declared that the Fathers of Confederation did not consider women one of the country's founding sexes. Tim Creery of Southam News commented that no doubt Quebec would want exclusive jurisdiction over its women. In a CBC commentary, Jim Stewart pondered whether or not to call the inquiry the Commission on Bisexualism, since Canada was made up of men and women, discounting "the queers as we men call them…with their exotic postures and gestures," an odd-ball remark that might have been a reference to a new omnibus bill that was to legalize private homosexual acts between consenting adults.[76]

The Ottawa Journal admitted that the idea of an inquiry scared men and concluded, "Women may make advances on men if they want to, but let 'em do it in their own way, and one at a time." In his syndicated column, Eric Nicol declared the inquiry to be "for the birds" and had fun with wordplay on the topic of "women's briefs."[77]

From the male-centred language of some of these items, it is evident that some men just assumed their audiences were male, too. Even a straightforward news lead, and the placement of articles about women's rights, could signal a certain scepticism. When the Commission announced its hearings schedule, and mentioned it would welcome views from men, a reporter in the *Globe's* parliamentary bureau began, "Men will be given an opportunity next year to offer advice on what to do with the fair sex." When the Voice of Women presented a brief in Regina declaring the women's pages a sex-segregated institution and suggesting that news of the Commission should be on the general news pages, the group was criticized. George Bain, who must have read the more sensational stories about the western hearings on the wire or in the newspaper, exhibited his blind spot about the extent of women's interests. He declared that there was nothing wrong with special sections of the newspapers, and that the rationale behind having the women's pages was no different in essence than having business and sports pages. "At one time, you'd have got thrown out of a saloon for discussing aloud what gets discussed every day on the women's pages now. The whole sex carries on like a lot of raging beasts. But they've got the bit in their teeth, and where it's all going to end, God knows."[78]

The news stories about the Commission's appointment, its financial state, and the *Report* originated in the Parliamentary Press Gallery. The men there tended to be seasoned journalists and broadcasters who worked 10–12 hours a day, and often spent weekends travelling on assignment as well. It was a demanding schedule which, Tom Earle of CBC News recalls regretfully, did not leave much time for their families. The very few women working there in the late 1960s, such as Susan Becker of CP, did not have the same privileges as the men. No battles were more divisive than the ones over whether the women should be allowed to play host to politicians, as their male colleagues did, at the annual Press Gallery dinners and be accepted as members of the National Press Club. Becker remembers that the Press Gallery women abstained when the members finally voted in 1967 to allow them to fully participate in the annual dinners, because if the vote was close, their opponents would blame them. They wanted the men to decide. Speirs of CP remembers visiting the National Press Club around the time of the Commission hearings and being startled when the bartender barked at her to move away from the long wooden bar that graced the main drinking area because women weren't supposed to touch it.[79]

Anthony Westell, then a political columnist with the *Toronto Daily Star*, was one of the men behind the move to allow women to participate in the dinners as a matter of "principle" and supported their membership in the club. Westell, who had earlier worked as a reporter and an editorial writer on *The Globe and Mail*, recalls that there was a very masculine, hard-drinking atmosphere in the Press Gallery at the time, that the dinner was basically "a drunk" where male journalists and politicians poked fun at each other, and the Press club was similarly a "boys' club" where some men went to find respite from the women in their lives. His own view was in line with "a sort of mood of the times, that things were changing, and ought to change...and journalism ought to change with them.... Women ought to have equal status."[80] Similarly, Tom Earle, the CBC newsman who was a Gallery colleague of Westell's, recalls, "Once you saw how unfair it was, the window opened. That's all."[81]

When the men first considered allowing women to become members of the National Press Club, however, in January of 1970, well after the Commission hearings, their vote, cast secretly rather than by a show of hands, was 58-53 against any change. The vote, broadcast on the CBC TV program, "Weekend," showed a procession of men coming to the microphone to present their positions, pro and con, most of them in jocular tones. One young newsman from CBOT in Ottawa said he was opposed to women members because he was afraid that "they're going to take control." After the vote, a group of news and sports reporters from the same station cheered the result.[82]

Women journalists, including Eleanor Dunn for the Guild, their liberal male colleagues like Westell, and NDP politicians and women's liberation activists subsequently took part in a noisy, 60-person demonstration during the club's annual ball, a well-attended, high-profile event held at a local hotel. Media coverage and commentary, which was generally critical of the Club, also took its toll on its reputation and the vote was subsequently and resoundingly reversed at its annual general meeting in May. As Ron Collister of CBC TV News said of the original vote, the Press Club had "'made a spectacle of ourselves.'" The first woman to join the National Press Club was Susan

Becker, who had recently married the Club's new president, a CP newsman.[83]

In the meantime, tensions were reportedly high inside the local media because of the Press Club issue. One female reporter, who had covered the original vote remarked, with some hyperbole, in the CWPC's *Newspacket*, "The Battle of Waterloo was never like this and some newsrooms have forbidden the subject to be mentioned in case of bloodshed."[84] Gail Scott was genuinely shocked at the result of the first vote and, when called upon, would passionately defend the equal rights of media women. Anthony Westell remembers being challenged by another male columnist who resented his stance.[85] After the vote was reversed, there was a minor skirmish when a *Citizen* editor, Charles King, who claimed he supported the women, publicly accused the CWPC of refusing to admit men to its membership. His column set off an internal debate within the women's club which was resolved when the members agreed to change the 1906 bylaws that mentioned only female members and to allow males to join. It was renamed the Media Club of Canada.[86]

A Divided Profession Tackles Women's Issues

There can be no doubt that there was antagonism over equality for female journalists, regardless of how well individual men and women got along together. The briefs from the CWPC and Eleanor Dunn made it manifestly clear that, like many women in the workforce, the women journalists were segregated from the men as a rule, were often not treated fairly in hiring, pay or promotions, and were operating in an atmosphere in which their work was denigrated or dismissed. Several of the women responded by becoming involved, either directly or indirectly through the CWPC, in the very story they were covering because it was important to them as well as to their audiences. The same situation applied at the CBC, where the conflict of interest stemmed partly from its position as a crown corporation.

It appears that what went on behind the scenes did not really matter as long as the journalists involved could present their work publicly in a "fair and balanced" way. But columns and editorials aside, when it came to contentious issues, such as women's rights, the objectivity ideal was honoured more in spirit than in fact. As Ericson et al., and Hackett and Zhao suggest, how journalists operate, and the values they bring to their craft, depend on several factors, including their relationships with official sources and with their own editors and colleagues, and their personal preferences and politics, no matter how well stifled under the professional rubric of "fairness and balance."[87]

Even so, those who covered the Commission regularly made sincere efforts to do a good job of it. Much of their work concerned the hearings, which were marathon sessions during which group after group presented its views on how the status of women in Canada could be improved. The reporters had to decide which briefs were worthy of attention and why, and then how to put the concerns expressed in them across to the public. The hearings were really about issues, not events or personalities, however, and for journalists used to working with accepted news values, that was the biggest challenge of all. They tried to get past that basic difficulty by using standard journalistic techniques, such as presenting conflicting points of view, spotlighting unusual ideas, and personalizing the very real dilemmas many women faced every day.

Chapter 3

"Ladies Reminded They're Women": Framing Feminine/Feminist

Be pretty, be pleasant, use mouthwash and deodorant, never have an intellectual thought, and Prince Charming will sweep you off to his castle, where you will live happily ever after. Such is the carrot and behind it is the stick: "Men don't make passes at girls who wear glasses," "wall flower," "spinster," "old maid," "loose woman," the list goes on, and its message is: to have caught a man is proof of a woman's desirability as a human being; to be without a man is a social and moral disgrace.[1]

—Bonnie Kreps, brief #373

$\mathcal{I}$ t was a June morning in Toronto, and 28-year-old Bonnie Kreps was presenting her brief to the Commission, then at the mid-way point of its tour across Canada. She was trying to impress upon the commissioners and the women attending the hearing how the traditional view of femininity limited women's real abilities and ambitions. The press described Kreps as a former university lecturer in English, a would-be broadcaster, an American immigrant, the wife of a physicist, and the mother of a five-year-old daughter, the priority of her personal and professional credentials varying according to the publication.[2]

Notes to Chapter 3 are on pp. 269–74.

Bonnie Kreps was also the future leader of the New Feminists, a later offshoot of the Women's Liberation Movement (WLM) in Canada. The WLM was then a fledgling group in Toronto, which favoured Marxist analyses of class structure in its interpretation of women's equality. The New Feminists, on the other hand, would regard patriarchy as the main force behind the inequality of gender relations but were still much more sensitive to class inequalities than were most liberal feminists.[3] In essence, Kreps was a woman in transition, as were many Canadian feminists at the time. Her role model, whom she quoted extensively in her brief, was Simone de Beauvoir. She also cited Friedan.[4]

Several days later, Kreps told a reporter, "I toned down some of my arguments. I didn't want to frighten them." It is not clear from the story whom she meant by "them." It could have been the commissioners, women attending the hearing, or the reporters who covered it. But clearly even the outspoken Kreps saw that discretion was the better part of valour, when, as a woman and a feminist, she presented strong ideas that challenged the traditional status quo, and, in particular, criticized the cultural ideal of femininity as limiting for women.[5]

Feminine Culture and the Media

American feminist writers, such as Tuchman and Douglas, disagree on the extent to which the media oppressed women in the 1960s, but it is clear that an emphasis on personal attractiveness, especially for young women, was still firmly embedded in the culture.[6] In Canada, the same mores appeared to hold sway, and were apparent in numerous news and feature stories about women that celebrated their desirable "femininity," and dismissed or downplayed any qualities that might be described as "feminist," its presumed antithesis. This dichotomy fit the general "conflict" model of news discourse, but made few allowances for the idea that perhaps a woman could be both "feminine" and "feminist," and gave little space or time to the mature woman of accomplishment without playing up her maternal role. A Commission study, for example, noted that 89 percent of female images in newspapers and magazines were of "young, elegant and beautiful" women under 35 years of age.[7]

The Royal Commission hearings presented a real challenge to journalists and commentators who were not always capable of changing the old news discourse about gender relations to reflect women's real concerns, rather than their images. While the interpretative objectivity of the 1960s allowed the reporters to analyze the cultural belief behind the women's testimony, they themselves were not immune to a certain defensiveness about the real meaning of womanhood, or the threat that "radical feminism" might present to it. This uneasiness manifested itself in story leads and angles, headlines, visual images and even music that both reflected and, sometimes, reformulated old labels and stereotypes.

With the exception of *Chatelaine*, Canadian mainstream magazines did not pay much attention to issues affecting women in the two years between the CEWC's lobbying and the Royal Commission hearings, but there was a definite interest among male writers in "liberating" women's sexuality. Even a young woman who was intellectually gifted could be framed according to her beauty, not her brains. *Weekend* magazine, for example, did a photo essay, mainly consisting of pictures and captions, on a young marine scientist who was photographed doing her research work wearing a bikini. The feature was entitled, "They Laugh when I Talk about My Seaweed," and noted, "Susan has an IQ of 150, which is about 30 points above what most people score, but she's blonde and pretty."[8] A reader sent the article to the Commission as "an example of what is wrong with present day attitudes towards women who have high I.Q's," adding that the text should have read "*and* she's blonde and pretty."[9] The Commission also received many complaints about gratuitous wisecracks and cartoons aimed at women in the press as well as advertisements and commercials that portrayed them as sex objects, or as homemakers and mothers who often needed the soothing, voice-over advice of a male expert.[10]

The Female Look

According to the media record, women who sent in their complaints or appeared at the hearings were not arguing against personal standards of attractiveness. They were searching for a new definition of femininity that would allow them to reject the worst of the old media stereotypes while still allowing women to retain their female credentials and a sense of optimism. As Myra Macdonald points out in her recent study of current myths about femininity in the media, "When women complain about the lack of realism in the media's representations of themselves, they are criticizing lack of diversity in portraying and defining women's lives and desires, not asking for a hall of mirrors."[11] When these same criticisms surfaced in briefs at the hearings, the reporters recorded them, and, in some cases, deflected them through their own use of sexist imagery in their coverage of the hearings, and through their resistance, which was shared by Florence Bird, to anything that smacked of government "censorship" of freedom of expression. They also too easily labelled any woman who was too forthright as "feminist," usually of the "militant" or "radical" variety, whether or not she embraced that term for herself.

Regardless of their gender, reporters and editors tended to respond defensively to any activist who strayed too far from the feminine ideal in presenting her case for equal status. At the same time, there was a certain fascination with the "militant feminist," representing, as she did, both the deviant and negative side of the "feminine" and, possibly, a threat to the social order. As many scholars have pointed out, the news media tend to exaggerate any deviancy from accepted cultural norms, which results in a news discourse that often distorts the message or intent of the groups or individuals concerned. As Ericson et al. explain: "They shape the moral band contours of social order, providing an ongoing articulation of our senses of propriety and impropriety, stability and change, order and crisis."[12]

While there is some truth to the argument that the men who ran the media were the ones who were concerned about how the women's movement would strip women of their femininity, in fact, women journalists reflected those concerns as well, which, as Macdonald notes, is not unusual.[13] There were differences among those who covered the Commission, but it was a matter of degree. Certainly, cultural understandings of "femininity" resonated strongly at the press table, as it did in society at large.

According to writer Susan Brownmiller, the ways in which a woman presents, adorns and moves her body, uses her voice, shows her feelings and expresses her ambitions, including a desire for motherhood, are all time-honoured indicators of that elusive quality considered most attractive in her, her "femininity." A feminine woman wears makeup, jewellery and skirts, perfumes and depilates her body, moves gracefully, smiles often, does not glare or shout, flatters men, and wants more than anything to have children, even when she also has a career. But, Brownmiller argues, allegiance to femininity restrains women in the ways they look, move and speak. "Femininity, in essence, is a romantic sentiment, a nostalgic tradition of imposed limitations," which really serves to underline and flatter the contrasting "masculinity" of men. A woman who refuses to play the game takes a substantial risk of losing masculine attention and approval, however, "for a woman found wanting will be appraised (and will appraise herself) as mannish or neutered or simply unattractive, as men have defined these terms."[14]

In its coverage of women's issues at the Royal Commission on the Status of Women the media did not define "femininity" or "feminist" specifically. Nevertheless, in their descriptions of the female commissioners, women's movement leaders, women who presented briefs at the hearings or sat in the audience, and even women in their everyday lives, reporters and editors qualified or indirectly invoked those terms, both positively and negatively, with references to physical appearance, body language, tone of voice and rhetoric, marital status, and actual or potential motherhood. Regardless of her age, journalists of both sexes most readily denigrated or dismissed a woman as both "unfeminine" and as a "feminist" when she was not considered attractive or pretty, was dressed in an unconventional way, appeared firm in beliefs which challenged the gender status quo, was assertive or aggressive in her body language, was judged to be loud, bitter or angry, was unmarried, older or not a mother. The pictorial record, that is, photographs, TV film footage and cartoons, reinforced these notions.

Figure 3.1. Florence Bird (Anne Francis), R. Olsen, *Toronto Daily Star*, 19 Dec. 1967 and 20 Jan. 1971. Courtesy of *The Toronto Star*.

The media were very interested in the women sitting on the Commission, especially Florence Bird, who had the air of a woman apart. Reporters described her as "a tall, distinguished-looking woman with upswept, white hair," and "a plummy-voiced 59-year-old broadcaster." Most journalists and editors were also careful to note that she was "Mrs. John Bird," the wife of another prominent journalist, even when some of them persisted in referring to her by her professional name, "Anne Francis."[15] Allan Edmonds of Maclean's commented on her attractiveness: "She's a bewitching woman with a fabulous sense of humour, and a damned good professional as well." He added, "Above all, Anne Francis is not a feminist" of the CEWC type.[16] When other journalists noted that she was a career woman without children, Bird claimed maternal experience in that she took care of a British friend's two little boys in Winnipeg during the Second World War.[17] Her femininity, class and professional credentials included studio photographs issued from the Commission office that invariably showed her in dresses, skirts and pearls.[18] There were occasional unflattering counter-images, however, shot by newspaper photographers, in which her mouth was wide open, or she was grimacing (see fig. 3.1).[19] All of these photos became "stock" shots and were used more than once.

Similarly, the reporter's descriptions of the four other female commissioners noted their marital status often, but not always, before their professional credentials. Most women journalists wrote about them in generally approving ways, using all the professional tricks in the book to make their articles interesting for their readers, including the snappy "lead," or introduction. The results were sometimes flippant comments that actually devalued the qualifications of the woman concerned. For example, in a series she wrote to introduce the commissioners to her readers before the hearings began, Alixe Carter of *The Ottawa Journal* began her article on the only unmarried member of the Commission: "If you can call an intellectual academic careerist a Go Go girl, then Jeanne Lapointe is just that. She obtained her pilot's license a year ago, which also proves she is a career girl constantly on the way up."

It can be safely stated that Lapointe, who was a respected literary scholar in her middle years from Laval University in Quebec City, would hardly be found among the hosts of gyrating, skimpily dressed and sometimes literally caged young women dancing above the throngs in night clubs and dance halls during the 1960s. The strained parallel between her and the go-go girl says something, nevertheless, about a perceived cultural split in flattering occupational designations for women, regardless of reality: you were either respectably married or a glamorous "career girl" on the go. In the absence of a husband, it was duly noted that Lapointe's father was a prominent lawyer. It was

a sharp contrast to the way in which Carter described the male francophone professor, Jacques Henripin, as "one of the new breed of
enlightened French Canadian academics."

Figure 3.2. Members of the Royal Commission on the Status of Women. From
left, standing, Prof. Jacques Henripin of Montreal; Prof. Jeanne Lapointe, Laval
University; Lola Lange, farm unionist, Claresholm, AB; Dr. John Humphrey,
Montreal lawyer. Seated, from left, Miss Elsie MacGill, an engineer from
Toronto; Anne Francis of Ottawa, chair. Judge Doris Ogilvie of Fredricton, NB,
is not pictured. *The Montreal Star*, 10 June 1968. Courtesy of *The Montreal Star*.

Taken overall, Carter's series on the commissioners was supportive of their mandate, but she often mixed the personal and the professional attributes of the female commissioners, something all the
journalists tended to do when describing especially accomplished
women. According to Carter, Doris Ogilvie, a juvenile court judge
from New Brunswick, had a "sense of fun" that was not only going to
be an "asset" during long deliberations but received more attention in
this article than her professional credentials. Elsie MacGill, clearly the

most feminist of the group, took after her late mother, a juvenile court judge from British Columbia, in that each was "a dogged doer of things" who rose to the top of her profession. Carter did not explain why MacGill, an aeronautical engineer who had been married for many years to a "business executive," persisted in using her maiden name. Lola Lange of Alberta was framed as an accomplished musician, a rancher's wife and mother of three daughters, who had taken many courses in leadership training and continuing education. She was also "attractive," a personal appellation that Carter did not use in reference to any other commissioner. Her lead on her profile of Commissioner Humphrey stressed that he wasn't "phased" [*sic*] at having to work with a predominantly female Commission.[20]

Figure 3.2a. Judge Doris Ogilvie, member of the Royal Commission on the Status of Women. NAC Florence Bayard Bird Collection #1975–440.

The Commission was presented in the media, and in fact, represented itself, as a calm, rational sounding board made up of very accomplished, well-bred, understanding and generally open-minded people who would do their best to make sure that all viewpoints were heard. (see fig. 3.2) They even observed all the social niceties between the sexes in public; for example, the men invariably held doors open for the women. The Commission's female members were ladies, and the male members were gentleman.[21]

While reporters invoked the "feminine" ideal in their descriptions of the female commissioners, and many of the women who presented briefs, they used the more negative and antithetical stereotype of "feminist" to describe any woman who did not seem to fit the accepted female norms. In their recent discussion of the media coverage of the American women's movement from 1966-1986, Ashley and Olson argue that during those years the news media presented feminists as less important, less legitimate, and more deviant than women who were anti-feminist.[22] This is a somewhat different argument than the one presented by Barker-Plummer, who writes that when feminist leaders cooperated with the media, their issues received better coverage. Nevertheless, supportive female journalists could not always persuade male senior editors that these stories were important.[23] While much of the coverage generated by journalists covering women's issues in Canada at this time was sympathetic, there were instances during the Royal Commission hearings when journalists and commentators misrepresented, dismissed and even insulted various women as "feminists," invoking time-honoured stereotypes to do so.

In an essay on the "tyranny of stereotypes," Canadian philosopher Lorraine Code explores how preconceived notions about women's abilities have limited their aspirations. She writes: "Despite the obvious inadequacies of their characterizations, (stereotypes) serve to define what it is to be a 'good woman,' they contribute to keeping women in their proper place in society, and they provide reasons for condemning as aberrant those who do attempt to defy their prescriptions."[24] Although they are based on limited, cultural understandings of women's nature, stereotypes have a certain currency, especially when they are repeated by individuals who are considered authorities or experts. Code notes that "a certain facility in their usage often masquerades as knowledge, both for a stereotype-user, and for listeners or readers of that person's discourse."[25] Thus, as van Dijk explains, stereotypes and prejudices can be represented in news discourse as general information about a social or ethnic group, such as its appearance, as well as its purported norms and attitudes, regardless of the facts of the matter.[26] Stereotypes about "feminists" as aberrant or deviant have been formulated and promulgated in the news media in just this way, especially by conservative males but also by women uneasy with the threat that they believed "feminism" poses to their "feminine" sense of security.

There was already a public expectation before the Commission hearings began that they would be dominated by professional and club women, whose leaders had already been tagged in the media as "vocal" and/or "militant feminists." Given that the Women's

Liberation Movement had not yet been firmly established in Canada at this point, the "feminist" label was actually a stereotype based on cultural memory of the middle-class, "first wave" feminists of 50 years earlier who had fought for the vote. Chief among the mid-to-late 1960s generation of club women was Laura Sabia, whose perceived militancy stemmed from her outspokenness on women's issues and, especially, her threat to lead a protest march of two million women to Ottawa if her request for an inquiry was refused.[27]

Figure 3.3. "Intent feminists…listen to speakers at women's status probe." *The Vancouver Sun*, 19 Apr. 1968. B. Kent, photographer. Courtesy of *The Vancouver Sun*. City of Vancouver Archives 443-68-1324 Frame 15.

The media construction of Sabia was interesting, considering that she was, in appearance, a model of well-groomed, ladylike decorum. It was her outspokenness that raised eyebrows. As Brownmiller has noted of a former British prime minister, Margaret Thatcher, "A woman on a soapbox with a microphone in her hand, even if she is perfectly coiffed, will still be called strident, hectoring or 'somewhat shrill.'"[28] Recalling the context of the middle 1960s, when "ladies" still wore hats and other accessories, Margaret Weiers of the *Toronto Star* comments: "Whether you're wearing white gloves and presiding at a tea party and proposing something quite outrageous that hasn't been done before, you can still be radical. And later on what you've done may not seem to be radical at all but was at the time it was being done.... Laura Sabia was what I would call a very radical feminist and she always looked the perfect lady."[29]

The labelling of Sabia was sometimes extrapolated to media descriptions of the hundreds of CEWC members as "militant feminists" as well. A male reporter saw the group's intention to keep an eye on the Commission proceedings as a threat from "militant watchdogs" waiting to "pounce" on the investigation.[30] The fact that many of the groups who later presented briefs were members of the CEWC added to the perception that "feminists" were running the show, regardless of whether they saw themselves as such, or what they actually said. Even women who showed up at the hearings just to listen were defined by their very presence as "feminists." A photo in *The Vancouver Sun*, showing a row of older women sitting in the audience, most of them wearing hats and one of them knitting, carried the caption, "Intent Feminists...listen to speakers at women's status probe" (fig. 3.3).[31] As the Commission prepared to move on to Alberta, *The Calgary Herald* warned its readers that the war between the sexes was out in the open with the headline, "Men Main Target of Commission on Women." The story makes it clear, however, that it was several women at the hearings, not the Commission itself, who criticized male attitudes.[32]

In prime time current affairs programming on the CBC, at least two programs dealt with the Commission in a dismissive way, using stereotypes to do so. The one that annoyed Florence Bird the most was called "Eve '67," and was aired on CBC *Newsmagazine* shortly after the inquiry was announced. The program began with an animated cartoon drawn by Duncan Macpherson of the *Toronto Daily Star*, that showed what looked like a sarcophagus in the shape of an outmoded woman, possibly from the Middle Ages, creaking open slowly to reveal a naked young woman cringing inside.[33] The program featured interviews with Bird, Sabia and other female experts on women's rights, intercut with comments from women under hair dryers, gyrating at slimming machines in beauty spas, defending wife-and-motherhood at a suburban coffee party and admiring and modelling dresses at a fashion show. Although all the women had interesting things to say about women's place in the world, the visual presentation clearly suggested that this place was not at the office. The host, Gordon Donaldson, opened and closed the show sitting in a botanical garden meant to represent the Garden of Eden. He insinuated that women were somehow guilty of some sin, and that the Commission was judging them. He ended the program by observing dryly, "It was, I think, the Queen in *Alice in Wonderland* who demanded that offenders be punished first and tried afterwards. This could be the case for the Canadian woman, who's just now, after 100 years, going on trial before a Royal Commission of four women and two men. Whatever it produces, it's certainly a worthwhile Centennial project. Perhaps we should have one every 100 years to find out what they're up to, and, of course, how to stop it." As Donaldson ended the program, the camera focused on him biting into an apple, cut away to several shots of flowers in the garden, and then caught the discarded apple as it was being tossed into a pool with a splash and what sounded like a spitting noise.[34]

Some viewers considered Donaldson so offensively patronizing that they sent copies of their complaints to the CBC to Florence Bird at the Commission. She told one of her correspondents that she was "distressed" by the program, which she thought was "cheap, superficial and sneering in a petty way. Why is it that we are not taken seriously?" She told another sympathizer that the many comments she made in the original interview were edited and spliced to the point where she felt that she sounded incoherent on the air. Bird had a few defenders, including Nancy Millar of *The Advocate*, in Red Deer, Alberta, who liked her straightforward comments, and criticized Donaldson's "jokey" approach and the segment in the beauty salon. "A sense of humour is a Good Thing, but not when it pokes fun at my favourite subject (or hadn't you noticed?)," Millar wrote.[35]

Another television program appeared to prize the Commission solely for its entertainment value. In the spring of 1968, the CBC's *The Way It Is* presented "a light look" at the hearings in BC, which it referred to as a "super-klatch." This segment consisted of short, intercut bursts of silent footage and sound clips of women, many of them older and wearing hats, at the hearings. The film was edited and timed to match the beat and lyrics of a Peggy Lee song extolling women's ability to do several tasks at once, "because I'm a woman, W-O-M-A-N." The grinning host acknowledged that this wasn't the original angle the producers had in mind and suggested that they might do another program on the hearings later on. Angela Burke wrote a polite letter to the program, pointedly enclosing the Commission's terms of reference and other background material, just in case they were planning to do a serious job of it.[36]

TV commentators were not the only ones to frame women inter-ested in the Commission in humorous or derogatory terms. Several male newspaper columnists did so too, including Mackenzie Porter of the Toronto *Telegram*, who in one column, tellingly headed, "Women Shall Remain Women, and That's That," spoke out about "brassy fem-inists." He wrote, "As a class, such women tend to be frumps, icebergs, bookworms or fishwives, seeking in the cause célèbre a pitiable sub-stitute for a more potent power they have either foresworn or been denied—the power that is exercised over men in the boudoir."[37] Newspaper columnists and broadcast commentators are not subject to the usual constraints, of "objectivity," but are expected to give readers an informed assessment and opinion of events in the news, even while giving free rein to their own individuality. Porter's column was a prime example of distortion, stereotyping and labelling, and was an irresponsible abuse of the journalistic freedom such a platform allows.

Given the negativity of that kind of media coverage and com-ment, it is not surprising that, as Rosemary Speirs observed, many women felt ambivalent and confused about losing their feminine cre-dentials and antagonizing men when they appeared before the Com-mission.[38] Their unease was underscored by women who came to the hearings to specifically "remind" other women of their proper place in life. At a hearing in Edmonton, a 30-year-old woman who referred to herself as Mrs. Trevor Anderson came with her husband and well-scrubbed young children in tow to defend traditional roles for wives and mothers. Speirs reported that she wore a bright pink dress, with ribbons tying back her long black curls. In its own story, *The Edmonton Journal* introduced her, on page one, as a "Man's Woman" while headlines in other newspapers read: "Ladies Reminded They're Women," "Femininity Plea" and "Married Women Told to 'Rely on Female Instincts,'" reflecting the cultural discourse of the proper female role.[39]

Anderson's appearance prompted Ed Reid of the CBC to invoke the classic "conflict" model of journalism is his account and, indirect-ly, raise the issue of "objectivity" as well. There was, he reported, a clear split on women's issues between traditionally minded women and more progressive ones, although they did not confront each other directly at this hearing. The progressive forces, he reported, included the women journalists at the press table.[40] On the next program, he elaborated. It opened musically with the lyrics, "it was good enough for grandma, but it ain't good enough for us," which Pat Patterson commented might make "a good rallying cry" for the Commission. Announcer Rex Loring then introduced Reid by describing him as the program's "beleaguered male on the scene," implying that he was somehow caught in the middle of a female mêlée. Reid let it be known that Anderson's appearance displeased some of the "press girls."

"Frankly they're aghast, I think, when someone says the man should be the lord and master."[41]

But men covering the story had taken sides as well. Lorna Wright, a reporter for *The Edmonton Journal*, revealed that "men reporters brightened visibly" at Anderson's appearance. According to Wright, one of them, "snapping his notebook shut with a relieved air," commented: "'Oh well, that is all that has really happened.'" A photographer murmured, "'Ah—that's your story. She's really got something to say.'" The gender split among the various media workers was apparent when it came to this story, as was the tenuousness of the "objectivity" model of reporting.[42]

Regardless of their personal feelings concerning traditional female values, however, the women reporters still tended to mention the qualifications of the women they covered in feminine terms. Even when a woman worked outside the home and espoused more liberal beliefs than Mrs. Anderson, the journalists frequently described her personal attractiveness, her marital status and even what she wore, sometimes in the same sentence as her professional or other qualifications. During the Ottawa hearings, one reporter noted in detail the particularly fashionable attire of a prominent union leader. Huguette Plamondon, the vice-president at large of the Canadian Labour Congress, "looked like a chic fashion-plate" but "spoke with ringing conviction" at the Ottawa hearing in October. Readers were told: "Miss Plamondon wore a smart, jaunty black hat, a black and white ensemble and gold jewellery. She also answered questions from the Commission on employment, discrimination, retraining, maternity leave and daycare centres." In the short, three-paragraph article, the unnamed reporter gave no details of the questions Plamondon was asked or her replies. But there was a head-and-shoulders photo of her at the hearing which took up twice the space of the copy.[43] Plamondon, described as "fiery" by another reporter, also let it be known that she was "not one of those fanatic feminists," even while she declared that unions could do more to help their female members. Reid also picked up her comment in his coverage on *Take 30*, but focused on gender conflict on the executive, illustrated when Plamondon forthrightly corrected her president, Donald MacDonald, after he defensively told Florence Bird that there was no discrimination against women within the unions affiliated with the Congress.[44]

Flattering descriptions of a woman's apparel, and taking particular notice when they spoke out, were common social and journalistic conventions at the time, and point to the fact that reporters were not immune to the conventions of their own culture when it came to women's roles. Even self-declared feminists such as Speirs commonly used expressions such as "pretty young mother" to describe women appearing at the hearings. Speirs herself caught at least one, presumably male, magazine editor's eye. The caption for a Canadian Press photo of her sitting at her typewriter, which accompanied her *Toronto Life* article about the hearings, described her as an "emancipated woman" and "a gorgeous redhead who is 27 and single," even while noting that she was just completing her PhD in labour history.[45] Elinor Reading remembers that this kind of descriptive information was mandatory at CP; however, reporters were not allowed to refer to men as "balding,"[46] presumably because that descriptive adjective, no matter how factual, might detract from their masculine self-esteem.

The Female Voice

It is apparent from the media coverage that, aside from youth and beauty, another measure of "femininity" was the way in which a woman conducted herself in public, with the emphasis not just on what she said, but how she said it. For many women, the very act of speaking out, especially at public meetings, was risky to one's "feminine" sense of self. At the Commission hearing in Halifax, Nova Scotia, one woman scheduled to present a brief felt so intimidated that she refused to get up and do it. As Eleanor McKim, the women's editor of the *Evening Telegram* in St. John's, Newfoundland, wrote on a similar occasion, speaking out in public was a challenge to the bravest of women, especially when men were present. "We're still immobilized by the long held tradition that it is unfemminine [*sic*] to be forthright....It's going to take a new kind of courage for women to overcome this sub-conscious hurdle."[47]

The women who found the courage to speak up at the Status of Women hearings were aware that they might appear strident or shrill, even when their anger was justified. One reporter recorded an interesting exchange between two women at a hearing in Calgary, Alberta. While one complained that "'women have become very shrill in saying they are mistreated and misunderstood,'" another woman countered "that if female demands sound strident and shrill, 'it may be that we have been asking for changes so long our voices have become shrill with repetition.'" Rosemary Speirs maintained that the occasional "whining" or "petty, querulous tone" that crept into the discussions resulted from the guilt these women felt at making demands, as much as from their unhappiness.[48]

Some journalists at the hearings seemed uncomfortable with anything but the most ladylike presentations. In Ottawa, one reporter describing a summary of the discrimination suffered by female professors at universities, a brief opposed by their own male-dominated associations, seemed to need to reassure her readers that the presentation was "calm in tone and free from feminist lecturing." When Carrie Best, a Black activist and newspaper columnist from Pictou, Nova Scotia, challenged the commissioners on the lack of racial minority and aboriginal women at the Halifax hearings, and later made a few comments in Ottawa about Black women and education, her white colleagues at the press table praised her interventions as "even-voiced" and "dignified." Their readings amused the usually outspoken Best, who wrote in her autobiography that it "may be the last time I shall be so described." Their response to her also begged questions about their expectations of a woman of colour, whom white culture often framed as unattractive and domineering.[49]

"Feminists" and "Suffragettes"

Not only did a woman have to watch her tone of voice when she spoke out in public, she had to be very careful not to threaten men in what she said if she wanted to be taken seriously and not be vilified in the media as a "feminist." In Vancouver, a sociologist, Norma Ellen Verwey, was labelled "some kind of nut" (her own words) after she suggested, in apparent seriousness, that all young men of 16 and over be forced to undergo compulsory vasectomies which, she said, were reversible. Since men had the superior status in society, she argued, they should take the main responsibility for birth control. Signalling the "unusualness" and unconventionality of her presentation, CP gave the story priority, flagging it as a "(SPECIAL)," and some newspapers carried it on the front page,[50] using rhetorical and pictorial strategies that immediately presented Verwey as deviant. The front page story in *The Vancouver Sun* included a picture of the middle-aged woman, who had short hair and was not conventionally pretty, with her mouth wide open and the caption, "Norma Ellen Verwey...pleads to commission" (see fig. 3.4). The story noted that Verwey was married but childless, as if this had something to do with her position. The CP version that appeared in *The Globe and Mail* was headlined "Compulsory Vasectomies at 16 Advocated by Feminist Sociologist," and referred to Verwey's "ardently feminist presentation." To balance her assertions, it included counter-testimony from a local medical specialist who said vasectomy could be reversed in fewer than half of cases.[51]

The media's coverage of Verwey's appearance at the Commission hearing was not entirely accurate. The original photograph of Verwey, which was taken in Vancouver and distributed by CP, actually showed her sitting in the audience, apparently reacting to someone or something off-camera. It was cropped to a close-up, making it look as if she was actually presenting her brief. The woman in the background appears to be looking disapprovingly at Verway, but she is actually talking to a companion. Moreover, the audio tape of this hearing reveals that at no time during her testimony did she refer to herself as a feminist. She even told the commissioners that although she favoured equality, she accepted discrimination as a sociologist; it happened in society and it was futile for women to expect much change in the near future because that would take generations. She did not "plead" but stated her case calmly: she was looking for alternative ways to lighten the load on women in the meantime. The feminist commissioner MacGill, who believed in the healing influence of education, seemed taken aback by her fatalism.[52] Given the media spin on Verwey's presentation, it is not surprising that other women appearing before the Commission, including a teaching order of nuns from Quebec, would support only "those feminist movements" which could demonstrate that they were "'truly feminine and not excessively radical.'"[53]

Figure 3.4. "Norma Ellen Verwey...pleads to commission." *The Vancouver Sun*, 18 Apr. 1968. B. Kent, photographer. Courtesy of *The Vancouver Sun*. City of Vancouver Archives 443-68-1324 Frame 5.

But what was "excessively radical"? When the media want their audiences to grasp an idea instantly, they sometimes use a historical reference, a supposed shared memory already embedded in the culture. In this case, the media compared the "feminist," especially of the "militant" variety, with the radical "suffragette" of a half-century earlier. In fact, Canadian "suffragists," as they were properly known, were a much more decorous group than the real suffragettes, the members of the Women's Social and Political Union in Britain, and were not given to hunger strikes, stone throwing or arson in order to win the vote. But the modern media saw parallels between the violence of the suffragettes and the determination of the assertive modern-day club woman, using a historical reference that did not really fit the case to label the women concerned.[54] One writer, for example, urged Canadian women to become active in the women's movement, but assured them that they didn't have to become "suffragettes" to do so. Marilyn Anderson, in her column in the *Niagara Falls Review*, wrote "while we don't have to resort to the tactics of suffragettes, tying ourselves to lamp posts to get what we want, we do have to get ourselves involved in fighting for our rights."[55]

The "suffragette" motif continued throughout the media coverage of the Commission and after it, in both small and large publications, and was accepted by journalists and some readers alike. After the Toronto hearings were over, Elizabeth Thompson's advice column in *The Globe and Mail* featured a debate among herself and a number of readers variously identifying themselves as "Sick of Suffragettes," "A Suffragette," "A Woman," and "Another Suffragette," and all espousing viewpoints that ran the gamut from traditionally conservative to socialist.[56] According to "Another Suffragette," many upper and middle-class women "are bought off by luxury, by fear of losing their 'femininity' in the eyes of the control group, by token reforms, and by permission to perform self-flattering charities." She argued that until they learned to stop behaving like pampered pets, and started challenging their men, there would be no equality.[57] A contrary opinion was expressed by a young reader of *Chatelaine*, 17-year-old Cathy Scaife of Burlington, Ontario, who asked: "Is the age of chivalry completely dead? Women must face the fact that man's role in society has always been dominant. If women cannot put up with a degree of inequality, the day may come when the roles of men and women are interchanged. We will have nothing then, for Femininity will be extinct."[58]

Scaife's was an unusually young voice in this media discussion, as most of it was aimed at mature women. Although some young women showed up at the Commission hearings, others appeared reluctant to do so. The media investigated and concluded that many of them were uncomfortable with the whole idea of feminism. The Toronto *Telegram* actually set up a panel discussion featuring female students from York University and the University of Toronto, who thought "'feminists' are old hat." One student was optimistic that her generation could change things without an "aggressive" women's movement. She is quoted as saying, "I react violently to this suffrage thing—I don't think it will solve anything."[59]

Not all young women rejected the "suffragette" image, and shunned feminism and women's issues. Another young woman who felt very differently appeared before the Commission in Vancouver. She was Kathyrn Keate, a student at the University of British Columbia (UBC), who was also the daughter of the *Sun's* publisher, Stuart Keate, and who worked during the summers as an intern journalist. She had earlier spotted a Commission ad in a newspaper and decided to complain about the frustrations she experienced as a bright undergraduate. *The Vancouver Sun* played up her contention that there were unofficial quotas that worked against female students in some faculties at UBC. The newspaper apparently saw accusations of unfairness against a local institution as having more "proximity" for its readers, especially when the Dean of Women apparently backed her up.

Sexist Imagery in the Media

Rosemary Speirs of CP was more interested in what Keate had to say about another issue that had come up at the hearings: media images of women, especially on TV and in the ads in women's magazines. This was the story that received the most play across the country. In Speirs' lead, Keate blamed mothers and the media for instilling certain attitudes about how young women were expected to behave. She was also quoted as saying, "I think this causes a lot of suffering in girls as they are growing up." Keate, whom Speirs referred to as "a pert brunette university student," also said the men of her generation were willing to consider women their equals, or could at least be persuaded that they were competent. As if to underline the idea that a supporter of women's rights does not have to bully men, Speirs quoted her further: "You can be firm in a ladylike way and get good treatment. You don't have to go tromping all over men with jackboots."[60]

Keate's appearance at the hearing was also laced with irony, considering that her father's newspaper had just published a vitriolic editorial declaring that the makeup of the Commission and its terms of reference "doom it to be a wailing wall for every scatterbrain, malcontent and frustrated pope in skirts....What is harmless trivia and self-pity over the back fence or underneath the dryers is an embarrassment when it is entered as official evidence." Keate remarks today, "It made an interesting story, a good ironic story, gave it a good angle," but her father had never talked to her about the *Sun's* attitude toward the Commission. She recalls that he looked "embarrassed" when he read of her brief in the newspaper the next day, but that might also have been because he was an alumnus of UBC and was then on one of its governing bodies.[61]

He did give her the original of one of Len Norris' editorial cartoons which ran in the *Sun* and has been kept in the family since. It depicted a father, playing cards with his cronies in the family living room, yelling at his bratty young daughter, attired in sleepers, who is glaring defiantly at him from the doorway, "I don't care what they said at the Royal Commission on the Status of Women...get back to bed!" (see fig. 3.5). Norris did not remember the story behind this specific cartoon when asked, but said that there were no little girls among his regular cast of characters at the time. "I needed her to be a girl because it was the Status of Women and she was down there to demand to get in on the game."[62]

"I don't care what they said at the Royal Commission on the Status of Women...get back to bed!"

Figure 3.5. Norris, *The Vancouver Sun*, 20 Apr. 1968. Courtesy of Len Norris and Dr. Kathryn Hazel.

The real-life Keate, who was, of course, several years older than the little girl in the cartoon, felt that the Commission at least took her seriously. "That's what the Commission did for me. It said the way you see the world is valid and true and the wrongs that you're angry about are definitely wrongs that should be righted." The experience had an impact on Keate, who did not always separate her role as a fledgling journalist from her burgeoning feminism. A few months later, she covered a Commission hearing in Toronto for the *Telegram*. The next day, after an impromptu invitation, she appeared on a panel on a local CBC program, *The Day It Is*, discussing the Commission with other panelists and, in her case, criticizing *Playboy* magazine for its impersonal attitude towards women and sexuality.[63] No one at the *Telegram*, she recalled, questioned her actions. Later, as a graduate student in Toronto, Keate became an active member of the Women's Liberation Movement, occasionally acting as a media contact. She was one of the organizers of the Abortion Caravan, a pro-choice demonstration that resulted in the protesters holding a sit-in inside the House of Commons in May 1970, bringing the day's business to a halt.[64]

It was not just some young people like Keate who were fed up with sexist images of women and a lack of role models for them in the media. There were many older women who felt the same way, including Wilma Brown of Regina, a public school teacher who declared to the commissioners that some advertising, especially on television, amounted to "hate literature" against women. *Matinee* that day began with a song with the lyrics, "How lovely to be a woman," and included a segment featuring Brown. She said legislation should be applied against images of women that depicted them as "senseless idiots." She said she did not favour censoring good literature, but some control should be exercised on the air, at least at the CBC. She was speaking particularly of the kind of commercials that showed "some brainless woman snipping another one's clothesline." Bird asked if it would not be difficult to "impose this censorship on advertising," and who should decide what images women wanted. Brown agreed that the issue was a problem and she was not sure how it should be resolved.

On *Take 30*, Reid ran roughly the same excerpts of the exchange between Brown and Bird, and, on both programs, reinforced the point with comments from Humphrey who challenged another group, the Voice of Women (VoW), over the same issue. Humphrey asked them rhetorically if it wasn't women themselves who form the attitudes of men when they are children of an impressionable age. He said men learn everything from women. "Now, if there is this insidious plot, who is responsible for it?" One of the group's spokeswomen responded, "we" all were, "from Genesis to 'Dick and Jane.'"[65] A similar exchange concerning censorship later occurred between Bird and Marjorie McEnaney during the presentation of the Toronto CWPC brief, but was not included on the program. After Bird pressed her on the issue, McEnaney also agreed that censorship was not desirable, and not even the CBC should be told what to broadcast. Their discussion was edited out at the time, possibly because, given the coverage of Brown, the point had already been made, and to repeat it might have been considered giving too much space to "old news." But it is clear that Reid was picking up and reinforcing Bird's perspective on censorship, presumably because it matched his own and that of other journalists like McEnaney. It is also possible that, because the CBC's current affairs staff had recently been at loggerheads with management over the corporation's public image as a national broadcaster, they were particularly concerned about that kind of control.[66] Nonetheless, Bird's and Humphrey's exchanges with McEnaney, Brown, and the VoW about censorship and sex-role stereotypes serve to illustrate Ericson et al.'s contention that shared perspectives among officials and journalists can limit challenges to the status quo, including the way women are portrayed in the media.[67]

Program hosts, journalists, interviewees and other experts are not the only people who interpret stories about women's roles, however. The people who work behind the scenes can also contribute to a discourse that is polarized and contradictory. A *Take 30* camera crew, in a telling sequence about women in Quebec, projected their own ideas about femininity, which either deliberately or inadvertently challenged women's complaints about media stereotypes. Reid introduced it on the air as the crew's "visual report on their reactions to the status of women." The camera followed several women, most of them young, pretty and in mini-skirts, as they walked along the street. Part of the sequence showed closeups of their faces, hair, knees, legs and behinds, with medium shots allowing for fuller frontal and rear effects. Other shots lingered on women rubbing their noses or otherwise playing with their faces. A group of nurses and a pregnant woman also appeared briefly. There was only one counter-image to this "femininity" mosaic, a young woman striding comfortably along in pants who did not fit a feminine stereotype. The entire sequence closed with a tall young man, filmed from behind, protectively clasping his much smaller girlfriend to his side.

Earlier in the same program, Reid had gone out to the streets of Montreal, gleaning complimentary comments from mostly male tourists to Expo '67 about the legendary feminine charms of Quebec women. The two segments seemed out of sync with the rest of the program, which concentrated on serious discussions about the status of women.[68] The executive producer of the program, Glenn Sarty, after watching the film sequence of the women years later, commented, "It is a beautiful statement in favour of the status quo, at any time." He theorized that perhaps the crew "felt that little tingle in the back of their necks" at the prospect of the changes in gender relations that might result from the Commission hearings.[69] As for the women of Montreal being more attractive than anywhere else, Paul Soles comments frankly: "That's how the whole world looked at the women of Montreal at that time. Which is why, of course, the Royal Commission was necessary, and why the feminist movement arose....I'm not defending it, or condoning it. But that is in fact the way we were."[70]

A certain unease with feminist radicalism, real or imagined, was also reflected in the coverage and analysis from women journalists who didn't question the cultural attitude that women's rights advocates should not be too forceful. When the hearings ended in October of 1968, Yvonne Crittenden of the *Telegram* was able to report, with some satisfaction, that the Commission had made a real difference to the aspirations of Canadian women, partly because the women presenting briefs were not, by and large, what one vituperative male columnist, Dennis Braithwaite of the *Telegram*, called "all those feminist harridans who projected their hatred and envy of men into a holy crusade."[71] Crittenden was telling her readers, many of whom were housewives, that ordinary Canadian women had legitimate complaints, even while she seemed to buy into the "militant" stereotype of the feminist then popular among male columnists. In her award-winning, front-page analysis she wrote that the Commission's eventual recommendations would be "One report Ottawa can't ignore." She noted that the issues brought before the Commission during the hearings, such as the need for daycare, equal pay and job opportunities, reproductive freedom and tax reform "have been in the news for years and are favorite targets of militant women's groups." But what had happened at the hearings themselves made a difference to how these issues were being heard now. "When the commission was first announced, many people, mostly men, announced openly that it would be an exercise in futility, that the feminists and 'flowered hat brigade' would dominate the hearings, that all one would hear were whines and gripes." She used quotes from the Commissioners to reassure her readers that most women who appeared before the Commission were not resentful or bitter, that there was no "battle of the sexes" and that the women simply talked about their day-to-day problems. There were ordinary women who were "scared stiff" about getting up and speaking in public, and others with "private, heartfelt briefs," some of whom had travelled hundreds of miles to get to the hearings. That, according to the Commission's records, was what Bird was hoping the media would say,[72] and, judging from the audio tapes of the hearings, was also generally accurate.

The Journalists' Conflict over Feminism

No matter how hard they worked to be "objective," the journalists who covered women's concerns at the Status of Women hearings were unable to step outside the attitudes of their own culture and time when interpreting the terms "femininity" and "feminism." The juxtaposition of these terms also fit the "conflict" model of reporting, and did not allow much room for highlighting similarities rather than differences. According to their accounts, the female commissioners, and most of the women who appeared at the hearings, confined themselves to standard, "ladylike" behaviour even while presenting the toughest arguments. The emphasis on their perceived "femininity," including descriptions of how they looked, their marital and motherhood status, what they said and how they said it, was derived from feminine culture, and from what Brownmiller perceives as the strategy for survival that suffuses it.[73]

It was important to most of these women, and to the journalists who reported their words, to believe that one could gain equality with rational, humanist arguments, without sacrificing one's "femininity" or, at the very least, important that men be placated in the process of "revolution." In other words, women were going to have to win their rights by looking attractive, by not raising their voices, by not challenging the status quo too abruptly, and by not overtly threatening men. That meant distancing themselves from more impatient women who did raise their voices, did threaten to shake up the status quo, and did challenge men. These women became, by definition, "feminists," usually of the "militant" or "radical" variety, a label that was difficult for many women to accept for themselves, at least publicly, regardless of their personal feelings and actions. Their resistance was underscored by images of women, even in the media coverage of the hearings, that bolstered old attitudes towards women and disputed new ones while giving support to the Commission in general terms. At the heart of the matter were fears that demands for "equality" in the workplace, at home, and in the bedroom, would irretrievably alter relations between the sexes.

Chapter 4

"Accept Us As Individuals in Our Own Right": News of "Equality"

Either you are a woman and entitled to the privileges this entails, or you are "just one of the boys" and you can get down off your perch and start scrambling for a living with the rest of them.

—Joyce Donovan, *The Sunday Reporter*[1]

The terms of reference of the Royal Commission on the Status of Women gave priority to "equal opportunities" with men, but there was some confusion among columnists and reporters over what that meant. They used the term "equality" and its variants quite often in the coverage of the briefs presented to the Commission, but gave it several uncertain and disputed meanings. This confusion was particularly evident in relation to the many complaints about the lack of "equality" for women in education, on the job, and in politics and public life. It was not surprising, given the cultural context of a rapidly changing Canadian labour force, especially for middle-class women. This uncertainty over meaning was a constant discursive thread in most of the headlines, story leads and quotes from the hearings, and challenged the journalists' personal perceptions, which tended to be liberal, as well.[2]

Notes to Chapter 4 are on pp. 274–81.

Much of the coverage stressed a dominant news discourse of "equal rights," regardless of what the Commission's terms of reference actually said. According to the journalists' accounts, many complainants declared that they suffered "discrimination" and were treated as "second-class citizens," often comparing the situation of Canadian women to that of "negroes" in the United States. Journalists, using standard news values, were easily able to play up various instances of "conflict" between, for example, government and civil servants, owners and unions, and male and female employees, which made for good news stories. Another very effective way of getting the issues across was to personalize the stories of certain women, so that one woman became symbolic of sex discrimination in her own field. Journalists also tried to use the simplest language to explain some very complex issues concerning labour legislation and what it meant. These tactics, well-regarded as professional practice, both helped and hindered the cause of women's equality in liberal feminist terms.

The professional bounds of "objectivity" were strained to some degree in that there were inconsistencies in how the journalists approached different aspects of the "equality" question. Some journalists, especially those writing for liberal publications and the CBC, did better than others at explaining the difference between equal pay for "equal work" and "work of equal value." As a group, they appeared less keen on the idea that women needed "discrimination in reverse," "preferential treatment" or "special status" in order to catch up to men, but seemed to favour the argument that women take "equal responsibility" with men, and be treated as "persons," or "humans" rather than as "women." This rather complex media rendering of women's demands for "equality" may have reflected the journalists' own concerns as women trying to make it in a man's world, and their essentially liberal politics as well.

"Equal Rights" in Education

A key concern for Canadian feminists of the 1960s was the need to update the traditional education of girls and young women so that they could take office jobs in the expanding business sector, earn post-secondary degrees, develop professional careers, and run for public office. Female students were not groomed to be professionals or skilled workers; they were educated, by and large, to be good wives and mothers. Usually, they were cast in supporting roles, which was evident in every aspect of the way they were taught, from the pictures and lessons in their textbooks to the advice their guidance counsellors gave them in high school. As they got older, girls tended to concentrate on social studies, home economics and commercial courses, while boys took mathematics, science and vocational courses such as welding or carpentry, a pattern that was repeated in trade schools.[3]

Much of the discussion about education at the Commission hearings focused on universities, which, generally speaking, were bastions of the upper and middle-classes. There were few female graduate students, and the female undergraduates, about one-third of the total, tended to take degrees in arts or education. They were often assumed to be there for their "MRS," that is, to look for a suitable husband, not to pursue a higher degree or embark on a career.[4] Although university authorities denied that quotas against women existed, or that female applicants had to have higher averages than the males, some law and medicine faculties had formal and informal barriers, the effect of which was to limit the number of women students, based on the assumption that they would leave their professions once they married. The Commission's executive secretary, Monique Bégin, discovered this when she met with several education officials in Quebec. In Nova Scotia, the School of Medicine at Dalhousie University decided not to bring in a quota after research revealed that most female doctors were still in practice. In Ontario, it was a matter of common knowledge, and even acceptance among some teachers, that quotas against women still existed. The Faculty of Education at the University of Toronto sponsored and provided trainee teachers for a publicly funded secondary school which excluded women altogether.[5] The Dean of the College of Education, D.F. Dadson, cited historical precedent, lack of financial ability to expand, and lack of will to divide the school's enrollment of 420 equally between male and female. He argued "it would mean the end of a school which has proven its worth over the years, and the substitution of another with doubtful potential." The end result of such systemic discrimination, however, was wasted intellect and ability.[6]

Despite the importance of this issue, it is apparent that the media gave it second billing to other briefs presented at the same time, partly, perhaps, because they felt it was a provincial matter, and other matters such as abortion and bilingualism, were more apt to make headlines.[7] The reporters tended to pay more attention when students themselves, or one of their educators, complained to the Commission that young women were being held back by university tradition, unofficial quotas and outdated social attitudes.[8]

Attention to those briefs did not always translate into a focus on those particular complaints, however, especially when there were competing media agendas. In Ottawa, for example, Janet Kestle, an executive member of the student council at the University of Western Ontario, told the Commission that universities should lead in changing outmoded social attitudes concerning women's intellectual abilities and interests. Perhaps because male faces were in short supply at the hearings, one of the reporters who covered her brief chose three males from a class of over 20 journalism students from Carleton University to comment on it. When one of them responded that more men should have been at the hearing, his remarks were captured in the lead of the story, which was headlined, "Says Men Affected by Commission," which had nothing to do with women and education. Nor did the comments of his fellows. A student from India said women in his country were treated equally in the workforce and would not have needed such an inquiry. A third said he came to the hearing expecting "another tea party," and was surprised at the "excellent quality" of the briefs and to find a man among the commissioners. The story, reverting to its supposed focus on education, also said that "many" of the journalism students, who were there on a class assignment, were unhappy with Kestle's contention that male students in general thought women went to university to find husbands. The reporter did not give a gender breakdown of the class or quote any of the female students, although there were several women in this particular journalism class. Kestle's point was buried in the last paragraph of the story in the *Journal*, and her complaint that as an intelligent female interested in math and physics she was often made to feel like a "phenomenon," received a mere three lines in *The Ottawa Citizen*.[9]

Similarly, in another story, the *Citizen* chose to highlight a quote from a Carleton student that female deans hindered rather than helped their female students. The unknown reporter did not elaborate on this point, but went on to say that the student, Rosemary Hooey, also had "harsh words" for her "fellow co-eds." She said they felt they were expected to be "flowery" and emotional in class, or risk losing their Saturday night dates. In contrast, Rosemary Speirs of CP, who wrote a longer story using the same material, quoted Hooey as saying that the situation was improving and that this kind of "brainwashing" was disappearing. There was a place for the female student who wanted to be intellectually equal as long as she was persistent; it was employers "who make a mockery of the universities' career placement programs."[10] Speirs, who earned her own PhD, obviously thought Hooey's viewpoint was worth a story. But the local media's relative dismissal of it, and of Kestle's complaints, may also have had to do with other aspects of media agenda-setting. Ottawa, which was the last stop on the Commission's tour, was the venue of high-profile, national organizations and unions, and the federal public service, and the emphasis and space in the local coverage and on the CBC were generally reserved for those briefs.

In other stories about young people and education there was an underlying "conflict" pitting separation from male students against integration with them as measures of equality and social progress. A striking example of this occurred in Halifax where the head of Mount Saint Vincent University, Sister Alice Michael (later known as Sister

Catherine Wallace), presented a brief. Not only was Sister Michael prominent locally, she had ideas the media considered progressive, especially in unspoken contrast to the conservative stereotype of the nun and the Roman Catholic church. According to headlines over the CP version of the story, she suggested that "All-girl Universities a Thing of the Past" and "College President against Separate Life for Females." The local *Chronicle Herald* also focused on her ideas about integrating educational institutions: "Women Cannot Stay in Isolation." These stories suggested a certain irony: here a prominent nun, who was the head of an all-female institution and herself lived a life largely segregated from men, seemed to be saying that everything she stood for was wrong. The CP story, the more detailed of the two, contrasted her views with those of other briefs presented earlier during the Commission tour, which suggested that girls and young women would have a better chance of succeeding if they were trained for the "masculine" professions in their own institutions where their needs would be given priority. On *Take 30*, Sister Michael chided Ed Reid for the media's obsession with radical student politics rather than putting extra effort into letting them know about the hearings in Halifax. "You know, you publicize what's new, but you are not making news." The students were also at fault, she said, adding presciently, "I think they are going to be protesting things later that they could have talked about here so they would not have to protest them later."[11]

At the time, when some students were taking over university buildings on campuses across the western world, anything that smacked of anti-authoritarian and youthful rebellion was grist for the media "conflict" mill. Campuses were slowly but surely becoming a major breeding ground for a new brand of outspoken feminism as well, not to speak of Marxist analyses, which most mainstream newspapers dismissed.[12] For example, in Toronto, the Commission heard from four Young Socialists who seemed to some uneasy journalists to represent a real threat. They had several suggestions that struck the reporters as radical, even though more mainstream groups or individuals had suggested similar ones. These suggestions included free tuition for everyone, no restrictions on scholarships, free access to birth control and childcare on campus, and an end to the practice of streaming female students into arts programs. The delegation connected "student power" with more say in the curriculum, a common demand at the time. They believed it would result in equality for women students, who would no longer be made to feel by their professors and guidance counsellors that their real place was in the home. The free tuition suggestion was not new, however. It had also been made by a member of the Liberal Party Women in Calgary, Alberta.[13]

The media, however, viewed the Young Socialists with great suspicion and immediately set up a "conflict" model for the story. *The*

Telegram began its account of their presentation: "The seven commissioners looked apprehensive as the militant delegation composed of three mini-skirted girls wearing huge Che Guevara buttons and one serious looking youth wound their way through flowered hats in St. Lawrence Hall. The Young Socialists began quietly and then let loose a wild diatribe against society which they said suppresses and degrades young Canadian girls."[14]

In contrast, another newspaper, *The Globe and Mail*, took the same confrontational tack but approvingly declared in its headline, "Commission Keeps Cool under Young Socialists' Fire." The lead was: "An unflappable group of commissioners kept their cool last night amid a shower of fireworks" from the students, some of whom "raised their voices to a shout" when questioned. Furthermore, as if to emphasize that these young people were unconventional, one story described one of them, Jacquie Henderson, as "a 21-year-old blonde in a low-cut blue dress and orange sandals" while another mentioned that one of her co-presenters, Kate Porter, had "hair cut so short she looked more like a boy than a 21-year-old woman."[15] CP said "Political activists wearing yellow, pink and blue mini-skirted sun dresses Thursday asked the royal commission on the status of women what it plans to do about student power."[16] The *Toronto Daily Star* chose another angle— that Florence Bird angrily squelched the students' attempts to discuss Canada's policy on Vietnam.[17] The most straightforward lead was in *The Montreal Star*, which noted that the Young Socialists examined the "basic foundations of Canadian society" and quoted them as saying that "women are raised from infancy to play 'second fiddle' with the blessing and encouragement of the capitalist system."[18]

Because they were so caught up in the stereotype of the radical student, most of the journalists missed the essence of an interesting discussion about equality versus special treatment for female students in the education system. The Commission's own audio tape recording of the hearing reveals that, at one point, commissioner MacGill, referring to the students' recommendations, asked them, "You don't believe in what is called reverse discrimination—giving women an edge." Jacquie Henderson, who raised her voice in emphasis but did not shout, replied, "Yes, I would be in favour of giving women an edge. After so many thousands of years of men having the edge, I think a few years of women having the edge would do a hell of a lot of good." Her frankness was greeted with laughter and applause from the audience who seemed to appreciate what the students were trying to say about discrimination against young women, whether or not they agreed with their socialist perspective.[19] Only Lillian Newberry of CP included any mention of that part of the discussion and Henderson's comment, but those paragraphs were edited out in subsequent versions.[20] Certainly, the portrayal of the Young Socialists is an example of journalists bringing their own subjective attitudes to their work, especially when it concerns groups considered "deviant." In this case, they replaced a discussion about equality versus special treatment, which was an important issue for the Commission and the students, with a more confrontational one about student radicalism.[21]

The discussion concerning "reverse discrimination" in the university system also came up in the case of female professors who were in a distinct minority, routinely paid less than their male colleagues and treated dismissively. One of their spokeswomen was Pauline Jewett, who had experienced gender discrimination first-hand as a lecturer at Queen's University in Kingston, and as an assistant professor at Carleton University in Ottawa.[22] One account in *The Ottawa Journal* began, "Carleton University Professor Pauline Jewett says the academic community will have to practise 'discrimination in reverse' if women university teachers are to receive equal consideration." It further quoted Jewett as saying "preferential treatment" was necessary; however, "I don't mean preferential treatment in the sense that you would take a lousy woman instead of a good man." The reporter further quoted her as saying that the problem was "getting in there in the first instance," in this context, into senior positions. Once that was attained, the woman was given, according to Jewett, "absolutely equal treatment" with her male peers.[23] Other stories, however, made it clear that Jewett and her three colleagues who accompanied her to the hearings were referring to problems at all hiring levels. In the CP version, Jewett said that it would take 15 years of "reverse discrimination" before employers would get used to the presence of women and automatically hire on the basis of merit. The CP version also provided telling statistics from 30 universities showing that male professors outnumbered females by about ten to one, most of the women were in the junior ranks and, regardless of length of tenure, were paid an average of 1,200 dollars a year less than the men.[24] Both local papers reported that the all-male boards of the Association of Universities and Colleges of Canada, and the Canadian Association of University Teachers, for which the brief had been prepared, refused to endorse it. The *Citizen* and the *Journal* included a revealing detail about students' attitudes as well. It was not unusual for a female professor to be greeted at the start of the term by a chorus of groans when her students realized they were going to be taught by a woman.[25] This brief was not covered on *Take 30*, but it was discussed on *CBC Matinee*, where Ed Reid and Ruth Worth, another reporter, focused on the professors' comments that universities were no more forward-looking than governments when it came to outmoded attitudes about women.[26]

Even though there was some confusion about the real meaning of "reverse discrimination," it was clear from the evidence the reporters chose to include in their stories that women on campus were not treated fairly. Still, in some quarters there were suggestions that women themselves were to blame. In one of his columns in the Winnipeg *Tribune*, Val Werier had earlier cited an American study which seemed to indicate that female college students were prejudiced against female authors of academic texts. Werier took this study at face value, and projected it onto Canadian women, asking rhetorically, "Do women not like women?"[27]

Elementary school teachers, unlike university professors, were a majority in their profession, but lost ground to male colleagues at the high school level. News stories about their issues, including that few women were appointed principals no matter how much education and experience they had, effectively revealed what we would now call "systemic discrimination" in education. This was especially true when the media linked sexist attitudes against both girl students and female teachers to demonstrate how both were treated as "second-class citizens." In Toronto, for example, several reporters covered a brief from the Federation of Women Teachers Associations of Ontario, using the comments of spokeswoman Florence Irvine. Maggie Siggins of *The Telegram* began, "How do you tell a 12-year-old girl she is second rate, and that no matter how hard she works, she likely won't be among the top in her profession?" The teachers, she added, were "sick of being rated as second class citizens simply because they're women."[28]

Canadian Press began, "How do we tell girl pupils they will always be second-class citizens," before adding a rider from Irvine, "'It's a rhetorical question of course. We don't tell girls that. We encourage them to try for the best future careers they are capable of.'" Irvine went on to reveal, however, that privately she wondered how many of her Grade 8 students realized that no matter how capable they were, "they are going to reach dozens of dead ends."[29] Both *The Globe and Mail* and the radio news service of the CBC focused on the Federation's criticisms that had to do with federal jurisdiction, but the *Globe* also posed the question of how to tell a "bright young girl" that she is a "second class citizen."[30] One of the smaller newspapers in Ontario, the *Owen Sound Sun-Times*, seemed to misinterpret the CP story, running it with the headline "Girls, You're Second-Class Citizens: That's What Women Teachers Say." Based on its understanding of the story, which it had received second-hand from the CP reporter on the scene, the same newspaper editorialized, "the statement that girls are 'doomed' to second rate citizenship is unwise. The major role for girls must be that of homemakers.... They should not be made to feel that this is a second rate career."[31]

At the time, women teachers in Ontario were officially given "equal pay" but in reality were often relegated to lower-paying positions in the education hierarchy, as were their colleagues elsewhere.[32] Several of the stories also included telling statistics reflecting female and male teachers' real status, but the *Toronto Daily Star's* was the most detailed. It included the Federation's contention that although they ostensibly received equal pay, the women tended to be more skilled and better trained than their male colleagues who were promoted over them. Again, "Women Appear to Be Recognized as 'Second Class Citizens.'"[33] In Ottawa, reporters covering a brief from the Canadian Teachers' Federation focused on discrimination against teachers hired by the federal government and their general status in the profession. One story included a photo of four teachers who, according to the flippant caption "talk turkey" to the Commission.[34]

The "Equal Pay" Debates

Women's groups appearing before the Commission made a concerted effort to expand the boundaries of "equal pay" legislation. They argued that while women doing exactly the same jobs as their male counterparts deserved "equal pay for equal work," those who were sex segregated into separate jobs from men but were doing equivalent or comparable work should be given "equal pay for work of equal value." Most of the professional women who appeared at the hearings complained that regardless of whether they supposedly received "equal pay" on paper, in reality they were paid less than their male counterparts and were not hired or promoted at the same rates. Despite the laws that did exist, the principle of "equal pay for equal work" was not being applied, even by the courts. For example, early in 1968, in a decision which upset many feminists and unionists, a judge of the Ontario Supreme court denied equal pay to Lois Beckett, a police officer in Sault Ste. Marie, on the grounds that it was "common sense" that she should be paid less than her male counterparts.[35] Similar workplace issues affected other middle-class professionals, such as business women and civil servants, although they had higher salaries and generally more job security than other women, especially if they also had bargaining rights. The 1962 (Glassco) Royal Commission on Government Organization barely discussed female civil servants at all, but did say the federal government was not making the best use of their skills and abilities. Discrimination was not "official" but was there in practice.[36]

The media stories from the Status of Women commission served to reveal the underhanded tactics even the federal government used to keep women in inferior positions. In Vancouver, a young biochemist working in the federal forestry department complained that she was doing the job of a lesser-paid technician on the specious grounds that research work was more physically strenuous.[37] In Ottawa, the National Council of Women of Canada accused the federal government of denying well-educated and qualified women the chance to reach senior positions in the civil service: "The 'not qualified' aspect of the situation changes to 'lacks personal suitability.'"[38]

Other stories underscored the problems of women in other professions who were generally paid between 60 and 85 percent of male salaries and did not have the same chances of being hired or promoted once they were. Those in sex-segregated occupations, such as nursing, wanted equal pay with women with similar education in other professions, and in some cases, with nurses in other provinces, as well as with men with medical training similar to their own. At the time, there was a shortage of nurses in Canada, partly because the job was badly paid and opportunities were opening for women in other fields.[39]

The fact that women were usually paid less than men and discouraged from succeeding in their careers was a legacy of nineteenth-century social attitudes which held that men needed a "family wage" to support their dependants, while women, regardless of their real circumstances, only needed pin money to pay for extras, or, at most, a "living" wage to support themselves. While these pay practices persisted, suggestions were being made by the end of World War II that since the workforce was largely sex-segregated, women should receive equal pay for "comparable work."[40] By the 1960s, when more women were supporting themselves or their families, the "equal pay" discussion took on an additional urgency, both at the federal and provincial levels. None of the existing "anti-discrimination" laws, with the exception of Quebec's, included sex as a prohibited grounds of discrimination, and Newfoundland and Prince Edward Island had no such laws at all. There were federal and provincial equal pay laws, except in Quebec and Newfoundland, but they were not enforced. In addition, BC and PEI had separate minimum wage acts for men and women, while in Nova Scotia, the existing minimum wage act covered both sexes but stipulated different rates for males and females. The Yukon had no legislation forbidding wage discrimination against women at all. Where legislation did exist across the country, it was up to the employee to prove discrimination.[41]

Groups like the Federation of Business and Professional Women (FBPW) were able to argue before the Commission that not only had the UN recently supported the principle of equal pay "for work of equal value," so had the new Convention 100 of the International Labor Organization (ILO).[42] It was a complicated issue but in their coverage the journalists working for the more liberal media made genuine efforts to differentiate between, and explain, certain terms. For example, Margaret Weiers of the *Toronto Daily Star* used the FBPW's "hardhitting" brief to outline the rather confusing differences in human rights and labour laws across the country. In her article, Weiers cited the FBPW's statistical information, that underlined the extent to which men and women received different rates of pay, which also varied from province to province: a junior accounting clerk in Montreal received $77 a week if male and $65 a week if female; this compared respectively with $86 and $72 in Toronto and $88 and $69 in Vancouver. Weiers paraphrased the Federation's president, Louise Card, who, using the example of a typical department store, explained how employers got away with paying women less. Simplification was one way to get the message across. "They pay a woman sales clerk less than a man, she said, because the man sells men's shirts, ties and socks while the woman sells women's blouses and sweaters. Or they vary the job description so that it indicates a man may do an additional assignment which, in fact, he never does." Weiers' story as it appeared in the *Star* did not mention, however, the FBPW's recommendation that Canada ratify the new Convention 100 of the International Labour Organization.[43] As Sheila Arnopoulos of *The Montreal Star* explained to her readers, it "enunciates the principle of 'equal remuneration of men and women workers for work of equal value.' There is no doubt, they [the FBPW] said, women are doing jobs which if done by men would command a higher salary."[44] According to Mollie Gillen of *Chatelaine*, the FBPW was suggesting that the wording of the federal act be changed from "identical or substantially identical work," to "work of comparable character done in the same establishment."[45]

But readers of other publications were either misinformed, or not told about the differences. According to the *Daily Times and Conservator* in Brampton, Ontario, the FBPW complained that Canada was reluctant to ratify Convention 100 of the ILO "giving equal pay to men and women for equal work." This story said the Convention had been in effect since 1953 and had been ratified by 37 other countries. In fact, some of Canada's existing laws were based on that old Convention, but had not been updated to comply with the new one.[46] *The Globe and Mail's* only reference to the ILO was that it stipulated the inclusion of the word "sex" in anti-discrimination legislation. The Toronto *Telegram* gave no information about the ILO Convention at all.[47]

The media response to the equal pay discussion at other hearings was inconsistent as well. In Vancouver, the United Fishermen and Allied Workers' Union raised the question of whether or not certain jobs should be reserved for men or women, and if they were, why this should imply lesser value for the "female" ones with a corresponding difference in pay.[48] On *CBC Matinee*, Ed Reid ran a clip of a union representative Mrs. Mickey Beagle, who argued: "The work that women do, in fact in most cases, is work that is certainly equal, but sometimes is *entirely different*. But that doesn't mean that it isn't equal. It can be equal in training, and it can be equal in production, equal in value to the total production, and equal in a whole number of ways, and the only thing that isn't equal about it is that it pays a lower rate."

This was the only media coverage that gave Beagle the time and space to explain how she saw the issue. Although Reid used essentially the same segment of the union's testimony before the Commission on both *Matinee* and *Take 30*, this particular passage was inexplicably omitted in the TV version.[49] In his report, Brian Kelleher of CBC Radio News succinctly paraphrased the union's brief: "If a woman contributed as much to production or efficiency as a man, she should get the same pay even if their jobs were not exactly the same."[50] Rosemary Speirs of CP, without getting into semantic distinctions between "equal work," and "work of equal value," used a specific example. She focused on the fact that a highly skilled female fish filleter made three cents an hour less than an experienced male general worker. She made $2.34 an hour while he made $2.37. The union, Speirs wrote, wanted "an elimination of the standards which set arbitrary divisions between what should be women's and what is men's work."[51] The local press, however, gave the distinction short shrift, being more interested in potential "conflict" between male and female workers, and union and management. One newspaper focused on the hypothetical question of whether the men would go out on strike to support the women, while its competitor flagged Beagle's assertive demand that the government put some "teeth" in the current "equal pay" legislation and drastically increase the fines for those employers who broke the law.[52]

In another instance, the media coverage of the equal pay discussion was hijacked by a national union's bitter recriminations against the federal government's policing policies. In Ottawa, the Canadian Union of Public Employees (CUPE) appeared before the Commission to demand that the Female Employees Equal Pay Act of 1956 be amended. This large union included 40,000 women, or one-third of the total membership, who worked mainly as support staff for municipal, provincial and federal institutions such as city halls, hospitals, school boards, government commissions and the CBC. Most of the press reporters, however, were far more interested in a dramatic accusation from the president, Stan Little. He and an associate, Gilbert Levine, said the Women's Bureau of the Department of Labour was a "sop" to women. It had no real power and was inadequately staffed to enforce the Act. This accusation, and Little's blunt admission that unions did not support their female members, took precedence on CBC radio news and in most newspaper headlines over his discussion of how the law should be changed.[53] It was an adversarial story, again based on "conflict," that had some educational value in that it suggested that the two agencies, government and union, which might be relied upon to defend the principles of "equality" for women, were not doing so. Huguette Plamondon of CUPE said much the same thing about unions during her testimony,[54] as did Eleanor Dunn of the *Citizen* in relation to the Newspaper Guild.[55]

The media also took notice when working-class women appeared before the Commission, especially when they criticized their unions, as this denoted yet more "conflict." Although union membership among women more than tripled between 1965 and 1981, most of them were public sector workers. In the late 1960s, only about 17 percent of women in the labour force, including some who worked on "women's" assembly lines, were unionized. Gender segregation was the norm in many factories, which the women experienced as destructive. It had led to massive layoffs for the female employees of McKinnon Industries, a subsidiary of General Motors of Canada in St. Catharines. The company transferred its "women's lines," including those producing shock absorbers, horns and spark plugs, to the United States or other parts of Canada after the two countries signed the 1965 Auto Pact. It was around this time that the United Auto Workers (UAW) women began to view gender equality as a specific goal.[56]

In Toronto, Ann Thomson Fast, a former chain-cutter who led a 12-woman delegation of laid-off workers from McKinnon Industries to the Commission hearings, angrily denounced her local of the UAW for not allowing them to "bump" less experienced men on the "male" production lines, for not fighting for the women's jobs, and for discouraging them from taking leadership positions in the union. This particular conflict was headlined in newspapers such as the *Globe*, which announced, "Discrimination Study Urged: Laid-off Women Say Unions Won't Aid Them."[57]

Another case coupled a personal story and strong rhetoric to bring out the fact that some women got equal pay but not equal benefits. In Toronto, Christine Bennett, who had worked as a solderer at the Continental Can Company of Canada Limited for more than 20 years, declared angrily that the Canadian Bill of Rights was "nothing but words that don't mean a damned thing" and her own male-dominated union was no help to her. The headlines were not exactly impressive; one of them was ungrammatical and the other was a pun, which suggested that she was not being taken seriously: "Says Bill of Rights Don't [sic] Mean a Thing" and "Christine, the Solderer, Is Burned Up."[58]

The reporters rarely told the stories of groups of poorly paid, unorganized workers, such as secretaries and clerks, apparently because they rarely appeared at the hearings. Women who worked in offices did write to complain to the Commission, however. According to Florence Bird, many women submitted confidential briefs because they were afraid they might lose their jobs if they spoke too openly, and these women may have been among them.[59] On *Take 30*, Reid featured one secretary who showed up at a Vancouver hearing to complain that she made less than a "ditch-digger."[60]

"Equality" in Public Life and Politics

Education and paid work were not the only areas the media high-lighted. They also covered briefs that pointed out the ways in which women were virtually shut out of public life and politics, underscoring the debates which centred on questions of "equality" versus "special treatment." This coverage also involved another question: Was it better to be a "woman" or a "person," a question the journalists were trying to grapple with in relation to their own working lives.

At the time there were no female bank directors, few women on boards of directors, and Canadian stock exchanges actually barred women from occupying seats or working as brokers, situations Laura Sabia had targeted for immediate action. Very few women were appointed to government commissions, and media commentators could only point to "firsts" for women, such as the appointment of the first woman director of the National Art Gallery of Canada, Jean Sutherland Boggs. But high-profile appointments such as hers were few and far between even on government boards and commissions, and, despite the publicity, did not really signal a brand new world for "career women."[61]

The same situation applied in party politics, where most women were either segregated into separate auxiliaries, as in the case of the Conservatives and the Liberals, or not encouraged enough to take an active role in the party itself, as was the case in the New Democratic Party (NDP).[62] Political analysts believed that most women were ill-equipped for an active political life outside of the "helpmate" model because they tended to lead domesticated lives, a factor which nonetheless was construed as their own failing. As Charlotte Whitton, social worker, alderman and former mayor of Ottawa, said, "The doors are open now if women did [sic] not want to be sissy-pussies making sandwiches in the ladies' auxiliary."[63]

The fact that the media and the public could be hard on female politicians and tended to emphasize their personal rather than pro-fessional qualities[64] might also have had a chilling effect on their ambitions. It was difficult for them to win party nominations during elections, and they could not even count on endorsements from women active in volunteer groups that pressured the government on specific issues, because these groups wished to be seen as non-partisan in terms of party politics. Only the most determined women, like Judy LaMarsh or Pauline Jewett, the professor from Carleton, ran success-fully; Jewett served as a Member of Parliament first for the Liberals and then for the New Democrats.[65]

By the late 1960s, many party women were debating whether they should join the men in the main organizations, stand for election and press for more female representation in the Senate and on federally controlled councils, boards, committees and commissions. Only 20 percent of the delegates at party conventions were women, and no more than one woman at a time had served in the federal Cabinet.[66]

For all the media excitement the Commission hearings had engendered, the election year 1968, when "Trudeaumania" was at its height, was not a good one for women. The headline over one of Doris Anderson's editorials in *Chatelaine* expressed her disappointment at the outcome of the federal election in June: "Justice: 1 Woman to 263 Men?"[67] There were 34 female candidates in the election, including 19 New Democrats, six Conservatives, one Liberal, and two each running under the banners of Creditistes, Social Credit, Communists and as independents. Of the four female MPs in the previous Parliament, only Grace MacInnis of the NDP was returned to the House.[68] As Jean Sharp of Canadian Press noted wryly in her "year-ender" feature in December, "Certainly federal election results seemed to indicate that, however high (the Commission) may rank as a conversation-starter, that status isn't up to much otherwise."[69]

The question of what to do about women's poor record in politics came up at the hearings several times. While some women criticized the main political parties for the dismissive ways in which they treated women, others, like the Alberta Liberal women, were quick to defend them. There was some discussion as to whether the parties should adopt strategies which we would now refer to as "affirmative action," that is, quotas, dual male-female constituencies or proportional representation, a debate which was already taking place in the United States as well.[70]

In Victoria, the Voice of Women (VoW) made the front page of the local paper after it told the Royal Commission that one-third of government jobs should go to women. According to Brian Kelleher of CBC Radio News, the pacifist VoW believed that, in his words, "with women having a real voice, there would be less chance of a nuclear war or a world paralysis caused by pollution, plague, starvation or overpopulation." The VoW believed that women were more able than men to protect basic values, but the media saw the suggestion of quotas as unusual enough to give it prominent coverage.[71]

Sometimes the news reports left the impression that the commissioners themselves were in conflict with people prepared to give women "special treatment." In Halifax, the vice-president of Nova Scotia's New Democratic Party, Peggy Prowse, replied to a question from Commissioner Humphrey about encouraging more women to enter politics: "What we ought to do is cut our present ridings in half and set up dual constituencies across Canada. Then we could run a man and a woman in each one." She acknowledged that it would mean a lot of seats in Parliament, "but we have to start somewhere." Humphrey responded that there would be a danger that people would say that the women were elected only because of their sex: "They might be treated as second-class politicians." But Prowse, noting that in the current Parliament only one MP was a woman, replied undaunted, "It looks to me as if the men who got there, made it simply because they are men."

Rosemary Speirs framed Prowse's position as "offbeat," possibly because it ran counter to the national NDP's position.[72] Speirs had earlier signalled her own scepticism about this kind of suggestion when the Alberta Farm Women's Union told the Royal Commission that 65 House of Commons seats should be reserved for women. Speirs noted in an analysis article that their spokeswoman could not explain, in response to a commissioner's query, "how this could be implemented in a democracy." She also picked up on a critical comment from a Liberal women's organizer, Mrs. Bruce Longmore of Calgary, that some women presenting briefs at the hearings were "fuzzy thinkers" because they had not thought through recommendations like the one from the farm women. Her sentiment was reflected in a headline in *The Vancouver Sun*, which, editorially, was not friendly to the Commission: "Fuzzy Presentations Galore At Women's Status Hearings."[73] Florence Bird scrambled to do damage control, insisting at her next news conferences that the briefs were well done and commending women for their courage in coming forward.[74] It seems that her husband was premature in his private comment to her that she had obviously "captivated" Speirs.[75]

"Equality" or "Special Status"?

A sub-theme in the discussion about work, politics and public life was the idea that women were holding themselves back, especially when this admonition came from prominent women like Longmore. *The Calgary Herald* quoted her as saying that women were mistaken if they believed that they were being mistreated and misunderstood. Her comments as presented in the *Herald* were ambiguous, however. The next paragraph quoted her: "Women want complete equality plus special status because they are women, " but it is not clear if she meant this as a criticism or an affirmation. In the next paragraph, she was paraphrased as saying that women who enter the workforce "expecting equality in wages and privileges must also be prepared to accept equal responsibility." The article seemed to confuse the issue as to whether women wanted equal or special status or both.[76] In a more dramatic and concise CP version, Longmore, who had a young daughter and worked part-time, was quoted as saying that women should "stop hiding behind their own skirts," and if they wanted to be treated equally they had to change their own attitudes and give the same time and effort to their jobs as men, "with no more excuses on the basis of sex or family obligations."[77] In an interview with Reid on CBC *Matinee*, Long-more confirmed his impression that women at the Calgary hearing were divided between "two poles," those who saw themselves as discriminated against because they were "women" and women who insist on being considered "a human being first, and a female second." The distinction between the two was again not made clear but she implied that women who complained that they were discriminated against because of their sex were simply making excuses for their own inadequacies.[78] In its overview of the Edmonton hearings, the local *Journal* headlined what it thought was the overriding sentiment expressed by the women there as well. "'Accept Us as Individuals in Our Own Right,' Women Petition."[79]

Similarly, Manitoba's first woman cabinet minister, Thelma Forbes, captured the day's headlines when she declared, during a short welcoming speech at the opening of Commission hearings in Winnipeg, that women must take "equal responsibility" with men if they wanted to get ahead in the world. Colin Hoath of CBC Radio News reported that Forbes "clearly surprised a few of the women in the audience with her argument that women were sometimes their own worst enemies when it came to getting ahead in the workaday world." Women were not, she claimed, making enough use of the opportunities and choices that they already had, and she implied that those who complained were basically whiners. Hoath ran an audio excerpt of her comments to underscore her point: "They must compete actively for advancement as opportunities arise, seeking out responsibility rather than passing it by. Too many girls and women are content with being a temporary member of the labor force, either before or after marriage. In this day and age, the world is her oyster for a single career girl, if she would but make the effort to prepare herself to improve her status rather than cry the blues about being passed by."

Hoath ended his report abruptly and mysteriously by interpreting Forbes' remarks as "a word of warning for the Royal Commission on the Status of Women,"[80] while the local *Tribune* headlined the story, somewhat snidely, "Thelma Tells the Girls to Stop Complaining."[81] Mollie Gillen later picked up on the "responsibility" theme in an article she wrote for *Chatelaine*. It warned, "Watch out for absenteeism, lack of ambition, low mobility, fear of responsibility. In advance of the Status of Women report—a startling look at the other reasons why women don't succeed in business." The media's coverage of the remarks of these prominent women lent a strong tone of self-blame to the discussion of equal rights, and suggested that there were only two camps of feminist thought, and they were in conflict with each other.[82]

Throughout the discussions during the hearings, there was a sub-theme that came up in several briefs and in the media coverage which, in a racial context, begged an essential question about the nature of "equality." Several speakers made patently inaccurate and simplistic parallels between the struggle for women's equality rights in Canada and the struggles of the American "negro." For example, Margaret Butters of the *Welland-Port Colborne Tribune,* a local weekly in Ontario, discussed the briefs presented in Toronto in a very supportive way, adding: "Throughout all of the sittings, either spoken or inferred, is the feeling that women in Canada are in the same situation referring to civil and legal rights as the negro in the United States. They have been termed 'second class citizens'; 'cheap or slave labor.'"

Any reasonable woman would fight for her rights under those circumstances, or so Butters implied.[83] She may have been referring to a specific and unusual brief, in this case, from a white male, 47-year old Bruce Mickleburgh, who caught reporters' attention in Toronto when he declared that Canadian women in general were being treated like "slaves" and it was time for them to fight their oppression.[84] The same kind of misplaced language came up in other stories.[85] It appeared to be part and parcel of the "human rights" approach to equality issues and ignored several key facts; for example, there had once been slavery in Canada and the majority of Black people in North America, including those in southern Ontario and Nova Scotia, were poorer than white, middle-class women, most of whom did not carry the double workload of most Black women.[86] Yet, when Carrie Best, the Black activist from Nova Scotia, spoke at the Commission hearing in Ottawa, the media gave no details about her comments on education and Black women.[87]

In their opinion and analysis articles, women journalists took the same attitude towards equality as many of the prominent women whose remarks they had covered. They were unanimous in declaring that women should not have "special status" or be treated as anything "less" than a human being, even when they disagreed on the extent to which women were discriminated against. In her assessment of the responses on equality issues from the reader survey in *Chatelaine,* which was "pro-woman" to begin with and elicited the hoped-for responses, Mollie Gillen acknowledged "the need you feel to be recognized as *persons.*" Although there were no specific questions on "special" status for women as such, there were enough comments to lead her to conclude that there was some reluctance to appoint women "*as women*" to positions of authority.[88]

Linda Curtis of *The Albertan* wrote that if men reversed roles with women for just one or two weeks, "they might get some idea of the obstacles with which women are confronted every day in their efforts to be treated simply as human beings." In her scenario, a businessman who makes the role-switch finds that every talent and advantage he thought he had was suddenly ignored or dismissed. He winds up on a psychiatrist's couch, tearfully pleading, "I'm a human being. Why should I be treated like a second-class citizen?" The psychiatrist tells him that "normal women don't want to compete with men" and recommends tranquilizers to calm him down. Here it is clear that being treated as "a human being" meant being treated equally with men, and being treated "as a woman" meant "second-class" status.[89] Similarly, Shirley Hunter, writing in a Roman Catholic publication, wondered how long it would take before "defensive" men realized that women "don't wish to be men," or to threaten their masculinity. "We simply want to be persons with the freedom and dignity that word implies."[90]

Pat Dufour of the *Victoria Times* recognized what she called the "quiet anger" behind the briefs to the Commission that demanded "more just interpretation of the equal work, equal pay laws." But she also believed that, rather than blame men for their circumstances, Canadian women should start to act like "people." Each woman must throw off the "shrinking violet" tendencies which prevented her, for example, from running for public office: "why should she settle for the 'pink tea' and coffee party ignominity [sic] of an auxiliary when she can play an effective role in the group which it feeds?"[91]

Sheila Kieran, writing in *Maclean's*, wanted "more realistic equal-pay-for-equal-work laws" but did not think Canadian women were discriminated against enough to need a commission of inquiry. She accused both "professional Friedanites" and "incompetent" women politicians of trading on their femaleness, and argued vehemently against "special" status for women, which she saw as a symptom of both "second-class" citizenship and a kind of apartheid as well. She resented the comparisons being made between the situation of Canadian women and that of American Blacks. In a period in which the term "nigger" was adopted by various non-Black groups who wanted to signal that they, too, were being oppressed, she defined it as a "bigoted, unflattering term for a second-class citizen...(who)...in the inverted bigotry of modern liberalism, is someone you have to make allowances for." She disdainfully compared the suggestion from the Alberta Farm Women's Union that 65 seats in the House of Commons be reserved for women to South Africa's practice of reserving some of its Cape Province seats for "coloureds."[92] Clearly, many female journalists, despite their philosophical differences on the extent of discrimination against women, felt that being regarded as a "human" or a "person" implied more status than being thought of as "female" or as "a woman."

When they commented on the prospects of women in the workforce and in politics, columnists and editorial writers of both sexes rarely made the subtle distinction between "equal work" and "work of equal value." There were few male editorial writers or columnists who dealt seriously with equality in the workplace or in politics at all, at least not when the hearings were going on. An exception was Harry

Bruce, writing in the *Star Weekly* magazine, who posed the question "Are women better than people?" Bruce ridiculed the idea that women were naturally more compassionate than men and should have reserved seats in the House of Commons, among other recommendations. While he agreed that there generally was discrimination against women in Canada, "virtually every successful woman in Canadian political history got where they got, not by demonstrating some female monopoly on compassion but by working hard, being smart and, yes, fighting like hell. They do not make peace, they make trouble."[93] In none of these columns was there any mention of the difficulties faced by women who were trying to succeed in politics.

Figure 4.1. Macpherson, *Toronto Daily Star*, 7 June 1968. Courtesy of Mrs. Dorothy Macpherson.

A less subtle kind of male defensiveness was apparent in cartoons that commented on "equality" for women in general. Regardless of what individual media correspondents wrote or said about the Commission, the cartoonists most often invoked the timeless stereo-

type of the feminist as bully in their depictions of the women who testified or were even interested in the inquiry. In one Macpherson cartoon, a female buffoon, hands above her head in a fighter's stance, prepared to deflate "the big lie of male superiority" before the
Commission, while simpering club women wearing ridiculous hats
looked on approvingly (see fig. 4.1). This cartoon, published in the
local *Daily Star* as the hearings reached Toronto, clearly represented
this federal inquiry as no more than a forum for silly older women
who were misguided in their quest for "equality."[94]

Public opinion made itself apparent in media surveys, as well as
in letters to the editor. In the *Chatelaine* reader's poll, 81 percent of the
mostly female respondents agreed that "equal pay" laws should be
strengthened to eliminate loopholes and that men should accept
women as "individuals" capable of performing as well or as badly as
men. About 76 percent said that men get ahead faster than women of
"equal ability." About 57 percent said women should take more
responsibility at work and in public life, but women were divided
(22/26%) or undecided (48%) about whether there should be protective legislation for women on the job.[95] The *Toronto Daily Star* surveyed
its male readers about the status of women and equality issues in general, garnering some interesting and mostly negative responses. A fear
that women would steal men's jobs underscored a curt response from
one reader, who said, "I do not see why women should receive a guaranteed minimum wage equal to that of men…unless they are prepared
to dig ditches." Another reader asked rhetorically, "If women want the
same rights as men, why should men not treat them as men?" while
someone else declared, "Women are too emotional to be given too
much responsibility."[96]

The "man in the street" surveys and letters to the editor were a
little more revealing, and some published responses were probably
chosen for their amusement value. None differentiated between
"equal work" and "work of equal value," or among "persons,"
"humans" and "women." They did dismiss the idea of "special status" which, several men argued, women enjoyed already. Some
women suggested, however, that it was men who were privileged,
and in some very basic ways. Patricia Young of Vancouver wrote that
women already did all kinds of things, including smoke and drink,
"like a man" and did not have a "divine 'right'" to Parliamentary
seats. If they wanted to enter such "highly competitive areas," they
should be "equally prepared to take their 'equal' chances with their
male counterparts, without asserting their femininity for a share of
the pie plus all of the cherries on top."[97] But several women felt, in the
words of Betty Walsh, who worked in a bank in St. John's, that "A
woman has to work much harder, she has to prove herself much more
than men."[98]

R.W. Haynes of Kitchener-Waterloo sneered at Peggy Prowse's suggestion of dual constituencies shared by men and women, using it to demand that the hearings be halted. "This is the intellectual level of this inquiry....Let's save money and let's spare everyone—particularly the women—further embarrassment." Another reader, B. Smith, replied to Haynes that the media reported "some of the nonsensical suggestions coming out of the inquiry" because "it makes amusing copy," but this was no reason to end the investigation.[99] Diane Dopking, a student at McGill University in Montreal, said she did not think it was true that women did not want to go into politics, and that "if there were really equal opportunities, we'd have many more women candidates."[100] Percy Maddux of Calgary took every complaint working women had made before the Commission to date, substituted "men" for "women" and argued, apparently in all seriousness, that, in the words of the heading over his letter, "Men Take Second Place in Today's Working World."[101] In Toronto, the anonymous "Old Man Who Knows" wrote to Elizabeth Thompson's column in *The Globe and Mail*, arguing that it was men, not women, who were getting the short end of the stick now that there was competition for jobs between the sexes. "There is nothing more confusing than women who want to be like men, and yet want to be treated like women. How crazy can they get?"[102] Mrs. Alixe Dobby of Ottawa related an amusing anecdote that relayed her dismissal of the traditional view that men should be paid more than women because they were supporting families; women and men should be paid for their on-the-job performances, rather than in relation to "the products of our extra-curricular hobbies."[103] Mrs. Deirdre Graham of Ottawa declared that there was "one small area of outright discrimination" that particularly upset her: the fact that women often had to pay ten cents to use a public toilet, whereas men did not. "Surely we can do no less than stamp out such horrid inequality between men and women in this enlightened country?"[104]

The answers to the *Chatelaine* survey and the one in the *Daily Star*, the "man in the street" interviews and letters to the editor generally reflected the responses that pollsters were already getting on somewhat differently phrased questions on the role of women in the workforce and public life and "equal pay for equal work." Generally, female and better educated respondents were more liberal than male and less educated ones, but much might have depended on the context of the questions asked.[105]

Mixed Messages

The media produced very mixed messages about the discourse of "equality." Sometimes the journalists allowed themselves to be distracted by more exciting issues, such as "student power," but several of them also made a real effort to help their audiences understand what the briefs were saying, especially concerning the equal pay debates. Philosophical assumptions about equal rights, and the logistics and practical aspects of newswriting, may also have had something to do with the way in which the discussion was played out in stories in which the fine distinctions between "equal work" and "work of equal value" were not made. Yvonne Crittenden of the *Telegram* comments today, "You've got to get the more glaring inequities out of the way first," and, at the time, few people thought that there might be "more sophisticated sort of inequities that we should be looking at."[106] It may also have been easier to write or say "equal pay" as a kind of familiar shorthand, than go through the litany of qualifiers every time one did a story on the issue.

The constraints of "objectivity" aside, their analysis and opinion articles reveal that several women journalists had definite reservations about "special treatment" of any kind. From their perspective as professionals, being treated like "a woman" had often really meant that they were relegated to segregated work spaces, organizations and gathering places, which many of them experienced as humiliating. They were no different from other white collar women that way and could relate to the same sentiments. Far better to be treated as a man's "equal" and insist that one was a "person" or "human" just like him, rather than as "a woman" who needed "special privileges."

What is really noticeable is how both female and male journalists picked up on the admonitions of prominent women, like Longmore and Forbes, who blamed other women for not taking their "responsibilities" seriously. Aside from the impetus to report what prominent people said, the media also had a duty to convey this discussion in the interests of balance. This approach, however, served both to blame women and hide the extent to which men were also responsible for the barriers which held them back.

Taken together, the news discourse of "equality" that peppered the media coverage of the Commission hearings was not in any way conclusive, and was sometimes misdirected and confusing, but did seem to relay the message that "equality" was a desirable position to attain, whether in education, the workforce or in politics. The reporting techniques the journalists used in getting the women's stories across to the public—such as simplification, an emphasis on conflict, and a focus on personalities—limited their scope and were somewhat contradictory, but still highlighted the cause of working women of all classes in Canada. On the other hand, editorial commentary, including cartoons, could negate much of the positive publicity and make women's aspirations seem laughable.

Another underlying factor in the media coverage examined here was the Commission's "democratic," "human rights" and "equal opportunities" agenda. There was a revolt against the conservatism of the 1950s, but most people, and certainly the media, were not willing to embrace a vision of personal freedom for women that stepped outside the boundaries of liberal democracy and "equality," as opposed to "special treatment." The reality, however, was that women could not model themselves successfully on men, especially if they wanted to be wives and mothers.

Chapter 5

"Please Don't Price Me Out of My Status!" The Media and "Conflict" in the "Marital Status" Debate

It is contented wives who are out. The Thinking Wives, the Dissatisfied Wives, the Wives Who Understand that their potential, their identity and their integrity are being mangled beyond recall—they are in.

—Jeann Beattie, in *Chatelaine*

*T*he writer of this observation, Jeann Beattie, was a single woman who well recalled the 1950s, when it was women like her who were "out" of the cultural mainstream and the married woman who was "in."[1] But, by the 1960s, when Canadian women were questioning the forces that kept them underpaid and in segregated workplaces, there was also a growing realization and some debate over the idea that the institution that used to both challenge and shelter them, marriage, was due for some fundamental changes. Where being the wife of a man once conferred social status on a woman, the cultural climate was shifting to reflect a new reality. Many upper- and middle-class housewives felt that they, also, were legally "second-class citizens" or less, especially compared with women who had careers or paid work outside the home.

Notes to Chapter 5 are on pp. 281–86.

The ways in which the journalists at the Commission hearings covered these issues, and how columnists and others commented on them later, revealed their ambivalence about the accepted cultural roles of married women. Most of them had little difficulty reporting women's complaints that they held an "unequal" position in marriage, and were badly treated when they were widowed, deserted or divorced, especially when they had children. The journalists were less comfortable with new ideas that signalled a shift in fundamental cultural attitudes, whether it was something as simple as changing the way in which a married women was addressed, or as serious as exposing the evils of spousal abuse. It is difficult for journalists to operate outside of dominant cultural norms, or what Shudson refers to as the "cultural air" of their own society,[2] which, at the time, regarded honorifics as simply polite, and wife-battering as a private, domestic issue. While this factor alone raises questions about "objectivity," two reporters actually spoke up at the hearings about their own marital circumstances, which, while informative, did violate professional standards of reporting.

All the journalists employed the usual techniques to help their audiences understand the complexity of the issues married women faced, but their continued focus on the "conflict" model did not leave much room for variations in women's experiences. According to their stories, married women were primarily at odds with the legal system, but also with their husbands, and with other women, particularly those who took up careers, an idea already prevalent in the media.[3] For example, there was not a lot of discussion about married women who were already in the workforce, and the double load they bore.

Again in their news discourse, the reporters simplified some of the complex legal issues using strong and direct language and pithy quotes, and personalized them by using the testimony of experts and ordinary women alike. They juxtaposed the ringing rhetoric of "equality" with hard luck stories that were quite educational in the scope of the inequities they brought to the public eye. There is also a tradition in journalism to entertain as well as educate, using the "human interest" story as a vehicle,[4] and so the reporters at the hearings treated some briefs as unusual or amusing, which detracted from the seriousness of the issues which underlined them.

Editorially, male voices seemed to dominate the discussion on marital status, a sharp contrast to what had happened with the equal pay issue, where women commentators had the most to say. The male writers used the more "unusual" suggestions, especially those made by women, such as a "bachelor tax" to criticize the more serious attempts to equalize the marriage relationship. Although there is no survey available that would reveal the marital circumstances of male journalists and editors, there is nothing to suggest that they differed from the norm at the time, and it is likely that most of them had wives who worked primarily in the home. Formal and informal survey results and letters to the editor were mixed, with many women supporting more rights for wives, and many males opposing them.

The laws in dispute were based on the traditional social attitude that a wife was her husband's dependent,[5] an attitude that many women at the hearings roundly criticized. The journalists picked up on, and relayed to their audiences, a new discourse surrounding the meaning of marriage and "marital status," much of which criticized traditional views, but some of which upheld them. They quoted women who told the Commissioners that they did not want to be treated as their husband's "chattels," but as their "equal partners," language that was reflected in many stories and headlines. These women were becoming more aware that they were not equal in law to their spouses and suffered economically as a result.

Financial Dependence

As in the "equal pay" debates, several journalists made considerable attempts, before and during the hearings, to help their audiences understand Canadian law as it affected married women. They recorded much of the detail that was important for readers to know, including the fact that federal and provincial laws concerning marriage, divorce and widowhood sometimes overlapped and were applied differently across the country. Eunice Gardiner, writing in *The Ottawa Journal*, reported on the main points of the wide-ranging brief from the Canadian Federation of University Women. It said that the provisions of the federal Income Tax Act clashed with provincial Married Women's Property Acts, which was a problem for wives who worked for pay outside the home. Under federal legislation, a wife was allowed to make only $250 a year. If she made up to a total of $1,250, her husband was taxed on the extra income; beyond that amount, she was taxed as a single person. Yet, provincial legislation said a married woman's property was her own.[6] Other stories noted that the federal Carter Commission on Taxation had recently recommended that husbands and wives be taxed jointly as a "family unit." Many of the women's groups opposed this on the grounds that, since the wife who worked outside the home usually made less, the tax on her income would really be based on her husband's salary and would thus be disproportionately high. She should be taxed as an individual, equal to her husband, not as his dependent or "chattel."[7] The headlines from the Commission hearings also reflected the women's concerns and the language they used, for example: "Income Tax Act Regards Wives as Chattels: Brief," and "Financial Equality of Wives Spotlighted."[8]

Other journalists brought out the ways in which business attitudes, rather than the law, presented economic barriers to married women, even those who were self-supporting. *The Albertan* in Calgary reported on a survey of financial institutions that consistently refused married women credit. The survey was conducted by the local branch of the Voice of Women, which told the commissioners that mortgage officers and credit managers came up with all kinds of petty excuses as to why a wife with property or an income of her own needed her husband's signature for a loan, even though it was not required by law. *The Albertan* published some of their more infuriating comments: "One man dared to express the hope that there would be a Royal Commission inquiry on the Status of Men to investigate why so much property was owned by women in the first place."[9]

Another way of bringing out the issues was to personalize them by giving a voice to the women who were most affected. *CBC Matinee* carried the comments of one unnamed woman, speaking from the floor at the Regina hearings, who listed the ways in which she felt at a disadvantage. She was supporting her husband, who was in graduate school, on a salary of eight thousand dollars a year, but it was only worth 10 percent for the purposes of a credit rating, even though she had been paying the mortgage herself for four years. The house was not in her name and she could not get a homeowner's grant; nor could she deduct the cost of a housekeeper from her income tax. She also criticized laws which assumed that a wife added no economic value through her work at home, froze her husband's assets immediately upon his death and later forced her to pay estate taxes. "But has she not been there doing the dishes, cleaning the floors, doing everything and earning her half of that money?" she asked.[10] In Toronto, Ruth Tait of the League for Socialist Action won warm applause from her audience when she suggested that all wives should receive a salary from the federal government and that the "family has become a prison for women."[11]

Legally, once a woman married she was generally considered the economic dependent of her husband in the eyes of the law. The resulting inequities were particularly hard on "farm wives," who worked in both the kitchen and the fields but received no remuneration for their labours. Like other Canadian wives, they were not automatically given an equal share in the assets accumulated during marriage, not even a legal share in the marital property. At the time, the husband tended to dominate farm life, making all the important decisions no matter how much his wife helped him, and the laws reinforced this attitude.[12] Some farm wives wrote detailed letters to the Commission, outlining the work they did on the farm. One reported that, aside from inside domestic chores and keeping the financial records, she drove tractors and other farm equipment, did heavy and light yard chores and the gardening, trucked grain and cared for as many as 100 head of cattle at a time.[13] It was the same kind of work done by Iris Murdoch of Alberta who, in 1968, unsuccessfully demanded a share of the family ranch as part of her divorce settlement on the grounds of her unpaid contribution.[14]

The Farm Women's Union of Alberta, which represented 20,000 members, complained to the Commission, in the words of the Calgary *Albertan*, that "Canadian law regards a wife as her husband's dependent when in reality she is a responsible contributing partner to the economic enterprise." A wife who helped her husband in the fields, replacing a paid hand in effect, could not claim wages and her husband could not deduct them from his income tax. He could deduct wages paid to his farm hands but neither he nor his wife could deduct the cost of a housekeeper. The farm women's union president, Paulina Jasmin, asked that the wives be entitled to half the family income and half the estate if the husband died, no matter what he stipulated in his will. *The Albertan* headlined the story: "Make us Equal, Say the Girls from the Farms," denoting that the media discourse of "equality" could apply in the case of married women as well as those with careers, even when they were still being referred to as "girls."[15] In other provinces, the headlines over other stories also reflected the idea that marriage should be equitable. Readers were told, "Women Bitterly Protest Current Status Imbalance," "Downgrading Charged by Women," and "Marriage Should Be a 'Partnership' Rather Than Maintenance Institution."[16]

A story about local conflict brought home the fact that a farm widow could be hit particularly hard if her husband left her without financial support and she had no other male relative to help her. Izzette Mitchell, a prominent citizen of Medicine Hat, complained that male ranchers treated widows like herself badly. Mitchell said that the men sometimes took financial advantage of these women rather than provide sound business advice or act as guarantors for mortgages and loans. She suggested a cooling off period of six months before a farm widow's property could be probated, regulations that would allow a credit company to extend her a loan during that period, and a commission made up of women to help her assess her property. Her accusation that "ranching was a closed shop for men" made the lead in the CP copy, although, unaccountably, the local *Herald* did not mention it in one account and played it down in another.[17]

Quebec women also suffered under the laws of that province which governed property within marriage,[18] but in one case, their concerns were superseded by the media's sensitivity to the simmering tensions concerning political jurisdiction between Ottawa and Quebec. When Pat Patterson asked Ed Reid on *Matinee* for a "distinctively" Quebec brief, he introduced Michel Hétu of the Quebec Chamber of

Notaries, who explained that its request that Ottawa transfer its power over marriage and divorce to Quebec and other provinces was meant to streamline the legal system, particularly regarding marital property rights, and was not a political power grab. Perhaps because he was admittedly unsure of his ground on legal issues, Reid did not challenge him further.[19] Although the press also covered the Chamber's submission, Sheila Arnopoulos of *The Montreal Star* was the only journalist who reported a glaring omission brought out under questioning from Commissioner MacGill: the Chamber spokesmen admitted that they had not consulted any women while preparing the brief.[20]

Marital Breakdown

Marital breakdown was another complex legal area for the media and their audiences to negotiate, especially when the women concerned received no remuneration for all their labour in the home and no financial support from their husbands afterwards. Divorce rates had risen steadily after the war, and took another jump after the legislation was liberalized in 1968, to allow for "marriage breakdown"; before that, the main grounds for divorce was usually adultery.[21] In the article which accompanied its survey questionnaire a few months before the hearings began, *Chatelaine* went into a great deal of detail about the laws affecting married women, including divorce legislation. Mollie Gillen brought home each injustice with direct, sometimes jolting language: "The law that will garnishee a man's wages for unpaid instalments on a car or television set won't do so for the subsistence of his deserted wife and children."[22] Because the courts tended to believed that children belonged with their mothers, with or without financial support it seemed, separated and divorced women from all parts of Canada were faced with almost insurmountable problems when they had children to support.

As with the equal pay debates, the reporters present could also be touched by these discussions, since some of them had experienced the same problems, but it was rare for any of them to take part. An exception was Nancy Brown of the *Victoria Colonist*, who was apparently covering the hearing there when a woman at the floor mike said to the commissioners: "I know that the press is supposed to remain silent but there is a Miss [sic] Nancy Brown who has taken this issue up very seriously and I would like her to speak if she would." Brown, a deserted wife with five children, rose and questioned the priorities of the courts when it came to men who deserted their families. "If he was to have a fine in police court or something and didn't pay it, he would be brought back. But when it's a question of his moral obligation to support his own children, nobody does anything." She also told the commissioners that even women like her who had good jobs could not get help from a financial institution without a man's signature.[23] The press covered Brown's intervention, using her complaints about finance companies and the legal system, although not quite accurately in the direct quotes. Still, the intent was there, and helped underscore the problems women like her faced, even if, strictly speaking, it was a professional conflict of interest for her to accept the invitation to speak.[24]

Prominent experts are another favourite media source, especially when members of the elite use straightforward and outspoken language, a discourse that is often reflected in direct quotes and headlines, and in this case helped to expose the problems many women were facing.[25] In Saskatoon, Judge Mary Carter of the magistrates' court spoke in the direct, slightly offbeat language reporters love when she told the Commission that separation and divorce often brought poverty to the woman and her children. "Most women come into marriage with only their false teeth and maybe a fur coat. Unless they have a kind and loving husband who puts all future property into their joint names, it is his." She had had women in her court "who have worked and saved for 30 years on a farm, putting up with drunkenness and brutality and complete indifference" for the sake of the children and to acquire some joint property. But, in fact, they were usually not entitled to it, and if they left the marriage after the children were grown, or even before, they were often left empty-handed. Judge Carter pointed out that a wife could get maintenance from a magistrate's court but had to prove desertion or cruelty first. It cost the wife a lot of money to hire lawyers to go to the higher courts that granted divorces and child custody, and she could claim nothing from the property she helped her husband build up, not even a bed or a refrigerator. *Take 30* ran a clip in which Judge Carter intimated that she tried to help some of these women find their way around the laws; she revealed that the advice she gave as a judge and "as a woman" were not always the same.[26] She recommended that all property acquired after marriage be jointly owned. Although the Deserted Wives and Married Women's Property Acts were provincial, most of them were similar to Saskatchewan's and she felt that exposing their "terrible flaws might do some good." The term, "terrible flaws" in divorce, showed up in a *Globe and Mail*, headline, based on a story from CP, while the local newspaper's headline, which summed up the entire day's proceedings, was bland in comparison: "Status of Women Enquiry Begins Sessions in Saskatoon".[27]

The testimony of lesser-known women also helped clarify the issues and brought a personal tone to the reporting as well. In Winnipeg, Ed Reid of the CBC sympathetically interviewed several separated and divorced members of "The Minus Ones," who had been left without financial support but were determined to fight back. One of them, Cathy Tay, told Reid that she had just spent four years tracking down her ex-husband. She said that he had defied a court order to pay her maintenance for their three children, who were one, two and three years old when he left. When she finally got him in front of a judge on a contempt of court charge for non-support, two weeks before the interview with Reid, it was thrown out on a technicality. "So I've given up because it's just a waste of time." Reid told his *Take 30* audience that he realized that the problems of sole-support mothers was not the only issue that was brought up at the Winnipeg hearings. "But I thought it was important because it pushed some people to the microphones and toward the *Take 30* cameras who aren't normally heard from, and I think it is a good thing to hear their side of the case." He added that just because these women had their say did not mean that their problems would end. While Reid cited professional reasons for taking this angle on the Winnipeg hearings, it is also clear that his personal sympathy for the women concerned, as much as his "objectivity," was a factor here as well.[28]

Spousal Abuse

A related issue that the reporters shed little light on, especially at first, was wife abuse. At the time, it was considered a "social problem" and was often swept under the rug. In fact, Florence Bird signalled early that the Commission would not be dealing with spousal abuse, by telling women outright not to write to the Commission about it,[29] apparently because it was supposedly covered under the Criminal Code. But, in fact, women whose husbands beat them had little protection.

It was a journalist appearing as a private citizen who first drew the Commission's attention to the issue. In Edmonton, Karen Harding, the editor of *The Edmonton Journal*'s family section and the mother of three children, presented a formal brief on behalf of herself and five other divorced and separated women. The media did not cover her discussion of spousal abuse but concentrated on what she had to say about the problems of getting financial support. According to the Commission's own audio tapes, however, she said that she had heard stories as a journalist, and as a member of her separated wives' group, about women who could not get the police to help when their husbands beat them. They were told that charges would not be laid unless their husbands really hurt them because the police could not walk into someone's house and interfere in a domestic dispute. In one case, Harding said, a man went berserk and smashed up the furniture with an axe, forcing his wife to flee to a neighbour's house with the children. The wife threatened to go back home herself after notifying the newspapers so that if there was a problem the police chief, whom she had already contacted, would get into trouble. In this way, the woman was able to persuade the police chief himself to go to the house, get the husband to take the nails out of the doors and open it up.[30] None of these comments were covered in the media, however.[31] It was only later in the hearings that the reporters seemed to catch on that wife battering was a serious issue. Before that, it did not seem to be part of their agenda of newsworthiness, perhaps because the police at the time considered it a private, "domestic" issue rather than a criminal one, and, as Ericson et al. have pointed out, journalists tend to treat sources like the police and other representatives of the law as authorities.[32]

When the problem of spousal abuse came up again later in the hearings, the media described battered women as living in poverty or with alcoholic spouses, not as women from all classes whose husbands or boyfriends wanted to control them. Perhaps because little gender analysis of battering had been done at the time by experts in family counselling, the media did not question that approach.[33] But neither did they really explain the legal issues involved for battered women, which they certainly had the opportunity to do. For example, as part of her presentation on poverty, Mrs. Anne Ross, who ran Winnipeg's only community health clinic, brought 10 women to the hearing, all of whom had been abused by their husbands. Mrs. Ross suggested a domestic police force which would come under the family court as an alternative to the regular police, who she said were ineffective in handling a problem husband in his own home. These new officers could charge the husband themselves, rather than leave it up to his frightened wife. But, again, the reporters did not explain why the city police often claimed that they had no power to act against a husband in his home until he actually committed a crime.[34]

In Charlottetown, Ruth Cudmore tabled but did not speak to a brief that recounted a dramatic tale of a farm woman she knew who more than once had to hide with her children in the fields to escape her drunken husband. Cudmore suggested a government wage would help such battered wives, wives who were ill, were supporting their spouses, or had been deserted. Rosemary Speirs of Canadian Press led with her anecdote about the frightened wife, but the local press apparently considered the idea of wages for wives more interesting than the problem of violence within families and did not mention wife abuse specifically.[35]

When the Commission reached Fredericton, Ed Reid mentioned, in a telephone call to Pat Patterson on *Matinee,* a brief from three anonymous wives of alcoholics "talking about what they called this abused and neglected part of society." He told her that these wives said that when their husbands were drunk, they would turn "as wild and dangerous as an inmate of a mental institution." But the police could not help them unless the husband actually hurt them or the children. Patterson cut him short at that point, because the show was running out of time.[36]

On the next program, Reid elaborated, using an interview with one of the women concerned to discuss the problem of alcoholism in families. The woman, who asked for anonymity, said the families of alcoholics suffer from the danger of physical violence, financial deprivation and a lack of government support because "he's working."[37] Again, Reid's sympathy helped to bring their problems to public attention, and he did a much better job of it than did the press.

Even though they requested anonymity, it was no small act of courage for the wives of alcoholics to appear in such a public forum, especially in a small Maritime city. But fuzzy writing and careless errors by reporters, editors or both, resulted in embarrassing mistakes in the local newspaper coverage, which overshadowed the problems these women brought to the Commission and must have appalled them. In one version, they asked for understanding for their husbands and "shelter and protection" for their families. The story did not spell out why they would need it. They were also referred to as "alcoholics," rather than as women who were married to alcoholics and, according to the headline, they had declared to the Commission that alcoholism was a "weakness," not an illness, the reverse of what they had actually said. Another newspaper either deliberately or inadvertently named the lead spokeswoman, even though the women had asked that their names be off the record and the Commission guaranteed confidentiality to anyone who asked for it. The brief had been unscheduled, which meant that the reporters were probably working without the copies the Commission usually supplied, but a skilled journalist should have been able to cover it properly nonetheless.[38]

Social Status

The issue of marital status and what it meant involved not only the laws but also social attitudes, and for this aspect of the issue the media framed their stories within the "conflict" model of storytelling. This was difficult, in that there were very few direct confrontations at the hearings, especially among the women present. The reporters did not exaggerate the conflicts, but got at the underlying tensions by concentrating on the contents of the briefs, and by paying attention to the things women said when they were questioned closely by the commissioners or when they spoke up from the floor. In this way, the journalists were able to flag social conflicts between, for example, married and unmarried women, husbands and wives, and housewives and career women.

It is not surprising that in a culture that put a premium on marriage for women, women without husbands often felt that they did not have much social status in the eyes of those who did. This was brought home in a personal brief from Miss Nora J. Rowe, who was supervisor of social welfare services for the Department of Veterans Affairs in Calgary. She conducted an informal survey of 150 local women, half of them single. The younger women who answered her questions felt that they were not welcome among the social "in-group," the young marrieds, and that their single male friends felt the same way. Widows felt suddenly cut off from the social circles they knew well when their husbands were alive, "'as if they were contaminated,'" according to Rowe. The newspaper headlines emphasized the loneliness of the single state, for both women and men: "Female, Single—and Isolated," "Single People Suffer Loneliness," and "Unmarried Persons Treated as 'Inferior,' Hearing Told." For Rowe, it was also an issue of equality, and she used the appropriate rhetoric, which was picked up in a quote: "'Unattached men and women are treated as second-class citizens.'"[39]

Another area of social conflict the media tried to pinpoint was within marriages in which the husband was more traditionally minded than his wife. Men who were financially able to support their families often saw themselves as losing status if their wives went out to work. For example, just after the western hearings, Margaret Weiers of the *Toronto Daily Star* covered a speech about equal rights at a men's service club in Toronto. She reported that only one married man of the five sitting at one table said that his wife worked outside the home, and he was a newlywed. One of the other married men said he was "'dead set against' working wives."[40] When the Commission reached Montreal, Mrs. Lu Connor co-presented a brief on behalf of several homemakers in Rosemere, a local upper-middle-class suburb. On *Take 30* she was shown answering a question from Commissioner Lola Lange, who was curious about how relatively affluent husbands felt about their wives' desire to work outside the home. Mrs. Connor, who appeared to be a little nervous but quite determined, revealed that the husbands, including her own, often tried to limit how much their wives could make, what hours they could work, or whether they could travel, but some of her friends were "bucking" the men and working out more flexible arrangements with them. Connor also said it was time women took the "feminist" line with their sons and daughters and taught them not to expect to grow up in a world where men went to work and women stayed home.[41]

At some hearings there was an undercurrent of animosity between women who elected to stay at home and those who felt women could be making more of a contribution in the wider world. Ed Reid told his co-host on *CBC Matinee*, Pat Patterson, that there were several women who turned out at a hearing in Edmonton not to present briefs but to state their support for traditional values.

Reid: They haven't got anything to recommend but they want to make sure that women are reminded that women are not necessarily…shouldn't necessarily be equal to men. You know, it's a strange thing.

Patterson: Has this resulted in much argument on the floor?

Reid: (Pause) No, I think these people have come and made their point, and the women who are representing organizations have pretty much let it pass (chuckles)…It's a different point of view. The women who think that women's place is in the home and the women who think that women should be liberated, follow professions or do what they want. There is a *definite* split.[42]

In Regina, Rosemary Speirs of CP related, one unnamed woman "grabbed a [floor] microphone to say that real women could be fulfilled by home duties." This woman believed that equal pay would lower wages for men and that some of the other things that career women were demanding, such as tax breaks for household help and daycare centres, would mean higher taxes. All this would increase the financial pressure on her marriage and she would be forced to go out to work. "Please don't price me out of my status!"[43]

The media also gave some coverage to those housewives who clearly resented the idea that married women who stayed home did not work. In Toronto, Inez Baker told the Commission that being a housewife was an occupation which should be allowed for on all application forms. Mrs. Baker declared that society does not give the housewife and mother the credit she deserves. "To suggest that pounding a typewriter is a vocation and pushing a vacuum cleaner isn't, is ridiculous." She said many married women went out to earn pay cheques "simply to have tangible proof of her own worth." Mrs. Lawrence Farley of East York went to the Toronto hearings to present what she called "the lowly housewife's" point of view, complaining, according to the reporter, that women were considered "second-class citizens" and housewives were considered "third-class."[44] Another brief came from Mrs. Margaret Overweel, who found it "deplorable" that women no longer found satisfaction in homemaking, and suggested that a marriage contract would enhance the economic status of the housewife and give her more financial protection.[45] By the time the Commission reached Halifax, Ed Reid was wary enough of their sensitivities to ask a young married woman who had been in the audience at the hearing, "Now you're a housewife, a home-maker…what is the correct term to use?" She replied, laughing, "I don't know. I don't feel strongly about the term. It's the tone of voice that's used, usually." During this exchange, Reid also included a clip from another of the women who said that the Commission should also emphasize the value of being a wife and mother at home.[46]

In all these stories, the journalists presented career women and housewives as being at loggerheads, with little consideration given to married women who were working outside the home. It was apparently easier to use the "conflict" model than to look for subtleties and variations that married women experienced, even for some of the women reporters who were married. Occasionally, a brief suggested that a woman could be a housewife and a career woman, but did not discuss the strain the double workload placed on her, or what to do about it. That point was lost in headline-grabbing rhetoric about related issues. In Toronto, for example, Bruce Mickleburgh, who contended that most Canadian women were "slaves," also complained that local voters' lists in the federal election told a "rotten lie" because they designated every married woman on them as a "housewife," regardless of whether she had a paying job. His wife, Ann, was head of the English department in a Toronto school. Mickleburgh caught the media's attention because he was a man, and men rarely appeared at the hearings, and because he used strong language.[47]

Mrs. or...?

There were other stories that were designed to produce headlines, and perhaps point at society's cultural blindness, but offered little in the way of real information. In their quest to make the hearings entertaining for their audiences, as well as educational and provocative, the reporters also focused on what they considered to be unusual or amusing briefs, those seemingly offbeat suggestions that they were not familiar with, often presented by people they considered particularly outspoken. The people concerned were trying to make a point about how cultural attitudes towards a woman, both positive and negative, were often based on whether or not she was married, rather than on her worth as an individual.

The reporters made much of the idea that some women wanted to change the language and customs used to designate marital status. The term "Ms." had not yet been coined and suggestions for changing "Miss" and "Mrs." were few and far between; still, some people made an attempt to either abandon "Miss" under certain circumstances, or come up with a brand new expression that would signal respect for a woman regardless of whether she was single or married.

One of the first women to appear before the hearings was Iva Conboy, an older woman with white hair who, according to Ed Reid, showed up at the Vancouver hearing wearing an "elegant" pink outfit. Conboy objected to the use of "Miss" and "Mrs." to differentiate between a married and a single woman, especially, she told Reid, for career women as opposed to the "contented housewife."[48] Conboy said that names are important in business. Ann Barling of *The Vancouver Sun* quoted her as saying: "If a woman is to be a person in her own right, she will have to learn, and so will her husband, that the name under which she gains her status is too important for her to relinquish it on marriage." According to the Vancouver *Province*, Mrs. Conboy also criticized the institution of marriage itself as the basis of women's "inferior position" and questioned social customs such as giving the bride away at the wedding. The reporter, Terry French, quoted her as saying: "If they're not chattels, then why give them away? Why, on marriage, should women obliterate their identities and names?" She suggested "Mistress, Madam, Mistra, Mistrix or Persona" as alternatives.

These were brand new ideas to the reporters, who treated her brief as comic relief. Barling led her coverage of the day's hearings with: "If Judy LaMarsh married Norman Moody, she'd be Judy Moody. In fact, she would be Mrs. Norman Moody but why should she not continue to be Judy LaMarsh?" Rosemary Speirs led with the rhetorical question: "Can you picture a demure bridegroom being paraded down the aisle and the clergyman asking 'Who gives this man in marriage?'" Terry French of the *Province* did not lead her coverage with Mrs. Conboy's brief, but described her as "a lady lawyer from Chilliwack," whose brief had provided "a light touch to the generally serious hearing." A few headline writers took the reporters' lead. For example, the story appeared under "Royal Commission Ponders: Mistress? Respectable?" in *The Vancouver Sun*, while Speirs' version was headed "Who Gives This Man in Marriage?" in the Toronto *Telegram*.[49]

In Winnipeg, Deirdra DeGagne and Carolyn Garlick, both married, also argued that wives should not have to take their husband's names. The *Tribune's* headline suggested a dismissive attitude towards many of the complaints made at the hearings that day, not just theirs: "Dog Food, Divorcees...a matter of Women's Status."[50] The media also reported a couple of incidents in which women at the hearings openly criticized Florence Bird for using "Mrs. John Bird" as Chair of the Commission, rather than Anne Francis or Florence Bird. In Toronto, a woman identified as Miss Z. Ters declared during discussion from the floor, "It is like a slap in my face to hear her called Mrs. John Bird. Since when has a woman's first name been John?" For some reason, the reporter did not mention Mrs. Bird's reaction to this specific comment but, after a similar incident, the Toronto *Daily Star* noted that she remained "imperturbable."[51]

It would be some years before the term "Ms." gained any acceptance in the media and even that was limited. The 1974 version of the *CP Style Guide* admonished its writers and editors: "Certain militant members of the women's liberation movement wish to be known as Ms. (with period, pronounced miz or muz) rather than Miss or Mrs., which they term degrading. Such use is not common in Canada so use Ms. only when insistently requested. All stories using Ms. should mention the request and say whether the woman in question is married or single—not as a putdown but as a matter of news interest."[52]

There were other outspoken women who challenged the definitions of marital status. Ed Reid appeared at first to regard some of them as "characters," but his coverage, and that of other reporters, had a certain educational value. On *Take 30*, he ran a clip of an indignant young wife who told the Commissioners that she had made "quite a stink" when the Vancouver Public Library refused her a library card in her own name. She elicited sympathetic responses from Elsie MacGill and Florence Bird, who both assured her that changing one's name upon marriage was only a custom in Canada, not a legal requirement, something that perhaps not many women realized.[53]

In Edmonton, Dr. Margaret Van De Pitte was particularly outspoken about the indignities she and other career women endured simply because they married. Dr. Van De Pitte said that the immigration department treated her as part of her husband's entourage and did not ask her about her own professional credentials when she came to Canada from the United States two years earlier. Both she and her husband held doctorates in philosophy and taught at the University of Alberta, where they held the same rank and earned the same salaries. Yet, the students called the men in the department "Professor" while she was addressed as "Mrs.—as if my marital status were all that counts." She also said that she had to prove that the provincial Married Women's Property Act allowed her to be responsible for her own debts before a local credit company would give her a loan.

Judging by their coverage, some reporters, or their editors, seemed to be missing the point of what she was saying. While the local newspapers correctly referred to her as either "Professor" or "Dr.,"[54] CP called her "Mrs." throughout, possibly because the 1968 *CP Style Book* did not consider the possibility that a man's wife might have a title of her own.[55] Ron Smith of CBC Radio News called her both "Doctor" and "Mrs. Van De Pitte, who doesn't care for the label." He reported that she also objected to a federal income tax guide illustrated with a picture of a husband filling out the forms while his wife brought him coffee. Smith ended his story on a humorous note by quoting a quiet comment from a man in the audience: "I'll bring the coffee, if the wife figures out the tax."[56]

Short-Term Marriage and a Bachelor Tax

Other stories that the reporters noticed because of their "unusualness" also featured people who were canny enough to use highly quotable rhetoric, or who had particularly contentious suggestions. In Saskatchewan, a middle-aged "bachelor farmer," Elmer Laird, got an inordinate amount of publicity, mainly through Canadian Press, when he conducted an informal survey of some of his female neighbours, apparently while dating some of them, and concluded that short-term marriage contracts would be useful for a variety of reasons. A one-year contract, for example, would give an unmarried woman and her child social status, rather than have her face "barbaric" public censure, while a five-year contract might discourage marital infidelity.[57] On *Take 30*, in a brief film clip, Laird said a local lawyer had told him that it was possible for a country to pass legislation allowing for short-term marriages. "If this is going to correct the public attitude against the unmarried mother, I would say let's have it."[58] In an article about the hearings which appeared in an American newspaper, the reporter flagged some of the more radical suggestions that had come before the Commission, including Laird's. He was quoted as stating his case succinctly: "A woman must juggle the ring, the man, the altar and the arrival of the baby. If she doesn't get them to come down in the proper sequence, she's a lifetime loser."[59] Local press coverage mentioned several suggestions he made to the Commission, some of which were more conservative.[60]

Aside from Laird, the person who appeared to receive the most attention was Mrs. Frank Martin of Winnipeg, whom CP described as "a perky, 62-year-old housewife." Mrs. Martin suggested that all single men over the age of 21, who had no families to support should have to pay a "bachelor tax" that would help support widows and other women on their own who were in need. Most men, she said, were no longer virgins after the age of 16, and since "they must be having what they want," each bachelor could be contributing towards this tax "to salve his conscience."[61] On *Take 30*, Ed Reid ran his interview with Mrs. Martin as a "brightener" or lighter item near the end of the program, and joked with his co-host on *CBC Matinee*, Pat Patterson, that as a bachelor he was shaken by Mrs. Martin's suggestion.[62] In a follow-up story, a reporter for *The Vancouver Sun*, who didn't cover the hearing apparently misread the CP story and inaccurately wrote that "women" appearing at the Commission were out to get bachelors by taxing them. She interviewed several local single men who, naturally, opposed the idea.[63]

Husbands and Wives—the Public Debate

The few cartoons that commented on the marital status debates during the Commission's tenure mainly reflected the male point of view. Len Norris of *The Vancouver Sun*, who recalled that his own wife was actually a traditionalist, depicted a determined, middle-aged woman on her way to the hearings telling her resigned husband as he pulled on his coat, "and I say you'll go with me to hear our side of the story." The smaller details in the cartoon also underscored the husband's viewpoint. He had left his pipe smoking in the ashtray near a table lamp with a base replicating a man doing a handstand, while his newspaper, which headlined the Commission hearings, was on the floor. In the corner, a bird hung upside down in its cage, either dead or disoriented, suggesting that the husband's world was also shifting precariously (see fig. 5.1). There was one cartoon in *The Ottawa Journal*, published before the hearings began, that appeared to express some sympathy for the stay-at-home housewife, although it could just as easily read as making fun of Florence Bird. It depicted her thrusting her head into a room where a thin, tired-looking woman was on her knees scrubbing the floor while her husband sat behind a newspaper with his feet up. Bird, who was carrying a brief-case marked 'Royal Commission on the Status of Women', was simpering at her: "I have a wonderful surprise for you." The cartoon appeared with a story about a pre-release brief from the Office Overload employment agency, which said, in effect, that given a choice, its housewife-employees would rather stay home than go out to work[64] (see fig. 5.2).

"... and I say you'll go with me to hear our side of the story."

Figure 5.1. Norris, *The Vancouver Sun*, 18 Apr. 1968. Courtesy of Len Norris.

Male columnists and editorial writers tended to fulminate on the question of who had most status in the home, insisting that wives ruled the domestic roost and that their husbands worked hard and paid through the nose to support them. From their point of view, some women's complaints about certain laws were justified, but most wives were basically well off. This attitude was expressed with anger, condescension, and not a little paranoia, especially on the more unusual suggestions coming out of the Commission hearings.

Figure 5.2. Dow, *The Ottawa Journal*, 15 Feb. 1968. Courtesy of Dow Nieuwenhuis.

Don Cayo, who wrote for a small, Newfoundland daily, the Corner Brook *Western Star*, which was the sister paper to the *Evening Telegram* in St. John's, seemed quite indignant about the idea that married women did not enjoy equality with men. He declared that, compared to his own grandmother, women had plenty of status if one counted all the labour-saving devices they had at home, not to speak of the birth control pill. "Still, one guy gets hurt from this status thing. The man. He's the fellow paying for the new look on the old lady."[65]

The Sudbury Star in northern Ontario argued in the same vein: "The 'typical wife' is most certainly paid for her services. She draws as much benefit from her husband's toil in providing a home, food, clothing and comforts as he does himself. The husband may receive the cheques from his employer or from his investment earnings, but guess who's always nearby when it comes to spending the cash?" The *Star* was responding to a woman doctor's argument that wives should have a basic succession duty exemption of one hundred thousand dollars on their husband's estates, plus half the value of the home as payment for her services as a wife.[66] Similarly, the weekly *Portage Leader* in Manitoba questioned the opposition of women's groups at the Status of Women hearings to the Carter Commission recommendation that spouses' incomes should be taxed as one marital unit, saying this would benefit both men *and* women who were the sole supporters of their families.[67]

Another theme that ran through the male opinion pieces was the idea that women bore equal emotional and financial responsibility with men for marriage breakdown. During the hearings in Winnipeg, John Robertson, in his column in the *Free Press,* lashed out at women who demanded government support for deserted wives and their children. "I'm tired of women complaining about how they bore some lazy lump's children, and then were cast adrift. I'm tired, because just as many women fall in love with other guys and cast their husbands adrift. And I've never yet heard of a case where a rich woman was paying alimony to a poor husband, after he won custody of the kids."[68]

But the suggestion from Mrs. Frank Carter that bachelors pay a tax to divorced and widowed women raised the most masculine ire. James K. Nesbitt, who wrote from Victoria for *The Vancouver Sun,* appeared almost apoplectic: "It's a monstrous, cruel idea, designed to cripple bachelors and put them out of business." He demanded the same tax for "bachelor girls," who would support widowers and separated men, dismissing Mrs. Martin's point that the young women were busy saving for their marriages. Nesbitt argued that bachelors were already hard done by, since they had to contribute money toward baby bonuses and to educate other people's children. They were, he claimed, "second-class citizens," and he exhorted them, "Bachelors unite. The matriarchy is rushing in upon you, and if you don't watch out you will be financially stifled, or forced into a marriage of convenience."[69]

Some editorial writers used Mrs. Carter's proposal as a way to dismiss what was going on at the Commission hearings. The editorial writer for the *Brantford Expositor* declared: "The conscience money penalty is as outrageous as it is immoral," and added that the hearings "have been turned into a psychiatrist's couch for the release of pent-up female fears and frustrations." The editorial argued further that a bachelor tax would be unfair and would result, if anything, in more marriages and, eventually, divorcees and widows who had to be supported. Both Nesbitt and the *Expositor* put their faith in that most eligible of bachelors, Pierre Elliot Trudeau, who upon his presumed election as the next Liberal prime minister would be expected *not* to bring in such a tax.[70] Similarly, the *Daily Intelligencer* in Belleville, Ontario, declared Mrs. Martin's suggestion to be "an affront to the freedom that permits a man to remain single if he so wishes." The newspaper argued that taxing bachelors would simply divert blame for marriage breakdown and non-support from where it belonged, on the shoulders of recalcitrant ex-husbands or guilty ex-wives.[71]

Bill Trebilcoe, a columnist with the *Winnipeg Free Press*, wrote that the audience must have been very tired to applaud Mrs. Martin's suggestion the way they did, since it was after 10 o'clock at night when that hearing ended. But he then turned his attention to a recent column in *The Vancouver Sun*, written by Joan Foster, a "Burnaby artist-housewife." Mrs. Foster had commented on the suggestion that married women "be allowed to keep their maiden names if they so desire." Trebilcoe did not make it clear that there was no law to prevent them from doing so, but approvingly quoted Foster, who spoofed the suggestion. In what might today be considered a prescient commentary, she wrote that no one's gender need ever be referred to again: "Smith, A.C. and D.L. are proud and happy to announce the birth of a small person, 7 pounds, 6 ounces, on April 25.... A postman will become a postal-person, a paper boy a carrier child, then we'll have house-persons, garbage individuals, cowpersons, fire-bodies, police-mortals, and bunny-girls will have to become bunny-folk." The male reader who had sent the Foster clipping to Trebilcoe was a sales manager. The columnist thanked him and added, "Now what are we going to do to eliminate the word 'man' from sales man-ager?"[72]

Val Werier of the Winnipeg *Tribune* was another man who did not seem to get the point of the arguments concerning the use of "Miss" or "Mrs"; he commented mischievously: "It confers status on the women, depending how they regard each state. Some women have been known to switch from one to the other to achieve rank."[73] Harriet Hill of the Montreal *Gazette* wrote that most women in the audience at a hearing in Ottawa liked a suggestion from a young man that single women and those over 30 years old should all be called "Mrs." But, she said, that was because many of those women were both.[74]

On some other issues, the writers were not as angry or flippant. Werier of the *Tribune* acknowledged in another column that some laws did discriminate, and he mentioned Judge Mary Carter's brief on separated wives. He devoted much of his column to the plight of widows, however, especially those on federal civil service pensions, which gave them only half the amount their husbands had received. The headline over his column reflected his sympathy: "Widows Supposed to Half Live."[75] The *Brantford Expositor* noted Bruce Mickleburgh's complaint that all married women were designated as "housewives" on local voting lists and agreed with him that it was an arbitrary and unnecessary practice. The *Expositor* suggested that no one's occupation, male or female, be recorded, not just as a matter of justice but of privacy for the individuals concerned. "Women have every right to consider this method of enumeration a slur on their status.... Why should it be necessary to put down what work a person does in compiling voters' lists?"[76] The *Kamloops Daily Sentinel* in British Columbia took a similar tone in considering the brief that said single people were feeling isolated from those who were married. The real problem, the editor wrote, was that the generations in general, as well as specific groups of people, were becoming segregated from each other to an unhealthy degree.[77]

The media's surveys of public opinion on the specific issue of marital status, indicated a certain amount of antagonism between the sexes, and among women as well. Although the questions posed to male readers by the Toronto *Daily Star* survey were somewhat different from the ones in *Chatelaine*, about three-quarters of the men said that women earning salaries should be as legally responsible as their husbands for paying alimony and supporting their spouses; and a slim majority said the wife should be able to deduct the cost of household help from her income tax, but most of them added, only if she had children.[78] In contrast, about 90 percent of *Chatelaine*'s respondents felt that wives should be legally entitled to a half-share in the family home and wanted an end to real estate taxes for surviving spouses; just over 80 percent agreed that a man's wages should be garnisheed, or he should be jailed, if he did not support his wife and children; 74 percent said there should be tax deductions for all married women needing household help regardless of the reason, but almost 70 percent said they did not believe that housewives should be paid a salary.[79]

Some public opinion was expressed in unofficial polls or letters to the editor around the time of the hearings. Specific questions about marital status were not asked in most "man-in-the-street" polls, nor, with a few exceptions, were they discussed in letters to the editor. The exceptions included a woman who complained to *Chatelaine* that women were not thanked for their work in the home and did not get the pension benefits they had, in fact, worked hard for. Mrs. J. B. Dodds of Sorrento, BC wrote: "I have come to the conclusion that the status of being a good wife and mother is not a career as far as male or even female government is concerned."[80] A woman calling herself "Farmer's Wife" from Fiske, Saskatchewan, wrote to a local paper saying she had complained to Elsie MacGill on the Commission's short-lived telephone hotline that a farmer could pay his children for working for him and deduct it from his income tax, but couldn't do the same for his wife, no matter what she did on the farm. "A wife can help to build up the farm equity by hauling grain, working in the field, helping to make bales, hauling stones, fixing fences and feeding livestock yet get no recognition, and pay estate tax after her husband passes on that very sum that she has helped to earn." The letter writer suggested other women complain to the Commission as well.[81]

Other letters to the editor appeared to be responding to news reports from the hearings in which roles within marriage were discussed. Harry Rosenberg of Toronto said that marriage is a career and women have more going for them than men. "It is hardly amusing to think of the time and money being wasted by some ladies talking nonsense before the Royal Commission on the Status of Women."[82] A conservative woman from rural British Columbia based her assessment of marital relations on what she had gleaned from the Bible, but used the same rhetoric often heard at the hearings, and the language of the working world, to express her thoughts in a local newspaper. Ruby McIlwain of Wells, BC believed that a wife was there to support, encourage and inspire her husband. "This does not mean that a husband should view his wife as a mere chattel and his slave. Her position as wife is comparative to that of president and vice-president, principal and vice-principal, pilot and co-pilot."[83] Lillian Austin of Toronto, who was much more belligerent, resented some of the women who had presented briefs, calling them "self-centred," "dopey dames" with their "almighty higher education" whose husbands must be "a bunch of gutless wonders." She declared that she was "a housewife and proud of it. I am an equal partner with my husband and bear his name." In her letter to the *Telegram*, she suggested that these women stop complaining, roll up their sleeves and do some volunteer work.[84] Other readers, even those who supported equality for women, criticized some of the "ridiculous" suggestions coming out of the hearings, such as the bachelor tax. Wrote Mrs. R. Ditchfield of Vancouver to the *Sun*, "This is another way of requesting that a man who has wisely avoided a marital mistake pay for the woman who hasn't."[85]

Marriage in "Conflict"

Marriage as an institution had been undergoing some fundamental changes since the immediate post-war years, especially as women began to stay in or return to the workforce rather than retire to hearth and home for the rest of their lives, as middle-class tradition still expected many of them to do. Yet, Canadian law had not yet caught up to reality, and in fact, as the hearings unfolded, it became clear that even women who remained in the home after marriage were not as well protected as many thought they were. It was all very well if the wife was happy at home, and well-provided for both during her marriage and after it ended through marital breakdown or the death of her husband. But those cases were rare, especially when it came to divorce. Their "marital status" did not bring them "equality."

The media picked up on this theme, which was simple enough, but had to come up with other ways to tackle the complexities of the issues, especially because federal and provincial laws conflicted with and overlapped each other. The other techniques they brought to their work were effective in some ways, particularly when they allowed individual women to tell their stories. But when they brought out the underlying "conflict" between the sexes and among groups of women, they played both sides against each other and virtually ignored women who represented the middle ground. They were least successful when they glossed over important issues such as spousal abuse, or, conversely, allowed too much play to proposals that few governments or members of the public would ever take seriously, such as short-term marriage contracts and the bachelor tax.

The editorial commentary, dominated by men as it was, raises questions as to how much they secretly feared that the Commission would bring about substantial social and financial changes in the marital status quo. Given what we can assume to be their own marital circumstances, that is not surprising. Perhaps it was easier for them to deal with the offbeat than the substantial when discussing who should take responsibility for injustice against women. Most of these commentators did not attend the hearings but were going by stories filed or broadcast by reporters who were there. Their absence certainly blunted their insight and sharpened their paranoia, especially when it came to the proposal for a bachelor tax. At the same time, some women commentators seemed a little uneasy with what may have been a radical idea to them: no longer differentiating between "Miss" and "Mrs."

In the media coverage of "marital status," the journalists who covered the issues applied standard newsgathering techniques while relaying messages that suggested they themselves supported change in the legal system. Two of them actually rejected professional norms of "objectivity" by discussing their personal lives during the hearings. The other news reporters seemed, by and large, sympathetic, especially in their stories about women whose husbands had deserted them and their children. Cultural conflict and mixed feelings over the question of whether married women should be in the paid labour force in the first place, perhaps internalized by some of the female reporters themselves, became more apparent when the Commission and the media turned its attention to another question: should women with children, especially young ones, work outside the home.

Chapter 6

"Why the Hell *Can't* We Provide Daycare?" The Media and the "Working Mother"

Our society doesn't really approve of working mothers, so we punish them in the most vicious way we can—through their children.... Because they want to accuse her of neglecting her family, they're not likely to support public or private attempts to improve day care.

—Janice Tyrwhitt, a "working mother," in *Star Weekly*[1]

$\mathcal{W}$ hen the Commission hearings began in the spring of 1968, the media reported that the issue of working mothers was going to be contentious. In Victoria, they quoted male taxi drivers, hotel workers and radio open-line hosts who were apparently of the same mind: women "should tie on their aprons and go back to their kitchens." On one open-line show, listeners hotly debated the pros and cons of working motherhood, in what one reporter referred to as a "claws-in" and another as a "dial-a-gripe."[2]

There was a very heated public debate about "working mothers," which was reflected in the media coverage of the Royal Commission hearings, and many questions about the issue. Who and what was a working mother, how old should her children be before she took a job outside the home, and if they were still young, who would care for them in her absence? What if she had no choice but to get a paying job?

Notes to Chapter 6 are on pp. 286–91.

Cultural understandings concerning the meaning of the term "working mother" were shifting in Canadian society at the time. The news media saw the issue, quite rightly, as another area of "conflict," but also used terms and expressions, reflected in stories and headlines, that suggested serious challenges to the accepted social norms of motherhood and a shift in the discourse about "working mothers." The journalists covering the Commission hearings picked up on the ambivalence many women expressed on this issue, likely because several of them were also "working mothers" as were some of the opinion columnists who wrote about the issue. Nevertheless, little of the discussion in the media acknowledged the extent of the work done in the home by women from all walks of life.

Mothers in Canada

According to statistics, there were appreciable numbers of working mothers in Canada but, as a group, they did not earn much money. One in five of Canadian mothers with children under the age of 14, or 540,000 women, were working outside the home. That meant that about 908,000 pre-school and school age children, or 18 percent of all Canadian children, needed care. The median wage of the Canadian working mother was $50 a week. Since that was not enough to buy childcare, almost two-thirds of these women had to rely on their husbands, relatives or a housekeeper to look after the children in the home. Others found care outside the home, or combined several different arrangements.[3]

This picture was somewhat at odds with the media's construction of the mother who went out to work, focused as it was on the middle- or upper-class professionals, and poorer, "sole-support" mothers, who appeared at the hearings. But in other ways, the media discourse tentatively reflected some progressive possibilities, such as the idea that the age of the child concerned was irrelevant if it was being cared for well while its mother was at work. A corollary suggestion barely being raised at the time concerned a truly equal domestic and childcare role for fathers.

The assumption that mothers are always the ones who take care of their children was based on attitudes long ingrained in Canadian culture. As historian Katherine Arnup writes, the very word "motherhood...conjures up images of women and children glued together in a divinely ordained symbiotic relationship" regardless of the mother's personal and professional circumstances. For the better part of the century, Canadian women had been inundated with advice from child psychologists and other experts who declared that the early childhood years were crucial to healthy development. Mothers who did go out to work were made to feel guilty, for, they were warned, maternal absences were dangerous for children, both physically and psychologically.[4]

The debate among the experts intensified as more women moved into the paid workforce during and after World War II. The media of the time erroneously constructed the working wife as a middle-class woman who had a real choice as to whether she wanted to take on a double workload or not, and was working for luxuries. But they also castigated this same woman for even thinking about outside work once she became a mother, even though many women felt they must. Blue-collar women may have better defied these proscriptive norms, however, being able to plead economic necessity.[5] By the late 1960s, as more women began re-entering the workforce, the cultural construction of the working mother broadened compared with the immediate post-war years. Over 55 percent of the formal briefs the Commission received raised concerns about women's employment and childcare. Of those briefs, just over half advocated that someone other than a mother be allowed to care for he children, while the remainder were ambivalent. Now, the media began to examine a question previously considered almost unthinkable: could not a mother put her job or career ahead of her domestic duties *even while her children were young?* The question tested the limits of public opinion, as polls suggested that most Canadians preferred that mothers stay home until their children were more independent. The media discussion tended to focus on this question without much reference to the many kinds of work that women did inside the home, including paid work, housework, childcare, care of the elderly and disabled, organizing social gatherings and nurturing their sexual relationships with their husbands.[6]

According to the media reports, women with different perspectives came forward at the Commission hearings: those who felt mothers should stay at home; those who said that they simply had to work outside the home because of severe financial need; those who questioned what the term "need" meant when they wanted more financial security or felt intellectually frustrated by their domestic roles; and those who insisted that they should have a choice, regardless of the ages of their children, their own financial circumstances or what men thought of them. What was more, some of them said, men must do more around the house than help with the dishes occasionally; it was time they took an equal share in the domestic chores and childcare.

These women included suburban housewives, career women, immigrants, domestic traditionalists, "sole-support mothers," farm women, social workers and daycare activists. Regardless of their own positions or personal beliefs, most of them insisted on state supported childcare for women who found it necessary to work at outside jobs, although some of them believed that it might be better to pay mothers of young children to stay home. There was less enthusiasm for public daycare when a woman's husband was able to support the family, even though some progressive groups argued that a woman could not take her "equal place" in the workforce without it.

As the hearings began, the media were ready with statistics on the issue. Adrienne Clarkson and a co-host, Moses Znaimer, gave their *Take 30* viewers a quiz about the number of women in the workforce.[7] The print media also blitzed their readers with statistics, including the numbers of mothers who were working outside the home. By 1968, about half of the women in the paid workforce were married. Of these women, 24 percent were mothers, and one out of five of them had children under 14 years of age. Their average age was 37. Many of them had returned to work, often part-time, only after their children were in school, but between 6 and 8 percent were "sole-support mothers" who had to work full-time even when their children were very young.[8] Many of them had earnings that placed them below the poverty-line, which was then drawn at about $3,000 a year for a family of two.[9] As the hearings progressed, it became abundantly clear that the progress of Canada's "working mothers" was being stalled by discrimination in public and labour policy, and in social attitudes. The ambivalence women themselves felt towards the issue was reflected in brief after brief, whether it came from a well-heeled upper-middle-class woman, or a single parent struggling to get by on a paltry salary.

Hélène Gougeon Schull, a food columnist for *Canadian Magazine*, co-presented a brief on behalf of 12 mothers living in Rosemere, an upper-middle-class community not far from Montreal. Schull, who was 43, had three children but did not like being a homemaker because, she later wrote, she found it "frustrating to stand at the kitchen sink in suburbia watching life go by the window." Earlier in her career, she had been a reporter,[10] but was working as a food columnist when she appeared before the Commission and was not constrained by the same professional expectations of "objectivity" as were her colleagues at the press table. Her media prominence, class position and her strong rhetoric singled her out for attention, however.

At the hearing, she spoke of suburban women, "swaddled in mink" retiring to their "caves" to have children and then complaining of boredom. They were inhibited, she said, by their own laziness, lack of education, fear of community criticism and "an archaic concept of the female role" which glorified motherhood at the expense of all other activities, and kept them from venturing out to take even part-time jobs. She also pointed out that such social and class attitudes both restricted these women and veiled an important fact: that they weren't necessarily home for their children, either. But the women who spent most of their time curling or playing golf, Schull said, "aren't criticized because ostensibly they're at home, they're not involved in a job." Her comments raised an interesting question about the real role of the "stay-at-home mother," but that point was lost in most of the other coverage.

The media saw her comments mainly in terms of conflict among women and as another example of the woman-blaming going on at the hearings, using aggressive language to do so. CP read her brief as a "feminist backlash," and also assumed that the women in the hearing room who applauded Schull's comments that day were the same women she criticized. The headline over the CP story in *The Ottawa Citizen* was, "Retreat to Cave Flayed," while the lead read: "A feminist backlash struck the Royal Commission inquiring into the status of women yesterday, and the mostly female audience applauded agreement as they were told *they* were lazy, uneducated, fearful of criticism and had an archaic concept of themselves."[11] The Gazette announced: "Brief Blasts Women As Own Worst Enemies." The reporters dutifully noted that Schull and most of the women who spoke in favour of married women returning to the paid labour force, either full-time or part-time, were careful to say that it was important to them that their children and those of working mothers in general not be neglected.[12]

It was quite another matter, however, for a mother to state categorically that she did not like taking care of her own children at all and wanted someone else to do it for her, especially in response to criticism from an angry man. In Regina, the media recorded a heated exchange between Fay Calnek and Ben Hanson, which added a strongly gendered element to the "conflict" model of the reporting. Rosemary Speirs of CP described Calnek as "a 29-year-old mother who works as a physical education teacher." Ed Reid and his CBC television crew revealed Hanson to be a dark-haired man in his thirties who said he was not a Canadian but a Dane, and spoke tersely, as if speaking in English and controlling his temper were both an effort. The camera swung back and forth between the two combatants, while, in the background, Florence Bird could be heard hooting with amusement at every sally.

While Hanson acknowledged that women and men could both "plow" and "cook," he also liked to think of women as men's "comfort" at night. When he demanded to know how much responsibility women wanted to take in life, after all, the camera caught Calnek, who was waving a lit cigarette, vehemently replying: "I cannot *stand* cooking, I *hate* housecleaning and little children down there (pointing downward) drive me *absolutely batty*. Therefore I can go out of the home. My children are better cared for and looked after by a person who is more patient. I do better work for society by using my capability, my, well, whatever my talents are, they do not lie in the home. But I do feel I give society value....I will not stay in the house just because a man says that I should." Hanson replied, with thinly veiled sarcasm: "I am sure I don't want you to stay at home. I'm just wondering—

merely wondering—if you wanted to stay a woman." The segment ended there, allowing Hanson to get in the last word.[13] Aside from providing the perfect "conflict" story, it was one of the more dramatic moments at the hearings, which often featured briefs that the reporters experienced as repetitive and boring.

Immigrant Mothers

It was ironic that Hanson was a Dane, because at the time the Scandinavian countries, as well as France, were often mentioned in the media and elsewhere as models of progressive thought, particularly on the issue of working mothers and state-supported daycare; moreover, the Commission itself was quite interested in the experiences of women in those countries.[14] Several groups at the hearings used the experiences of women in Denmark, Norway and Sweden as a measure of what might be possible in Canada, but there were also times when women from these countries were framed as too radical and "foreign," meaning "deviant" in the lexicon of mass communication theorists such as van Dijk.[15] In at least two cases, the issue of "foreign-ness" and "working mothers" overlapped, resulting in competing media agendas and two very different pictures of who these women were.

In Toronto, Solveig Ryall, an immigrant from Norway with two daughters aged seven and nine, went even further than Calnek had. She told the Commission in Toronto that both parents should work part-time when their children were of pre-school age and should share their professional, domestic and child-rearing burdens equally at all times. The press quoted Ryall, a 38-year-old freelance photographer, as saying, "Emancipation of women cannot be realized until women actively pursue life-long careers and reject the housewife ideal and the idea that the family is a means of financial support." In her front-page coverage, Margaret Weiers of the *Toronto Daily Star* described Ryall as "a militant crusader for women's rights who wants to abolish housewives," and quoted her as saying, "'The key to freedom is the right to work.'" She also mentioned that Ryall had been in Canada for 11 years but had not become a citizen. While there was a certain hyperbole in the way Weiers presented the story, she also correctly signalled that the ideas Ryall presented were not commonly discussed in Canada at the time.[16] The other journalists' stories about Ryall suggested slightly different interpretations: the CP version was headlined, "Mother Would Make Housewives of Men," in *The Ottawa Citizen*, and somewhat more positively, "Housewife's Role 'Must Be Abolished': Father Must Share Responsibility for Raising Children, Royal Commission Told,"in *The Globe and Mail*.[17] Clearly, some of the reporters or their editors felt that men could not take on equal roles in the home without somehow becoming feminized, or without deleting the accepted description of what "housewives" did.

Earlier in the hearings, the journalists had framed the immigrant working mother in quite a different way after the Commission received a brief from two high school students, Loredana d'Elia and Alida Bianchi, who were refugees from an Italian-speaking area of Yugoslavia. They attended a multi-racial school in Vancouver's east end and, speaking on behalf of the students there, asked for English-language courses and technical training for the immigrant mothers of the area so they could get jobs and help support their families.

Figure 6.1. Italian-Canadian girls and teachers. *The Vancouver Sun*, 19 Apr. 1968. B. Kent, photographer. Courtesy of *The Vancouver Sun*. City of Vancouver Archives 443-68-1321 Frame 4.

Most of the women who came to Canada in the post-war years up the late 1960s were from Europe and the United States. Comparatively few women of colour were allowed into Canada before 1965. But all these women had varied experiences, many of them working at home, as well as in factories or in domestic service.[18] Nevertheless, all the news stories about this brief stereotyped these mothers, regardless of racial background and experience, as being of peasant stock, timid, isolated, deferential to their husbands and desperately in need of education and training. D'Elia's comment that they "are like birds who have lived in cages all their lives" was projected in the CP lead, which was also the only account to mention that these two young women wanted to combine marriage and careers themselves.[19] The local *Province* focused on the need for education for immigrant mothers, but the *Sun* decided the story was about the students' opinion that mothers who did not have to go out and work should remain in the home until their children were in their teens. The headline read, "Claim Students in Brief: Mothers Belong at Home." Their personal attractiveness also played a role in the coverage. Both local newspapers ran photographs of these two "beautiful young girls," one showing them standing together with the caption, "Speaking out for their mothers," and the other presenting their brief, with the support of two of their teachers[20] (see fig. 6.1).

The journalists missed another aspect of this story as well. According to the Commission's own audio tape of this hearing, both young women also made it clear that their own mothers were well-educated, middle-class professionals who had worked outside the home at some point and had more or less equal relationships with their husbands. But the news stories did not mention their own personal circumstances at all, or reflect the diversity of the immigrant experience. They made no reference to the skills immigrant mothers had, or the work they did inside their homes to support their families.[21] This lack of information contributed to the stereotyping and labelling of these immigrant women as working class, poor and ignorant, and also suggests a certain middle-class bias among the reporters.

The Mothering Debates

Since youthful faces were at a premium at the hearings, and many women spoke in favour of emancipated roles for the working mothers, the reporters were also happy to find Canadian-born and well-educated young wives who would present the traditional side of the story, providing "balance" to the overall coverage, especially as there was little open hostility at the hearings between the two camps.[22] These women saw the role of homemaker as a legitimate career, one which should be given a lot more credit than it was. Mrs. Robert R. Hudgins, whose expert credentials were underlined in a story which described her as "a pregnant young wife from Waterloo (Ontario), with a Master of Science degree and one child," complained about her perceived loss of status. Hudgins, a nutritionist who was married to an engineering professor, was quoted as saying that "the role of motherhood is becoming a less and less valued one," and that she was concerned by "'the feminists' all around her." She apparently believed that, while women should be given all opportunity to develop their potential, "family means responsibility, and for a mother it means a bigger chunk of life than for a father. Let's not forget this 'handicap' as women gallop off in an attempt to overtake men in the jobs sweepstakes."[23]

According to the media reports, then, Canadian mothers had both a responsibility to work in the world, and a responsibility to stay at home with their children, at least until they were old enough to go to school. The real situation was not so cut and dried, however, and journalists did reflect the ambiguity in the arguments among the experts, and in the real lives of women. There were medical and other authorities who declared that too many mothers at home were suffering from a "syndrome" called "housewife fatigue," and "nervous depression," a theme eagerly repeated in some briefs and reflected in the headlines. The New Brunswick Association of Social Workers, for example, found that local young housewives, stretched to the limit, were running to professionals for counselling. They were suffering stress and role confusion from all the work they did at home; relatively few of them went out to work as well. Nevertheless, their plight, and that of women in a totally unrelated study, was recorded in the local newspapers in evocative and confusing headlines which would have puzzled the inattentive reader: "More Women than Men Have Emotional Ills," "Working Mothers Have Problems," and "Non-Working Mothers' Frustration Factor in Mental Health Problems."[24]

The reporters still tended to see the issue as an either/or equation, rather than look for more subtle interpretations. An exception was an interview during which Ed Reid asked one of the New Brunswick social workers, Phyllis Keating, and her colleague, Pamela Tonary, which category of mother suffered the most stress. Keating replied that these women felt torn if they were at home and torn if they were at work. But the double workload was not necessarily a bad thing, Tonary added. Some working mothers were better able to give quality time to their children if they weren't with them continuously, a viewpoint and a discourse which was becoming more popular among social workers and which the bachelor Reid found interesting enough to include in both the *Take 30* and *CBC Matinee* versions of the interview.[25]

It was not an easy issue, and the media picked up on some of the inconsistency and confusion in the hearts of the women who discussed it before the Commission. Corrinne Bryers of the Ontario Jaycettes expounded at a Toronto hearing on the group's "100 per cent" consensus that mothers with young children should not work, "unless it is essential." But then she added a personal comment that belied her group's official position, with which she personally disagreed. "I work and enjoy it very much. I am not sure what they mean by 'essential'."[26]

Younger women could also feel torn, despite all the talk about sexual liberation that was going on at the time. On one *Take 30* program, Reid approached a group of young "hippies," sitting in a park in Winnipeg. A young woman carrying an infant confidently declared that women should have the freedom to do anything, but another young woman hesitantly confessed her own deep fears and ambivalence about the whole issue of working mothers. On the one hand, she wanted equality of opportunity. On the other, she believed that the absence of the mother at home led to family breakdown. She confessed, "It scares me."[27]

It can be seen, then, that the news discourse reflected the ambiguity that upper- and middle-class Canadian women, at least, felt about leaving their young children and going out to work.[28] Working-class women did not have that option, but the coverage rarely presented their points of view. An exception was the inclusion of comments from Lisa Fauteux of Hull, Quebec, a mother of two children, who told a reporter doing a street opinion survey that she knew nothing of the Commission and had never heard of daycare centres. "My husband is a construction worker and we can't live on his wages. I leave my children at a babysitter's. No kidding it's still a man's world. I wish I could stay home."[29] When the Commission was in Montreal, Bill Bantey of the *Gazette* interviewed Ibel Webb, an Irish-born cleaning woman who worked at the Montreal YWCA, the site of some of the hearings. She believed women were just as smart as men and should be equal to them.[30] The interviews with the "hippies" and Fauteux among others were examples of the so-called "man in the street" interview, in which reporters elicited the responses of the public to issues in the news. The interview with Webb was more suggestive of her as a character who could be presented as a foil to the presumably middle-class women who were appearing at the hearings. Both techniques were a common feature of reporting in the 1960s, and reflected the democratizing trend toward "analytical objectivity," which allowed journalists to include the perspectives of ordinary people as well as experts in various fields. As Ericson et al. explain it, it was intended as a corrective to the bias even journalists understood was inherent in the official sources they used.[31] But, aside from such isolated opinions, there was no real sense in the media coverage of the Commission how low-income women who had to work felt about women's issues in general, or "working mothers" in particular.

Single Mothers

The media did find a way to discuss the predicament of "sole-support mothers," women who had to bring up their children alone, including those who had been middle class but who suddenly found themselves poverty-stricken after their husbands left them. In Ontario, for example, women who received the Ontario Mothers' Allowance, most of whom were deserted mothers by the late 1960s, were not given enough money for their needs, and were subjected to intrusive moral scrutiny of their personal lives and their lifestyle choices. On the one hand, they were encouraged to support their children financially; on the other, they were told that their children needed them in the home.[32]

In telling their stories, the reporters often played on the sympathy they seemed to expect from their audiences, and may have felt themselves, especially Ed Reid. Fortunately for him, these women were quite outspoken about coping with life on welfare, trying to get court orders for alimony and child support from deceitful ex-husbands, and, most of all, their emotional anguish over others' accusations and their own fears that they were neglecting their children. The simple and straightforward language they used testified to the strength of their feelings, and the difficulty of their circumstances, and contributed strong broadcast clips and quotes to the news coverage. Reid, wisely, ran long segments, allowing the women to speak for themselves.

Rita Costello of Winnipeg, who had two children aged five and six, told him in an interview: "I've had some trouble with my oldest child, my daughter. She just started into school this year. Part of it was a physical problem but the last one I came across was—she took a few pills, we think, and I took her to the doctor, and I've had a hard time handling her lately, and have just been at my wit's end with her. And he told me he felt that she was neglected and she lacked parental supervision. And I'm in agreement with him and I feel very badly that I see this happening to my child. But there's nothing I can do because I can't be with her. I have to work to support her." Costello, who worked seven-and-a-half hours a day as a key-punch operator, also said that she came home so tired from her noisy job that she did not have the energy to pay attention to her children. She could neither afford help with the housework, nor to live on welfare and mother's allowance.[33] The press also paid attention to these women's stories, emphasizing that these women worked out of "need."[34]

In contrast, Reid perceived a lengthy brief by the Saskatchewan government on its willingness to share daycare costs with the federal government as "almost boring" in comparison to the personal testimonies of some of the women at the hearing. He did provide some coverage of the brief, which made front page headlines in the local press.[35] "Boring" it may have been as a media topic, but social policy was obviously lagging behind the demands for daycare, and when a provincial government challenged a federal one to share the funding, that was worth a story, even if, as *Time* magazine suggested, the challenge might have had something to do with the upcoming provincial election in Saskatchewan.[36]

Daycare and Other Options

Daycare topped the list of concerns at the Commission hearings despite the reluctance of the more conservative women to see it or other non-maternal childcare services as an option. From the perspective of the career women, however, daycare was the key to a mother's economic freedom. Among the progressive thinkers on the issues were members of the media. Reid was already sympathetic to the idea that daycare should be available, as was *Take 30*'s co-host, Adrienne Clarkson. They made no secret of that fact on the air, which demonstrates that strict objectivity was not required in CBC television public affairs as it was in the news service. On their first program about the hearings, as the two discussed with Paul Soles the issues that would likely come up, Reid mentioned the numbers of women going into the workforce.

Reid: I mean, what happens to all those children while their mothers are working? Do they get other women in to look after their children? I'm sure they don't.

Clarkson: Well, that really means that the problem of daycare is really one that has to be looked at very closely, right away. We're really behind, aren't we, Ed?

Reid: Well, I think we are.

Clarkson: Well, I do, too.

Reid then mentioned Russia and several Scandinavian countries which provided daycare, and also that money had been put aside for that purpose by the United States government. Clarkson scoffed at that, however.

Clarkson: Four million dollars in a country like the United States (laughs) to set up daycare centres...it's *nothing*.

Reid: I think there will be a big change, probably this year.

His was an ironic comment in retrospect, given the many unsuccessful attempts to get federal daycare in Canada since the 1960s. Perhaps the mixed media messages, which did seem to reflect public ambivalence, have had a lot to do with this official failure, even though progressive media personalities such as Clarkson and Reid were onside.[37]

The professionals who ran the few daycare centres that did exist had long argued that they benefitted both mother and child, arguments that were repeated by other supportive groups at the hearings. Here was a chance to use the media as a tool to educate the public about outmoded ideas concerning the "good mothering" ideal. In Toronto, Reid, eager by this time for a fresh news angle, was interested to hear what he thought were these "new points" from Barbara Chisholm of Victoria Day Care Services. Sheila Arnopoulos of *The Montreal Star* did a special feature on Chisholm, whom she described as "one of Canada's most respected child care authorities."

Chisholm blamed limited research for prejudice against working mothers and the lack of daycare in Canada. She explained that the fear of "maternal deprivation," that is, the idea that children would suffer badly if their mothers were not with them, was based on studies of infants placed permanently in institutions, not on those placed for a few hours a day in professional daycares. She argued that, in fact, a woman who is with her child 24 hours a day may be too irritable and harassed to be a good mother.

To illustrate her point, Chisholm told reporters a dramatic success story. Her daycare centre was able to help a deserted mother of six children with a difficult, three-year-old son after the mother had warned, "'If you don't help me with Gregory, I'm going to hurt him. Someday I will hit him and if I ever do I won't be able to stop.'" The staff not only kept the boy safe, Chisholm said, they pulled his mother back from the edge of a severe mental breakdown.

At this point, Reid, perhaps striving for "balance," took on the journalist's role of devil's advocate, reminding her that many people still feared that the availability of daycare simply encouraged mothers to go out to work and leave their children. Chisholm replied that it wasn't true. Canada, with its totally inadequate daycare services, was simply not at the point where "we could afford the luxury of worrying about the irresponsible mother.... Mothers have gone out anyway and we are not facing the issues of what is happening to the children." Most of the existing daycare centres, including Chisholm's, had few spaces and could accommodate only mothers who had to support their families, in other words, those who really were in "need."[38] Although other briefs, such as the one from the Day Nursery Centre of Winnipeg, argued for a broader definition of that term, they did not receive a lot of media attention.[39] Most of the discussion about daycare, reflected in the media assumed that only mothers who had to work should have help caring for their children.

The news reports of the hearings were peppered with suggestions as to what forms childcare should take; or, alternatively, with a range of other options. They included flexible work hours, professionally trained housekeepers, tax breaks for household help, paid and unpaid maternity leave, a guaranteed annual income for sole-support mothers, specialized training in home economics and childcare for homemakers, and volunteer work as a flexible alternative to paid labour. Several of these ideas might be presented within one brief, or within several in the space of one day, but did not take priority in the coverage.[40]

There appears to have been little detailed media discussion of maternity leave, for example, although several groups declared themselves in favour of it. Apparently the federal government was waiting to see what the Commission recommended before going ahead with its own labour legislation.[41] The reporters were marginally more interested in the idea that a woman should be paid for staying home and taking care of her children. CP's Rosemary Speirs was the only one, however, who covered a last-minute brief from Thora Wiggen and Betty Tait, possibly because she found their ideas "unusual." These "crusading farm wives," as Speirs called them, had travelled from Prince Albert to Saskatoon to outline their "'plain, common sense plan' for paying housewives $100 a month." According to Speirs, Tait told the Commission, "We are simply advocating pay for service given. After all, who gives more service than a mother of a family?" Wiggen said such a scheme would wipe out unemployment, as many women held down two jobs, at home and at work, while half a million people in Canada had none. They suggested the money to pay them could be raised through corporate taxes. The Edmonton branch of the VoW had already suggested that homemakers be paid to stay home at least until their children were 12 years of age and received a modest amount of media play for the suggestion. CP and *The Edmonton Journal* found it interesting enough to use as a lead. The women of the Saskatchewan Farmers' Union and other individuals and groups also suggested government wages as a way of encouraging mothers to stay at home with their children, which received a mention in several stories. None of these efforts were to any avail in the end.[42]

News Workers and Motherhood Issues

The news stories of the hearings, then, reflected the strong feelings and the ambiguity shared by many women about the place of the working mother in Canadian society and how much she was responsible for the care of her child. These women, regardless of where they stood ideologically, expected the state, if not their husbands, to help them be good mothers, whether they were in the home or in the workforce. The stories did not reflect, however, the multiple responsibilities that most of these women carried, especially those who had no choice but to work outside the home. Most of the discussion centred on middle-class concerns about how paid work would detract from care of one's children, and not how childbearing affected women's chances to be equal partners with men in the workforce.

As we have seen, many female journalists were working mothers, and used various strategies to handle their double load, which included staying with their children while they were young, arranging their work hours to accommodate their domestic duties, or hiring home help. The Vanier Institute survey of senior media executives revealed on the other hand that the men tended to disapprove of mothers in the paid labour force.[43] Consequently, opinion from female writers and columnists about the working mother debates varied, while the few men who commented tended to believe that mothers belonged in the home.

Eleanor McKim of the St. John's *Evening Telegram* reflected the ambivalence many women felt as she ruminated on the emotional tug-of-war that many working mothers, including herself, felt when even their adolescent children needed them. "Who will be around to provide tea and sympathy when it is required—and it is usually required unexpectedly and unobtrusively. Nobody says, 'Mother, I'm confused and unhappy or scared and guilty—can I make an appointment to see you over the weekend—say 2 o'clock Saturday to tell you about it? Mothers in a home develop a sort of emotional antennae which detects such trouble areas." McKim believed, however, that there had to be a workable solution that would allow women to be mothers and career women without anyone suffering unduly. But if she was unsure of what that solution was, she was quite clear that the demands of motherhood had more to do with cultural expectations than biology. In a subsequent column she noted that many men she knew were criticizing the Commission, but added "there's nothing in the chromosomes to make women want to do the dog work of the world," and that too many women had been "brainwashed into accepting the myth that motherhood means a sort of life-time of slavery."[44]

Thelma Cartwright, a *Matinee* commentator who also wrote for various labour newspapers, took a somewhat different tack. She felt that women were not owning up to the pressure the double workload placed on them at work and in the home. She believed that it was a mistake to insist on being equal to men in the workforce because women were not the same as men. Their reproductive biology meant they had "special needs" such as daycare, which must be provided if they were to take their places beside men in "top management and business jobs." But rather than fight for these needs, too many women were hiding their domestic and childcare concerns while at the office in order to prove they could do the same jobs under the same circumstances as men. Cartwright felt that daycare should be provided as part of the education system.[45]

Dorothy Dearborn of the Saint John *Telegraph-Journal* also believed that women's biology made them unique, but saw it in a different light. She was not entirely opposed to working mothers, but drew the line at paid maternity leave, which she believed was in crass opposition to the sacredness of motherhood, for "to make a paying proposition out of the privilege of pregnancy would be to reduce the stature of women to an all-time low." She did not mention the suggestions that mothers be paid to stay at home and look after their children.[46]

Linda Curtis of the *Albertan* noted the lack of childcare and other services available for working mothers, including part-timers, but hinted that male policy makers should help out. "What will the men do about it? Probably not very much…unless the women are persistent."[47]

The men were particularly resistant to the idea that husbands should share equally in the household chores. This suggestion barely came up at all outside of the Commission hearings until the fall of

1968, when, in a report that was well-publicized across North America, Sweden recommended to the United Nations that men take their place beside their wives. Sweden said both parents should provide for the family, and both should be responsible for domestic chores and child-care,[48] a reflection of the comments Soveig Ryall had made to the Commission several months earlier. In Toronto, the *Financial Post* dismissed the idea, and similar suggestions made to the Commission, as "a view which may turn a large number of fathers against working women, if not against fatherhood itself."[49]

Among the male columnists, one of the most conservative was Dennis Braithwaite of the Toronto *Telegram*, who nevertheless agreed that most women were exploited. His answer to the double workload was to endorse a reader's suggestion that the government pay women to stay at home and raise happy families, thereby giving them a sense of self-worth and reducing the need for outside professional intervention. Braithwaite ended his column somewhat piously with the hope that "with women restored, we shall be able to say, as Thackeray said, that: 'Mother is the name for God in the lips and hearts of little children.'"[50]

Some columnists took a humorous approach to the debate. Eric Nicol of the Vancouver *Province* pondered the conflicts working fathers felt between their duties at home and those at work, while Jack Hutton of the Toronto *Telegram*, who was more sympathetic, decided he should become "a walking exhibit" for the Commission after he spent a mere four days at home with the children while his wife was away.[51]

The same concern about women working outside the home was apparent in several newspaper cartoons about the Commission. Most of them satirized the idea that husbands should take over the household chores, a discussion that had likely arisen in some of their neighbours' homes if not their own. Sid Barron's cartoons of that period often portrayed the characters in a typical middle-class suburban family, not unlike those in Don Mills, near Toronto, where he lived. At the time he had a conventional marriage, but later moved with his second wife to BC where they both felt freer to be themselves. He has brought up several children.[52] In one of his cartoons in the *Toronto Daily Star*, drawn just before the hearings began, Barron portrayed a domestic scene in which a young girl came across her father doing the dishes. The kitchen walls and floor were littered with exchanges of notes concerning menus, the milkman, the garbage and a pair of slippers left on the floor, all suggesting an absentee wife and a certain amount of domestic chaos. Barron's trademark, a disgruntled cat, was off to one corner holding a sign which read, "Social Studies 401." The daughter was saying to the father, "Our teacher told us all about what a matriarchy is today and I pretended not to understand what it was"[53] (see fig. 6.2).

Figure 6.2. "...our teacher told us all about what a matriarchy is today and I pretended not to understand what it was...." Barron, *Toronto Daily Star*, 2 Mar. 1968. Courtesy of Sid Barron. National Archives of Canada C-147456.

Other cartoonists were less subtle about the male fear of changing roles within marriage. When the hearings opened in Ottawa, a *Citizen* cartoon, drawn by Rusins, depicted a husband coping badly at home with kids and pets who were out of control. An older child was telling a telephone caller, "Mum's out presenting a brief to the Royal Commission on the Status of Women." Her presence was still being felt, however. In her portrait on the wall, she was brandishing the age-old symbol of the female bully, a rolling pin[54] (see fig. 6.3).

Among the reading public at large there was a clear gender split when it came to views about appropriate domestic roles, and many of the women were clearly ambivalent. When *Chatelaine* had asked its mostly female readers what they thought, about 58 pecent, given a choice, indicated that they wanted marriage and a career. But their answers to a question about their preferred working hours showed a direct correspondence with the period during which children were in school. Nearly three-quarters of the women wanted daycare services and/or tax breaks for home help, although single women were not as enthusiastic as the married ones. Over 40 percent thought work inside and outside the home should be shared by both partners, while 22 percent approved a complete switch in traditional sex roles if the partners desired it. About 62 percent of the women thought that their husbands wanted them to stay at home, however.[55]

Figure 6.3. Rusins, "Mum's out presenting a brief to the Royal Commission on the Status of Women." *The Ottawa Citizen,* 1 Oct. 1968. Courtesy of Rusins Kaufmanis.

How to manage a job when one has children was a definite concern. In a letter to *Chatelaine* magazine on its reader survey findings, Mrs. R. Heider of Toronto wrote: "How can women be employed in key jobs when you don't know if they will be able to make it the week there is an outbreak of chickenpox? Day-care centres are fine when the child is healthy."[56]

In the *Toronto Daily Star* survey, the male respondents seemed to reinforce the message that mothers belonged with their children. "In 1968, Most Men Believe a Woman's Place Is in the Home," was one heading for the article, which said that close to 55 percent of the men who replied were emphatically of that opinion. Their responses included the following comments: "Anyone knows that a career and mother-hood don't mix any more than drinking and driving." Still, there were some who believed, in the words of one man, "Not enough men share in the responsibility of raising a family and doing housework."[57] Both surveys reflected middle- to upper-class opinion on the whole.[58]

The columns, editorials, cartoons and public opinion about working mothers indicate that there was a clear gender split on the issue, and some differences of opinion among the women journalists, although on the whole, they appeared to be more progressive than the men. These women were either working mothers themselves with their own conflicts over the need to juggle their dual roles, or had colleagues who were. The issue was evidently much closer to home for them than it was for the men, who were also in higher and better paid positions in the media hierarchy, or for women who worked full-time inside the home.

The Changing Profile of the "Working Mother"

The media coverage of the Royal Commission on the Status of Women indicates that, by the late 1960s, the social construction of the "working mother" had broadened to include, however tentatively, women from the middle and upper classes who were insisting on their right to work, either full-time or part-time, even when their children were young. There was also sympathy expressed for the poor woman who had to support her children, although these women had long been of concern for social workers. The working-class woman who laboured to help both her husband and family was rarely part of the media equation. Nor was the fact that women who juggled two roles were often responsible for all aspects of domestic labour in the home, and sometimes took care of their elderly parents as well. Immigrant women, regardless of class, were stereotyped as either radical or needy.

It was also clear from the media coverage that the mythology of motherhood and the culturally held ideals of "good mothering" were still strong enough to sow doubts about daycare in all but the most determined women. Many mothers, including those in the media, felt torn between traditional values, their own needs, and the new feminist rhetoric of individual freedom and choice for all women. Inside the media, however, there was a clear gender division over the issue. Men, including columnists and editorial writers, were more likely to resist any changes to the domestic status quo. The media discussion about the needs of sole-support mothers was less divisive, tied as it was to the liberal, "humanist" impulse that imbued the Commission, the political climate of the time, and some of the journalists themselves. Overall, there was a conflicted and complex news discourse about working mothers that reflected, by and large, the journalists' own concerns and sympathies.

Aside from childcare options, a related consideration for Canadian women who wanted careers was the ability to control both the timing of their children's arrival into the world and the size of their families. The Canadian government happened to be dealing with legislative changes in this area then the Commission's cross-country tour began.

Chapter 7

"Nobody's Going to Tell Me Whether I'll Have a Baby": The Language of "Freedom of Choice"

If you are pregnant and your health is in the balance, and you know you can't face the likelihood of bearing a deformed child, that you can't care for another child in an already over-burdened and underprivileged family, or that you'll live em-bittered by shame and resentment and lost opportunities for the rest of your life, or that your health may be impaired to the point of cancelling your enjoyment of living, you won't be allowed a personal choice.

—Mollie Gillen, in *Chatelaine*

*I*n the cultural discourse of the 1960s, if a woman was going to have "choices" about her education, her career and her home life, she had to have "control" over her own reproductive functions; however, until late in the decade, this was officially illegal in Canada. Mollie Gillen's indignation was directed, in this instance, at Canada's new abortion law, which came into being just after the hearings of the Royal Commission on the Status of Women were over.[1] Obviously, the insistence of the women who presented briefs demanding freedom of choice had only a marginal effect on Canada's male lawmakers at the time, who decided that a hospital committee, not the woman in ques-tion, would decide whether or not she would have the child.

Notes to Chapter 7 are on pp. 291–96.

Although abortion was, according to one newspaper report, "one of the most ticklish problems being considered by the women's inquiry," birth control and sterilization were major ones as well.[2] The news discourse brought out the real and varied meanings behind the general demand for a woman's "freedom of choice" and "control over her own body." But, with the exception of Norma Ellen Verwey's brief on compulsory sterilization, in which she emphasized that men should be made to take "full and sole de facto" responsibility for birth control, the media coverage of the reproductive choice issue at the Royal Commission hearings was actually muted, compared with other issues. There was less overt emphasis on "conflict," strained attempts at flagging "unusualness," and a general lack of personal stories, or overt opinions, especially from female columnists.

Generally, on matters of reproductive choice, the reporters were still operating according to the discourse and rituals described by Schudson, Ericson et al., and van Dijk, but in less pronounced ways than they did regarding other matters that concerned women.[3] There were several reasons for these differences: the then-proposed new legislation on birth control and abortion had already received a thorough and generally supportive airing,[4] women at the hearings appeared to go out of their way to avoid directly confronting each other, especially over abortion, and few women, including journalists, were willing to personalize their stories by speaking openly about such intimate matters. While these factors restricted the reporters' ability to frame the story within the "conflict" model, they were able to bring out disagreements over the issues in generally low-key ways by attempts to "balance" disparate points of view at the same or different hearings, and by recording the questioning of a participant who held one belief by a commissioner who was understood to hold another. They used the "unusualness" technique in relation to women who did speak out about these matters, either as groups or individuals; but given the prior publicity on the issues, and the realities of women's culture, the reporters exaggerated the "frankness" factor. Some of them found it newsworthy that farm women and "French-Canadian" women generally supported reproductive freedom, which suggests their ignorance of life in rural areas and in Quebec. In this case, they were taking the words of one of their most "authoritative" sources, Florence Bird, at face value. As with the other issues before the Commission, "radicalism" was duly noted as deviance, especially when it came from young people.

Sexual and Reproductive Issues in Canada

The political and cultural context in which the Commission hearings were held had much to do with how the reporters covered this issue.

At the time, the federal government was amending its laws on birth control, abortion, homosexuality and other matters concerning public control over private morality. During late 1967 and early 1968, the health and welfare committee of the House of Commons held hearings on proposals to liberalize the old laws. The matter was delayed during the election campaign of spring 1968, but the new majority Liberal government under Prime Minister Pierre Trudeau promised to renew its efforts. These factors were reflected in the briefs before the Commission, which often demanded that any new law accommodate the real needs of contemporary heterosexual women.

Their vision of "choice" did not include intimate relationships with women. In the late 1960s, private lesbian sexual activity between consenting adults was not illegal in Canada but was still considered deviant behaviour practised by women who were mentally unbalanced, criminals, or both.[5] No one who came before the Commission identified herself as a lesbian, demanded an end to discrimination, or argued for that kind of sexual freedom, because lesbianism was not yet generally regarded as a legitimate claim for equal citizenship. As Mary Louise Adams explains: "The ability to lay claim to a definition of normality was a crucial marker of postwar social belonging. To be marked as sexually 'abnormal' in any way was to throw into question the possibility of achieving or maintaining status as an adult, as a 'responsible citizen,' as a valued contributor to the social whole."[6]

Most progressive groups, and the media, too, regarded the old laws restricting birth control, sterilization and abortion as unnecessary, outdated and in many cases hypocritical. These laws made the advertising, sale and distribution of birth control devices as such illegal, even though drug stores normally carried birth control devices such as condoms, ostensibly to prevent venereal disease, and many doctors prescribed the "Pill" to women on the grounds that their menstrual cycles needed regulating.[7] Some groups complained that these laws not only made criminals out of people practising birth control, they made it virtually impossible to teach sex education in the schools, provide effective premarital counselling and set up family planning clinics. In addition, a woman's right to knowledge of and access to the means of controlling her own fertility had already been recognized by the United Nations, leading some advocates, such as the Family Planning Federation of Canada, to argue that this right was a fundamental measure of equality and human rights for women.[8]

The new law would come under the Food and Drug Act, not the Criminal Code, and would make it permissible to distribute information about birth control, provide counselling, and buy or sell any contraceptive device that did not require a doctor's intervention. There was little opposition to the government's plan to lift these restrictions, even from Canadian Roman Catholic bishops. In July 1968, the Pope issued an encyclical reinforcing the church's official stand against direct interference with conception, a position which disappointed many Catholics. Shortly afterwards, the bishops defied him by declaring birth control to be a "matter of conscience," although they retained their opposition to abortion under any circumstances.[9]

There were no specific laws against sterilization for contraceptive purposes, but no clear legal guidance, either, on the doctor's responsibilities, which made most members of the medical profession quite cautious. Normally, female sterilization was done when doctors felt that another pregnancy would threaten the health of the mother; for example, in cases involving repeated caesareans or serious disease. But the woman had to have her husband's permission. There were even fewer vasectomies performed, partly because of male squeamishness and fears of impotence. Some doctors maintained that these operations were not necessary for the health of the man and were reversible only in about 60 percent of cases.[10]

Abortion was illegal unless the mother's life would be endangered by carrying the pregnancy to term. But a 1967 Gallup poll indicated that 71 percent of Canadians favoured the legalization of abortion under some circumstances, a statistic which supported the government's decision to bring in limited changes to the law. Under the proposed new legislation, a woman's *life or health* had to be in direct, serious danger before her pregnancy could be terminated. The decision to abort would not be hers, however, but left up to a voluntary hospital committee. Advocates of removing abortion from the Criminal Code altogether argued that the new law would not put an end to illegal abortions, which some estimates put as high as 300,000 a year.[11]

Given the amount of influence and control that the church, state and the medical profession had over matters of sexuality and reproduction, it is not surprising that the news discourse reflected a major theme: "freedom of choice" for women. Nevertheless, it was often interpreted differently and stated with a great deal of caution. Many women and men supported the proposed government legislation, and even those who found it too narrow made it clear that, in most cases, birth control and sterilization were preferable to abortion, which was mainly discussed, even by its champions, as a "desperate" and "tragic" last resort.

At the same time, the reality of changing sexual mores, especially among unmarried women, brought with it ringing declarations of "the right to control one's own body" that included free access to birth control and abortion "on request," "at will" or "on demand." "Freedom of choice" was also understood, however, to include the right of an unmarried mother to keep her child with society's support, rather than have to give it up for adoption.

The Question of "Choice" and
Journalistic "Balance"

The media flagged the discourse of "choice" from the beginning of the hearings. Reporting from Vancouver, Ed Reid told his *Take 30* audience, "It's become very clear to me that women out here want freedom of choice. They want control over their own bodies." In his coverage of a brief from the Children's Aid Society (CAS) of Vancouver, he included a film clip of Catherine Collier, a social worker, telling the commissioners, "Freedom of choice is important" and that there were many extenuating and "extremely unfortunate circumstances" which sometimes made abortion necessary. Reid also noted that the CAS emphasized the importance of birth control as a way of avoiding abortion. On *CBC Matinee*, Collier cautiously elaborated in an interview: "Where abortion is a desirable thing in many cases, it shouldn't be provided freely. Ah, there should be some freedom of choice, yes, but that it shouldn't ever be taken lightly." She added that the woman involved should receive immediate abortion counselling and birth control information for the future "so that she would be better able to prevent this kind of thing happening to her again."[12] One CP version of the story emphasized the CAS's request for changes in the abortion laws, but also noted a spokeswoman's comment that abortions should not be performed "willy-nilly." Nevertheless, the story was headlined "Abortion Choice is Woman's, Group Argues" in *The Globe and Mail*.[13]

In their coverage of the CAS brief, a couple of the press reporters, using snappy leads, led with an interesting twist to the Christian rhetoric often brought to the debate by those opposed to reproductive choice, a twist which also shifted concern from the mother to the child. In one version of the CAS story, Rosemary Speirs of CP wrote: "A Vancouver group says the Ten Commandments might be rewritten to include the warning, 'Do not bring unwanted children into the world.'" Ann Barling of the Vancouver Sun led with a similar quote, describing it as "an 11th commandment." In another version of the story, Speirs explained that there were not enough adoptive parents for the 30,000 children born out of wedlock in Canada in 1967. According to Barling's report, in BC alone there were 4,000 of these children born in 1966-67, an increase of 46 percent since 1961. The *Sun's* headline put the problem in a nutshell: "More Birth Control Aid Asked: Unwanted Children Increase."[14]

This angle on the issue of reproductive choice anticipated arguments from those who held that it was immoral to do anything to prevent children from coming into the world, and that life began at conception. Not many of them presented briefs at the hearings, but when they did, the reporters, in the interests of "balance," gave them due coverage. In Edmonton, Rita Morin, the first woman to oppose any relaxation of the laws against birth control and abortion, argued her case on religious grounds as "a Christian woman." Morin, who was a nurse and a Roman Catholic, "suggested the pill leads to immorality," and that abortion should be seen "as the evil that it is." She warned, according to Rosemary Speirs: "A society that now advocates the pill for birth control might one day be willing to 'quietly dispose of all elderly people or misfits' with another pill." There seemed to be some confusion over how strong a stand she was taking, however. At the time, the Vatican was still pondering its position on contraceptives and Morin qualified her position by saying that Catholics were eagerly awaiting its guidance. Nevertheless, a local reporter paraphrased her as saying that "people should let conscience be their guide." Speirs' version of the story was transposed into eye-catching headlines in several newspapers across the country, such as "Permissiveness with One Pill Invites Extremes with Another, Commission Told," in *The Globe and Mail* and "Commission Told: After the Pill Legalized Murder," in *The Vancouver Sun.*[15]

Considering how strongly people like Morin held their views, it was surprising to the reporters that there was little direct confrontation at the hearings, even over abortion; rather, it appears that a conciliatory approach predominated much of the time. Sheila Arnopoulos of *The Montreal Star* wrote that many of the briefs presented in Toronto demonstrated "the concern of women in general for the varied needs and interests of other women." As an example, she cited a comment from Inez Baker, who had come to plead for the status of housewives, but had "strong recommendations for abortion reform even though she personally felt abortion to be 'deplorable.'"[16]

The headlines over some of these stories were sometimes more negative than the testimony before the Commission, but that had to do with the variable meanings of the words people used. *The Calgary Herald* headlined one story, "Abortion on Request Vetoed by Calgary Women's Brief." But a closer reading reveals that the local Jaycettes, the female auxiliary of the Jaycees service club, actually supported abortion on several grounds, including "proven rape and incest" and "untenable" economic hardship on the parents. What they were really saying was that a woman should not be allowed an abortion just because she asked for one. The Jaycettes felt that such requests should go to hospital committees so that abortions would not be made too easy for unmarried women who, in the words of their spokeswoman, Mrs. Scott Lamon, "just might see it as a way out. We're having trouble taming our teenagers as it is."[17]

More direct conflict might be expected between secular and Catholic groups, but this did not occur exactly the way some reporters played it. Take, for example, the brief from the conservative Catholic Women's League (CWL). Maggie Siggins of the Toronto *Telegram* wrote that their brief "emphasized several times that it did not want to impose their religious beliefs on the entire Canadian society." She quoted the CWL as saying, "We want only what is for the common good." Its brief, however, questioned the idea that the proposed amendments to the Criminal Code would minimize the number of illegal abortions, or that enough evidence had been submitted to the Commons committee concerned to help its members formulate "a prudent judgement on this question." It recommended a royal commission to study abortion, which Siggins interpreted as a slight shift in the CWL's usual stance that there should be no change in the law.[18]

Rosemary Speirs, however, interpreted the CWL brief quite differently, to the point that she or her editors appeared to manufacture a confrontation with another group holding the opposite perspective. In one of her analytical articles about the hearings, she wrote that the Catholic women wanted "more stringent penalties" for the performance of illegal abortions and "suggested widening the grounds for abortion might not be prudent." Further, she juxtaposed their views with those of the League for Socialist Action, "an independent group of Trotskyites," which had presented a brief that same evening. According to Speirs, the Catholic women's position "brought a sharp answer" from the Socialists, who declared: "Abortion should be available on demand and should be cheap so that those who need it most can afford it." The way in which the story was written, or edited, made it appear that the two groups actually confronted each other, but although they did appear at the same session, their presentations were quite separate. Similarly, Judi Freeman of the *Calgary Herald* contrasted one brief demanding that abortion not be legislated at all to another demanding abortion committees that had actually been presented the preceding day.[19]

A more obvious foil for the Catholic Women's League was the feminist Catholic group called the St. Joan's International Alliance, to which reporters also paid some attention. The two organizations, which had clashed earlier when Cecelia Wallace of the Alliance accused the CWL of planning to boycott the hearings,[20] did not meet face-to-face in Toronto as Wallace presented her brief a few days later. Nor did the media suggest a direct clash between the two at the hearings. They simply reported that Wallace, who had formed a local branch of the Alliance and was also on the executive of Laura Sabia's CEWC, wanted the church to rethink its position against birth control and abortion and give Catholic women more equality in general. According to Margaret Weiers of the *Toronto Daily Star*, Wallace said that "the laws of the country ought not to reflect moral positions of any particular group," which was not much different from the CWL's position. Wallace also stated that her liberal stance on abortion, that is, that the Criminal Code should deal only with "illegal abortions performed for gain," was her own, and not that of her Alliance.[21] Here, journalists could have presented the views of both groups in one analytical article as a way of examining diversity among Catholic women, but they did not.

Another area of potential conflict was disagreement among the members of a group presenting the same brief. But, judging from the reports of the hearings, it appears that many of them avoided conflict and alienation amongst their members by aiming for a middle-of-the road approach, one that was not necessarily shared even by its spokeswomen. Both Rosemary Speirs of CP, reporting from Calgary, and Harry Nuttall of CBC News, who covered the Toronto hearings, noticed the tendency of some organizations to agree with the government's stand that hospital committees should decide on whether or not a woman could have an abortion. Speirs said that boards were touted as "a common solution" by women's groups "who have said frankly they feel unprepared to give detailed recommendations on the tricky abortion question."[22] But, as Nuttall pointed out in one of his reports, some of the spokeswomen who presented the briefs privately held beliefs that, in his words, "go much further." This was true in the case of the Local Council of Women from Windsor, Ontario, which officially supported the government's position. Mrs. H. Carefoot, a lawyer and the Council's spokeswoman, nevertheless told Nuttall as she waited for her train that, personally, "I'm very happy to have this opportunity to put in a bid for the removal of *all restrictions on abortion.*"[23]

Another potential centre of conflict over the abortion issue was among the commissioners themselves; however, they wisely avoided confronting each other directly at the hearings. But when Elsie MacGill, who believed that abortion should be taken out of the Criminal Code,[24] closely questioned a woman who presented a brief with the opposite viewpoint, Ed Reid paid their discussion a lot of attention. It occurred in Halifax where Mildred Moir, the mother of 10 children ranging in age from 15 months to 17 years, appeared before the Commission. Using the discourse of justice, rather than religion, she began by saying that abortion was "a very degrading form of violence and one which is only fully understood by women." She complained that most of the publicity about abortion in the media had amounted to advocacy by people who dismissed the concerns of those who opposed it as the complaints of the religious or the unsophisticated. Moir maintained that there was "another side" to the issue that should be heard. "The government of Canada should not consider the question of abortion as a religious matter, or as a matter for private conscience, but that it should be examined in the objective, disinterested light of public justice" as applied to the unborn child, who, she maintained, constituted developing life. Reid explained to his *Matinee* audience that MacGill put what she called "the hard case" to Moir, asking her, "Is it a gross injustice to a woman to insist that she bear a child which results from violence such as rape?" Their exchange, carried out in quiet but firm tones, was broadcast on both *Take 30* and *CBC Matinee*.

Moir: I wouldn't agree that to provide such a woman with an abortion would necessarily assist her. I think that for her to have the experience of an abortion might very well compound the injury that she has already suffered.

MacGill: I see. And if in her opinion it would relieve her or assist her in the injury that she has already suffered, you will not be prepared to let her have that choice?

Moir: I don't see how we could permit her to have that choice, to choose whether or not someone should live or die.

According to Reid, Commissioner Humphrey called Moir's brief the best case against abortion he had heard at the hearings so far.[25] The only direct criticism of her position came from a man in the audience. He was identified in the local press as K.W. Fox, a civil servant, who, the *Mail-Star* said, took exception to Moir's remarks. During the general discussion period after the session, he argued that if women were considered "responsible adults" in other areas, they should have a "right of choice" in matters of reproduction. Reid did not identify Fox by name but recorded other remarks that he made that put an oppositional, ethical spin on the issue of reproductive rights. Fox said, "When the woman is moved by compassion and sincere consideration for others, to practise her Christian philosophy of love for others, by ensuring that she brings no more children into a life of poverty and hardship, she is condemned. She's considered not capable of deciding what she herself wants to do."[26]

"Unusual" Perspectives

As the "conflict" paradigm was only partially successful in bringing out the differences of opinion on reproductive issues, the reporters had to look to other methods of reporting the nuances of the discussion. One technique was to frame a person or a presentation as "unusual."[27] In this case, "unusualness" was applied to the general outspokenness about sexual matters that women from all walks of life brought to the hearings, regardless of which side they were on.

Harry Nuttall of CBC News reported that pro-choice women in the audience in Toronto tended to be more outspoken than those presenting briefs from groups, although that was true both of people who supported freedom of choice and those who did not. As an example, Nuttall ran an extensive clip from Margaret Hawkins of Owen Sound,

Ontario, who told the commissioners during the discussion period that she came 130 miles (210 kms) to Toronto especially to listen in on the hearing.

She told the commissioners:

> I feel very strongly that nobody but me has any right to say whether or not I'm going to have a baby. Not unless he's willing to come and help wash the diapers. It's nobody's concern but mine....I would like you to tell our legislators that they must not be so distrustful. There seems to be an idea in the minds of men that if they make it alright for me to have an abortion, I will promptly go out and have one every six months. Their mothers ought to be ashamed of them. Nature got to women before the legislators did. If a woman wants an abortion, she thinks of it as a tragedy and it's only in extreme circumstances that she would ever want an abortion. And I think her judgement should stand.[28]

The *Toronto Daily Star* headlined this story, "Nobody's Going to Tell Me Whether I'll Have a Baby, Status Commission Told." Apparently, there was no response from anti-choice people who may have been in the audience as well,[29] but they had spoken up just as frankly at other hearings. For example, an unnamed woman in Saskatoon said, according to one reporter, that "abortion was murder," and even doctors could not tell how badly a fetus might be deformed, or how the birth of an unwanted child might affect the mother's physical or mental health.[30] In Ottawa, Louisa T. Katspaugh (Eleanor Dunn) reported, descriptively, if dismissively, in *The Southeaster Times* that "one flowery lady from Sarnia attired in a flashy purple brocade outfit suggested that women using birth control pills were no better than 'drug addicts.'"[31]

Some reporters, mainly from the cities, appeared to be taken with the fact that so many women were not shy about discussing the "controversial" issues of birth control, sterilization and abortion in public and noted that even rural women supported reproductive choice. In this case, they appeared to be picking up on similar comments from Florence Bird during her news conferences. In reality, farm women had been concerned about controlling the size of their families for decades, but Bird appeared to think that it was something new. In Edmonton, she was quoted in one report as saying that she was "amazed at how extremely liberal and realistic about life the farm women are." On questioning from John Warren of CBC *Radio News*, she said that there had been a recent change in how women in general talked about sexual issues in public. "I think that there is a great liberalizing of thought in our society, that people no longer feel that sex is something to be shoved underneath the carpet. It is something that concerns the whole human race or we wouldn't be here, and that therefore it should be talked about sensibly and quietly. There was no silly giggling today as I'm sure there would have been even five years ago."[32]

As if to underline this interpretation, Ed Reid asked one member of the Farm Women's Union in Alberta, "I am just wondering, how recently is it that you can get up at a public meeting and *discuss* this kind of thing?" Perhaps unaware herself of the history of farm women's concern with this issue, the unidentified woman replied: "Perhaps only in the last five or six years, we are casting aside our Victorian scruples...so that we speak of this very openly in our women's meetings."[33] Earlier, her colleague, Paulina Jasmin, told the commissioners that every illegal abortion was "one woman's desperate attempt to solve her personal population problem." Certainly, the media reports of the rural women's briefs suggested that they were not at all reticent about these matters, and, moreover, that they felt that a woman's reproductive rights should take precedence over anyone else's, including a husband's opinion. The Women's Institutes begged for relief from yearly child-bearing for any "worn-out" mother who wanted to be sterilized after bearing several children. The Institute's spokeswoman, Paulina Jasmin, made it clear that this meant without the husband's permission, especially when husband and wife were living apart.[34]

The seemingly liberal attitudes of Quebec women who came to the hearings also caught the journalists' attention. By the time Quebec's "Quiet Revolution" came to fruition in the 1960s, francophone Quebecers had long begun to question the authority of the Roman Catholic church, especially over matters of private morality such as sex before marriage, birth control, abortion and divorce. In 1970, the province's birth rate was the lowest in Canada because Quebecers had begun to use various forms of birth control, not just those sanctioned by the church.[35] Yet, their willingness to embrace reproductive choice seemed to come as a surprise especially to Reid, although it is possible he was simply playing to an assumed ignorance on the part of most of his national audience.

Reid set a stereotypically traditionalist scene for Quebec in an opening sequence of *Take 30*, which showed him riding in the kind of open-air, horse-drawn carriage favoured by tourists in Quebec City. As he entered the old section of the city, he pointed out that it was founded around the time that Shakespeare died in England, well before Alberta and Saskatchewan were provinces. After thus invoking a simplistic, historical context for his anglophone audience, he added: "The thing we wondered about here was whether the difference in language and culture would be reflected by difference in attitude to the status of women." On *Matinee*, his co-host, Pat Patterson, was a little more specific about what she assumed their audience would want to know: "Would it be different in Quebec where people are mostly French-speaking and mostly Roman Catholic?"[36]

As far as Reid was concerned, one of the most surprising results of the survey done by *Chatelaine* and its French-language counterpart

was the support among Quebec francophone women for liberalization of the laws on abortion and birth control.[37] According to the
responses in both the English and French versions of the magazine,
about 55 percent of both francophone and anglophone readers
favoured liberalized abortion laws that would allow pregnancies to
be terminated when the mother's physical or mental health was in
danger, "and in the case of rape, incest, damaged foetus or too many
children to support adequately on the family income." Twenty-two
percent and 32 percent respectively wanted abortion on demand,
while 22 percent and nine percent preferred to keep the existing laws.
Almost all of the respondents favoured lifting the legal restrictions on
birth control, as did more progressive Catholic commentators, one of
whom clearly resented that church policies "are made entirely by
men." Moreover, 65 percent of francophone women favoured birth
control clinics open to any woman of fertile age compared with 54
percent of the anglophones.[38]

When Reid interviewed Hélène Pilotte of *Châtelaine*, he focused
on the survey results concerning the abortion issue, which he found
"especially surprising" and she enthusiastically regarded as "fantas-
tic." She also pointed out that Quebecers had been thinking about it for
quite some time. Rita Cadieux of the Fédération des Femmes de
Québec also made the same point to Reid about the abortion question.
But only the *Matinee* versions of these interviews included these pas-
sages, which meant that the subtleties of the discussion reached a limited radio audience. It was not included on *Take 30*.

On *Matinee*, Pat Patterson asked Reid if these issues had come up
in other briefs, which allowed him to introduce a businesswoman from
Quebec City, Micheline Goulet. On both the radio program and *Take
30*, he ran a clip of her responding to Commissioner John Humphrey,
who asked for her opinion on contraception and abortion. She replied
that people who wanted to use birth control information and devices
would do so. As a Catholic she found the abortion issue more difficult
but she was in favour of the proposed law that specified that a woman
whose life or health were in serious danger should have the permission of a committee of doctors. On *Matinee*, she explained that she felt
this might end the harm done through illegal abortions, but this part
of the interview was left on the floor of the *Take 30* film-editing suite.
Her comments as they ran on *Matinee* led Patterson to conclude, "So,
although the church has taken a stand, obviously individual Catholics
seem to be making up their own minds." Reid responded that not
everyone was a "free-thinker" like Goulet, a comment he also made on
Take 30. In the context of the *Chatelaine/Châtelaine* survey responses,
however, her views were not particularly progressive.

In contrast, the *Quebec Chronicle Telegraph* disregarded Goulet's
exchange with Humphrey and focused on material not included in the

CBC coverage, her own experiences of salary discrimination and the need for childcare for working mothers. Reid appeared to be the only journalist who mentioned Goulet's opinions on reproductive choice. On the other hand, he was also the only one who detailed a point high school students from Ste-Anne-de-la-Pocatière had made in their brief, although he used it only on *Matinee*. While there was a gender split among the students as to whether women could combine marriage and careers, almost all of them felt that using birth control was permissible after marriage.[39] The local reporter mentioned that the students talked knowledgably about premarital chastity, abortion, family allowances and birth control, but the story gave no details.[40]

Generally, most briefs presented by francophones who discussed reproductive choice were liberal, although some groups were split over the abortion issue. One brief did express the deep reservations of a group of conservative Catholic women, who saw reproductive choice as both immoral and a danger to the existence of francophones as an ethnic group. But according to a CP story, an unnamed "official" of the Commission dismissed these women's opinions "once thought typical of Quebec," as "quite a surprise" in the context of the other, more progressive briefs presented at the hearings there,[41] which was the reverse of what the reporters assumed. The general message was that the francophone women of Quebec were "typical," that is, not much different from their anglophone sisters in the rest of Canada, which helped the Commission's argument that women across the country wanted essentially the same changes in the law. Generally, the media coverage suggested that professional, French-speaking women also wanted equal pay, higher education, involvement in public life and daycare. Sameness was equated with modernity; the Catholic, francophone "new woman" was, if anything, a "more ardent feminist" than her anglophone counterpart in her thinking about relations between the sexes. At the same time, she wanted to be considered "a human being," as did anglophone women.[42]

Outside of Quebec, several outspoken women also bluntly challenged what they saw as the federal government's hard line on keeping abortion in the Criminal Code, especially given the loopholes in the legislation governing access to birth control and abortion devices. The reporters at the hearings did not always pick up on these stories, however. One challenge to the government's inconsistent approach to the letter of the law came in Regina, where the Saskatchewan section of the provincial women's committee of the New Democratic Party presented a brief from party women in 10 urban and rural constituencies. Their spokeswoman, Myrtle Surjik, said the present laws in Canada, which "made criminals" out of women who wanted to control the size of their families, "have been a farce in as far as anybody can go into any drugstore and purchase any contraceptive device." But she also challenged the proposed new law on the grounds that it would not stop unmarried women from seeking illegal abortions.

In an expanded version of her comments on *Take 30*, she revealed that, among the NDP women, "everyone was uncomfortable" with the idea that contraceptives should be made available to young women who were not married, but that they were also aware that the statistics on illegal abortions showed that "age doesn't seem to limit sexual participation." After a long pause, Surjik, who appeared to be a little nervous, said that they welcomed the proposed new law which would widen the grounds under which abortions could be performed legally, but: "On the other hand it didn't at all recognize the fact that the illegal abortions in Canada generally are, are [another long pause while she appears to be searching for words] that so many young women have abortions who could not qualify under these conditions, and [we] felt that this is the evil, the degradation and danger involved in abortion. Also, if we are prepared to expect women to go through this [bringing the fetus to term], we are then saying that motherhood is going to be used as a punishment."[43]

These were strong words, no matter how hesitantly put, but the local newspaper did not detail the NDP women's stand on birth control and abortion, while Rosemary Speirs, who described Surjik as "a pretty blonde mother of four," referred only to comments she made about divorce. It is not clear why more reporters did not emphasize her committee's position, as it took a harder line on the government's policy than many of the other groups which appeared before the Commission.[44]

Similarly, it appears that only one journalist picked up on another challenge to the federal government, made at an Ottawa hearing. According to Sally Barnes of the *Toronto Daily Star*, Mrs. Lore Perron of the Association for the Modernization of Canadian Abortion Laws, "waved a container of multi-coloured pills" before the Commission, charging that at least two local doctors were dispensing them to women wanting to abort fetuses. She said that the local health department, police, RCMP and a federal government minister all refused to have the pills analyzed. Finally, a local doctor sent them to a laboratory in Toronto, where they were found to contain estrogen and quinine sulphate, which, Perron said, could cause deafness or blindness in the fetus or the pregnant woman. She read a letter from Allen MacEachen, the former Minister of Health and Welfare, in which he refused to investigate her complaints on the grounds that they did not come under his department's jurisdiction. Perron cited what she called "non-involvement syndrome," saying that politicians liked to avoid the abortion issue because it was too controversial. She urged the Commission to recommend liberalization of Canada's abortion laws: "Let us remember that women are not animals or saints, but human beings who deserve a little bit of common justice." Neither the press nor the CBC offered immediate verification or follow-up of her accusations, however.[45]

Unwed Mothers

Public frankness also extended to several groups who questioned what they saw as the hypocrisy of old social attitudes, including those that vilified the unwed mother. For example, in Toronto, a group of social workers said that unmarried mothers were often stigmatized and ignored by government officials and others when they needed housing and other services. Several of them proposed that the legal marriage age for girls, which came under provincial jurisdiction, should be 16 or older and that exceptions should no longer be made when she was pregnant.

In 1968, there were 32,629 births outside of marriage in Canada, or 8.3 per 100 live births. The usual alternative to an early "shotgun" wedding was seclusion during pregnancy, often at a home for unwed mothers, and adoption for the child when it was born. The social stigma attached to being an unwed mother could be tremendous for, in the words of author Anne Petrie, who lived through this experience: "The warnings were loud and clear: your life would be ruined, you would be kicked out of school, perhaps out of home, and branded a slut or a tramp. You would bring indescribable shame on yourself and your family."[46] Nevertheless, by the late 1960s, about 20 percent of unwed mothers in Canada were raising their own offspring. This did not mean it was any easier to face down public criticism, as the reporters well knew.[47] For one such unmarried mother, who came to the Commission as an individual, it apparently took a great deal of courage to demand freedom of choice. Her testimony gave the reporters a rare chance to personalize what was essentially a private matter.

In Regina, Sherrie Tutt, a registered nurse who had become pregnant out of wedlock not once but twice, spoke before the commissioners and 150 spectators. Tutt, who was 32 years old, had decided to keep her six-year-old daughter and two-year-old twin sons rather than give them up for adoption. She said that unmarried women should be given more information about what their options were when they got pregnant rather than be "more or less forced" by public opinion to either get married or give the child up. The reporters who interviewed her afterwards, especially Reid and Speirs, were obviously impressed with her courage and, perhaps touched when she burst into tears as soon as her stressful presentation was over.

Reid told his audience that "it was obvious to everyone that she needed all the self-control she could muster" to present her personal story, which for him stood out above many of the other briefs he had heard. In an interview which ran on *CBC Matinee,* Tutt revealed that she had been so confused and scared about what people might do to her and her first child that, up to the moment her daughter was born, she planned to give her up for adoption. She quickly realized, however, that "I could no more give her away than fly to the moon." She told the reporters, "I don't feel very many girls realize what choices are open to them. Some girls get married in the situation simply because they don't see any other way out. And other girls give up their child simply because they don't see any other way out. I find most girls make the decision they do, not on any rational basis, but simply because the preponderance of attitude that they get is in one particular direction."[48]

Speirs focused on the financial hardship Tutt faced because of her position. Under the current regulations, if a mother wanted financial support from the father of the child born out of wedlock, she had to prove that he had fathered it. This was impossible if he denied paternity. Tutt felt that the man should have to prove that he was not the father before he was relieved of his responsibilities. Her nurse's salary left her no money for daycare, and she wanted to spend some time with her children, so she gave up her job and moved in with her parents, who were supporting them. Both CP and *The Leader-Post* also included Tutt's suggestions, using a model from Denmark, that single mothers be eligible for co-op housing and daycare, which they could both share and finance through part-time jobs.[49]

In contrast to the CBC and CP coverage, the local paper subtly implied a certain shame to Tutt's behaviour. The reporter, Ruth Willson, did not reveal her name nor that of the town near Regina where she lived, and also found it noteworthy that the hearing audience that day included a class of grade 12 students. Willson wrote that reporters asked Tutt directly why, as a nurse who must have had access to birth control, she didn't use it. According to Willson, Tutt replied that she "was not at all sure of her reasons." Speirs, on the other hand, quoted her more directly as saying that she had an "irrational personal aversion" to birth control and that its availability seemed to make no difference to most women in her position. Willson's story also paraphrased Tutt as saying that although she herself would not consider having an abortion, terminating a pregnancy should be "a free choice" and might well be less painful for most women than giving up their child.[50]

This story was interesting not only because it suggested that single motherhood might be a "choice," but also because Reid and Speirs, especially, took note of Tutt's courage in speaking out, thereby making her something of a heroine. Willson, on the other hand, seemed to be implying that she was something less than that. Clearly, the respectability of the single mother was still tenuous, even in the minds of the "objective" reporters covering the hearings.

Frank, Silent and "Radical" Voices

After the western hearings were over, Adrienne Clarkson asked Reid on *Take 30* if he had encountered any surprises. In his reply, he glossed over the more obvious objections to reproductive choice from Christians such as Rita Morin, and emphasized the frankness with which the issues had been discussed, especially abortion, again reflecting Florence Bird's viewpoint as well. He told Clarkson, "I expected people would argue this on the grounds that it was a criminal act, or that it wasn't, but there was none of that at all. And it reminded me of how fast things have changed in the last five years, you know. There's been such a change in attitude that people can get up and speak publicly with apparently very little sense of self-consciousness on issues of birth control, contraceptives and abortion." When Clarkson asked him if this was true of all age groups, Reid replied that a student group from the University of Alberta and the Farm Women's Union had both asked for the free distribution of information on contraception. "So, to me this is something that has spanned the generation gaps."[51]

His assessment and that of the other journalists was somewhat premature, however. Although there was plenty of support for freedom of choice of all kinds in the rest of Canada, there was a resounding silence from advocates of abortion in the Atlantic provinces. The journalists who covered or commented on those hearings made no attempt to explain why this should be, but appeared to take it as given that, as Florence Bird intimated to the media in St. John's, women on the east coast appeared to be more "conservative" than their sisters in other parts of the country. In Prince Edward Island and Newfoundland, neither birth control nor abortion were discussed at the hearings at all.[52]

Given the strong positions of several seemingly mainstream groups and individuals in the rest of Canada that women should have freedom of choice, it was difficult for the media to paint any of them as particularly radical. As Rosemary Speirs of CP had pointed out, one "hard-hitting" and "down-to-earth" approach to freedom of choice was set out "surprisingly enough not by a radical young exponent of the new morality," but by the majority of the 300 members of the CAS in Vancouver.[53] But young, unmarried people who took advocacy positions did provide such a model, especially when they were left-leaning men who claimed they supported women. Perhaps the reporters saw "radicalism" as a natural way to approach what were the undeniable effects of the so-called "sexual revolution" among the young.

In Ottawa, Ken Huband, a recent university graduate and management trainee in the civil service, "stunned" the Commission when, according to the Toronto *Telegram*, he declared that "boys" should undergo compulsory sterilization "at puberty." He qualified his remarks by saying that voluntary sterilization and a good sex education program might be preferable. As a corollary, he advocated birth control and free abortion "to all women on demand." But when Gail Scott of CBC News challenged him on how strongly he really supported compulsory vasectomies, he hedged: "It's a measure which I hope never becomes necessary because it's a very severe measure to be taken but I believe more strongly in the equality of the sexes than I do the right of men to not be vasectomized by the government—put it that way." He also said he expected medical science to advance to a point where vasectomies would not be "as traumatic" an operation, meaning they would become more easily reversible.[54]

Speirs paraphrased Huband as acknowledging that "some people might find his ideas radical" or question why he might want to fight for women's rights, but he felt that women should have "as much control and protection from birth as men, which means completely since I have not recently observed any men becoming pregnant." According to her coverage and other reports, Huband also declared in his wide-ranging brief that couples should perform their own marriage ceremonies, "on a beach, at a party or in a church. I don't care."

It is interesting to see how the print media and CBC Radio News latched on to this young man who, one journalist noted, wore sideburns, a bright green turtleneck and a wine-coloured jacket. Another reporter considered him "courageous" for venturing into such a predominantly female venue as the hearings at all. He did not get anything like the kind of criticism Norma Ellen Verwey had been subjected to six months before when she suggested compulsory vasectomies. In fact, only the *Telegram* led with his views on sterilization; Speirs and Scott gave precedence in their coverage to his comments about marriage ceremonies and other issues, while the two local newspapers didn't discuss his opinions on reproductive rights at all. Either they decided that the "compulsory vasectomy" angle was old hat, or he had more appeal framed as a young, radical male with opinions on just about everything, who had somewhat amused his audience.[55] Even so, he had not been the first young person to demand freedom of choice for all women, including those who were not married, in matters of birth control and abortion, or to question the institution of marriage. A group of medical students at McGill University in Montreal had done the same, as had other university students, both men and women, who were identifiably left-leaning.[56]

Media and Public Opinion

Compared with other issues brought up before the hearings, such as equal pay, marital status and working mothers, there was a distinct silence on the issue of reproductive choice among editorial writers and columnists. This could be attributed, perhaps, to the fact that, because of the Commons committee hearings, there had been so much media discussion about birth control, abortion and sterilization already. Given the support of her readers, as demonstrated in the *Chatelaine* survey, Doris Anderson was generally safe in writing an editorial against the Pope's stand on contraceptives, pointing out that problems of overpopulation affected women in families all over the world and it was poor, devout Catholics who would suffer the most. Her editorial also directed readers to an article in the same edition of *Chatelaine* titled, "A Catholic Mother Answers the Pope." The author, under the pseudonym of "Joan O'Donnell," wrote that after several difficult pregnancies and much agonizing, she had finally decided to practise birth control.[57] In September of 1968, cartoonist James Reidford of *The Globe and Mail* drew a cartoon that underscored the extent of male control over women's bodies, depicting clergymen on a see-saw with a huge birth control pill[58] (see fig. 7.1).

The few comments on sexual issues from male columnists, who questioned suggestions that men were irresponsible, were patronizing and tongue-in-cheek. Jan Kamienski of the Winnipeg *Tribune* regarded the idea that a man should be made to prove he was not the father of a child he didn't want to support as "a throwback to the Napoleonic Code."[59] Val Sears of the *Toronto Daily Star*, in a column about an imaginary Royal Commission on the Status of Men, made fun of several of the ideas presented in briefs to the real Commission. Sears wrote that since the bodies of male "victims of the sexual revolution" were carpeting marriage bureaus across Canada, young women should be made to undergo "temporary" sterilization until they were responsible enough to take on motherhood. "Even in the age of The Pill, Elizabeth Barrett Browning's love sonnet, Let me count the days, is not something a man can safely leave to a maid."[60]

There was surprisingly little public response in letters to the editor during the time the Commission hearings were being held, in the spring and fall of 1968, aside from a couple of letters attacking Norma Ellen Verwey's proposal for compulsory temporary vasectomies, and another suggesting that liberal abortion laws might lead to suicide among remorseful women.[61] But a few months earlier, Yvonne Crittenden of the Toronto *Telegram* had carried out what she referred to as "an informal poll among dozens of women all over Metro" on abortion. They were of all ages and stages of life, and included professionals and homemakers. Crittenden testified to the "tremendous emotional reaction" to the subject of abortion among her mostly anonymous respondents. Regardless of their own opinions, she noted, they were all sympathetic to the woman who wanted an abortion. Almost without exception they wanted the law changed, although their opinions varied as to the extent, and all of the women wanted abortion allowed when the woman was raped. There were other women, however, who felt that making birth control information more available was a better option than easier abortions.

Figure 7.1. Reidford, *The Globe and Mail*, 20 Sept. 1968. Courtesy of James Reidford and *The Globe and Mail*. National Archives of Canada C-147635.

While this poll was unscientific and limited to a large urban area, the answers several women gave expressed their impatience at male lawmakers and church officials because of the power they held over women's reproductive choices. Commented the one woman who did give her name, Margaret Renwick, an NDP member of the Ontario legislature, "The hilarity which some male members of the Legislature have greeted proposals on changes in the abortion law is unbelievable and deplorable to me as a woman." A prominent society woman asked rhetorically, "What gave men the right to make these decisions and pronouncements without consulting women?" Another woman, who had three children, declared, "It's a woman's right to decide [if she wants an abortion]. I resent being imposed upon by politicians and church groups." An unmarried teenager, who had had an illegal abortion, called it, "one of the worst experiences of my life, not just physically but because of the back-alley atmosphere surrounding the whole thing. Why should men have the right to put a woman through that?"[62]

The Different Meanings of "Choice"

The hearings of the Royal Commission provided what turned out to be a secondary forum on the issue of freedom of choice, given that the hearings were held after those of the Commons committee studying proposals for new laws. The same arguments were brought out by the reporters covering the Royal Commission but with less conflict and passion than might have been expected otherwise. It also appears that the people presenting briefs avoided or played down confrontations within their own groups, or with others present at the hearings, and, judging from her approach on other issues, Florence Bird as Chair was not one to foster open conflict on such a highly charged issue as abortion.

The overall coverage did appear to give precedence to those favouring less stringent laws, or removing matters of reproductive choice from the Criminal Code altogether, which likely reflected the viewpoints of several of the journalists there, and public opinion as well. Although more conservative and oppositional voices were present at the hearings, they were not there in as great a number, which may also explain the apparent lack of "balance" in the reporting. What did come out were the varying degrees of meaning attributed to the idea of "freedom of choice," especially as it pertained to abortion. According to the news discourse, the right to a "choice" could refer to married women only or to all women, while the meanings of "at will," "on request" or "on demand" varied according to the circumstances of the pregnancy, or could mean that there should be no legislation forbidding a woman to an abortion under any circumstances. But the word "choice" could also mean access to birth control, or refusing to give a child born out of wedlock up for adoption. The reporters, even as they strained the journalistic formulas of "conflict" and "unusualness," and attributed outspokenness to farm women and Quebecers, nevertheless managed to underscore how united mainstream Canadian women were in wanting to lift some restrictions on their freedom of choice and to what degree the old laws were demonstrably outdated, paternalistic and hypocritical.

The emphasis on the idea, inspired by Florence Bird, that "all" Canadian women were experiencing essentially the same problems and demanding many of the same solutions, blinded the journalists, however, to the special circumstances of those who were regarded as marginal in English Canada, including aboriginal women. All the issues discussed at the hearings affected them, too, but not necessarily in the same ways as they did white women.

Chapter 8

"North or South, It's All the Same": The Media and Aboriginal Women

Oh it just burns me up the way some poor Indian women in this town living in one room house and they can't talk or write for themselves. I myself is even scared to turn to the welfare even if I had a chance to, scared that I'd get turned down like when I first came here.... What if I get sick what then?
—Mary Ann Lahache of Fort Smith, NWT, in a letter to Florence Bird as carried by Canadian Press.[1]

*T*he lives of aboriginal women on reserves, on urban streets and in Arctic villages were far more difficult, by and large, than most other Canadians realized. Several of them came to the hearings to appeal for better living conditions, help for their youngsters going to the cities, and a change in the federal law that stripped the women of their "Indian status" if they married anyone other than a First Nations man. In August of 1968, commissioners Bird and Lange visited, in the space of just a few days, Whitehorse in the Yukon, and Yellowknife and several small Inuit villages scattered around Hudson Bay: Baker Lake, Coral Harbour, Rankin Inlet, and Eskimo Point (now Arviat). They finished their tour in Churchill, Manitoba. Members of

---

Notes to Chapter 8 are on pp. 296–303.

the local media joined Ed Reid of the CBC and Elinor Reading from the CP bureau in Edmonton in providing coverage.

Cultural Theories about Race and Gender

Mass communication and cultural studies on media and racism, especially those that also take gender into account, provide stronger theoretical models for the media coverage of native women's complaints than do the more generalized analyses on news discourse and ritual. While the theories of Schudson, Ericson et al., van Dijk and others are still applicable, studies by Weston, and especially Burgess and Valaskakis, who discuss race and gender, lend themselves to a deeper understanding of the ways in which the media reported aboriginal women's issues in Canada 30 years ago.[2] These news stories should be considered against the backdrop of age-old cultural stereotypes about native people, especially the women, but also in relation to aboriginal-government relations at the time. The coverage about the concerns of these women, while they sometimes exploited these stereotypes, resulted in a complex news discourse about the similarities and differences between aboriginal and white women, and among native women as well. The media often followed the assimilationist line apparently favoured by the Commission and the federal government, yet, even so, there were stories in which the importance of cultural differences were stressed. Most of the reporters were not very familiar with native issues, but, as in their other articles and broadcasts about disadvantaged women, their less than "objective," liberal sympathies tended to filter through their professional attempts to present "fair and balanced" coverage. Unlike other issues the journalists covered, the complaints native women brought to the Commission attracted little attention from editorial writers, columnists, cartoonists, or the general public in letters to the editor, perhaps because these women's concerns were not considered of enough interest, or a substantial threat to the gender status quo.

Writing and broadcasting stories about people of a different race presented the journalists with real challenges. Like gender, race is a socially constructed category; in other words, regardless of obvious physical differences, the ways in which native women are perceived are tied to specific historical and cultural contexts and the power relations of the society in which they live. Generally, sameness equates with acceptability. The more native people are perceived to be the "same" as whites in their lifestyles and aspirations, the more sympathy and acceptance they receive. The media most often projects racial difference as deviant,[3] although they can also present it as "exotic," or "noble." But, as Mary Ann Weston points out in her study, whether the media image is meant to be negative or positive, native people are most often presented in relation to white values and norms, usually in "conflict" with them.[4] For their part, native women have sometimes appropriated positive stereotypes for themselves for their own purposes during certain cultural time periods, as Burgess and Valaskakis observe.[5]

A brief Canadian discussion about more recent events suggests that the media still tend to frame native women according to a simplistic princess/squaw dichotomy, the princess being what Weston describes as the Pocahontas model of maidenly, self-sacrificing virtue. A native woman was expected to be shy and self-effacing, and was seen only in relation to the men around her.[6] Her foil, the "squaw," was, in the words of Canadian writer Daniel Francis, culturally regarded as everything the "princess" was not, "ugly...debased, immoral, a sexual convenience," and often living "a squalid life of servile toil."[7]

Aboriginal People in Canada

Native women's testimony to the Commission about their circumstances, as relayed by the media, must be seen in light of the political events of that time. During the 1960s, the Canadian government adhered to an acculturation model considered desirable for the aboriginal people; that is, it assumed that improved living standards and an adequate education were the tools that would help them both survive and achieve equality. From this white perspective, all "Indians," "Eskimos" and Métis[8] naturally aspired to the same housing, education, work opportunities, and medical services as other Canadians. Aboriginal children who came under federal jurisdiction were given a "white" education in schools on the reserves or in their villages, or were sent to white-run residential schools away from their families. This education not only caused wrenching alienation between the generations, it did not prepare the girls to take on jobs any more financially rewarding than a nurse's aide, hairdresser or domestic worker. Since there was little work for them on native reserves or territory, they went to the cities, which many experienced as alien and frightening.[9]

The aboriginal people formed their own organizations to bargain with the federal government over the miserable living conditions and unemployment on the reserves, which led to poor health and early deaths; treaty rights, land claims and the changes they wanted to the Indian Act of 1951, which was just being revised.[10] The Act gave the federal government control over reserve land, money, the system of government and even who was legally designated an "Indian." Native organizers and writers were also very much concerned with "Indian" identity, and were resisting any attempts at cultural assimilation, which they saw as a byproduct of the ideal of "equality" within the "Just Society" philosophy of the new Liberal Prime Minister, Pierre

Trudeau. They insisted that they deserved "Citizen Plus" status; in other words, their legal status under the Indian Act should be retained and, in addition, their "special history, rights and circumstances" should be recognized.[11]

At the time, the Dominion Bureau of Statistics did not keep population records for native people. But some unpublished studies written for the Commission suggested that there were about a quarter of a million registered, or "Status" Indians in Canada, about half of whom were women. It was much more difficult to track the non-status population, including the Métis. There were, apparently, about ten thousand Inuit people in the Northwest Territories (NWT). As of this writing, there are few studies by and about native women in Canada, especially for the 1960s. Those that do exist are mostly in the oral history tradition and present a valuable perspective on their lives, but little that is specifically about the Commission.[12] At the time of the hearings, those in the south were starting to form their own associations through which they asked the Commission for equality within the broader legal system, as did white women. But, from their perspective, decent housing, healthy living conditions, education that would not rob their children of their languages and cultures, and, for some on reserves, equal status with First Nations men, took priority. The Indian Act, in line with other white legislation, assumed that a woman would take the nationality of her husband, and stripped her of her Indian status if she married anyone other than a "Status Indian." It also gave band councils the right to pass laws which further separated these aboriginal women and their children from their communities. Conversely, any woman who married a "Status Indian" attained Indian status.[13]

The Media and Aboriginal Women's Issues

As Weston has pointed out, "conflict" and "unusualness" are the most common frames for media stories about native people.[14] Similarly, the journalists who covered the Commission hearings framed most of their stories about aboriginal women according to the conflict model, often between white bureaucracy and native reality, native women and men, and "modern" and traditional ways; in the media's parlance, both a "generation gap" and a "Stone Age" culture gap existed, especially in the North. Admiring accounts of aboriginal "new women" who were becoming better educated than their mothers overlapped with dramatic portrayals of the activists among them, and less-flattering stereotypes of those who deviated from so-called "white" moral and family values. Several stories focused on their common-law marriages, high "illegitimacy" rate[15] and the addictions, sexual exploitation and imprisonment, which appeared to be the lot of "tragic" and "destitute" aboriginal women on urban "skid rows."

The journalists also allowed well-meaning white authorities to provide "expertise" about the lives of native women, who, they claimed, wanted the same things other Canadian women wanted. This approach invoked the "proximity" model of newsworthiness in that it could be said that women of vastly different cultures had common concerns which fit the Commission's "human rights" mandate. Aboriginal voices demanding more say in their own social welfare, health and education filtered through, however, along with supportive comments from sympathetic whites, including journalists, lending a more nuanced tone to the message which equated human rights with sameness.

The word "racism" did not appear in any of the media coverage considered here, which suggests that it was not used then as commonly as it is now. But some stories and commentaries using the word "discrimination" linked the struggles of Canada's aboriginal peoples with those of Black people in the United States and Canada; denial of their human rights, these articles said, could result in violence at worst and at the very least was unjust. Contemporary Native leaders looked to the civil rights struggles of Black people for inspiration, but the media tended to conflate their issues.[16]

During the Commission hearing in Edmonton, for example, Jack Thorpe, a white man who, together with his wife, fostered several teenage Métis girls, appeared before the Commission. Thorpe, a businessman, said that he had interviewed over 70 Métis and "Indian" women living on "skid row." He was quoted as saying that the federal government did not "give a damn" about the Métis, who did not even have the admittedly inadequate protection that "treaty Indians" did. Drawing a parallel with the recent riots involving Black people in the United States, he predicted "violence" if something was not done. Rosemary Speirs of Canadian Press quoted him: "Metis and Indian men are not going to stand by much longer and watch their women become the scum of white society.…If we do nothing, in 10 years we will have problems that will make the Watts and Detroit riots look like small stuff." What he actually said was, "Because the Métis and Indian men are not going to stand by and see these women become the victims of the scum of white society, " which is not exactly the same thing. The story ran in several newspapers with startling headlines which drew attention away from the point of his brief, the problems facing these women: "Violence Forecast at Hearings: Métis Problems Serious, Says Edmonton Manager," in the Regina *Leader-Post*; "Métis Will Explode—They Can't Take Much More Degradation [sic]," in the Calgary *Albertan* and "Help Métis Now or Face a Watts Riot in 10 Years, He Warns," in the *Toronto Daily Star*. While the quote used in the CP story was a close approximation of what Thorpe actually said, according to the Commission's own audio recording of the hearings, the threat of violence was not something Thorpe dwelt on during his testimony. He seemed most concerned that the women be helped which, in turn, would help their families.[17] In their coverage, neither the local *Journal* nor Ed Reid of the CBC made any reference to Thorpe's predictions of violence, but rather concentrated on the plight of the women as he had described it.[18]

CP also ran a related story about "Mary," a woman Thorpe interviewed, using his tape recording as a reference. She had run away from her home in Lac la Biche, Alberta, to find a new start in Edmonton after she and her mother became pregnant by the same man. She wanted to be with her own people in the city and wound up on "skid row," where she lived with a procession of men who often beat her. The story reinforced the image of the Métis woman as a tragic figure or, in the words of the headline in the Fredericton *Gleaner*, "Commission Hears Tragic Story of Destitute Métis Women."[19]

Thorpe also claimed that 75 percent of the women in the Fort Saskatchewan jail, where prisoners from Alberta were sent, were aboriginal or Métis, a claim later confirmed in a brief to the Commission from the Saskatchewan government, which also said most of them were there because they could not pay liquor fines. At the time, the federal government kept few statistics distinguishing white from native inmates, but police often arrested aboriginal people of both sexes if they were drunk. They could also pick up any young woman they suspected of being a prostitute on a charge of "vagrancy," even if she was just walking down the street. When the women couldn't pay their fines, they were jailed.[20] The media exposure of this situation led an editorial writer on the *Red Deer Advocate* of Alberta to exclaim, under the heading, "Our Colored Problem": "It is hard to imagine a more damning indictment of Canadian Indian and Métis policy, white society's values or the judicial process...and this in a country which pretends to be horrified by other countries' treatment of colored people." This kind of coverage, although sympathetic, tended to reinforce the stereotype of the aboriginal woman as "squaw," a hopeless drunk with loose morals, and again conflate the issues of native people in Canada with those of Blacks in the United States.[21]

The media image of the native woman as a tragic victim overlapped, however, with more admiring accounts of young women who were trying to "make something" of themselves, and of women of all ages who were fighting for better housing, education and health services. These women complained to the Commission about their living standards, but the media focused on the question of how they could survive without compromising their chastity.

In Edmonton, Emily Yellowknee, then 19, appeared on behalf of her mother, Clara, who was secretary of the local Métis-Indian association on the five Wabasca reserves about 250 miles northeast of

Edmonton. Through her daughter, Clara Yellowknee said that local women were dying of poverty and asked for training for the younger ones so that they could becomes cooks, nurses or teachers on the reserves, rather than quit school and live common-law: "How can girls raised in such conditions become respected Canadian mothers of tomorrow?"[22]

At the hearings, the media spotlight turned on Emily, who was the eldest of 12 children and in Grade 12 in a school in Edmonton. She wanted to get a degree so that she could teach, which the media represented as evidence that the key to solving the problems on the reserves was education. In fact, many native women desired a balance between white and native-oriented education for their children, one that would help them cope in a white world but still impress upon them the values of their native elders and spiritual leaders. For the media, Emily presented a success-story foil to her former grade eight classmates on the reserves. The following exchange among Emily, Florence Bird and Floyd Griesbach, a white, provincial development officer at Wabasca, brought this out on CBC TV's *Take 30*. Bird listened sympathetically as Emily, filmed in medium close-up, said that she wanted to complete university and go back to the reserves to teach.

Bird: What do you think your friends feel about this? Do they have that kind of dream or hope?

Emily: Not the friends from back home, I don't think.

Bird: What do they dream about?

Emily: I don't know.

Griesbach: I think if you want to get some light here you ask Emily about the girls who were with her in grade eight.

Bird: What happened to them? Please tell us.

Emily: I'm the only one that doesn't have a baby. They've been shacking up, all my classmates from grade eight.

Bird: Shacking up...with any old person?

Emily: Mm-hmn.

Bird: Any time?

Emily: Yes.

Bird: I understand.[23]

Of the media that covered Emily's brief, only the local *Journal* gave her the space to explain their circumstances. They dropped out of school because there were no jobs for them to go to, they had to take care of younger children in the family, or because they didn't want to be sent away to a residential high school. Even so, the headline implied that they were on a one-way street to an immoral lifestyle: "1-Way Street Leads to Common Law."[24] The story explained to the Commission, but not told in the media, was that Emily wanted them to be able to go to school in the place where they lived.[25]

The media coverage of the hearings did not always present these women so negatively. There was space for a native-centred point of view, and the women concerned used a human rights language that the Commission, the reporters, and their audiences understood. After 300 native women met for a conference in Edmonton in March 1968, two Cree women, Alice Steinhauer and June Stifle, and a Métis, Christine Daniels, took the delegates' suggestions to the Commission. Their brief, Wayne Erickson of CBC News reported, would deal with health care, education and housing, rather than issues white women were concerned with such as equal pay and daycare. Steinhauer said that aboriginal women were not very familiar with the Commission, although some of them had been involved with white women's organizations. She told him: "I don't think the native women are ready for this type of advancement or whatever you call it." Erickson ended his report by saying rather condescendingly that although the Commission was a "mystery" to the aboriginal women, Steinhauer felt they could bring their problems to it. They would accomplish nothing, she said, by being silent.[26]

Steinhauer and her two companions told the commissioners that the women were tired of federal interference in their lives, a message that came through clearly in the media coverage. They had had enough of seeing their families torn apart when their children were sent to residential schools away from their reserves and villages, an experience that stripped them of their language and heritage. The three women also asked for better living conditions on the reserves, but they also made it clear that aboriginal and Métis women were working together to find solutions to their problems. Steinhauer was quoted as saying, "No one else can do that for us, nor do we want them to." In a local version of the story, June Stifle asked for half-way houses for aboriginal women coming to the city, but specified that they should be run by "Indian counsellors.... Otherwise it will be just another do-good program." Clearly, the aboriginal spokeswomen were demanding agency over their lives, and the media coverage was beginning to reflect this point of view.[27]

Ed Reid apparently did not cover their brief, but he paid a great deal of attention to Mary Ann Lavallee from the Cowessess Reserve near Regina. Lavallee, whom he described as "the short Indian woman in a simple, purple dress" really seemed to surprise and impress him when she appeared at a Regina hearing. Reid was apparently unaware that she had received a lot of media attention at the native women's conference in Edmonton. Florence Bird, clearly expecting her to be hesitant and shy, tried to reassure her: "So could you just try to tell us very simply, and we will listen with the greatest interest." But Lavallee stunned the reporters and won their sympathy with a hand-written, last-minute submission, which Reid called "the most eloquent brief of the week." Her "very moving" and "fighting" presentation, he said, had many women in the hearing audience in tears.

Lavallee's speech embodied some of the liberal expressions that would have been familiar to the white women there, even though she was speaking in a specifically aboriginal context. Her opening remarks, which Reid used on *Matinee*, captured that spirit.

> Ladies and gentlemen, what I will say concerns the people of the reserves but particularly the Indian women. As Canada lit a flame to light the way to her centennial year, may this brief presented to the Royal Commission on the Status of Women light a flame for native women, to light the way for her emancipation, her recognition and acceptance as an individual on her own merit. As an ally and partner for the struggle for the human rights for the Indian and Eskimo and Métis. [Pause] And last but not least it is secretly hoped that this brief and the moral support it can earn will help open the way for Indian man, to give to Indian woman the dignity and respect and recognition which is hers by virtue of birth, by virtue of being wife and mother, and individual, and by virtue of 20th century standards.[28]

The local press appears to have misunderstood her message, however. Lavallee began by saying that her comments concerned the people of the reserves, especially the women, but Ruth Willson of *The Leader-Post* saw her brief mainly as a plea "for status for Indian men," and, in one version, contrasted this approach to white women's demands for equality *with* men. She also paraphrased Lavallee as saying that Indian women wanted respect from their male partners. Lavallee actually saw the problem as one of economics, which affected all her people, and aboriginal women as the key to helping the larger native community. She said the Indian Act "emasculated" the men of the reserves and overprotected them to the point where they could not provide for their families themselves. This system had led to "favoritism, apathy, alcoholism and local political patronage." Once the status of the men improved, so would their own. The women, she said, had been silent for too long; it was time for them to act.[29]

Rhetorically, one of the strongest comments Lavallee made was: "It is a well-established fact that the Indian woman has been the work-horse, the doormat and the baby machine." On *Take 30*, Reid started his segment on Lavallee with a medium-shot of her reading these same words from her brief. In her story, Speirs focused on the women's lives on the reserves and quoted Lavallee's contention that they were expected to "blend with the scenery." Some newspaper editors picked up on her "doormat" comment in the CP version and put it in the headlines; for example, the story appeared as "Indian Women Just Doormats Status Commissioners Told," in the *Toronto Daily Star* and "Society Uses Indian Women as Doormats, Commission on Women's

Status Is Told," in *The Globe and Mail*. Other headline writers focused on her "plea for understanding."[30]

Her strong sentiments and the way the media highlighted them served again to underline a stereotype of the native woman as inadequate, a risk which Lavallee acknowledged. Speirs of CP quoted her as saying: "But for Indian women my description of them as subordinated in an extreme way, carries an extra sting and a deeper hurt than is apparent."[31] In an interview with Reid after her presentation, Lavallee added, more colloquially, "I don't know why it is that before Indian people are noticed, before anybody pays attention to what they say, they have to…expose their dirty laundry."

In the same interview, Reid asked her about her dreams, a question he put in the context of Martin Luther King's dream for the Black people of the United States. The *Take 30* version of her reply assumed the context of the substandard living conditions on the reserves and suggested that Lavallee aspired to the values of the white, middle-class housewife: "Sometimes I dream that I could own a beautiful house and it has red brick tiles on all the floors and there's elegant furniture, and that we could live graciously, and that I could be the lady of the house." The longer *Matinee* version casts a more complex light. After "lady of the house," she added: "author, Nobel Prize winner [she laughed]. I'd like to win a Nobel Prize some day."

In this rendering, Lavallee did not fit any handy media stereotype of the aboriginal woman. She was not a tragic figure and certainly no doormat. Reid made a point of saying that she was the mother of five well-educated children, one of whom had won a scholarship to medical school, but he and the other reporters at the hearings did not mention that she was writing two books at the time and completely missed the fact that she was already known as an activist among the aboriginal women of the Prairies. For her part, she told Reid that native women had taken note of the publicity white women were getting for their demands. "Well, we see through the TV and the radio and all the news media where certain women are doing this, and women are doing this across the country, you know, so we wanted in on it, too."[32]

Lavallee and the other women from the Alberta native conference were not the only women with fighting spirit to appear before the Commission, even though, in at least one case, it put them at risk. In Ottawa, six months later, three women from the Kahnawake reserve (then known as Caughnawaga) outside of Montreal led a delegation of 30 Mohawk women to the hearings. Mary Two Axe Earley, Betty Deer Brisebois, Cecilia Ouimette and Charlene Bourque, who was just 15, came to complain about the section of the Indian Act which stripped them and their children of their treaty status if they married non-First Nations men.

According to the archival records, this was one of the briefs the Commission staff meant to downplay,[33] possibly because of the recent media coverage of a Mohawk activist, Kahn-Tineta Horn, who lived in Montreal but was also from Caughnawaga. In September 1968, just before the Commission hearings in Ottawa, Horn dumped a dead rat and several live ones in the middle of a meeting with Indian Affairs officials in Ottawa to demonstrate how common the rodents were on the reserves. Horn, who said she spoke only for herself, opposed assimilation and intermarriage with whites, and said that all whites should pay rent for living on what originally had been aboriginal land.[34]

But Mary Two Axe Earley and her delegation did appear at the hearings and received a lot of attention from the press, although not, it appears, from the CBC. The newspapers reported their complaints that aboriginal wives or widows of white men had no voting, property or burial rights on the reserves and were often threatened with eviction, even from property they had inherited. Their children were not allowed to go to school on the reserve, or even swim in the community pool with their friends who had aboriginal fathers.[35] The coverage, however, did not make it clear exactly what loss of privileges were stipulated in the Act and what were the rules imposed on non-Status residents by the band councils interpreting it.

Most of the reporters took essentially the same angle on the story: that the women were in conflict with their councils as much as with the federal bureaucracy, and were demanding the same rights for themselves and their children as First Nations men who had white wives. When the women stated that they were risking eviction from the reserve by complaining,[36] Wendy Dey of *The Ottawa Citizen* led with, "Thirty Mohawk women are afraid they'll be 'kicked off' their reserve for bringing their beefs to the Royal Commission." The *Toronto Daily Star* mentioned that the native women had asked two prominent white women, Grace MacInnis and Thérèse Casgrain, to sit with them. From the media accounts, they were reaching out to these and other white women for moral support.

The "pretty" and "attractive" Bourque, the daughter of a Mohawk mother and francophone father, also caught the eye of the reporters, who framed her as a youthful advocate of aboriginal pride. Although the journalists stopped short of describing her as an "Indian Princess," Dey of the *Citizen* mentioned that she was wearing a headband, also apparent in the accompanying photo (see fig. 8.1), and CP noted that the women who accompanied her and her companions were "sporting headbands and feathers." Dey said Bourque made a "passionate plea" to the Commission, which the *Toronto Daily Star* quoted at length: "I look like an Indian. I feel like an Indian. I want to be an Indian but this law says no.... I want my rights—I want my heritage. I am very proud that I am an Indian and that is what I am in my heart."[37]

This quote was, however, only a rough approximation of what Bourque, who was "50% Indian," actually said at the hearing.[38] It was either phrased this way for dramatic effect, or was actually a quote from an interview done immediately afterwards, but that is not indicated in the story. The *Toronto Daily Star* headlined the story, "Indian Women Want to Be Indians," which could have either been a simplistic play on words, or an acknowledgement of the native demand for special recognition as well as their rights under the Indian Act. The story included a photograph of the delegation.[39] A *Montreal Star* headline writer, on the other hand, used strategically placed quotation marks to question the women's contention that they were discriminated against: "'Discrimination' in Indian Act Aired by Women."[40]

Figure 8.1. Mohawk women addressing the Commission, *The Ottawa Citizen*, 3 Oct. 1968. Courtesy of *The Ottawa Citizen*.

The coverage and commentary of the Mohawk women's brief taken as a whole, reveals both journalists' sympathy with their demands for "equality" and consciousness of their differences, especially in appearance. The references to headbands and feathers were included, presumably, to add "colour" to the story, and underline the idea that while these women wanted legal acknowledgement of their marital status, they were otherwise exotically different from the white women in the room. Those descriptions could also be read, however, as an acknowledgement of their insistence on their "Indian" identity.

There was no mention of their comparative lack of political, social and economic privilege in Canadian society, which was the real effect of their difference. Rather, the reporters' emphasis on their fears about being ejected from their homes for complaining to the Commission inevitably set up a conflict model which centred on the women versus the men and any white or Métis woman who had married a First Nations man. The conflict approach also underscored the idea, as *The Sudbury Star* editorialized, somewhat snarkily, that the problems with the Act notwithstanding, "discrimination is not entirely a white man's failing."[41] In reality, both the band councils and the federal government were working together at that point to resist any changes in the Indian Act which would have given the women back their status. In the meantime, the women continued their fight for recognition.

After the hearing in Ottawa, Earley wrote to the Commission saying that the women had been harassed on their return home and that Bourque had been given such a hard time by other young people, some of them "whiter" than she was, that the women arranged for her to leave the reserve for awhile. They formed an organization called "Equal Rights for Indian Women" and appealed through the media for support from other native women across the country. They met twice with the Minister of Indian Affairs and brought their issues to native conferences. Harassment continued, apparently from white women who had married aboriginal men, as much as from anyone, and they cautiously asked the media not to used their names.[42]

The Media and Native Women in the North

The complaints that aboriginal women from the reserves brought to the Commissioners, especially about their need for better living conditions and a suitable education for their children, were echoed in the north. But the words of northern native women were muted in comparison, partly because hardly any appeared at the formal hearings, and the Inuit women in the villages spoke through interpreters, both native and white. In almost all cases, the white people who intervened to speak for them had quite a different set of concerns.

Before Commissioners Bird and Lange arrived in Whitehorse, the local *Star* published advance stories about the hearings. It also devoted a full page to the issues it was interested in, such as equal pay and income tax deductions, but nowhere were native concerns specified. It is perhaps no surprise, then, that in Whitehorse, a city of five thousand with well-appointed, middle-class housing segregated from the poor "Indian" shacks, the Commissioners heard only from elite white women and men who discussed the issues already aired in the south

as well as their "different" issues, which mainly stemmed from the isolation newcomers to the north experienced.[43]

Ed Reid covered the hearings in Whitehorse and Yellowknife on
Matinee, and the trip to the Inuit villages on Hudson Bay on *Take 30.*
According to his and other media accounts, the Yukon "Indians" and
Métis made up about one-fifth of the population, while in the
Northwest Territories it was split roughly three ways among "the
Indians, the Eskimos and the whites." While the two CBC programs
were very different, on both of them white people expressed a great
deal of well-meaning concern about the lives of the aboriginal peoples,
who, generally speaking, led a segregated existence from them.[44]

On *Matinee* there were definitely mixed messages about assimilation, and some conflict among the whites. In Whitehorse, Councillor
Gordon attributed the high "illegitimacy" rate to "Indian-custom marriages" and common-law unions between natives and whites. But
while she questioned the idea that any child should be considered
"illegitimate," she and others asked for legislation that would "validate" these arrangements. Doctor Hilda Hellaby, who was in her sev-
enties and the Director of Divinity at the Anglican church in
Whitehorse, was also concerned about common-law unions. She said
that the native women who willingly became involved with transient
white men were acting to protect their own status as Indians and as
mothers by not marrying them. This would suggest a great deal of
agency on the part of the women concerned, but Hellaby believed it
embittered and alienated young native men who had to wait for "a
white man's leavings." Dedie Dodds, who had grown up in a multi-
racial, working-class area of Toronto, said that all the people of the
north should integrate and be called "northerners," not "Indian,
Eskimo or Others. I'm tired of being an 'Others.'" At the same time,
according to the local paper, "she deplored the fact that native young
people are being forced to adopt our standards and way of life. 'All
these kids are coming out like little peas in a pod now in the Hostel
system.'"[45]

This segment of *Matinee* moderated what could have been an
unremitting emphasis on the need for aboriginal people to integrate,
assimilate, or otherwise change to fit the current federal model of
"equality" for all Canadians. It also underscored some conflict and disagreement among white people, including journalists, as to what
assimilation, equality, and respect for racial differences really meant.
Flo Whyard, who had been the editor of the local *Whitehorse Star* for 11
years and covered this hearing, broke the "objectivity" rule by commenting to Reid in an interview. "Who are we to come in and say to
these people, 'look, unless you have a piece of paper signed, your
children are illegitimate.' I mean they've been doing this for centuries,
and it's the way they're accustomed to setting up a union and a fami-

ly." Reid, also dropping his "objective" stance, even told Pat Patterson on the air that he, too, was uncomfortable with the idea that white people should be telling native people how to live.[46]

As they had in the south, Commissioners Bird and Lange heard several people speak about sexual exploitation of native women, and their degrading living conditions. In Yellowknife, however, the coverage shifted to questions about white men and some of their brutal sexual behaviour towards aboriginal women, which was a new angle on the issue. Marilyn Assheton-Smith, a regional program director for the Company of Young Canadians, and a progressive thinker, seemed genuinely puzzled as to why transient men, considered respectable husbands and fathers in their home communities, exploited vulnerable native women who were new to town. She claimed that these native women, and white women in similar circumstances, were "considered fair game for normal and respectable men" who had "learned unconsciously to differentiate between women whose social status permits them to be abused and those whose social level does not." As an example, she cited the cases of two "Indian" women she had encountered in the Territories and in northern Alberta respectively who, she believed, had probably been gang-raped by transient men working on construction or survey crews. Her comments, as quoted in the media, underscored the violence they must have experienced: "I don't know exactly what happened to either of them. I am sure it involved sex, and quite sure it was not so kind as simple rape, and quite sure they were kept mercifully drunk most of the time. Whatever it was, it destroyed them."

Assheton-Smith also said, according to Elinor Reading of CP, that "such incidents cannot be explained away by blaming men" and suggested a study of "relatively normal men, not deviates, destroying relatively normal women" as a way of understanding their behaviour. Some headlines played on her contention that women who lacked social status were regarded as fair game by respectable men, sometimes in ways which seemed to excuse the men: "Non-Status Women Considered Fair Game for Respectable Males," in the *Oshawa Times* in Ontario, "Non-Status Women Claimed 'Fair Game,'" in *The Star-Phoenix* in Saskatoon, and "'Non-Status' Women Make Fair Game, Commission Told," in the *Winnipeg Free Press*.[47] The reporter, Reading, comments today that most people, including herself, were not as aware of the power dynamics of sexual exploitation as they are now.[48]

Only one woman held these men accountable for their actions in using the women and then disparaging them. This woman was Rosemary Thrasher, an Inuit woman from Paulatuk on the Arctic coast, who, at 22, was working as a typist for the Northwest Territories government in Yellowknife where she presented a brief to the Commission. In an interview with Reid, she said that when the young women, new to town, could not find jobs, "they either starve or give themselves away for food or a place to sleep." Even so, white people should bring up their male children to respect them. "I mean, to teach a guy how to be polite, especially to a native girl, not to make fun of her just because of what she did, or what she used to do, things like that. This making fun of her and whatnot makes a girl feel low and then she goes out and keeps doing what she always does." But her objections received limited media play as, apparently only Reid asked her to expand on this aspect of her brief. The press coverage of her comments emphasized her concern with the poor living conditions of the native people, although the local paper mentioned briefly that she thought "Girls should be able to live without having guys bugging them all the time."[49]

It was difficult for the native women to discuss their most personal problems, including the conditions in which they lived, in a room full of white people. For example, the letter from Mary Anne Lahache which opens this chapter was apparently meant as a personal letter to Bird. Although it effectively underscored Lahache's frustration and fear, its publication raises questions about how much their privacy was respected.[50]

Reid had found the absence of native women at the hearings "disappointing" and somewhat puzzling. In his interview with the local announcer-operator in Whitehorse, Jim Millican, he attributed it to their reluctance to be outnumbered by whites at such gatherings.[51] There may have been another reason, however. Aside from their need for privacy, perhaps they saw the Commission as just another white inquiry into their circumstances; moreover, their recent meetings with government officials to discuss possible changes to the Indian Act had not been particularly successful.[52]

In their reports from the northern hearings, none of the journalists directly pitted whites against aboriginals in a "conflict" frame, but there was some tension evident concerning race relations in the North. At one point on *Matinee*, Reid mentioned to Patterson that when native people did show up at the hearings, "you could feel the bitterness behind what they said." As an example, he quoted Rosemary Thrasher as saying, "Everybody knows this country belonged to the native people before you came." At another point in the program, he ran another audio clip of her asking for adult education courses for native women rather than domestic training. Thrasher insisted that aboriginal women, who had been badly educated as children "have ability to do something better than just being a waitress or a chambermaid or babysitter." She was actually responding to a comment from a white woman from the local YWCA, Alison McAteer, who had suggested that native women should be given domestic training, but this was not made clear in any of the coverage. At other points, both Thrasher and

Dedie Dodds suggested that white women new to the north could learn a lot from mixing with the aboriginal women as peers, comments which were included on *Matinee* but not in the press coverage.[53] Reid's sympathy for the native women, and that of some of the whites he interviewed, suggested conflict between the races but also suggested that changes in attitudes towards aboriginals were overdue. It also had the effect of bringing the issues out, rather than simplifying them, especially on *Matinee,* where he had the time to do so. Privately, he told Reading over lunch one day, referring to native people but perhaps speaking generally as well, that "human problems were 'out of hand.'" "Those were the words he used," Reading noted, "'Out of hand.'"[54]

When the commissioners visited the Inuit villages on Hudson Bay in the Keewatin district of the Territories, the focus shifted again to an assimilationist view that more closely matched the approach of the Commission and the federal government. It was clear that the southern reporters knew little about the area. Reid, who had cut his vacation short to go north, had managed to read one book and several newspaper clippings on the Territories and the Yukon. Reading was eager to visit these villages, but still considered herself a "green" reporter. Several northern journalists and broadcasters, who may not have travelled to the more isolated areas all that often, were also on the tour. All of them, and the two commissioners, had to rely on briefings from white experts such as Bob Williamson, an anthropologist, and member of the Territorial council in NWT.[55]

The villages were quite small compared with other possible venues such as Frobisher Bay on Baffin Island, but since all of them had airstrips that could accommodate the party's DC-3, they were ideal locales. Bird, not wanting to rely solely on research reports about these areas, was also concerned that the Commission would be criticized if she did not pay them a visit. To help with financial costs, she arranged with Mr. Justice William Morrow to share an airplane on one of his regular trips to these settlements. She was pleased when the CBC decided to pay half the cost of the charter, as the presence of Reid and his crew, and a CP reporter, would mean good publicity for the Commission. According to Glenn Sarty, the executive producer of *Take 30,* sharing such costs was a common practice and not perceived as a conflict of interest. Reid even mentioned the arrangement on the program.[56]

On the trip to the Inuit villages, Reid came into closer, more prolonged contact with Bird than he normally did at the hearings, and this, as well as his unfamiliarity with the area, may have unduly influenced his approach. Bird, apparently feeling protective of the women in the villages, deliberately tried to keep the reporters away from "shy" Inuit women and white civil servants. At one point she said to Reid, somewhat apologetically, on camera: "Yes, the women are shy and I don't think it's easy for them to talk with cameras running and the press all over the place. And I also think that when you talk to some of the girls at the nursing station or the wives of people here that they ought not to be quoted because they are, in a way, civil servants, and I never like to quote a civil servant or put them on the spot. I hope you understand. I just feel if you could just—when I'm talking quietly to people—lay off?"

This request, and the language barrier which already existed, meant that Bird or Lange did the interviewing while the reporters stood by or went off on their own to talk to young Inuit who spoke English, and white people who had made their lives in the north or were conducting research there. At one point, Reid even referred to Bird by her journalist's name, Anne Francis, as if she had switched roles. The fact that he used the clip of Bird's intervention on the air suggests that he wanted it understood how his work as a journalist was being constrained.

Most of the other clips he used tended to reflect the Commission's concern with integration and similarities, a sharp contrast to what had transpired on *Matinee*. In one segment, Bird said to Williamson that she didn't think the Inuit women had any conception of what "status" meant and wondered how to get through to them. She liked the French translation, "situation," better. At another point, he assured her that the native people were ready to embrace the best of white culture, and wanted the same opportunities as other Canadians. She replied that the mandate of her Commission was "to give equal opportunity to women in every aspect of Canadian life, and this is an aspect of Canadian life, surely." These exchanges had a certain "staginess" about them, which suggests that Reid was more under the direction of Bird that he might have liked.[57]

Visually, the northern setting at least gave him more scope than the formal, static hearings in the south, but it also allowed him to juxtapose the "new," white ways with the "old," aboriginal ways. The *Take 30* camera roamed freely, alternating between shots of a Hudson's Bay store, government housing and a tuberculosis (TB) clinic, and fishing boats, native crafts and the weatherbeaten faces of the older Inuit women. Most of the *Take 30* and press stories about this trip had to do with the housing and services the federal government was providing; for example, medical screening for tuberculosis at Eskimo Point and an arts and crafts workshop at Rankin Inlet.[58] *The News of the North*, however, was most critical of shoddy government planning and housing, an issue that did not come out as clearly in any of the CBC and CP coverage. At Coral Harbour, for example, local people complained that government surveyors were inept, and that houses were built on swamps, were badly warped, or were fire traps, but only the *News* emphasized these problems.[59] According to Lange, who wrote a separate report on the north for her fellow commissioners, part of the problem was that each settlement was different but the federal government treated them all the same.[60]

Instead of dwelling on such criticism, *Take 30* and CP focused on how important it was that the Inuit adapt to white standards of health and hygiene, and to the bureaucracy that federal government intervention inevitably brought to their lives. On *Take 30*, government housing was presented as a desirable alternative to the tents and igloos which Williamson blamed for the high infant mortality rate among the Inuit, even though he insisted they were "not dirty people." They just had to be taught how to manage hygiene in their new homes.

Another theme was respect for local customs which could easily be adapted to the needs of white bureaucracy. Inuit couples who had several children, for example, would give one or two to family or community members who had none of their own, or who needed a child of one gender or the other to provide a balance of job-sharing within the traditional family structure. On *Take 30*, there were scenes of parents with their children in Judge Morrow's court, where he legalized these adoptions, 92 of them in four days on this trip.[61] The signed papers made it possible, Reading's story said, for the women to collect mother's allowances from the government, "innovations the Eskimos are as quick to appreciate as power toboggans." According to one headline over her story, "There's Always a Happy Ending" to a day in Judge Morrow's court, a rather congratulatory approach, based on an interview with the judge himself. *News of the North*, however, using Morrow, Williamson and a local priest as authorities, emphasized that love for children and a strong sense of community lay behind the Inuit adoption custom.[62] As Reading remembers it today, the court procedure "satisfied both our desire for a lot of federal records and respected the customs of the community." Personally, the generosity of the birth parents impressed her profoundly and made her reassess white culture's view of children as possessions.[63]

In their visits around the villages, Bird and Lange appeared anxious to connect with the Inuit women, and tried to do so by discussing things they might have in common with them. In one film sequence Bird reported to Reid that she thought she had been successful in striking a rapport. She understood that older women were respected in Inuit society and their advice was often sought, and pointed out to them that she, too, was an older woman. She told the younger women that she had been young once herself and understood their problems. Even so, her perspective was inevitably that of a white outsider looking in. She said that she explained to them "that all of the problems of women were basically the same because we're interested in what happened to our men, our home and our children. And this was something that you were talking to them [about] very directly. And they are very direct people, I find, the Eskimos. They have tremendous humour and sly jokes and many of their jokes are very much like ours. You ask them who is the boss in their family and they say, 'Well, my husband thinks he is, ho, ho,' with this wonderful toothless grin, you know."[64]

Reading's stories, too, emphasized similarities rather than differences, although her version of the "woman as boss" angle was not the same as Bird's. A group of nine women at Rankin Inlet had started out discussing adult education over coffee with Bird and Lange but soon began to talk about who really ran their homes. According to Reading, Lange said that she was boss inside her home and her husband was boss outside it. Most of the women appeared to agree: "Smiles and nods ran around the circle." The lead on this story read: "North or south, it's all the same—Canadian women rule their homes or think they do." It was published as "Women Rule Roost in the North Too," in *The Edmonton Journal* and "Eskimo Women Boss in the Home," in the *Telegraph-Journal* of Saint John, New Brunswick.[65]

Reading remembers that she was quite aware of the large gaps between the two cultures, even though there were some commonalities. "I think everybody felt a connection. I felt a connection but I must say, I also was uneasy about going into people's houses," such as the tents that most Inuit still lived in at Coral Harbour. She adds that it takes a lot of experience for anyone, including anthropologists, to bridge cultural difference when they're the ones with all the advantages and come "bopping in on a plane" and out again.[66]

In several interviews and at news conferences following Bird's meetings with aboriginal women in the south and the north, the media continued to pick up on her emphasis on the similarities rather than the differences between aboriginal and white women. She told a reporter back in Ottawa that when one young woman told her how hard it was to be a widow, "it sounded just exactly like our society. I almost cried at this point." Bird could also be quite romantic about the Inuit women, with whom she was clearly quite fascinated. When she recalled a meeting at Eskimo Point, on another *Take 30* program over two years later, she enthused about the "most wonderful experience" of witnessing the younger women caring for their infants. One mother had flipped her crying baby out of her hood and over her head to nurse her while another quieted her squalling child by "doing a little dance back and forwards that must be as old as time. Yes, I think that's something I'll never forget." At the time, *Take 30* simply filmed Bird and Lange, with Williamson translating, talking to a room full of Inuit women and their children, apparently about co-ops, judging by the background sound track.[67] In her version of the meeting at Eskimo Point, Reading focused on the women's enthusiastic response to Lange's suggestion that they set up a co-op store rather than have to rely on the local Hudson's Bay outlet. The women were not happy with the local manager, but that did not come out in the CBC coverage.[68]

The local newspaper saw the issues more closely from the perspective of the Inuit women than did the southern reporters. According to *News of the North,* when Bird suggested to the women at Eskimo Point that "the problems of women are the same everywhere," they did not entirely agree. "But the Eskimo women sitting in a circle inside a government building, their babies on their backs and their older children seated beside them, pointed out that they also have some problems quite different from those of southern women." According to the *News,* they told the commissioners that they wanted their children to learn English in order to act as mediators between the people and government agencies and staff, but they did not want them to lose their own language and culture. They would be a lot happier if their older children did not have to go away to school, could have trained Inuit teachers rather than transient white ones, and they themselves would be interested in adult education if they could help choose their own courses.[69]

Bird passed their concerns about their children along to Reid and his *Take 30,* audience, and added, in reference to the teenagers who were sent away to school, "These people are the in-betweens. They haven't yet become a part of our culture and they are beginning to leave their own culture and this is a problem which those women were very much concerned about." Even so, adopting white ways was still presented as the most desirable alternative. Near the end of the program, the camera focused briefly on three young Inuit women, a stewardess, a public health nurse and a typist accountant, none of whom were interviewed. Reid commented, "The Commissioners hope that these girls are beginning to typify the new woman of the north."[70] For her part, Reading did a profile of Alice Ningeongan, Bird's 14-year-old interpreter in Coral Harbour, whom the reporter framed as "a link between cultures." *News of the North* ran a photo and brief item about the stewardess, Charlotte Karetak, who "may be the only Eskimo airline stewardess in Canada," and who was described as a "slim, attractive 19-year-old," and "bilingual" in the northern sense of that term.[71] The "generation gap" theme was a common concern among observers of the north at the time, and one which might well have resonated among southern media audiences concerned that their baby-boomer teenagers were turning into hippies and radicals. Adrienne Clarkson provided yet another perspective, commenting that the concern in the north was similar to "the immigrant problem" among newcomers to Canada. Reid replied that he had spoken to one young, educated woman, whose parents grew up on the land, who wanted to introduce fashions to her home settlement. "And it's just unbelievable, the leap from virtually the Stone Age to the present in one generation." Paul

Soles, who had visited Frobisher Bay the year before, interjected, praising the "adaptability of these incredible people." No one on this program questioned the idea that the Inuit were the ones who had to do most of the changing.[72]

The Media, Human Rights and "Difference"

The news stories about native women did not present a clear-cut "princess/squaw" dichotomy, but were much more complex than that. Generally, but not always, stories were framed along the journalistic models of white culture: conflict, personalization and efforts at proximity or familiarity which seem almost laughable in retrospect, especially regarding the so-called "Stone Age" Keewatin women of Hudson Bay. Attempts to fit disadvantaged people into a "human rights" framework was part of the spirit of the times for the liberal-minded journalist. With the best of intentions, perhaps, the reporters took white experts at their word, or confused aboriginal issues with those of other minorities such as the Black people of the United States. When native women did speak out for themselves, using the human rights language that white reporters understood, it could still have repercussions. They became easily framed as "doormats," or tragic figures disenfranchised from their native heritage, media messages that must have added to the sense of betrayal in aboriginal communities. For every successful "Emily" there always seemed to be a destitute "Mary" waiting in the wings.

Given the disadvantaged position of aboriginal women in Canadian society, the journalists' interpretations certainly had some basis in reality. But their emphasis on conflict and violence, tragedy and redemption, poverty and pain, meant that one woman, or a few, became symbols for many, and the values of their native culture became lost. These media representations were particularly painful for aboriginal women, as the letters to the editor in *Chatelaine* revealed in one instance unrelated to the Commission. In February 1968, the magazine published a group profile, "Women of British Columbia," that included the sad story of Georgina Archie, who had worked as a prostitute on skid row. Three readers protested, pointing out that there were non-natives who shared the same fate and criticizing *Chatelaine* for singling out a native woman that way. Wrote Ethel Brant Monture of Middleport, Ontario, "We continue to wonder why the Canadian news media deny us the racial courtesy given to other citizens." In response, the editors, invoking the journalistic model of "fairness and balance," replied that they had profiled successful aboriginal women in other recent stories about the women from the various provinces. "However, not all Indian women have happy stories to tell and with Georgina Archie we presented the other side."[73]

At the same time, the strong presence that women like Lavallee, Thrasher and other native delegates brought to media coverage of the Commission hearings clearly signalled the desire of aboriginal women to claim citizenship and identity on their own terms. The result of their interventions were breaks in the usual story lines, mainly the voices of these insistent aboriginal women and of the more progressive white people, including reporters, who suggested that the issues of equality and difference, in terms of "human rights" news discourse, were not at all clear-cut, regardless of the Commission's mandate, and the journalistic mandates of "objectivity" and "balance." As Marilyn Assheton-Smith, who had appeared at the Yellowknife hearings, wrote to the local newspaper, "Maybe we in Canada can build a Canadian society that will allow people to be different, to be extraordinary. Can you tolerate that? Even as a dream? Maybe then we can talk about integration and not mean 'they' must become just like 'us.'"[74]

Those same issues of "equality" and "difference" were to reappear in a more general context of relations between the sexes later on in the commission's mandate. It was the essential problem the Commissioners had to tackle in respect to all Canadian women once the hearings were over and they turned their attention to producing their recommendations.

Chapter 9

"Too Little...Too Late": The Coverage of the Commission's Report, 1970

The report on the status of women is a peculiarly feminine document—intriguing, expensive, a little late, wisely illogical and its beauty is in the eye of the beholder. The basic theme of the report is that women should be the legal, moral and social equals of men—except in one or two instances where women should be more equal.

—*The Tribune*, Winnipeg

The Tribune's editorial response to the Commission's recommendations on equal opportunities for women deliberately adopted a patronizing and unflattering tone which likened the document to women themselves. Specifically, it referred to key criticisms from within the Commission's own ranks, women's movement leaders and other media, criticisms the editorial writer was apparently only too happy to seize upon. In *The Tribune's* eyes, not only had the Commission taken too much money and time to produce its *Report*, rendering it expensive "old news," it was also inconsistent in its approach to "equality" because it stipulated that women's differences from men justified "special treatment."[1]

The media's reactions to the *Report*, which was finally tabled in the House of Commons on 7 December 1970, were contradictory

Notes to Chapter 9 are on pp. 303–10.

211

and somewhat confusing, well illustrating the drawbacks of professional news discourse and newsroom ritual, including the "objectivity" regime.[2] Editorial and opinion columnists aside, if the journalists concerned could previously claim any objectivity in the way in which they covered the Commission, which is doubtful, they certainly could not in relation to its recommendations, despite their attempts at "fair and balanced" reporting. They were operating within their own cultural milieu, and their coverage reflected its changing attitudes towards women's roles, a process that is never straightforward or easy.[3]

Primarily using the "conflict" frame, they focused on any criticism from any quarter, but especially complaints about recommendations which suggested that women should be given short-term, preferential treatment. They highlighted only these and a few other contentious issues, and conflated or downplayed others that, it could be argued, were just as important to the women of Canada. There was little strong analysis of the *Report*, or of the feminist movement which precipitated it and had, in the meantime, been supplanted in the media by the women's liberation movement. In fact, journalists tended to conflate the Commission and the old and new manifestations of the movement for women's equality, which added to the semantic confusion in the news discourse about women's rights.

Not that there was no praise for the *Report*. While there were differences on both sides of the sex divide and among individuals, women journalists tended to support it while the men tended to be more sceptical. Their gender biases, pro and con, permeated their coverage, underscored by the apparent tensions between male and female journalists over the women's rights issues in their own profession. They were also constrained by their own work routines and rituals that demanded that they shift their attention all too quickly from the Commission to other pressing issues in the news. In short, the *Report* was headlined, debated and quickly dismissed.

Initially, there was a short-lived explosion of media coverage which lasted about two days in the daily press. These stories appeared in three formats: summaries of the *Report*; focus stories on specific recommendations and the reactions to them, including the positions taken by the various commissioners; and editorial commentary, including cartoons. Inevitably, many of these stories were repetitive, adding more weight to the criticisms of the *Report*. The CBC coverage also concerned itself with the more contentious recommendations.

The Debate over "Special Treatment"

According to a journalist who attended her news conference the day the *Report* was tabled in the House, Florence Bird was "testy" and unsmiling, a defensive image.[4] Bird had been thrust into the uncomfortable position of having to put a positive spin on the Commission's work in light of the serious gender and philosophical splits among the commissioners. Journalists were particularly intrigued that John Humphrey had refused to sign the *Report* and had issued a 17-page minority document of his own. He charged that the Commission was not committed to equality but "special treatment" for certain classes of women over both men and other women in hiring and promotion, and that it favoured women in the labour force over women at home. Three other commissioners, Jacques Henripin, Elsie Gregory MacGill and Doris Ogilvie, signed the *Report* but issued separate statements which served to bring out their major disagreements over the abortion issue, and, for Henripin and MacGill, other matters as well.[5]

Playing up the "conflict" angle, the journalists paid particular attention to the gender division among the Commissioners and to the recommendations that the men, especially Humphrey, did not like. *The Globe and Mail* announced, "One Male Member Issues Minority Report: Commissioners Divided by Their Sex on Recommendations on Woman's Roles," while other headlines in the *Winnipeg Free Press* made the specific point that it was a male Commissioner in opposition.[6] A closer reading of the *Report*, Humphrey's minority report, and the separate statements of MacGill, Ogilvie and Henripin indicates that their disagreements did not always fall so clearly along gender lines, although it was true that the men had more objections and reservations than the women. Nevertheless, all the commissioners did agree on many of the recommendations.[7]

The recommendations Humphrey disliked were specific measures that would help women attain higher positions or better pay in politics, public life and the workforce, such as the appointment of two female Senators from each province, efforts to put female civil servants in line for promotions, the appointment of more women to public boards, and their admission into non-traditional jobs in the Royal Canadian Mounted Police (RCMP) and the military. He also objected to suggested changes in the tax structure that would reduce the amount of the marital status exemption, a new child allowance of $500, a proposal for a national network of daycare centres, mandatory and paid maternity leave funded through the Unemployment Insurance system, and, indirectly, to a guaranteed income for sole-support parents, 90 percent of whom were women. The child allowance, $40 per month or $500 dollars a year for each child under 16, would be payable to the mother and would replace both the current family allowances of eight dollars per month per child and the standard income tax deduction of $300. The Commission felt this would give mothers the financial freedom to either stay at home with their children or pay for childcare. Humphrey said that not only would the child allowance encourage a population explosion, but it, and paid maternity leave discriminated against childless people who also had to contribute to these measures financially. He also preferred a guaranteed minimum income for everyone, not just sole-support mothers. In fact, the majority *Report* stated that the recommendation concerning sole-support parents was only a first step towards the goal of universality.[8]

The media, and Humphrey himself, played on his credentials as an international legal expert. Citing the UN Universal Declaration of Human Rights, which he had helped to draft, he acknowledged that discrimination against women existed, but he appeared not to see it as a systemic problem, preferring to accept the masculine status quo as a measure of what women could achieve rather than try to change it. The journalists paid a great deal of attention to Humphrey's argument that women did not need what he and they called "quota systems" in the Senate, the judiciary, the civil service or the workforce because, according to the lead in the Montreal *Gazette*, "Canadian women are quite capable of standing on their own feet and should not be treated as 'wards of society.'" It was a good quote which made a snappy headline as well. Other headlines, which emphasized that the Commission wanted "special treatment for women," which Humphrey thought was "discriminatory" and "unfair," were equally damning from a public relations perspective: "Commission's Prescription: For Women: 'Special Treatment,'" and "Commissioner Feels Report Discriminatory to Both Sexes." Humphrey actually agreed with the principle of what he called "preferential treatment which is extended to the end that there should be real equality," but only in relation to certain racial or ethnic groups or individuals. He did not believe, however, that women had the "psychological characteristics of a minority," a term he did not explain.[9]

At her news conference and in subsequent interviews, Bird used all her skill in handling the media to counter Humphrey's objections. She kept insisting that "special treatment" would only be temporary and would not set a precedent in public policy, as he argued. In reference to proposals that called for numerical targets, she avoided using the word "quota," the term Humphrey insisted on and which, he noted, was avoided in the *Report* as well. According to Bird, "We didn't think in terms of quotas.... Once a better balance is achieved then there would be no need for these provisions to continue." In reference to women in managerial positions, she said that even though a special effort should be made to bring them forward, they still have to get those jobs and promotions "on merit—they have to compete on the open market." In later interviews, she said there were many misunderstandings about some of the recommendations, especially from people who had either not read the *Report*, or had not read it carefully.[10]

Part of the problem was that journalists are trained to write linear accounts of events, not complex philosophical discussions about feminist issues. Consequently, they were not quite successful in getting the philosophy behind the majority *Report* across in their stories. To them, what the Commission was saying seemed to be contradictory, at least when placed within the human rights framework it and many women's movement leaders had espoused all along. As Leone Kirkwood of *The Globe and Mail* explained, the Commission claimed "no special status for women, no separate realm, only full acceptance in the present world." Nonetheless, it thought that "special treatment" would always be necessary in the event of pregnancy and childbirth, and "women will, for awhile, need special treatment to overcome discriminatory practices" in public life and the workforce. This position deviated from classic liberalism in that it was essentially an argument, which is still contentious, about "equality" versus "difference"; could women be allowed to be "different" from men and still be "equal" to them, and if so, how?[11]

The excitement over Humphrey's intervention to some degree stole the spotlight away from the Commission's recommendations on equal pay. In their stories about professional and other working women, the journalists did not bring out the extent to which the Commission wanted changes in the equal pay laws so that women working in sex-segregated occupations could benefit. The fact that it asked that the federal, provincial and territorial governments eventually adopt the International Labour Organization's Convention 100 concerning equal pay for work of equal value was mentioned specifically in very few stories and commentaries. Most referred simply to "equal pay." An exception was a story written by Rosemary Speirs, who had left CP for the *Toronto Daily Star*, which mentioned that the Commission wanted women to earn the "same wages for jobs of comparable skill."[12]

The "Unrecognized" Housewife

Humphrey's other main accusation was that the Commission had ignored the housewife without children at home, whom he called, in a follow-up interview, "the forgotten woman," a term also used in the lead to the CP story and headlines in both *The Montreal Star* and *Winnipeg Free Press* versions. The journalist interpreted his phrase to mean the "large segment of the female population which did not submit briefs to the Commission, and which had no major complaints." This interpretation was an oversimplification; married women without children were not a particularly "large segment" of the population compared with those who did have them, and, in any event, their nonappearance before the Commission did not necessarily signal indifference, or lack of problems either. There was no discussion of whether these women had written any of the one thousand letters the

Commission received, perhaps because none were cited in the *Report*.[13] Other stories said that Humphrey, in his document, had accused the Commission of treating these women as "social parasites" and said that its attitude towards them was "unfair." This comment was in reference to his feeling that a reduction in the marital status tax benefits would force the childless wife into the workforce, and that the value of her contribution to the home should not be equated to that of a servant.[14] These very expressions lent an extremely negative tone to this coverage, all the more so because Humphrey was an authority, and a male one at that.

At her news conference, Bird also dealt with this aspect of Humphrey's intervention. According to Yvonne Crittenden of the *Telegram*, she "repeatedly stressed the 'enormous and largely unrecognized' contributions made to society by women in the home. She said many of the *Report's* recommendations would benefit them as well as the working woman"; for example, a recommendation that they should be able to contribute voluntarily to the Canada and Quebec Pension Plans. Bird repeated the Commission's essential argument that a wife should not be considered the husband's "'dependant' when the work she did was of invaluable use to him," an argument she repeated in an interview with Ed Reid on *Take 30*, broadcast the following day.[15] The media's juxtaposition of the views of Humphrey and Bird underscored the conflict frame, while still allowing "balance."

Abortion "On Demand" and Daycare for All

In its treatment of reproductive choice, the media framed the abortion issue not only in the context of the split it caused among the Commissioners, but also in relation to the recent demands of the women's liberation movement. In both their overview and focus stories, many of the major newspapers headlined the news that the Commission was asking for "abortion on demand," an expression that seems to have originated with socialist feminists. Strictly speaking, the story was wrong, however. The words "on demand" never appeared in the Commission *Report* although that intent was clear, at least for the earlier stages of pregnancy. The Commission asked that the Criminal Code be amended "to permit abortion by a qualified medical practitioner *on the sole request* of any woman who has been pregnant for 12 weeks or less." After that, abortion should be permitted "*at the request of a woman*...if the doctor is convinced" that continuing the pregnancy would endanger her physical or mental health, "or if there is a substantial risk" that the child would be "greatly handicapped, either mentally or physically." The hospital abortion committees which had been set up under the most recent law could allow abortions if they thought the pregnancy would endanger the life or health of the mother, but the Commission argued that they should be disbanded as they did nothing to solve the problem of illegal abortions and often resulted in delays. They legally protected the medical profession but did not necessarily help the woman. Still, *The Montreal Star* headline for the abortion focus story read, "Another Chants 'Abortion on Demand,'" which might have suited a story about a women's liberation protest better than the *Report,* and the Toronto *Telegram* headline also claimed that the Commission had asked for "Abortion on Demand," although the stories themselves qualified the term correctly. Most of the journalists mentioned that Elsie MacGill had filed a separate statement but did not point out that what she said actually did amount to "abortion on demand" in the cultural discourse of the day, in that there should be no conditions placed on a woman's freedom of choice at all. MacGill felt that abortion was a private matter between a woman and her doctor, regardless of how advanced the pregnancy. Only *The Telegram* noted that her position "probably will be echoed by the women's liberation groups across Canada" as the recommendations in the *Report* still did not meet their demands.[16]

In the focus stories, little attention was paid to Henripin and Ogilvie's position that human life should be protected, except in a newspaper headline over a CP story published in Ogilvie's home province of New Brunswick. This was an illustration of the "proximity" news frame at work, and also invoked Ogilvie's legal expertise even though she was not acting in her capacity as a judge: "Moncton Judge Doesn't Support Relaxed Abortion Laws." The less controversial recommendations that would have the effect of making sterilization and birth control legally supported and as widely available as possible were generally included in the stories about abortion.[17]

A headline in the Montreal *Gazette* flagged another issue which was just as big as abortion in its estimation: "Abortion Rights, Day-Care in Top Issues." The Commission made several recommendations that would make childcare easier for women at home and in the labour force. The headlines made it clear that the Commission had listened to the progressive authorities in the field, as well to the many groups who asked for daycare. As *The Globe and Mail* noted, it "came out strongly in favor of daycare centres...and attacked some long-standing beliefs that mothers are the best people to bring up their children." A headline over a CP story in *The Ottawa Journal,* "Not Just the Working Mother: Day-Care Centres for All Who Need Them Suggested." The Commission wanted the federal government to provide the provinces with much of the operating and capital costs, although parents who could afford to pay the fees would do so. This suggestion, and the two male Commissioners' reservations, received a fair amount of media play, both separately and taken together with other recommendations. The men argued that any daycare should become part of the education system and thus come under provincial, not federal, jurisdiction. Moreover, tax money should be spent on more important social needs and, from Henripin's pro-natalist perspective, children should be cared for in the home as much as possible.[18]

Journalists' Gender Conflicts and Workplace Equality Stories

The journalists no doubt would have felt delinquent in their duty if they hadn't pointed out these "conflicts" and differences among the Commissioners. That was their job as they saw it. Permeating these stories, however, was another kind of gender conflict, among the journalists themselves, who were transparently less than "objective." There was already some tension evident between the men and women who covered the story, owing partly to the controversy over the integration of the National Press Club earlier that year. On the day the *Report* was released, this tension manifested itself in the boorish behaviour of some of the male journalists at Florence Bird's news conference.

Several female reporters who had covered the hearings were sent to Ottawa for the occasion. Or, as Yvonne Crittenden of the *Telegram* observed, "every newspaper worthy of the name trotted out its token women reporters and sent them up for their day of glory on Page One—before retiring them back to the Women's Pages." Crittenden was annoyed enough about the behaviour of some of the men to write about it in an opinion column. She revealed that one unnamed male staffer from *The Telegram* "screamed 'discrimination'" when told he could not go to Ottawa to cover the *Report* and "whined" that it was because he was a man. He threatened to bring the issue to the Toronto Newspaper Guild.

In Ottawa, not only did the MPs sitting in the House seem distracted by a stronger than usual female presence in the press corps, the press gallery was "a-twitter" with male reporters "making the predictable double-entendres to their female colleagues" about the recommendations. Although Crittenden believed that newspaper men tended to be more liberal than other males, some still made the kind of remarks that would turn "even a moderate female into a rabid she-wolf or a Betty Friedan." She noted that while the "militant feminists" there could easily be spotted by "the pantsuits, the rimless glasses, the aggressively challenging questions…you could tell the male chauvinists by their refusal to take the report very seriously."

Florence Bird had to contend with, among others, columnist Charles Lynch, who, Crittenden remarked, "made our womanly hearts beat a little faster with his clever remarks…. 'You and I both know that women loathe one another,' puffed Charlie on his pipe and was not quelled when Mrs. Bird shot him her frostiest glance."[19] Zoe Bieler of

The Montreal Star later wrote that the reactions of the male journalists to the *Report* "ranged from good-natured quips to the more belligerent 'what do you women want, when you've got everything?'" Noted Anthony Westell, who was there, too: "the depth of male chauvinism has seldom been more obvious."[20]

The news discourse about the recommendations, reflected in the very words the journalists used, transmitted their respective, gendered viewpoints. Perhaps it is not surprising that the stories about the Commission's *Report* that were written by the female journalists tended to emphasize Bird's claim that Canadian women faced a "horrifying" amount of discrimination. Crittenden picked up on her comment that women in Canada were "treated like children." Lillian Newberry of CP observed in her opening paragraphs that the "long-awaited report tells Canadian women they have come a long way, but still have a long way to go." Newberry emphasized what is "wrong with their world—dead-end jobs, economic subservience, blatant discrimination in employment standards and a lack of freedom to control their destinies." Another CP story cited the *Report* as saying that to suggest that discrimination against women was systemic was often to "encounter resistance, disbelief and even derision. Perhaps no prejudice in human society is so deeply-imbedded or so little understood."[21]

Some of the focus stories on specific issues also presented the Commission's case strongly, sometimes using telling statistics. For example, Newberry of CP pointed out in an article concerning women in politics: "Since Agnes Macphail was elected first woman member of Canada's Parliament in 1921, only 17 other women have been elected to the Commons." Stories about the recommendations concerning marriage and divorce, which stressed the rights and responsibilities of both parties, emphasized that "equality" would work both ways. Or as Eleanor Dunn put it in *The Ottawa Citizen,* would also "go a long away to end discrimination against men." Essentially, the Commission had recommended a one-year waiting period for an uncontested divorce rather than three, that assets accumulated during a marriage be shared equally upon divorce, and that both wage-earning wives as well as husbands should be legally responsible for supporting dependent spouses and children during and after marriage.[22]

A certain amount of scepticism showed up in the news discourse the male journalists used. Tom Earle of CBC News, well aware that male reaction might not be so welcoming, did try to use "balance" but with a wry, masculine twist. He began by saying that if all levels of government were to accept the Commission's 167 recommendations, "the change in the nation's pattern of male-female relationships would be drastically altered." His focus was clearly on his male listeners as he went on to say: "For the good if you believe that women are discriminated against in Canada, for the worse if you believe otherwise. If the latter you better put your head under the pillow tonight and hope that this whole nightmare of giving women an equal chance with men in jobs, opportunities, security and anything else you care to add will just disappear. But I've got news for you—I don't think it will."[23]

Time magazine's Canadian edition referred to the *Report* euphemistically as "A Call to Arms" which "ticks off discriminatory practices and male-orientated attitudes with a barely subdued ferocity." Ben Tierney of Southam observed more carefully that some of the recommendations "cannot fail to raise male eyebrows across the nation" and that "the extent it goes to in seeking equal opportunity will come as a surprise to some." Here he referred to recommendations that women be eligible to become officers in the RCMP, "a bastion of the male to date" and that they be accepted, regardless of their marital or family circumstances, in military trades. Wayne MacDonald of *The Vancouver Sun* wrote in a more negative overview that the 167 recommendations "would substantially increase the federal budget" and "range the full course from ridiculous to sensible." The story initially ran under the headline, "'End Discrimination; Give Equality,'" which a *Sun* editor changed in the final edition to the misleading "Paid Vacations for Housewives." What the Commission suggested in its general discussion about women in the home was that since they worked around the clock and needed a break, they might also benefit from childcare services.[24]

In a couple of cases, journalists demonstrated a lack of sensitivity in their treatment of the recommendations concerning sexual offences and the Criminal Code. Essentially, the Commission wanted the vagrancy provisions removed because they allowed the police to arrest girls and women on suspicion of prostitution. It also wanted some of the anomalies in the law which discriminated against one gender or the other abolished, including instances of sexual assault and sex with a minor. Nick Hills' focus story led with the statement, "The present criminal code is unfair to men because it gives them no protection against being seduced by women." The *Toronto Daily Star* took essentially the same angle. Both stories were reflected in headlines such as "Criminal Code Unfair to Men—Commission." In contrast, CP's coverage of criminal matters led with a related recommendation, that the Kingston Prison for Women close because women were generally not violent offenders and needed open institutions closer to their homes where they could get rehabilitation and vocational training.[25]

A certain amount of gender tension was also evident on *Take 30*, although it was presented in a friendly manner. After unsuccessfully pressing Florence Bird on Humphrey's issue of "preferential" treatment for women outside the home, Reid brought the issue up again in the studio with Adrienne Clarkson. Clarkson thought that the *Report* was "just great" because it allowed women to take more responsibility for themselves, but that the press coverage left "a lot to be desired." When Reid mentioned the Commission's position that "special treatment" was necessary for "an interim period," he added, "They want women pushed forward. There is some fear that it will bring in a kind of quota system." Clarkson replied: "But for a time, however, this isn't a bad thing. This has happened with the Blacks in the United States, and so on...in companies. Well, Ed, you say 'stay-tus', I say stat-us. I think we agree on equality if not sameness." They smiled at each other as he reached across the desk, offering his hand to her, "Let's shake on that, kid!" To which she replied, "Yeah!"

Aside from Reid's reference to the thirtyish Clarkson, who was also visibly pregnant, as "kid," this amicable image of man and woman meeting over their differences, which ended the program, dissolved, ironically, to a very different one. It was a dramatically rendered promo for a TV trilogy of Somerset Maugham's plays, including *Women of the World*, who, intoned the heavy-handed voice of a male announcer, "use all their instincts, intuition and guile to manipulate and scheme, women who take but never give." When the promo was over, the *Take 30* credits appeared, rolling over the girl-watching film of Montreal women that was shot during the Quebec hearings. These final images could have been taken as *Take 30*'s last word on the Royal Commission, despite the general support of Reid and his co-hosts.[26] It also underscored the intransigent nature of sex-role stereotypes, which contributed to what the Commission referred to as the "cultural mould" within which most women lived.[27]

The Commission actually discussed the problem of sex-role stereotyping in the media, but offered no specific recommendations, an omission only Rosemary Speirs mentioned and, even then, only in passing.[28] As we have seen from the hearings, the commissioners and the media seemed uncomfortable with any suggestion of censorship, but this reservation was not referred to in the *Report*. The problem of stereotypes did come up in relation to the education of girls and how they were perceived later as adult workers, however. There were several stories written by individual journalists which underlined the Commission's proposals aimed at ending sex-role stereotyping in school textbooks and in other aspects of the school system because they favoured domestic and childbearing roles and discouraged girls from seeking challenging careers. Even so, CP buried the angle on stereotyping in education and led the same story with the more exciting and "unusual" recommendation that girls should be allowed into military colleges, which, again, was reflected in most of the headlines.[29]

The ways in which sex-role stereotyping affected women on the job, including the ghettoizing of women's work and the relatively low pay they consequently received, was, given the number of briefs about it, not explored fully in the media coverage of the *Report* either. Sexist attitudes towards the "stewardess" was one of the Commission's most telling examples concerning stereotyping on the job and its effects, but it was treated in a somewhat cavalier manner in the press during the hearings and afterwards. At the time, Air Canada's female flight attendants were hired young on 10-year contracts, which the Commission regarded as discriminatory because this emphasis on their female workers being young and beautiful adversely affected the terms and conditions of their employment. Southam and CP ran with focus stories saying the Commission wanted the airlines to drop their "bunny club" philosophy, a term that the Commission did not actually use but included in a passage cited from the original brief presented by the Canadian Airlines Flight Attendants' Association, one that received little publicity at the time. *The London Free Press* transmitted a decidedly mixed message in its headline: "Ugly Air Hostesses?—Insistence on youth, beauty called unfair."[30]

Absent Issues

Among the most glaring absences in the media coverage of the *Report* was of issues affecting aboriginal women. The commissioners integrated their concerns into several chapters in the *Report* and the media followed its agenda, rather than do separate focus stories on native women's issues, again reflecting journalists' tendency to follow the lead of their most authoritative sources.[31] There were only a couple of exceptions. *The Globe and Mail* discussed aboriginal women in terms of the Commission's comments on education, declaring, "Nowhere is the report more sympathetic than when dealing with the 'problems of Indian and Eskimo women.'" It listed the several recommendations which asked various levels of government and the universities to provide education and training to help "bridge the gaps between their children who go away to schools and the parents who remain behind." It also mentioned that the Commission wanted the Indian Act changed so that aboriginal women who married non-Status men would not lose their own Indian status. The Winnipeg *Tribune* added specific recommendations concerning education and management training for aboriginals to the CP story on educational opportunities for women in general. This story included Henripin's objections that the proposals pertaining to education for native women were paternalistic, hastily considered, focused on the North and were outside the Commission's jurisdiction.[32] The absence of coverage was a stark contrast to the attention the aboriginal women received when they presented briefs, or were visited by Bird and Lange in the North. In the coverage of the *Report*, their "differences" were subsumed within the "equality" framework. The reporters apparently did not see native women's issues as a priority, and devoted most of their energies to the conflicts among the commissioners, and various observers.

The Responses of Feminist and Other Leaders

After the initial flurry of media coverage of the *Report* itself, there were extensive follow-up stories focusing on the reactions of feminist leaders and other commentators, including female politicians. These and other accounts were riddled with clichés that showed up in the leads and the headlines about the *Report*, and resurrected the news discourse used when the Commission was first established. Those women who essentially supported it did not want it "pigeonholed" or "left to gather dust." Depending on whether they were optimists or pessimists, various commentators regarded the *Report* as a "step forward," "revolutionary," "explosive," or, alternatively, "too little, too late," mainly because the more recent demands of the women's liberation movement had "far outstripped" the feminists who had fought to get the Commission established. Most commentators agreed with Grace MacInnis of the NDP, however, that it was "going to be up to women" to get anything done about it; in other words, it was their responsibility. Other women had "mixed reactions," meaning they agreed with some recommendations but not others. Although some journalists tried to differentiate between the various women's leaders and their philosophies, a certain amount of conflation also occurred.

In the meantime, MacInnis, still the only woman in the House of Commons, urged Canadian women to start a letter-writing campaign to get the proposals implemented even if they did not agree with all of them, a request which the established women's groups immediately supported. But she and other female politicians gave mixed reviews to some aspects of the *Report*, which the media immediately picked up on. For example, at the time, the NDP wanted to get rid of the Senate, but, even so, MacInnis told the *Toronto Daily Star*, she did not support the recommendation that two women from each province should automatically be appointed to the Senate as seats became vacant until more gender equity was achieved. "'When you fence off a hen pen you get condescension—and that's not equality,'" a sentiment reflected in the headline. Similarly, using a CP story, *The Vancouver Sun* declared that "Grace Asks You to Goad Pierre." The Winnipeg *Tribune* flagged her admonition, "Status Now up to Women" in its headline, which might have been read as letting the male politicians off the hook.[33]

CP did two major stories on the reactions of feminists with a national profile, the second one more negative than the first. The first CP story began with the news that Canadian women were being urged to work hard to prevent the *Report* "from being pigeonholed." The story noted that it received "generally-favorable reaction from leading spokeswomen who described it as only a first step toward full equality." It also noted that Laura Sabia "adopted a pessimistic tone." She was quoted: "as far as I'm concerned, the women's lib has way outstripped us. Three years have gone by and I think the whole report is outdated, is too late." Nevertheless, she was still eager to get the recommendations implemented. The story appeared under various headlines, including, "Step Forward for Women Reaction to Commission *Report*," "'No Pigeon-Hole' for This Report—Women Vow," and "Women Urged to Press Cause."[34]

The second version of what was essentially the same story, however, resulted in a more negative impression, which was underlined in the new lead and the headlines that ensued. In the new version, the editor led with Sabia's pessimistic comment but added another from Bonnie Kreps, which may have been picked up from a story in *The Globe and Mail*. CP's new lead was, "The woman who began the moves that led to a royal commission on the status of women said Monday the women's liberation movement, 'has way outstripped us.'" The report added that Kreps agreed with Sabia and quoted her, too: "I didn't expect much from it and the money (an estimated $1.9 million) could have been spent much better." The story ran on page one of *The Calgary Herald*, along with a photo of Sabia which bore the caption "...too late." *The Daily Gleaner* in Fredericton ran both versions as "Waste of Time," and "Outstripped, Late and Also Outdated," also on page one. According to the *Toronto Daily Star* story, Kreps, who was no longer with the New Feminists, believed that the Commission had not "attacked the institutions which stand in the way of the progress of women" and only served to maintain the political status quo. She called the recommendation for a child allowance of $500 dollars "a whopper, a horror. It's a disaster encouraging more babies at a time when there are too many people in the world," and said the government should be putting more money into fixing the real causes of female problems, including the cultural and psychological biases against them which they learned in school. Kreps added that "'there was a fundamental flaw' in setting up the commission when it added two men" as there was "disagreement from the beginning.... 'Men can check into what's wrong with them. Leave the women to the women.'" She also said that the "only new thing in report" was the Commission's request for an ongoing status of women council to monitor women's progress, which did not received much attention in the media at the time. She believed that other groups had done better in lobbying for legal changes concerning reproductive choice.[35]

The *Star* ran Sabia's comments in another story, with the headline, "Other Women's Groups Praise It: Militants Scoff at 'Crumbs' in 'Half-hearted' Report." The lead more or less said the same thing as the headline, but the reporter confused the older and newer feminist groups with the assertion: "Few of the 167 recommendations...won praise from the 'Women's Lib' movement whose agitation for emancipation from a male-dominated society helped spark the $1,800,000 study." Here, Sabia, who was once cast as Canada's most militant feminist, was described as a representative of the "less radical of the women's rights groups." Ten days later, Elsie MacGill met with representatives of some of those same groups, apparently on friendly terms. The headline over that story said, "Women's Status Report 'Better than Expected.'"[36]

Other stories, from Toronto, Montreal, Vancouver, the Prairies and the Maritimes all recorded the same kinds of reactions from local women's leaders, anonymous women, and several men. Some of them did not agree with the recommendations that Humphrey and other commissioners also did not like, but had their own reasons. Grace Hartman of the Canadian Union of Public Employees, for example, saw paid maternity leave as the "weakest" recommendation because the Commission wanted it calculated according to the woman's contributions to date rather than give her full unemployment insurance. CUPE did agree, however, to work toward implementation of the *Report*, as did the Canadian Labour Congress.[37]

No aboriginal women were identified or quoted in the reaction stories. The only native representative was Stan Daniels, president of the Métis Association of Alberta, who told CP he welcomed the idea that native women be trained to operate co-operatives and small businesses and be given greater opportunities in the teaching profession. But his comments were edited out of several versions of the same story, which perhaps illustrates how quickly news editors dismissed aboriginal concerns. The activist Kahn Tineta-Horn, however, called in to the CBC's national open line radio show, *Cross Country Checkup*, to angrily denounce the recommendation that women who married non-Status men be able to retain their Indian status.[38]

Public and Editorial Reactions

Most of the local newspaper stories, perhaps striving for "balance," stressed a mixed public reaction of "cheers" and "jeers," or their equivalent, such as those in *The Vancouver Sun*, which appeared on a two-page spread under the banner headlines, "Jeers, Cheers, Doubts Greet Status" and "Some Hopes Soar, Some are Dashed." The smaller headlines over separate stories told much the same tale: "Men are Laughing Themselves Sick"; "I Take the Lumps with the Men"; "'Women Are Their Own Enemies,' Says Bank Manager—a Woman"; "A Strong Preamble Would Speed Equality, Says a Clubwoman"; "Should Husbands Pay Alimony? Why Not, Says an Alderman"; "Women Directors? OK at Hydro."[39]

The Calgary Herald, however, seemed to go out of its way to find people who made very negative comments about the *Report*, underscoring these quotations with its own antagonistic hyperbole. Its headline announced that "In Calgary, The *Report* Is Just 'Ho-Hum.'" The unidentified reporter began: "Calgary has greeted the Bird report with a collective yawn and comments of '...the Royal Commission on what?'" The story goes on: "With a resounding thud of nothingness" the report has "stirred the city's women into a buzzing mass of lethargy." Negative comments followed from unidentified women: "The damn thing's been out of date since the day after it was set up" and "Everything's being done. They're asking for things already in the works." The story implied that housewives did not like the recommendations that would have affected them. "Listen, I'm changing a diaper. One mess at a time is enough, thanks." All these extremely negative comments were based on a *Herald* "survey" of opinion, apparently conducted by phone and on foot. The reporter noted that even women's rights activists did not want to "turn cartwheels" over the *Report*. In contrast, *The Edmonton Journal* was much more "balanced" in its approach. The headlines included, "Edmontonians Surveyed Support Many of Commission's Proposals," and "Abortion Still Contentious."[40] Reporters sought out the opinions of men as well, including predictable comments from the founder of the newly formed "Men's Movement of Canada," which devoted itself to defending the rights of husbands and fathers after marriage breakdown.[41] The public opinion expressed on the CBC's *Cross Country Checkup* generally reflected the same kinds of opinions that were evident in the more equitable newspaper surveys.[42]

The news discourse in the stories about the Commission's *Report* relayed the conflicts among the commissioners, feminist leaders and the public over its recommendations regarding Canadian women's concerns, which is to be expected. The emphasis on conflict, however, also served to camouflage or downplay other important issues and recommendations, such as the suggestion that many women should receive equal pay for work of equal value. The news coverage not only served to expose the gender divide that existed on certain issues among the commissioners, but reflected the same female/male split among many of the journalists, whose lack of "objectivity" leaked through in their accounts, to greater or lesser degrees.

In the overtly opinionated editorials and columns, almost all of the writers acknowledged that the Commission had been thorough and did uncover instances of discrimination. At the same time, several tended to dismiss its recommendations as "old news," which, in journalism practice, is not worth repeating, and also signals the media's ongoing, impatient and often precipitous quest for novelty, uniqueness, "unusualness" or, at the very least, a new angle, on fundamental issues.[43] For example, the *Albertan* called the *Report* "thorough, conscientious and unflinching" but added that it "somehow misses being big news...it seems that so many things have changed" since the Commission was appointed, and that almost all of the recommendations had the "grey look of things accepted in principle if not in fact, or in the process of being debated to death." The exception, that women should be able to join the RCMP, "just proves the point."[44]

The *Report* may have been "old news," but just about any change that stemmed from the Commission's recommendations would actually have been "new" news since, outside of the new abortion and divorce laws, and limited progress on equal pay and related issues, very little had actually changed for most Canadian women since the hearings were held two years earlier. Not only would it take years for some of the recommendations to be implemented, there are several, such as a national daycare system, that are still outstanding to this day.

The lengths to which the editorial writers were willing to go to support the recommendations varied, and so did the attitudes that underlined their various writing styles. One of the most dismissive was the editorial from the Winnipeg *Tribune* which opened this chapter. Other commentaries were more subtle, but also damaging to the Commission's credibility. The *London Free Press* backed Humphrey's position that the *Report* was discriminatory because it would allow "quota" systems for women in some areas, and force homemakers out into the workforce, among other problems. The *Free Press,* using overtly negative and misplaced terms for female outspokenness, decided that "The *stridency* of much of the Status of Women report greatly diminishes its value as a basis from which to work. Some of it seems *outrageous* and guaranteed to win a deaf ear from many males."[45]

Several other newspapers and columnists admired the *Report* in the main, but still had reservations about "special status" as applied to women in political life, especially. *The Edmonton Journal* referred to the "quota" for appointees to the Senate, which did "indeed go beyond equality to a kind of special status" and probably would not work. The newspaper argued that the real political power was in the Cabinet and House of Commons, a point also made by a *Gazette* columnist, Arthur Blakely, who questioned whether women really wanted it. The *Journal* believed that women had not used their vote, with the result that the power to do anything concerning these recommendations was in the hands of men. It warned men, however, that "the more extreme members of the women's liberation movement" were not the only ones who were unhappy with the obvious injustices and inequities in the system, and women as a group did have the power to "shake up all the cozy centres of male government."[46] Other editors and columnists questioned the wisdom of specific recommendations, such as daycare, pensions for housewives and abortion.[47]

Although the commissioners, with the possible exception of MacGill, were hardly "women's libbers," the spectres of suffragists and other feminists pervaded the editorials and columns to a startling degree. An editorial writer for *The Telegram* in Toronto wrote, "As with the militant feminists of 50 years ago, Susan B. Anthony and Carrie Chapman Catt," Bird and the other commissioners "tend to speak at the top of their voices in order to be heard." Conversely, *The Ottawa Journal* noted that Florence Bird "is too wise to have allowed the report to adopt the extremes or even the rhetoric of a Betty Friedan." Both newspapers underlined the idea that the traditional family was an essential bulwark of Canadian society but took different views as to whether some of the Commission's recommendations were a threat to it or not.[48] One of the most negative editorials, in the Fredericton *Daily Gleaner*, called the *Report* "unrealistic" and "far-fetched" because it "ignores the fact that most Canadian women are content to be mothers and housewives and happy to have their husbands be the bread-winners." The *Daily Gleaner* backed both Humphrey and Ogilvie wholeheartedly and concluded with, "We are all for women but not the greedy, grasping, aggressive Amazons which this report depicts the women of Canada as being." It did not believe that most Canadian women would support it.[49]

Not surprisingly, Doris Anderson of *Chatelaine* praised the *Report* as "a bristling DBS [Dominion Bureau of Statistics] of facts about women, a handbook for the feminists and an historical indictment on the lack of progress by women in Canada." She added that if Canadian women wanted Parliament to follow through on the recommendations, they must write to their MPs; otherwise, the report "will molder away on a shelf. It's up to you."[50] Among the newspaper women, Marney Roe of *The London Free Press* was among the very few who supported proposals that would give women in politics a boost because, she said, it would give other women the confidence to follow in their footsteps, something the isolation of the female pioneers to date had not. Even though she had reservations about the "militant" tactics of some women's liberation groups, she also felt that women of all feminist persuasions should work together and be "relentless" in demanding the changes they needed. "Just because it is now down in black and white doesn't mean things will change."[51]

In an analysis story, which featured a picture of Bird juxtaposed with one of a women's liberation protest, Leone Kirkwood of *The Globe and Mail* posed the question: "Loud echoes of women's lib in the status report?" Kirkwood drew strained parallels between the Commission and "women's lib," specifically the New Feminists, because of their similar critiques of sex-role stereotyping in textbooks. She did not mention that this was also a major complaint of the more established women's groups, including teachers' associations, who had appeared before the Commission.[52] Other women journalists believed that feminism had grown and become a lot more radical since the Commission hearings had ended, and the recommendations were, in the words of Margaret Weiers of the *Toronto Daily Star*, "too little, too late." Weiers was disappointed with the *Report* on several grounds; essentially, that it was too vague, and not progressive or imaginative enough. She opposed the idea of "special treatment" for women in politics because she believed that most women would resent it as "tokenism"; moreover, she felt that it might be more useful to have all candidates' campaign expenses paid out of public funds. Weiers was the only journalist who commented, even briefly, on the proposals concerning aboriginal women, suggesting that one of them, to set up native-run friendship centres, was inadequate to help them cope with poverty. She also said the Commission could have taken a much stronger stand on helping battered women, another problem it virtually ignored. In a brief article that was closer to an editorial than a news story, the *Star* suggested that the selling price of the *Report*, $4.50 a copy, was too expensive for many of the women the Commission had been trying to reach.[53]

Other journalists, on the other hand, saw the *Report* as revolutionary, in one way or the other. Elizabeth Dingman, the women's editor of *The Telegram*, wrote that it was a "good, hard-hitting report. Far from lagging behind the Women's Liberation Movement, it surpasses the movement in its revolutionary tone and its recommendations." Dingman felt that, unlike the WLM, the Commission made recommendations that recognized the "validity of the family unit." She was also ready to try the affirmative action suggestions. "As abrasive and artificial as this action may seem, there is no reason it should not be tried as a catalyst to break up discriminatory practice."[54]

Anthony Westell wrote in his column in the *Toronto Daily Star* that the *Report* was a "time-bomb...primed and ticking" and should be taken seriously by politicians. Westell says today that the bomb as metaphor likely reflected the political climate of the time. In Canada, the struggle for Quebec's independence had reached the stage where separatists associated with the FLQ had been blowing up mail boxes. In October 1970, when terrorists murdered Quebec cabinet minister Pierre Laporte, and kidnapped British diplomat James Cross, Prime Minister Trudeau declared a State of Emergency, suspended normal civil liberties and sent armed soldiers into Quebec.[55]

Identifiably left-wing columnists among the men disagreed specifically with Humphrey's intervention. Douglas Fisher, writing in the Toronto *Telegram*, saw it as "more surprising than damaging....I think they are right and he is wrong in terms of political and social reality." James Eayrs, a political science professor with a regular column in the *Toronto Daily Star*, was more contemptuous. "A pity that out of 11 million Canadian males a commissioner could not have been found a little less eager to keep the mothers of confederation up against the wall."[56]

"COFFEE, TEA OR HOMEMADE MUFFINS?"

Figure 9.1. Ting, *The London Free Press*, 9 Dec. 1970. Courtesy of Merle Tingley.

A few male columnists were blatantly antagonistic towards the Commission, but none to the same degree as Ray Guy of the St. John's *Evening Telegram*. Erroneously blaming "women's libbers" for the inquiry in the first place, the usually humorous Guy slid into crude invective, calling them names like "rag bags" and describing them as having "faces like brass monkeys and dispositions like cornered wolverines." He noted that one of the male commissioners, meaning Humphrey, "came out wiser than he was when he went in" and had produced his own report "contradicting the five harpies and the other miserable wretch." He also referred to "Anne Francis of Ottawa" as "the chief biddy on the panty hose commission."[57]

Norm Ibsen, an editorial writer for the *London Free Press*, took the opposite approach. His humorous column consisted of the comments of a group of fictional men, made as they drank through the supper hour at a bar, about feminists and women in general. "Give women too much status and the next thing they'll want is respect." Another male columnist who expressed support for both the *Report* and equal relations between the sexes was Christopher Dafoe of *The*

Vancouver Sun, who believed, "If we don't make it together, we won't make it."[58]

"With a motto like 'We always get our man' recruiting is no problem!"

Figure 9.2. Uluschak, *The Edmonton Journal,* 9 Dec. 1970. Courtesy of Edd Uluschak.

Cartoonists, as could be expected, adopted a lighthearted approach to the recommendations that they found easiest to spoof; in fact, most of the cartoons about the Commission were in response to its recommendations. Ting of the *London Free Press* portrayed a travelling businessman reading a newspaper account of the *Report,* being offered "coffee, tea or muffins" by a rotund, elderly woman wearing a stewardess cap, an apron and bedroom slippers (see fig. 9.1).[59] Several other cartoonists played on the idea that romantically inclined women would be attracted to the RCMP because of its well-known motto. Uluschak of *The Edmonton Journal* drew three nubile and busty female recruits lined up before an older officer who had been sitting at a desk perusing a newspaper account of the Commission's *Report* and was looking up at them appreciatively. Another older, male mountie is saying to him, "With a motto like, 'We always get our man' recruiting is no problem." In the background, a third officer with a horse in tow is questioning a memo, "The musical ride...sidesaddle?"[60] (see fig. 9.2).

Figure 9.3. Collins, *The Gazette*, Montreal, 9 Dec.1970. National Archives of Canada C-107232.

John Collins of the Montreal *Gazette* suggested, perhaps hopefully, that lawmakers would drag their heels over putting what appeared to be air-headed women in men's roles[61] (see fig. 9.3) while the fearful effect the *Report* might have on gender relations was an undercurrent in several other cartoons. The most subtle was one by Chambers of the Halifax *Chronicle-Herald* who drew his balding, middle-aged man sitting at one end of a couch, sweating and looking apprehensively at his wife who is sitting at the other end reading the *Report* with an angry look on her face[62] (see fig. 9.4).

Figure 9.4. Chambers, *Chronicle-Herald*, Halifax, 9 Dec. 1970. Courtesy of Mrs. Anita Chambers. Public Archives of Nova Scotia.

The Lack of In-Depth Analysis and Other Shortcomings

Taken together, the media response to the *Report* of the Royal Commission was initially extensive, but could not be considered especially positive, regardless of the articles that expressly put forward the point of view of Florence Bird and the majority. The value of conflict, so embedded in the journalistic tradition, was a primary factor here. While the media is rightly expected to cover contentious viewpoints, it could be argued that they paid too much attention to Humphrey's "expert" intervention at the expense of other issues which he and the other commissioners actually supported. This factor, and deadline pressures, also meant that there was little time or space to consider recommendations that the Commission could have made.

With some exceptions, the *Report* was covered by Parliamentary Press Gallery reporters who had not been at the hearings, most of them men. The apparent gender tensions aside, all the reporters approached it much as they would the results of any other federal inquiry, with a concise 80-page summary to hand and immediacy in mind. The summary, which was prepared by the Commission, had an "embargo" placed on it until after it was tabled in the House. After that, they were free to release the story.

Tom Earle of CBC *Radio News* does not specifically remember filing his seven-and-a-half minute story on the *Report*, which was also the first headline on *The World at Six*, but speculated that he would have attended Bird's news conference and then recorded a quick interview with her afterwards. Armed with that clip, he wrote a summary of the recommendations and recorded the item in time for the newscast. He does remember that, given the pace of life in the Press Gallery, it was a story like any other, and was over as soon as he met his deadline. There would have been little time for follow-ups, perhaps not even one on Humphrey's minority report.[63] A few days before the Commission *Report* was tabled, James Cross had been released by his FLQ kidnappers; two days later, Senator Keith Davey brought down his report on the mass media. There was enough going on in the news that week to eclipse the Royal Commission on the Status of Women.[64]

At any rate, once the Commission's *Report* was tabled, there was little for the Press Gallery correspondents to report from the House. The Prime Minister and his ministers, questioned by MacInnis and her fellow NDP members on 7 and 8 December refused to commit the government to follow through on any of the recommendations, saying that the Cabinet needed time to study them. Prime Minister Trudeau also quipped that perhaps responsibility for women's labour concerns should go to the Minister of Health and Welfare. *Chatelaine* magazine, among others, took his laughing pun as a sign of disdain.[65] The Opposition did not bring the matter up again until after the December break. When Parliament reconvened on 11 January 1971, the acting Prime Minister, Mitchell Sharp, would only tell them that the Cabinet was considering the *Report,* and it was not clear if a specific minister would be designated to handle the task of implementation. He also added a wisecrack: "I may say I do not know whether anyone in the cabinet wants to be responsible for women." To which Tommy Douglas of the NDP responded, "I am sure women do not want to be responsible for the cabinet."[66] These comments and exchanges raise questions as to how seriously the Liberal government, which had no woman MPs at the time,[67] took the Commission's *Report* in the first place. The cartoonist Yardley Jones mischievously illustrated this point by depicting Prime Minister Pierre Trudeau leering lustily as he pulled a centrefold from his copy of the Royal Commission *Report*[68] (see fig. 9.5).

It would be unfair to suggest that all the male members of the Parliamentary Press Gallery shared the government's dismissive attitude, or that they were unprofessional in their treatment of the *Report's* recommendations. At the same time, they did not have the informed hindsight of journalists such as Rosemary Speirs and Ed Reid, who had covered almost all the hearings, or of Margaret Weirs, Yvonne Crittenden and Eleanor Dunn, who had covered women's issues extensively over the intervening years. There were also divisions among the journalists over the issue that seemed to provoke the most negative response, "special" treatment as a catch-up mechanism for women. The men were clearly sceptical, while women were divided over the relative merits of "tokenism."

Figure 9.5. Jones, *The Telegram*, Toronto, 24 Feb. 1971. Courtesy of Yardley Jones. National Archives of Canada C-107231.

When feminist leaders also expressed doubts about these, or other proposals, they set the stage for another round of news stories that were contradictory in tone at best and negative at worst. Most of them were commenting on what they heard in the media or were told by reporters, who did not always convey the exact intent behind the Commission's recommendations or the official reactions to them. Kathryn Keate, then of the Women's Liberation Movement, told Maggie Siggins of *The Telegram* that the recommendations were "excellent," but she was "extremely angry" at reports that Prime Minister Trudeau and his cabinet "did not like the recommendations," which was not exactly what he said. She responded on that basis, however:

"Well, consider that Mr. Trudeau is a millionaire Roman Catholic bachelor, and like his Cabinet ministers he is completely out of touch with the lives of the women these recommendations affect."[69]

One of the striking things about the coverage of the *Report* is most media commentators' failure to distinguish among feminists, their various philosophies and what the *Report* actually said. This conflation of Sabia's CEWC, "women's libbers" and the commissioners resulted in both technical errors, exemplified by the stories implying that the Commission actually used the term "abortion on demand," and in some very superficial commentary about the *Report*. This was true whether the commentator concerned supported it, wanted to demonize it by framing it as militant in some way, or make it sound safely mainstream, or even passé. In any event, none of the coverage could be said to be "objective," and in some cases, the gender conflicts in the journalism profession itself filtered through what was written and broadcast about the recommendations. The public could have used more in-depth analysis of the *Report*, but that would take time and was not forthcoming, perhaps, again, because other news events intervened, and there was no immediate follow-up from Parliament once the journalists had covered the recommendations.

The essential conclusion in the Commission's *Report*, that Canadian women were not being given "equal opportunities" in Canadian society, was not a particularly radical statement in the context of the times, but was still presented in the media as highly contentious, especially suggestions that women deserved special consideration, even in the short term. There were many indications that this was a difficult area for most of the journalists and editors involved: the gendered nature of the "news discourse," the failure of "objectivity," the overriding use of the "conflict" frame, the positions taken by various writers in their editorials and columns, cartoonists' send-ups of women's concerns, and the rushed newsroom rituals and routines, all combined to create complex and contradictory coverage and limited analysis. In the meantime, women's leaders in Canada prepared for the next round in the equality battle, getting the Commission's proposals implemented. That is a campaign, and a news story, that has continued for the last three decades, and has also challenged the media in very much the same way.

Conclusion

$\mathcal{T}$his book combines feminist cultural media analysis and the social history of Canadian women during an important period in their political progress. The context—cultural, historical and national—of events and issues that affect the lives of women is crucial to the analysis of media and gender. As Hardt and Brennan and others have pointed out, cultural analysis is a useful tool in helping us determine the context in which journalists analyze issues of social importance in given time periods.[1] Ericson, Baranek and Chan's work on the social organization of newswork in a more modern period is Canadian in context and points to important considerations that historians can take into account when examining the interplay between officials, or other "authorized knowers," and journalists.[2] While this body of knowledge also accounts for the play of language in the way in which reporters cover the news, van Dijk's study of discourse and the news media is useful for understanding how newsroom rituals and language can resonate with each other.[3] Finally, as Jansen, van Zoonen, Henry and Weston, among others, insist, gender and race are fundamental categories of media analysis that, where appropriate, allow us to concentrate on white and native women's cultural understanding of their experiences and issues in a specific period, as relayed by news reporters.[4]

Notes to Conclusion are on pp. 310–11.

A Canadian Context for Feminist Cultural Analysis

This study provides a Canadian context that differs from the American experience and will be, I hope, a useful contribution to the growing body of literature in Canadian and international media studies. There is very little historical analysis to date on the news coverage of Canadian women's concerns specifically, and, aside from a few articles, there's nothing substantial on the news media and the "second wave" of the women's movement in this country. No other book-length Canadian study that I am aware of interviews the journalists concerned, or examines their attitudes towards professional "objectivity" in relation to the specific media environments in which they worked. While gender analysis studies of the modern media are an important area of research, so is the historical record, and that has barely been investigated. In Canada, for example, women have been involved in the news media since its earliest days, working for newspapers, magazines, and early radio and television, but little of that reporting has been analyzed in its historical and cultural context. We need to know how and why social attitudes about gender, ethnicity and other factors influenced media coverage, and how journalists of both sexes negotiated the tensions between professional expectations and their personal perspectives on the issues during different eras, specifically and comparatively. Only then can we more fully understand how the impact of the women's movement in all its manifestations has played out in Canadian history.

It is my hope that *The Satellite Sex*, with its focus on coverage of women's concerns 30 years ago, will suggest lessons that scholars and journalists can apply to historical research and to gender issues today. This book demonstrates that the media coverage of women's issues in late 1960s Canada was more complex and "fractured" than straight-forward.[5] It was open to social change to some degree, but was also limiting in its vision of what women could achieve. The reasons are highly complex and have to do with the cultural history of Canadian women, including female journalists, the mandate of the Commission that heard their concerns, the supportive coverage of most women's pages, the CBC women's programs and *Chatelaine*, and the discourse of newsgathering at the time, especially the professional limits of objectivity, fairness and balance.

The historical context of the general culture in which the media operate, and the accepted norms of that culture, must be considered as the primary environment in which journalists carry out their assignments. In other words, it is no longer enough for scholars to take American examples as given and assume they snugly fit the Canadian case. Our media were operating within a Canadian society which at the time was predominantly and moderately liberal in its political sympathies, although, certainly, pockets of economic and social conservatism were quite evident. More progressive ideas about women's roles in society began to gain credence as the economy expanded and their increased participation in the workforce was needed. It was different from the American experience in that women were not "symbolically annihilated" in our media coverage, feminists were not divided quite so neatly into "liberal and radical," and women's issues generally received more equitable recognition earlier in Canada than in the United States.[6] Still, despite more recent studies that argue that female audiences exercise "agency," that is, self-empowering interpretations of the news about women,[7] or that feminism has had a positive impact on the American news media,[8] it also appears that after about 1980, the media tended to favour conservative women's groups such as Canada's REAL women over feminists of any stripe.[9]

In media coverage of women's issues during the time of the Royal Commission, there were both a recognition that Canadian women had real grievances, and attempts to downplay those that might truly challenge the gender status quo in society. In fact, this federal inquiry allowed women their own public sphere in which to present and debate the issues. Several key factors encouraged the media to pay attention to women at the time. Historically, it was an era of rapid political and social change. In Canada, economic times were good, and a minority government that needed women's votes during the next election was in power. Another factor in the media coverage was the Royal Commission on the Status of Women's "democratic," "human rights" and "equal opportunities" agenda, which was firmly planted within a liberal democratic political framework. The United Nations' discourse of "human rights" pervaded politics, the philosophical approach of the women's group demanding a commission, and the language of the journalists who supported the inquiry. It was a handy news hook for the media, but also a measure of the spirit of the times. Certain segments of society were in revolt against the conservatism of the 1950s but, regardless of the demands of more radical social critics and protestors, most people were not willing to embrace a vision of personal freedom that stepped outside the boundaries of liberal democracy and the capitalist system.

The types of media available to audiences have a bearing on the coverage they receive. Although American magazines and TV competed for Canadian readers and viewers to an alarming degree, and were not particularly friendly towards the women's movement,[10] two outlets differentiated Canada's media scene from that of the US. One was a generally progressive and publicly financed broadcasting network, the CBC, which, despite competition from private broadcasters, was still dominant in many areas of the country. The other was *Chatelaine*, then Canada's only general interest women's magazine, which cannily combined traditional service articles and fiction with a pro-Canadian and pro-feminist editorial mandate. Although Joanne Meyerowitz argues effectively that Betty Friedan's initial analysis and condemnation of American women's magazines was too narrowly focused on a white, middle-class perspective, none of the US publications then circulating in Canada took *Chatelaine's* consistently progressive editorial line.[11]

The immediate, gendered journalism environment within which a reporter works, rather than just his or her sex, determines how a story is produced in print or on the air. Judging from their bylines, almost all of the reporters who regularly covered women's issues and the Commission were women. Some of them worked in the predominantly "male" news environments of the main print and broadcast newsrooms, but others were still confined to the women's pages of the newspapers, or worked in the editorial department of *Chatelaine*. One man, Ed Reid, regularly covered the Commission for the CBC's "women's" programs, whose predominantly female staff generally supported the inquiry. Sometimes Reid would find another man, usually a local print or CBC reporter, at the press table during the hearings, but otherwise most of the male journalists who wrote about the Commission itself did so sporadically, usually from the Parliamentary Press Gallery in Ottawa. Some of the reporters who attended the hearings also wrote analytical or opinion articles, while several men and some women who did not actually cover the Commission presented their own views on the proceedings in the form of columns, editorials, and cartoons.

Journalists of both sexes responded in various ways to the professional standards expected of them in their respective milieus. Their attitudes towards professional ideals, including "objectivity," no matter how highly regarded rhetorically, actually varied in practice. As Hackett and Zhao point out, it can be argued that journalists absorb the opinions of their owners and publishers and the expectations of advertisers, but there is not always a conscious, direct connection, and journalism culture values both freedom of individual thought and editorial independence as essential to the media's role in a democracy.[12] Recent events, such as the removal of the "objectivity" clause from the code of the ethics of the Society of Professional Journalists in the United States, and the insertion of value-laden words such as "truth," "accuracy" and "comprehensiveness"[13] testify that the debate over journalistic expectations is ongoing. It also suggests that media critics have succeeded to some degree in persuading practitioners of the inadequacy of standard notions of "objectivity" as an effective model for newsgathering.[14]

While reporters and broadcasters interviewed for this study agreed on a broad definition of professional "objectivity," the strictness of their interpretations varied not only according to where they worked, but according to their own political proclivities. Several of them admitted, either directly or indirectly, to a great deal of subjectivity in their own approach to women's issues and to feminism in its various manifestations, and impute the same to their colleagues. There were demonstrable differences among individuals, which also varied according to the specific circumstances in which the reporter found her- or himself when working on a particular story about the Commission. But all held to certain understandings about the import of the issues they were covering, which can be discerned in the very language of the stories they wrote or broadcast.

Finally, the structure and language of any story is determined, not just by the cultural attitudes and news practices of the news worker, but according to the genre or media format within which it is produced, whether in the form of a magazine article, newspaper story, editorial, in-studio discussion or film, video or audio clips on a news or current affairs program, or photographs, drawings and cartoons. There were accepted but sometimes contentious differences in professional attitudes and standards among journalists and their associates who worked on newspapers, on magazines, in broadcasting, or, even more specifically, between those who worked in CBC news and their colleagues in current affairs. There were also perceptible differences between the general newsroom and the women's department, *Maclean's* and *Chatelaine*, and prime time CBC current affairs and afternoon women's programming. What united the journalists was a general understanding of the importance of the "story" in conveying messages about women's issues, or any other matter, to their audiences. In other words, there is a common formula of storytelling that crosses the boundaries of both genre and gender. Moreover, as Hall, Langer and Barthes have pointed out, the visual is a strong component in the discourse of news, and relays, among other variables, labels and stereotypes in very direct ways, as can be seen in the various media images of women who brought their issues to the Commission.[15]

The news stories the journalists produced signalled their recognition of a pressing need for changes to discriminatory laws and practices against Canadian women that resulted in narrow cultural definitions of the nature of womanhood; limited educational opportunities; unequal status in the workforce, politics and within marriage; the absence of government-sponsored childcare; unnecessary limits on reproductive freedom; and the difficult conditions under which the marginalized, such as native women, lived. At the same time, there was some editorial resistance to the necessity of a public forum on women's grievances, which was also reflected in informal "man-in-the-street" surveys and letters to the editor. This resistance stemmed from a combination of cynicism about the government's agenda and concern about costs, and referred back to other commissions, especially the Royal Commission on Bilingualism and Biculturalism which, in 1967, had still not produced its own report. But the editorial disapproval of a federal inquiry into the status of women was also based on conservatism about women's issues within a profession which was itself sex-segregated.

While the Canadian media establishment prided itself on being a cornerstone of a free and democratic society, it had an obvious blindspot: the lack of equality for women within its own ranks. The "human rights" agenda struck a chord mainly with the liberal-minded journalists and broadcasters with the major urban dailies, the pro-feminist *Chatelaine* and the CBC. The testimony they heard at the hearings resonated with women journalists' own efforts to break through the gender barriers placed in their way. They were the ones most familiar with the issues that came up at the Commission hearings, partly because some of them had dealt with them personally or professionally themselves or had covered stories about women who had. These were *their* issues as women of Canada, even if they did not involve themselves directly in feminist politics because they considered it a conflict of interest in professional terms. This is not to say that all women journalists supported the cause of equal rights for women. Some of them, particularly columnists on the smaller papers, were more comfortable with traditional views of women's place in the world.

It could also be argued that the one man who covered the Commission on a regular basis, Ed Reid, was not typical of most male media professionals if only because he shared his journalistic duties with women as a matter of course. At the same time, his approach and that of his female co-workers was mediated by the fact that the CBC itself came under the Commission's purview, that the Chair, Florence Bird, was a former colleague, and that his male colleagues, especially his camera crew and perhaps his editors, had a more conservative agenda of their own which he felt obliged to accommodate in his coverage. While he was personally sympathetic to the less privileged people in society, a perspective which came through clearly in his coverage of sole-support mothers and aboriginal women, he was also uncomfortable with radical expressions of feminism.

Most of the other male journalists and broadcasters took a more sceptical view of the Commission, perhaps because they were not as engaged in it as were Reid and the women reporters. Few of these men actually covered the inquiry, and when they did, their stories were usually one-day affairs that focused on a local hearing or related the Commission to other political goings-on on Parliament Hill rather than to the situation of Canadian women as such. But these men still had to confront gender issues as, more and more, they found themselves working beside women in their newsrooms and on Parliament Hill. Some believed that these women should be treated equally, while others resented their presence. Depending on their personal circumstances, the male journalists likely had to confront the same kinds of issues in their private lives as well.

For journalists of either sex, then, the Commission and its agenda was not something they could be purely "objective" about, try as most of them did to present the arguments in the accepted "fair and balanced" way. Although the appointment of the Commission, every hearing and the tabling of the *Report* were all separate "events," the journalists were essentially grappling with "issues" that had far-reaching implications for themselves and their audiences. As far as professional practice was concerned, the essentially subjective conventions of reporting—for example, the frames of "conflict," "unusualness," and "proximity"—were the only models they had to go by. At times, these conventions served to distort the stories they covered, but at other times they helped bring the issues out. This was particularly true when "personalization" was used, through which women were able to tell their own stories, at least to the limited degree prescribed by the journalistic demands of time and space. Because the media demands expertise and leadership from its sources, the reporters would have normally sought out those people who were most often considered authorities on the legal, economic and social life of Canada; in other words, men. The vacuum caused by male absence from the hearings, it could be argued, provided an unprecedented opportunity for the women there to finally become the media's experts of the moment as well as the symbolic representatives of other Canadian women who were dealing with the same problems.

This did not happen without some resistance, however. In some reporters' eyes, many of the women demanding change were "feminists," whether they identified themselves as such or not. As can be seen from the media's construction of "femininity" and "feminism," a certain defensiveness was apparent in the attitudes of both the women who appeared before the Commission and the media workers themselves. There was no real contradiction between the two cultural ideas; many women, such as the well-turned-out and outspoken Laura Sabia, could be said to be both "feminine" and "feminist." But because the media perceived a "conflict" between the two ideas, women like Norma Ellen Verwey were perceived as "feminist" even when they themselves were negatively fatalistic about women's immediate chances of attaining equal status with men. Other women, such as Mrs. Trevor Anderson, served as a cautionary foil for those who would abandon their femininity. What is more, despite the many complaints at the hearings about sex-role stereotypes in the media, some sardonic male broadcasters and journalists, the *Take 30* film crew in Montreal and several of the newspaper cartoonists relied on those same stereotypes to reinforce the idea that women should not venture too far from the accepted norms in their demands for "equality" and were laughable when they did.

One of the most complex issues that journalists—used to writing brief, straightforward copy or producing relatively short audio or film clips—had to deal with was conveying what "equality" meant. The Commission had stipulated "equal opportunities" with men, but the stories from the hearings signalled a broader context, a struggle in which some women at least dared to suggest that they be considered "equal" in education, paid work and politics and public life. In the context of liberal humanism, "equal" was defined as "same as," an easy generalization for journalists to make, given that part of their job is to deal with generalities and not specifics. Nevertheless some reporters did manage to signal that there might be such a thing as "equal pay for work of equal value," which was another way of saying that there were differences between the work men and women did in what was essentially a sex-segregated labour force. The reporters also relayed the suggestions made by several women appearing before the Commission that women should be the beneficiaries of "reverse discrimination," or special treatment, in order to catch up to the men. It was a position that most of the women journalists were clearly not comfortable with themselves. They would rather be treated as a "human" or a "person" who was "equal" with men, than as a "woman" with "special privileges" who clearly was not. Male journalists who commented on this discussion tended to agree with them.

Many briefs the journalists covered considered what happened to this vision of "equality" when a woman married. Although marriage bestowed "status" on a woman, in terms of social approval if nothing else, it became abundantly clear from the coverage of the hearings that for many women it meant a loss of independence, property rights, economic freedom, and for some, their personal safety. Others faced poverty if the marriage dissolved or if the husband died. Only the well-off, the well-loved and the well-protected could be said to enjoy "status" under this arrangement. The discussion of status suited the "conflict" model of journalism, which brought out the tensions between homemakers and career women but did not allow for much discussion of the fact that many women, including several of the journalists who covered the hearings, played both roles. The marriage issue set up a false split between the two categories of women. The reporters seemed most taken by the idea that marriage was not an "equal" proposition in terms of legal and property rights, and some appeared genuinely surprised, as was the Commission, about how a woman could be reduced to poverty because of her marital status. This was the strongest educational message that the media brought to their audiences. "Unusual" and entertaining suggestions, such as Elmer Laird's marriage contract and Mrs. Frank Martin's bachelor tax, were perhaps welcome comic relief to the journalists who sat at the press table, day after day, hearing much the same depressing complaints. The publicity these two suggestions garnered, however, was out of proportion compared to the lesser coverage of wife-battering, which was also considered marginal at the time.

Similarly, the media played up conflicts surrounding the debates about working mothers without paying enough attention to women who had always worked outside the home to support their families because they had to do so. Although there was some mention of the burden of the double workload, there was also little detailed discussion of the many kinds of unpaid labour women did inside the home. The debate, as it was reflected in the media, became one about the right, or lack of it, to work when one's children were young, what role the federal government should play in providing daycare, and which "working mothers" should benefit from these services. The exception involved the plight of sole-support mothers who had a difficult time getting their ex-husbands to provide financial support for their children. Here, the media technique of personalizing their stories was the most effective way to convey the issues of sole support mothers, the implication being they, at least, "deserved" some support.

The discourse of "rights" was most apparent in the discussion about reproductive "choice," one which had already received a fair amount of media coverage due to the proposed new federal legislation. Key to a woman's freedom was "control over her own body," especially in the area of birth control but also in terms of female sterilization rather than vasectomy, where the debate had taken on exaggerated proportions. The media flagged abortion as the most difficult issue, with justification, and tried to tease out the major conflicts when individuals and groups refused to face off before the Commission. The news discourse used in these stories also reflected many women's insistence that abortion be liberalized, or taken out of the Criminal Code altogether. Polite arguments for "abortion on request" were giving way, in some instances, to the more aggressive rhetoric of "abortion on demand." The media coverage of these briefs also brought out another aspect of "choice," namely the right of an unwed mother to keep her child without public censure. An additional theme was the media's assumptions that farm women and Catholic Quebecers had mysteriously caught up to urban, English-speaking Canada, and that all Canadian women basically wanted the same right to control their own bodies, even though there were differences among them, particularly on the abortion question. The almost total silence on

another issue concerning women's sexual freedom, lesbianism, underlined the marginal status of lesbians and bisexual women, and ignored
the many injustices they suffered.[16]

Because the media and the Commission both emphasized the
"sameness" of the demands of Canadian women, real issues of "difference" did not come up in the coverage in any substantial way, even
regionally, until marginalized women, particularly aboriginal women,
became the focus of media attention. Here, there were competing messages as to how "equal" native women wanted to be, and whether or
not they had different perspectives from white women. The stereotype
of the aboriginal woman as tragic and somehow immoral was mitigated by other stories that pointed to her efforts to educate herself and
improve her living standards so that she could become, with her white
sisters, an active participant in all the best that twentieth-century
Canada had to offer. This was particularly true when she herself used
the "human rights" discourse familiar to the Commission and the journalists in order to fight for better living conditions or to regain her
"Indian status." Still, especially in the north, some aboriginal and liberal white voices, including those of reporters, filtered through the
predominantly assimilationist news frame, suggesting that native
women should not have to be just like white women in order to be considered "equal" in Canadian society.

When the Commission's *Report* was finally released, almost four
years after the inquiry had been established, journalists immediately
pounced on the "conflict" among the commissioners and particularly
on the minority report written by John Humphrey, who had refused to
sign the majority document. The real conflict was over "equality" versus "difference" in relation to men and women, especially in the workforce. The concept of affirmative action did not seem to fall into the
Commission's mandate, which was essentially a liberal democratic
one. The media discussion of that contradiction in the *Report* was to be
expected, as was the coverage of the split among the Commissioners
on the abortion issue, and the different reactions to the *Report* from
women's movement leaders and others, particularly as they were
framed in the context of "women's lib." But the "conflict" frame also
served to distract attention from some serious analytic writing on
issues such as, for example, "equal pay" versus "equal pay for work of
equal value."

The overriding problem with the media coverage of the *Report*
was twofold. One was the immediacy with which the journalists were
expected to cover it and then move on to other things, which limited
any real analytical discussion of the recommendations the commissioners did agree on, or of the women's movement and its evolution,
for that matter. The other was the gender tension evident among the
reporters themselves, who had that year battled their way through the

highly symbolic and contentious debate about female membership in the National Press Club. This tension was evident at Florence Bird's news conference and, in some instances, seeped into news coverage about the *Report*. Moreover, some of the stories and commentaries that greeted the recommendations were reminiscent of the kind of discussion that went on when the commission was first appointed, although the editorial response was somewhat more welcoming of the prospect of female equality by late 1970. "Women's lib" was the new, demonizing factor for those who did not agree with it, or who wanted to dismiss the ongoing concerns of Canadian women as "old news." The former media discourse of women's rights, then, had shifted somewhat to accept notions that were seen as suspect just a few years before, and balk at new notions of what was considered "radical," meaning "deviant." The overall effect was to draw boundaries around the aspirations of Canadian women while still allowing their suggestions of progress towards "equal opportunities," and even "equality with men," to reach the public.

Towards the Future

There are lessons to be learned from the news media's coverage of Canadian women's concerns as they were aired before the Royal Commission on the Status of Women 30 years ago. One of them is the fragility of the "objectivity" ideal, and the difficulty of maintaining, at the very least, "fairness and balance" when journalists cannot avoid becoming politicized to some degree by the society around them and the cultures of their own newsrooms. How to rectify that problem is another issue, one which has been taken up by mass communication critics, but not very effectively as far as everyday news practice is concerned.

Suzanne Strutt and Lynne Hissey question the whole concept of "balance" because it's supported by liberal-feminists who believe improvements in the ways the media present gender issues can be accomplished within the status quo. The authors argue, however, that presenting both sides of the story usually involves using conventional establishment sources, such as two MPs from opposing parties discussing national daycare. The authors' self-defined "radical" critique calls for the journalist to question representatives of different philosophies of feminism as well. They argue that as long as journalists ignore feminism or regard it as one movement instead of many, their coverage of women's issues will be inadequate.[17]

There is certainly something to be said for allowing feminists of different persuasions to debate daycare and many other issues, something which is done rarely, if at all these days, but actually did take place at the Commission hearings. The fact that there were separate women's pages on the daily newspapers, *Chatelaine* magazine, and the women's programs on the CBC allowed for these issues to be covered.

But other feminist approaches create more difficulties, especially for the media historian. One author, Meenakshi Gigi Durham, argues that journalistic objectivity is a form of relativism that depends too much on standard establishment sources and fails to consider the validity of diverse perspectives in society. Her model of journalistic inquiry, however, would see reporters automatically foregrounding marginalized groups or individuals in the story, rather than establishment ones, and bringing to their coverage their personal perspectives as journalists, including acknowledgement of their own class and cultural positions in society. Under this model, there is no one truth, of course, but many truths presented by the various participants, including the journalist writing the story. This approach, Durham maintains, "has the potential to fulfil the liberatory goals of feminism."[18]

The conventional reporter of the 1960s, immersed as he or she was in hegemonic corporate culture, middle-class consciousness, liberal values, standard and ingrained reporting techniques, and tight deadlines, would likely have little patience for such a theory of news practice. In today's neo-conservative climate, I suspect there would be even less patience with it. This is where the academics and the journalists part company. The academics come up with critiques of what journalists do, usually in academic language that is often inaccessible to the journalist, and promote what appear to be impossible suggestions that go against standard professional practice. In my experience, mainstream journalists are much more responsive to feminist ideas that can be adapted to everyday newsgathering effectively, such as Helen Benedict's thoughtful discussion of how reporters use gender-specific language and careless professional practices to label female victims of sex crimes, and how that can be changed.[19] In short, regardless of the value of the arguments more radical scholars bring to the debate about news practice, little is likely to change within the capitalist media unless journalists find the suggestions immediately workable. Certainly, the mainstream journalists of the 1960s would not have adopted these ideas, but managed, all the same, to expose a great deal of the injustices then perpetrated against women including marginalized aboriginal women.

The biggest sins that journalists still commit, when it comes to women's concerns that can be rectified, are over-emphasizing what is "new" or "in conflict" and conflating or reducing the issues and their proponents to their simplest common denominators. This is certainly true with respect to the real variations in political leanings among women. We saw it during the Royal Commission hearings and the coverage of its *Report*, and we see it now when some revisionist columnist or academic equates feminists of all political stripes with "radical" ideas that have supposedly gone mainstream. Of course, these pundits suggest that these ideas pose a danger to "taxpayers," who, for some mysterious reason, seem to occupy a separate category from ordinary working women who are often being paid less than they deserve. Similarly, some editors and scholars find a youthful "postmodern" (i.e., detached) spin on women's issues far more interesting than what the committed "old guard" has to say. In fact, there were assertive women who deliberately detached themselves from feminism in the 1960s, and young women today who are very committed to winning the victories that are still outstanding. Furthermore, there are many women of all ages who might never call themselves feminists, but still bristle at the suggestion that their concerns are not important.

We need more journalists and columnists of both sexes to cover gender issues more thoroughly and to interpret them clearly and fairly. Why is it that only a few feminist stalwarts, such as Michele Landsberg of *The Toronto Star*, continue to point out the inequities that still exist for Canadian women, information that has also been tracked by academics. Landsberg writes, for example, that despite three decades and more of trying, and the fact that two-thirds of Canadians are in favour, women still don't have a national daycare policy in this country. What's more, the media still blame "working mothers" for neglecting their children. As Landsberg points out, most mothers will work outside the home at some point. To suggest that there are two separate categories of mothers, "stay-at-home" and "working," is "hogswallop," in her words.[20]

Scholarly inquiry backs her up. Julia S. O'Connor, formerly of McMaster University, has traced the ongoing struggle for gender equity in employment from the Royal Commission *Report* in the 1970 to the 1990s. She notes that despite the influx of married women with preschool children into the labour force over the last 25 years, child care and parental leave and benefits are still inadequate. Moreover, large pay gaps between men and women remain in many occupations, and much of our labour force is still sex-segregated. She concludes that bureaucratic remedies have been largely ineffective but demands for more fundamental changes in our political structure are not going to be heard in an economic climate that favours downsizing and deficit reduction. In the same vein, Pat and Hugh Armstrong note in their ongoing assessments of the Canadian labour force that men still tend to leave most of the household work to women even when both partners work outside the home, and those who stay home with their children still receive no wages, no unemployment insurance, no pensions, no sick pay or other benefits and little leisure time.[21] In the universities, neo-conservatives are seriously threatening the gains women professors and students have made in the last 30 years.[22]

When it comes to gender issues today, both journalists and scholarly researchers should make a concerted effort to find out what is really going on, rather than dismiss them out of hand as old news or as the ranting of off-the-wall, "older" feminists that somehow threaten the ideal of "balanced" journalism. Reading and providing information on the latest statistics and academic studies should be basic homework for anyone who really cares about the facts. A little knowledge, especially of history, is a powerful tool in the battle for a democratic media and a society in which men and women are truly equal. Injustice is passé only if something concrete has actually been done to change the status quo lately, not because previous complaints have already been covered, or because that news angle has been "done." If the problem hasn't been fixed, it's still an issue.

Notes

Introduction

1 Examples include Danielle Crittenden, "Let's Junk the Feminist Slogans: The War's Over," *Chatelaine*, August 1990, 37-38, 62, and *What Our Mothers Didn't Tell Us*; Laframboise, *The Princess at the Window*; Roiphe, *The Morning After*; Manji, *Risking Utopia*. See also Strong-Boag, "Independent Women, Problematic Men."

2 Terence Corcoran, "Radical Feminism's Absurd Legacy," *The Globe and Mail*, 31 July 1998, B2. General coverage included Jack Aubry, "Pay-equity Win Worth Billions," *Ottawa Citizen*, 30 July, 1998, A1; Laura Eggleston, "Now Women Face Court Battle over Back Wages," *Toronto Star*, 1 Aug. 1998, B1; Edward Greenspon, "Pay-equity Costs Too High: Chrétien," *The Globe and Mail*, 18 Aug. 1998, A3.

3 Gingras, "Daily Male Delivery,"; and Robinson and Saint-Jean, "The Portrayal of Women Politicians."

4 Armstrong and Armstrong, especially Chapter 2; Arscott, "'A Job Well Begun'"; Burt, "Gender and Public Policy"; Tremblay and Andrew, eds., *Women and Political Representation in Canada*.

5 Frideres, "The Royal Commission on Aboriginal Peoples," and Williams, "Aboriginal Women in Toronto."

6 Actual statistics on lesbians in Canada are few and far between. A recent Quebec study is cited in CP, "Gay Women Are More Accepted but Still Hide, Study Finds." *The Edmonton Journal*, 3 Aug. 1998, 5.

7 Historical case studies are often based on institutional files, but I find this idea useful for my own research, partly because it sheds light on how Canadian women regarded gender issues at the time. For an example of Canadian case study literature, see Iacovetta and Mitchinson, eds., *On the Case*.

8 For example, McLaughlin, "Gender, Privacy and Publicity in 'Media Event Space,'" in Carter et al., eds., *News, Gender and Power.*

9 Leone Kirkwood, "Satellite Sex Called Good Title for Report on Status of Women," *The Globe and Mail,* 24 Mar. 1971.

10 *Report of the Royal Commission on the Status of Women;* Prentice et al., *Canadian Women: A History,* Chapters 12-14. Vickers, "The Intellectual Origins of the Women's Movement in Canada"; Burt, "Changing Patterns in Public Policy"; Baines, "Law, Gender, Equality"; Black, "The Canadian Women's Movement; Ursel, *Private Lives, Public Policy,* Period III, 1940-1968.

11 Timpson, "Royal Commissions as Sites of Resistance." Arscott, "Twenty-Five Years and Sixty-Five Minutes," "'More Women,'" and 'A Job Well Begun.'" See also Williams, "Re-forming Women's Truth." Masters theses include Speers, "The Royal Commission on the Status of Women: A Study of the Contradictions and Limitations of Liberalism and Liberal Feminism"; Cumming, "The Report of the Royal Commission on the Status of Women: A Liberal Feminist Analysis."

12 See, for example Bégin, "The Royal Commission on the Status of Women in Canada: Twenty Years Later." The study Bégin and other articles cite is Cerise Morris, "'Determination and Thoroughness': The Movement for a Royal Commission on the Status of Women in Canada." In her dissertation, Morris stated that the overall media coverage of the Commission improved over time, citing both Florence Bird and a report prepared for the Commission by its public relations officer, Angela Burke. This study, however, covered only the first half of the hearings and was written to reassure the commissioners that the initial, negative coverage was improving after Bird and Bégin had signalled their concern. Morris also cited some of the material she examined herself, mostly editorials and magazine articles, but did not actually analyze the daily news coverage, the editorial cartoons or any of the broadcast programming. Nor did she interview any journalists. Morris, "'No More than Simple Justice,'" especially 128-30; 209-15 and 279-83. See Angela Burke, "Public Relations Report on Press Comment on the Commission," August 1968, in National Archives of Canada, Papers of the Royal Commission on the Status of Women (hereafter NAC RCSW), RG 33/89, Vol. 35, file marked "Public Relations—Reports."

13 Gaye Tuchman argued that the mass media "symbolically annihilated" women through condemnation of untraditional female behaviour, trivialization through the use of demeaning sexual stereotypes, or by ignoring them and their contributions to society altogether. Tuchman, "The Symbolic Annihilation of Women," in Tuchman et al. (eds.), *Hearth and Home,* 3-38.

14 This is despite the fact that most women read the editorial and news pages, and about 45 percent of men read the women's pages, according to a 1964 survey of 11 major dailies conducted by the Canadian Newspaper Publishers Association. Cited in the *Report of the Royal Commission,* 9.

15 Barker-Plummer, "News as a Political Resource"; Bradley, "Mass Communication and the Shaping of US Feminism."

16 Tuchman notes that until the 1970s, it was men writing about and for men who commonly produced social studies, many of which concerned power and social stratification. Tuchman, "The Symbolic Annihilation of Women," 4.

17 Bradley, "Mass Communication and US Feminism."

18 Tuchman, *Making News,* Chapter 7.

19 Meyers, "Fracturing Women," 12.

20 Hardt and Brennan, "Communication and the Question of History," 130.

21 Ibid., 132-133.

22 Jansen, "'The Future Is Not What It Used to Be,'" 144.

23 Examples include Rutherford, *A Victorian Authority* and *When Television Was Young*; Sotiron, *From Politics to Profit*; Vipond, *Listening In*; Raboy, *Missed Opportunities*.

24 Freeman, *Kit's Kingdom*; Downie, *A Passionate Pen*. The latest is Lang, *Women Who Made the News*.

25 Robinson, "Monopolies of Knowledge in Canadian Communications Studies."

26 Durham, "On the Relevance of Standpoint Epistemology to the Practice of Journalism."

27 Strutt and Hissey, "Feminisms and Balance."

28 van Zoonen, "Feminist Perspectives on the Media," 41. See also, van Zoonen, *Feminist Media Studies*, Chapter 3.

29 van Zoonen, *Feminist Media Studies*, 40.

30 van Dijk, *News as Discourse,* 74.

31 Ibid., 119. Using a controlled study of readers in Amsterdam, van Dijk discovered that they remembered only the details of a news story which reinforced their original understandings and biases concerning a given situation. See Chapter 4.

32 Ericson, Baranek and Chan, *Negotiating Control: A Study of News Sources*; *Visualizing Deviance: A Study of News Organization*; *Representing Order: Crime, Law and Justice in the News Media*.

33 Hackett and Zhao, *Sustaining Democracy?*

34 Schudson, *Discovering the News*, 5; Schiller, *Objectivity and the News*. Mindich, *Just the Facts*.

35 Hackett and Zhao, *Sustaining Democracy?* Chapter 1 (written with Satu Repo) and Chapter 2.

36 MacDougall, *Newsroom Problems and Policies*, Chapter 5, "Presenting Facts and Opinions." On the history of "fairness" in journalism, see Schudson, "In All Fairness"; also Mindich, *Just the Facts*, 7. The late Professor Emeritus Wilfrid Kesterton once told me that the MacDougall text was used at Carleton University's School of Journalism and Communication in the 1960s.

37 *CP Style Book*, 1-2; Phelan ed., *The Globe and Mail Style Book*, 3rd ed,, Introduction.

38 Freeman interview with Scott; also with Arnopolous, Crittenden, and Sharp, among others.

39 Martin, *Communication and Mass Media*, 248 and Chapter 5. For a slightly different argument that it is more useful to examine the term "truth" in news stories about gender, see Allan, "(En)Gendering the Truth Politics of News Discourse."

40 van Zoonen, "One of the girls?" 35-38.

41 Schudson, *Discovering the News*; and Schiller, *Objectivity and the News*. Also, Ericson, Baranek, and Chan, *Representing Order*; Galtung and Mari Ruge, "Structuring and Selecting News"; Sigal, "Sources Make the News" in Manoff and Schudson (eds.), *Reading the News*; Gans, *Deciding What's News* and Fishman, *Manufacturing the News*.

42 Ehrlich, "Using 'Ritual' to Study Journalism," 14.

43 Meyers, "Reporters and Beats."

44 Hall, "The Determination of News Photographs."

45 Langer, "The Structure and Ideology of the 'Other News' on Television."

46 Gender relations are discussed in Cumming, *Sketches from a Young Country*, Chapter 10; Burr, *Spreading the Light*, Chapter 4. Studies that don't examine gender include Morris, *The Jester's Mask* and *The Carnivalization of Politics*, and more general interest surveys, such as Desbarats and Mosher, *The Hecklers*, and Hou and Hou, *Great Canadian Political Cartoons, 1820-1914*.

47 "Mythical speech is made up of a material which has *already* been worked on so as to make it suitable for communication: it is because all the materials of myth (whether pictorial or written) presuppose a signifying consciousness, that one can reason about them while discounting their substance. This substance is not unimportant: pictures, to be sure, are more imperative than writing, they impose meaning at one stroke, without analyzing or diluting it. But this is no longer a constitutive difference. Pictures become a kind of writing as soon as they are meaningful: like writing, they call for a *lexis*." Barthes, "Myth Today," 93-95, 116, 132.

48 Arguing from a Marxist perspective, Graham Murdock sees labelling as serving a dual function. "First, it reasserts the existence of a basic set of shared assumptions and interests, and secondly, it clarifies the nature of 'consensus' by pointing to concrete examples of what it is not." Murdock, "Political Deviance," 156-75.

49 Barthes, "Myth Today," 141.

50 de Beauvoir, *The Second Sex*, Introduction.

51 Warner, *Monuments and Maidens*, xx.

52 For example, see Smith-Rosenberg, *Disorderly Conduct*.

53 Davis, "Women on Top," in *Society and Culture in Early Modern France*, 129.

54 The "blue-stocking' was a common stereotype in the eighteenth century, when women demanded equal rights to education. Daumier, *Intellectuelles (Bas Bleus) et Femmes Socialistes*.

55 Franzen and Ethiel, *Make Way! 200 Years of American Women in Cartoons*; Sheppard, *Cartooning for Suffrage*, 58-64. Cumming, *Sketches from a Young Country*, Chapter 10.

56 Freeman interviews with Norris and Barron.

57 Biographical sketch of the late Robert Chambers from Robert W. Chambers Fonds, Public Archives of Nova Scotia, MG1, Vols.3661-3666.

58 Sangster, "Beyond Dichotomies."

59 Henry, "Changing Media History through Women's History."

60 The briefs are in NAC RCSW, microfilms C-4878 to C-4883 and C-6798 to C-6803.

61 Dubinsky and Marks, "Beyond Purity: A Response to Sangster"; and Iacovetta and Kealey, "Women's History, Gender History, and Debating Dichotomies." See also Iacovetta and Valverde, eds., *Gender Conflicts*, Introduction.

62 Scott, *Gender and the Politics of History*; Pierson, "Experience, Difference, Dominance and Voice"; Parr, *The Gender of Breadwinners*.

63 *Report of the Special Senate Committee on Mass Media*, Vols. 1-3. See also Porter, *The Vertical Mosaic*; and Clement, *The Canadian Corporate Elite*.

64 Most of them are in scrapbooks in NAC RCSW, RG 33/89, Vols. 40-45.

65 See list of audio-visual material in the bibliography.

66 NAC RCSW; NAC Florence Bayard Bird Papers MG 31 D 63; NAC Elsie Gregory MacGill, Papers MG 31 K7.

67 Arscott, "Twenty-Five Years and Sixty-Five Minutes," 36-38.

68 NAC RCSW, audio tape recordings of public hearings, numbers C9902 to C10009.

69 Steiner, "Newsroom Accounts of Power at Work," 148.

70 NAC Media Club of Canada Papers (Canadian Women's Press Club), MG 28, I 232, especially Vols. 18, 22, 29, and 32.

71 See Bégin, "The Royal Commission on the Status of Women in Canada"; Arscott, "Twenty-five Years"; Dumont, "The Origins of the Women's Movement in Quebec"; and Lamoureux, "Nationalism and Feminism in Quebec." Examples of English-language CP articles which appeared in French included Rosemary Speirs (CP) "Les hommes adoptent une attitude hautaine

a l'egard des femmes" in *La Presse*, Montreal, 23 Apr. 1968, 20. They were translated at the news agency's Montreal bureau. Freeman interview with Stewart.

72 For example, van Dijk, *News as Discourse*, Chapter 4.

73 Eaman, *Channels of Influence*, especially Chapter 11.

74 Boyd, "Canadian Attitudes towards Women."

75 Letters to the editor from Mrs. Edna Toth and Patricia Williams under heading, "Feminists No Threat to Housewives," *Toronto Daily Star*, 8 Dec. 1970, 61. Another came from a pro-choice activist: Ruth Evans (ARCAL), "'Our Abortion Laws Should Be Repealed,'" *Toronto Daily Star*, 1 Nov. 1970, 7. Several feminist advocates phoned in to a CBC open-line program after the release of the Commission's report. *Cross Country Checkup*, 13 Dec. 1970.

76 Ericson et al., *Negotiating Control*, 343-76; 397-98.

77 Comments of Lu Connor of Rosemere, *Take 30*, Montreal hearings; and from Mary Anne Lavallee, *Take 30*, Regina hearings.

78 *Canada House of Commons, Debates*, 3rd Session, 28th Parliament, Vols. II and III.

79 Osler, "The Evolution of a National Press Policy" and Hannigan, "Canadian Media Ownership and Control." It is too soon to tell if the proposed Canwest Global take-over of the Hollinger newspapers, headed by "arch conservative" Conrad Black, will result in a shift towards more liberal editorial policies. See Shawn McCarthy, "Megadeal Creates Canada's Largest Media Empire," *The Globe and Mail*, 1 Aug. 2000, A1.

80 In the American context, Susan Faludi has argued that the media simultaneously blame feminism for ills that beset modern women, while downplaying the movement's accomplishments. Faludi, *Backlash*, especially Chapter 4.

81 Trimble, "Coming Soon to a Station Near You?"

82 The authors note that the proportion of women is higher in TV, partly because of federal affirmative action policies for broadcasters. The print media are not regulated in the same way. The study does not cover radio. Robinson and Saint-Jean, "Women's Participation in the Canadian News Media."

Chapter 1

1 Her emphasis. *Take 30*, RCSW hearings in Victoria and Vancouver. See also (no byline), "Women's status study would break barriers," *The Tribune*, Winnipeg 11 Dec. 1967; Weise, "Status study a probe into society's future," *The Tribune*, Winnipeg, 1 June 1968, 3.

2 Ericson et al., *Negotiating Control*, 16-17.

3 See, for example, Landes, "The Public and the Private Sphere," in Johanna Meehan, (ed.), *Feminists Read Habermas*.

4 Marshall, "Communication as Politics," 465.

5 Ibid., 467.

6 Bothwell et al., *Canada since 1945*, Part 5; Stanley, "The 1960s"; Little, "'No Car, No Radio, No Liquor Permit,'" Chapter 6.

7 Costain, *Inviting Women's Rebellion*, Chapter 1 and Conclusion; May, *Homeward Bound* and Gitlin, *The Sixties*.

8 Findlay, "Facing the State," 34-37.

9 McRoberts, *Quebec*.

10 Grant, *Lament for A Nation*; Cook, *The Maple Leaf Forever*.

11 Clement, *The Canadian Corporate Elite*.

12 Lumsden, ed., *Close the 49th Parallel*.

13 Kostash, *Long Way from Home*; Laxer, "The Americanization of the Canadian Student Movement," 275-86.

14 Miller, *Skyscrapers Hide the Heavens;* and Hamilton, *Arctic Revolution.*

15 *Report of the Royal Commission,* Chapter 2.

16 Armstrong and Armstrong, *The Double Ghetto,* 16-24.

17 Prentice et al., *Canadian Women,* 354, 394-98.

18 Prentice et al., *Canadian Women,* 381-82, 426-27; McLaren and McLaren, *The Bedroom and the State,* 131-38.

19 Friedan, *The Feminine Mystique,* 2; Meyerowitz, "Beyond the Feminine Mystique".

20 Rosen, "The Feminist Generation Gap"; and Kostash, "The Rising of the Women," in *Long Way from Home.*

21 de Beauvoir, *The Second Sex.*

22 Crowley, "Did Canada Miss the Enlightenment?" 3.

23 Pierson, *"They're Still Women after All,"* 11-21, and Chapters 1 and 2; Prentice et al., *Canadian Women,* 214-25, 323-24, 353-54, 410-14.

24 Von Heyking, "Red Deer Women"; Cassandra Sanders, "The Decline and Fall of Women's Clubs," *Chatelaine,* Oct. 1967, 43, 73-76, 78; Jean Sharp, Canadian Press (CP), "Thinning Ranks Concern Clubs," *Winnipeg Free Press,* 13 Aug. 1968, 14.

25 The Jaycettes were affiliated with the male service group, the Jaycees.

26 Prentice et al., *Canadian Women,* 409-14; Griffiths, *The Splendid Vision;* Bashevkin, *Toeing the Lines;* Kinnear, *In Subordination;* Stewart, *Women Volunteer to Go to Prison;* Roberts, "Women's Peace Activism in Canada"; Macpherson, *When in Doubt, Do Both.*

27 See, for example, Jean Sharp, Canadian Press (CP), "Snowballing Consumer Revolt Aimed to Upset Status Quo," *The Ottawa Citizen,* 22 Dec. 1966; Martin O'Malley, "The Time of the Consumer Is at Hand," *The Globe and Mail,* 25 Feb. 1967, 9; Canadian Press (CP), "Housewives across Canada Waiting to Say Their Piece," *London Free Press,* 17 Feb. 1967, 15. Parr and Ekberg, "Mrs. Consumer and Mr. Keynes in Postwar Canada and Sweden."

28 Adamson, "Feminists, Libbers, Lefties and Radicals"; for the United States, see Echols, *Daring to Be Bad.*

29 On the Presidential Commission, see Linden-Ward and Hurd Green, *Changing the Future,* 2-10; and Mead and Kaplan, eds., *American Women: Report of the President's Commission on the Status of Women.* Friedan, *The Feminine Mystique;* Evans, "The Women's Movement in the United States in the 1960s," in Backhouse and Flaherty, eds., *Challenging Times;* Echols, *Daring to Be Bad.*

30 Vickers, "The Intellectual Origins of the Women's Movement in Canada," in Backhouse and Flaherty, eds., *Challenging Times.* See also Black, "The Canadian Women's Movement: The Second Wave."

31 On post-war reconstruction, see Brandt, "Pigeon-Holed and Forgotten."

32 National Archives of Canada, Papers of the Royal Commission on the Status of Women (hereafter NAC RCSW), Vol. 39, file marked "United Nations—International Instruments," copy of the Declaration on the Elimination of Discrimination against Women, reprinted by the Women's Bureau of the Canada Department of Labour, n.d. Bothwell et al., *Canada Since 1945,* 271, 366, 196, 343; Arscott, "Twenty-Five Years", 34-36.

33 Sabia quote in "Minutes of Exploratory Meeting of Canadian Women on Human Rights and a Commission on the Status of Women," University Women's Club, Toronto, 3 May 1966. Copy in National Archives of Canada, Media Club of Canada Papers (then known as the Canadian Women's Press Club and hereafter referred to as NAC CWPC), MG 28, I 232, Vol. 18, File marked "Status of Women, 1967-73."

34 Canadian Press (CP), "Women Organize for Rights," *Toronto Daily Star,* 4 May 1966, 75.

35 "Minutes of Steering Committee," 27 May 1966; letter from Sabia to the presidents of the women's groups, 1 June 1966; minutes of the Second Meeting of representatives of National Women's Organizations," 28 June 1966. Copies of these documents are in NAC CWPC, Vol. 18, "Status of Women, 1967-73" file.

36 Canadian Press, "Group Urges Quebec Inquiry for Women," *The Globe and Mail*, 29 1967, 17; Lewis Seale, "Women's Liberal Federation: Group Urges Provincial Inquiries on Status of Women," *The Globe and Mail*, 5 Apr. 1967, 11.

37 (No byline), "Women Protest All-Male Committee," *The Globe and Mail*, 28 June 1966, W2.

38 Submission to the Government of Canada from the Committee for the Equality of Women in Canada, 15 Sept. 1966, copy in NAC RCSW Vol. 37, "Report of the Commission—Outlines, etc." file. It was presented on 19 Nov. 1966.

39 Sabia made her "protest march" comment in response to a follow-up inquiry from a reporter two months later. Barry Craig, "Women's March May Back Call for Rights Probe," *The Globe and Mail*, 5 Jan. 1967, 1.

40 On LaMarsh, see Rudy Platiel, "Stop Harping about a Royal Commission, Judy LaMarsh Warns Women's Group," *The Globe and Mail*, 9 Jan. 1967, 13. LaMarsh, *Memoirs of a Bird in a Gilded Cage*, 301-302. LaMarsh apparently raised the question of such an inquiry in most of her speeches to women's groups during the mid-to-late 1960s. See NAC RCSW, Vol. 34, "Press Releases" file, text of speech by Judy LaMarsh to the Canadian Federation of University Women, 1 June 1967. Reidford, *The Globe and Mail*, 10 Jan. 1967.

41 For example, CP, "Gov't Calls Royal Probe on Women, " *The Ottawa Journal*, 3 Feb. 1967, 1, 27. Tom Earle, reporting for CBC Radio News, *The World at Six*, Tape #670203-0(1), 3 Feb. 3 1967.

42 Morris, "Determination and Thoroughness," 20, n21, citing an interview with Margaret Hyndman, one of the leaders of the CEWC.

43 Bird, *Anne Francis*; NAC Bird Papers; Peter Stursberg interview with Florence Bird, NAC ISN #163396, recorded 23 June 1976; Jean Bruce interview with Florence Bird, NAC ISN #163393, recorded in October 1980; NAC MacGill Papers, Vol. 3, File 1, Appendix "E", Biographical Notes on the Commissioners, Mrs. John Bird (Anne Francis).

44 Freeman interview with Bird, 18 Nov. 1992; NAC Bird Papers and Commission records concerning public relations cited below. Bird, *Anne Frances*, 263-318.

45 NAC RCSW, Vol. 1, File SW 1-5-1-3, news release from the Office of the Prime Minister, 6 Feb. 1968; Andrea Goeb, "Human Rights Commissioner's Life Concern," The Gazette, Montreal, 8 Feb. 1968, 10. Telephone conversations between Freeman and Bird, 20 July 1994 and 20 June 1996. NAC MacGill Papers, Vol. 3, File 3, 24-26 May 1967, Appendix "W," Memo from Bird to the Commissioners, 11 May 1967.

46 Davey, *Report of the Special Senate Committee on the Mass Media*, vol. 1, "The Uncertain Mirror, 3-12. MacDougall, *Newsroom Problems and Policies*, Chapters 1, 2 and 6; Tuchman, *Making News*, Chapter 8; CBC, *Journalistic Policy*.

47 Ericson, et al., *Negotiating Control*, 2, 389.

48 CP, "Status Probe Set," *Winnipeg Free Press*, 4 Feb. 1967, 1, and CP, "Women Hail Status Study—except Charlotte, *The London Free Press*, 4 Feb. 1967, 3. Regarding the RCSW mandate, the words "equal opportunities" were specified in the minutes of a Privy Council meeting 16 Feb. 1967.

49 Submission to the Government of Canada from the Committee for the Equality of Women in Canada, 15 Sept. 1966, copy in NAC RCSW, Vol. 37, in file marked "Report of the Commission—Outlines, etc." Arscott, "Canadian Women and 'Second-Class' Citizenship, 1970," 2; see also Arscott, "Twenty-Five Years."

50 Code, "Feminist Theory," 38.

51 NAC MacGill Papers, Vol. 3, Folder 4, Minutes of the Third Meeting, 24-26 May 1967, Appendix N, a RCSW news release, 9 May 1967. See also item 18 and *Report of the Royal Commission*, vii-xii.

52 Coverage and commentary included CP (Ottawa), "Status Probe Set—Women Win Fight for Commission," and (no byline), "Local Women Favor Study into Status," *Winnipeg Free Press*, 4 Feb. 1967, 1, 6; (no byline) "Most in Ottawa Think Probe Will Accomplish Little," *The Ottawa Journal*, 4 Feb. 1967, 3. A supportive editorial, "One for the Ladies," *The Ottawa Citizen*, 4 Feb. 1967, 6, versus a sneering one, "Women in Bunches" in *The Ottawa Journal*, 4 Feb. 1967. There was criticism from Conservative MP Jean Wadds and a former Ottawa mayor, Charlotte Whitton, among others. See (no byline), "MP Claims Commission Funds Could Have Gone Elsewhere," *The Ottawa Journal*, 6 Mar. 1968; CP, "Women's Status Study Inexcusable: Whitton." *Ottawa Citizen*, 4 Feb. 1967, 18. Further comments included an editorial, "Those Royal Commissions," *Claresholm Local Press*, Alberta, 16 Mar. 1967; Richard Jackson, "In-Depth Study of Women's Status," *Brantford Expositor*, Ontario, 7 Nov. 1967; editorial, "A Reluctance to Act," *St. Catharine's Standard*, 18 Feb. 1967; Concerns about costs were noted in CP, "Study's First Year Costs $218,946," *The Gazette*, Montreal, 24 Jan. 1968; (no byline), "$218,946 So Far: Commission Salaries Questioned," *The Ottawa Journal*, 27 Jan. 1968; (no byline), "Status Awards Contracts," *The Edmonton Journal*, 27 Jan. 1968; Donna Anderson, "Explains Whys and Wherefores: Commissioner Clears the Air," *The Vancouver Sun*, 5 Mar. 1968.

53 No byline, "Most in Ottawa Think Probe Will Accomplish Little," *The Ottawa Journal*, 4 Feb. 1967, 3.

54 "Costly commissions," *The Telegram*, Toronto, 12 Nov. 1968.

55 Letters to the Editor, Dundas *Star*, Ontario, 19 July 1967.

56 Letters from Jean Nowland, "Women's Status," and Iris Craig, "Women's Rights, " objecting to editorial "Women in Bunches," in *The Ottawa Journal*, 8 Feb. 1967. The editorial appeared 4 Feb. 1967. Letter from Elizabeth Miles, objecting to an editorial on homemakers in the *Uxbridge Times Journal*, Ontario, 23 Mar. 1967. The editorial ran 16 March 1967.

57 On delays in the "Bi and Bi" Commission report, see editorial, "Lingering," *The Globe and Mail*, 6 Apr. 1970, 6.

58 On the RCSW, see (no byline), "Commission Burns Midnight Oil," *The Windsor Star*, 10 Mar. 1970; CP, "No Report Yet: Women's commission to cost 1,779,868," *Toronto Daily Star*, 10 Mar. 1970. Commentary included editorial, "Inflation and Inertia," *Sarnia Observer*, Ontario, 18 Mar. 1970; editorial, "Tell us Anne!" *Halifax Mail Star*, 11 Mar. 1970; editorial, Maurice Western, "The Cost of Royal Commissions," *Lethbridge Herald*, 15 Apr. 1970; "Too Many Shrill Voices," *Prince George Citizen*, BC 3 April 1970.

59 Len Norris, *The Vancouver Sun*, 26 February 1969.

60 Porter, *The Vertical Mosaic*; and Clement, *The Canadian Corporate Elite*.

61 Freeman interview with Gordon, Jr.

62 NAC RCSW, Vol. 1, File SW1-5-1-1 "Press Comments and Clippings" file. News release from the Canadian Labour Congress (CLC), 21 Feb. 1967. See, for example, CP, "Women Need Commission Unionist," *The Ottawa Citizen*, 28 Feb. 1967; MP Grace MacInnis followed up on the suggestion after Gordon resigned. See CP, "Suggest Commission Replacement," *The Ottawa Journal*, 30 Jan. 1968. Behind the scenes, Bird, concerned about giving the CLC too much influence, reneged on her suggestion that it act as an official advisor. NAC RCSW, Vol. 36, "Relations with Associations" file, memo from M. Bégin to F. Bird, 6 Sept. 1967 and from F. Bird to M. Bégin, 7 Sept. 1967.

63 Other criticism concerning lack of representation on the Commission came from, among others, an anti-poverty activist at the Commission's first hearing in British Columbia and from three young people in Edmonton. CP (Victoria), "Dream World: Lacks View of Poor, Grandmother Tells Probe," *The Globe and Mail*, 17 Apr. 1968, 10; Rosemary Speirs (CP), "Status of Women: Students Condemn Outdated Concepts," *The Montreal Star*, 29 Apr. 1968.

64 Freeman interview with Bird.

65 Robert Chambers, in *The Windsor Star*, Ontario, 14 Feb. 1967, among others.

66 Freeman interviews with Bird and Bégin. NAC MacGill Papers, Vol. 3, File, 1, "Guidelines for the Royal Commission," item 7(d), adopted at the Sixth Meeting of the Commissioners, 13-14 Dec. 1967, made the Chair responsible for carrying out policy and programs concerning publicity. On Bird's final authority over news releases, see MacGill, Vol. 3, File 8, Minutes of the Fifth Meeting of the Commissioners, 1 Nov. 1968, 3. NAC RCSW Vol. 34, "Notes of Meetings with Mrs. Bird" file, containing Bégin's notes of their meeting held 2 May 1967 refers to Bird writing press releases. NAC RCSW, Vol. 34, Commission Guidebook, "Relations with the Media," 1-9; Vol. 31, File 8,—Administration: Personnel (1), Memo from Bird, dated 22 June 1967. It appears Bégin did some liaison with the francophone media, although she believes Bird, who was bilingual, handled most of it.

67 Several files, NAC RCSW, Vol. 1 contain the details of this well-orchestrated campaign.

68 The letters are in NAC RCSW, Vol. 1, File SW 1-5-2-1, Requests for Information from Private Individuals; Vol. 2, File SW 1-5-2-4 Requests for Information—Others; and Vols. 7, 8 and 9.

69 NAC MacGill Papers, Vol. 3, File 2, Minutes of the Chairman's and Commissioners' First Meeting, 1-3 March 1967, #5(f).

70 NAC RCSW, Vol 35, "Public Hearings—Advertising and Publicity" file, Came to Bégin, 20 Sept., 20 and Vol. 31, File 8—Administration: Personnel (1)," Came to Bégin, 1 Nov. 1967. On Kirk, see column, "Just What Was Spent: Horrible Stories (X), *The Globe and Mail*,30 Apr. 1969; NAC MacGill Papers, Vol. 5, File 33, 16th meeting of the Commissioners, 22-23 Jan. 1969, Appendix "C," Report of the Chairman; NAC RCSW, Vol. 36, file marked "Relations with Gov't—Privy Council Office", Bird to Leo Lafrance, 15 Apr. 1969; NAC MacGill Papers, Vol. 4, 21st meeting of the Commissioners, 7-9 May 1969, Appendix "C", Report of the Chairman, 30 April 1969; Arscott, "Twenty-Five Years," 49. Neither Gordon nor Bird would discuss the reasons for the resignations. Gordon does say Kirk and Bird did not get along. Freeman telephone conversation with Bird, 20 June 1996 and interview with Gordon.

71 News stories included Susan Becker CP, "Tension Said Rising among Commission's Staff; 3 Quit." Halifax *Chronicle Herald*, 23 Dec. 1967, 3; and "Status Commission Loses Three Members, Low Morale Suggested," *The Globe and Mail*, 23 Dec. 1967, 26. The original story about Gordon's resignation included CP (Ottawa), "One Male Member Resigned," *The Montreal Star*, 24 Nov. 1967 and (Special to the Globe and Mail), "Resignation Leaves a Lone Male on Women's Status Commission," *The Globe and Mail*, 24 Nov. 1967.

72 NAC MacGill Papers, Vol. 4. Commissioners' meetings. File 1, 8th meeting of Commissioners: minutes, reports and submissions, 13-15 Mar. 1968, Addendum to Appendix D, Report of the Chairman, 12 Mar. 1968, #10.

73 Freeman interviews with Becker, Bird, Davidson and MacDougall.

74 Freeman interview with Speirs.

75 Commissioner Lola Lange went to Prairie cities twice. Her first report is in NAC MacGill Papers, Vol. 3, Folder 7, 5th meeting of the Commissioners, 1-3 Nov. 1967 (Part 2), Appendix "II." Reports on meetings, conferences, etc.

attended by Commissioner Lola Lange indicates she was welcomed by the media. Press coverage of her trip included: Lorraine Moore, *Herald* Women's Editor, "Claresholm Mother Probes Status of Women: Continuing Education Vital Says Commission Member," *Lethbridge Herald*, 21 Oct. 1967, 20; (no byline), "Royal Commission on Status of Women: Representation from All Women Requested," *The Leader-Post*, Regina, 20 Oct. 1967; and (no byline), "Lola Lange: Woman's New Role," in the "Newsmaker" column, *Western Catholic Reporter*, 26 Oct. 1967; (no byline),"PM's Choice a Natural for the Job," *The Edmonton Journal*, 27 Feb. 27 1968, 18. On Commissioner Doris Ogilvie, see CP (Halifax), "Commission Will Help All Women," *The Ottawa Citizen*, 9 Mar. 1968. NAC MacGill Papers, Vol. 3, File 10, 7th Meeting of the Commissioners, Appendix "G," Report of the Public Relations and Press Officer, and reports from MacGill and Ogilvie. See also, NAC RCSW, Vol. 34, "Management Team, #1," File, Report from Doris Ogilvie to Commissioners and management team, 26 Jan. 1968.

76 Linda Curtis' column, *The Albertan*, Calgary, 29 Nov. 1967; Beth Raugust, *Herald* staff writer, "'Status of Women' Chairman Hopes To Breach Barriers," *The Calgary Herald*, 8 Dec. 1967; (no byline), "Barriers 'Prevent' Female Equality," *The Albertan*, Calgary, 6 Dec. 1967; and Lyn Schankerman, "Status Of Women Study Will Focus On the Young Says Mrs. John Bird," *Winnipeg Free Press*, 9 Dec. 1967.

77 Margaret Weiers, "The Forthright Woman Who Ran the Inquiry" *Toronto Daily Star*, 7 Dec. 1970, 49.

78 NAC RCSW, Vol. 35, "Public Hearings — Preparation" file. These remarks are also recorded on the audio tapes of the hearings, which are held in the NAC as part of the RCSW collection under acquisition number 1971-0016.

79 Ibid., "Public Hearings—Advertising and Publicity" file, Sandra Came, "A Plan For Press Relations—Working Paper 1," November 1967, 6. Freeman interview with Bird, 18 Nov. 1992.

80 No byline, "Queen Cover-Up Clarified," *The Calgary Herald*, 23 Apr. 1968, 1, 2; CP, "'Stupid Misunderstanding': Queen's Portrait Hidden for Women's Hearings," *The Montreal Star*, 24 Apr. 1968; (no byline) "Probe Follows After Royal Portrait Covered," *The Edmonton Journal*, 25 Apr. 1968, 1; Eva Reid, "Why no protests?" *The Albertan*, 26 Apr. 1968, 7. Editorial, "This Is Inexcusable," *The Calgary Herald*, 24 Apr. 1968, 4. NAC RCSW Vol. 31, File 10— Administration: Personnel (3) Letter from F. Bird to Mr. D Williams, Manager of the Palliser Hotel in Calgary; and Vol. 36, "Relations with Gov't—Privy Council Office" file, letters from Bird to Mrs. Isabelle Harland of Winnipeg, dated 14 May 1968, and from Bird to Leo Lafrance of the Privy Council Office with a copy of the question from Stanfield to Prime Minister Trudeau, 14 May 1968.

81 NAC RCSW, Vol. 35, "Public Hearings—Preparation" file, memo from Public Relations Officer (A. Burke) to the Executive Secretary (M. Bégin), 9 May 1968, "Report on Media Response on Western Hearings Tour." Burke felt, at the mid-way point in the hearings, that the coverage had improved. NAC RCSW, Vol. 35, "Public Relations—Report," Angela Burke, "Public Relations Report on Press Comment on the Commission," August 1968.

82 Ibid., "Public Hearings—Preparation" file, memo from Public Relations Officer (A. Burke) to the Executive Secretary (M. Bégin), May 9, 1968, "Report on Media Response on Western Hearings Tour." Memos between Bégin and Burke, 10 May 1968 and Burke to Frances Coté, 21 May 1968 in the same file. NAC RCSW, Vol. 31, File 5, "Administration: Budget estimates for the Commission (2)," and memo to the Executive Assistant, (M. Bégin) 26 July 1968 from Jocelyne Ellichuk. The Commission on Bilingualism and

Biculturalism had hired two journalists in the Parliamentary Press Gallery either to provide similar summaries or help write its report. NAC RCSW, Vol. 34, "Notes of Meetings with Mrs. Bird—Confidential," Notes on Meeting between Mrs. Bird and Miss Bégin, 19 July 1967, ref. 9.

83 NAC RCSW, Vol. 35, "Public Hearings Atlantic Provinces" file, letter from Jean Clavel, Vice-President, Public & Industrial Relations Limited, Montreal to M. Bégin, 29 May 1968.

84 CP, "Few Men Attending Commission Hearings," *The Ottawa Journal*, 20 Apr 1968. Margaret Weiers, "Status of Women Hearings Open Here Today," *Toronto Daily Star*, 3 June 1968, 49; Mary Bletcher, "Commission Chairman Sure Men Will Support Findings," *The Tribune*, Winnipeg, 29 May 1968, 30. Interview with Bird on "The Day It Is," 6 June 1968. Donna Flint, "Chairman Outlines Aims of Commission on Status of Women," *The Gazette*, Montreal, 10 Jan. 1968; (no byline), "Mrs. John Bird Seeks Men's Views," *The Telegram*, 20 Dec. 1967, and Alixe Carter, "Even Men Are Writing to Anne Francis," *The Ottawa Journal*, 9 Feb. 1968, 22. Commissioner MacGill also emphasized the need for male opinions. Kathrine Thomas, "To Hold Public Hearings on Status of Women: Commission Due Here in April," with a photo of "Miss Elsie MacGill and the caption, "hopes men will take an active part in the inquiry." *Victoria Daily Times*, 5 Dec. 1967, 19.

85 Rosemary Speirs, "Will This Woman Change Your Life?" *Chatelaine*, July 1969, 32, 52-53.

86 NAC RCSW, Vol. 38, 14th meeting of the Commissioners: minutes, reports and submissions, 30-31 Oct. 1968, Appendix "K," Report of the Chairman, items 4-7; NAC MacGill Papers, Vol. 4, File 5, 16th meeting of the Commission: Minutes, Reports and Submissions, 21-22 Jan. 1969, Appendix "C," Chairman's Report; File 6, 17th meeting of the Commission: Minutes, Reports and Submissions, 12-13 Feb. 1969, Appendix "H."

87 LaMarsh, *Memoirs of a Bird in a Gilded Cage*, 302. NAC MacGill Papers, Vol. 4, 20th Meeting of the Commissioners, 16-17 Apr. 1969, Report of the Chairman, 11 Apr. 1969. It appears that the CBC did not keep a copy of this edition of *Cross Country Checkup*.

88 Freeman interview with Bird; CP, "Anne Francis Denies Differences between Members: Commission on Status of Women Likely to Hand in Report by Spring of 1970, Its Chairman Says," *The Globe and Mail*, 6 Oct. 1969, 12. Press comment included editorial, "Expensive Commissions," *Port Arthur News Chronicle*, 29 Oct. 1969; (no byline) "Our Men in Ottawa," *The Vancouver Sun*, 6 Nov. 1969, 5; Richard Jackson, "Expensive Offices, 'Fat Cats' Mark Trudeau regime—MP," *The Ottawa Journal*, 28 Oct. 1969. Gordon Pape, "Are the Days of Royal Commissions Gone?" *Monetary Times*, Nov. 1969, 62.

89 NAC MacGill Papers, Vol. 4, File 5, 16th meeting of the Commission: Minutes, Reports and Submissions, 21-22 Jan. 1969, Appendix "C," Chairman's Report; File 6, 17th meeting of the Commission: Minutes, Reports and Submissions, 12-13 Feb. 1969, Appendix "H"; File 18, 29th meeting of the Commission: minutes, reports and submissions, 8-9 Oct. 1969, Minutes, 1-6, Appendix "CA," Report of the Chairman, and Appendix "D", Report of the Executive Secretary; File 20, 31st meeting of the Commission: minutes, reports and submissions, 22-24 Oct. 1969, memo to the Commissioners from the chairman, 14 Oct. 1969.

90 Ericson et al., *Negotiating Control*, 378.

Chapter 2

1 Christina Newman, "What's So Funny about the Royal Commission on the Status of Women?" *Saturday Night*, Jan. 1969, 21-24, citation from 21 and 22.

The absence of men at the hearings did not go unnoticed by other writers. See Pauline Jewett, "Where Were the Men When Canada Set Out to Find What Makes Life So Tough for Its Women?" *Maclean's*, Dec. 1968, 12. Wendy Dey, "The Silent Sex," *The Ottawa Citizen*, 5 Oct. 1968, 39. Frank Jones, "200 Women Talk about Equality—4 Men Listen," *Toronto Daily Star*, 2 Oct. 1968, 5, 72.

2 There appear to be no Canadian sociological studies of journalists before 1981. Even then, men outnumbered women 75 percent to 25 percent. Robinson, "Women Journalists in Canadian Dailies," 2-4; see also, Robinson "The Future of Women in the Canadian Media" According to a US study conducted in 1971, most American journalists and broadcasters were young, white, middle and upper-middle class men who outnumbered women 4 to 1 in the print media and about 9 to 1 in broadcasting. There was systemic wage discrimination against women in journalism, regardless of several mitigating factors. Johnstone, Slawski and Bowman, *The News People*.

3 Armstrong and Armstrong, *The Double Ghetto*, 131.

4 Haig, *Brave Harvest*.

5 On education, technology and the influence of advertisers on nineteenth-century newspapers, see Rutherford, *A Victorian Authority*. For an historical overview, see Lang, *Women Who Made the News*. Some women who made their livings from journalism, such as the CWPC's first president, Kathleen ("Kit") Blake Coleman of the Toronto *Mail*, shied away from becoming active participants in the fight for the vote. Others, such as Alice Freeman ("Faith Fenton") of the Toronto *Empire* and Cora Hind of the *Winnipeg Free Press*, did not. Freeman, *Kit's Kingdom*, especially Chapters 2 and 5; Downie, *A Passionate Pen*; Haig, *Brave Harvest*; Rex, *No Daughter of Mine*. On the early *Chatelaine*, see Sutherland, *The Monthly Epic*, 153-63. On women journalists during World War II, see Freeman, "Mother and Son"; Arnold, *One Woman's War*.

6 Crean, *Newsworthy*, Chapter 3. Kate Aitken's radio scripts for her women's programs are in NAC Kate Aitken Papers, MG 30 D 206, Finding Aid #1299. See also, for Abbie Lane, Public Archives of Nova Scotia (PANS) Film and Sound Division FSG1 CBHT Film Collection, S 2126, "Around Town with Abbie Lane, Monday Oct. 27, 1958; See also PANS Family Papers, Lane Collection, MG 1 Vols. 535-539. Freeman interviews with Bird; Creighton, formerly of the *Victoria Colonist*, *Victoria Daily Times* and *The London Free Press*; with Sharp Cochrane, formerly of *The Hamilton Spectator* and CP; and with Arnopoulos, formerly of *The Montreal Star*. See Bird, *Anne Francis*; Crean, *Newsworthy*, Chapters 2 and 3; Mott and Others, *New Survey of Journalism*, 133-137. On women in the post-war years, see Strong-Boag, "Their Side of the Story"; Sangster, "Doing Two Jobs"; Meyerowitz, *Not June Cleaver*; Spigel, *Make Room for TV*, especially Chapter 3, "Women's Work."

7 NAC CWPC, Vol. 22, File 32, Survey of Women's Page Trends, 12 Nov. 1969. See also, Vol. 32, *Newspacket*, No. 3, April 1970, 4, 5, 6. On the "nature vs. nurture" debate, see Armstrong and Armstrong, *The Double Ghetto*, Chapter 5. American women journalists had similar experiences and were also sympathetic to the women's movements of the time. See Barker-Plummer, "News as a Political Resource."

8 Kimmel, *Manhood in America: A Cultural History*, Chapter 8.

9 Repo, "End Women's Page," *Toronto Daily Star*, 11 June 1968.

10 Letter from Harold J. Levy under the heading "Unipaper?" *The Globe and Mail*, 2 Feb. 1970, 6.

11 Letter from Barbara M. Coutts of Toronto, under the heading "Unipaper?" *The Globe and Mail*, 16 Feb. 1970, 6.

12 Hackett and Zhao, *Sustaining Democracy?*, 54.

13 Schudson, *Discovering the News*, Introduction, and 184-186. See also Schiller, *Objectivity and the News;* Tuchman, *Making News*, Chapter 8.

14 Hackett and Zhao, *Sustaining Democracy?*, 1.

15 Ericson et al., *Visualizing Deviance*, 350-55. They discuss medium and genre at length in Ericson et al., *Representing Order*, Chapters 2 and 6.

16 *CP Style Book*, 1-2; Phelan, ed., *The Globe and Mail Style Book*, Introduction. Freeman interview with Sharp Cochrane, and with Stewart, former Bureau Chief at CP Montreal. On CP's standards, see *Report of The Special Senate Committee on Mass Media*, "The Uncertain Mirror," 229-35.

17 MacDougall, *Newsroom Problems and Policies*, Chapter 5, 169-201.

18 Steiner, "Construction of Gender in Newsreporting Textbooks," and "Body Language." On "objectivity" as an Aristotelian male construct, see Code, "Feminist Theory," and Baines, "Law, Gender, Equality" in Burt et al (eds.), *Changing Patterns*; also Creedon, "The Challenge of Revisioning Gender Values."

19 Johnstone et al., *The News People*, Chapter 7.

20 Sangster, "Telling Our Stories," 6.

21 Freeman interviews with Bird, Burke Kerrigan, Bégin, Henripin, Lange, Lapointe and Ogilvie.

22 Exceptions include Stone, "Getting the Message Out"; Ericson et al., *Visualizing Deviance*. American studies include Benedict, *Virgin or Vamp*; Tuchman, *Making News*.

23 The error is in Morris, "A Matter of Simple Justice," 223. Correct information from Freeman interviews with several journalists, as cited below. See also (no byline), "Star Women's Pages: They're for Every One," *En Ville*, Montreal, 29 Apr. 1968.

24 Freeman interview with Sharp Cochrane. Jean Sharp, "Women's Rights: Canadian Women Function under Diverse Provincial Legislation," *The Ottawa Journal*, 2 Feb. 1968, 24.

25 Quotes from Freeman interview with Speirs. An unnamed journalist from Victoria told Bird during a CWPC gathering in Toronto that the same kind of incident had happened to another woman when she was assigned to cover the BC legislature in Victoria. The men who started the petition in the gallery there were afraid that her presence would interfere with their "social life." NAC MacGill Papers Vol. 3, Minutes of the Fourth Meeting of the Commissioners, 29 August - 1 Sept. 1967, Appendix "D," Report of the Chairman, 14 Aug. 1967. One of the men Speirs considered supportive of her was William Stewart, who headed the Montreal bureau of CP in the 1960s. While he acknowledges that it is possible women were paid less than the men, he believes "the management wouldn't have stood for that" and reporters were paid according to their competence. He was "hostile" to the Guild and still does not want to talk about the unionization of the agency. He does not remember the deskmen's walkout but declares he would not have tolerated such rebellion against what was a management decision. Fraser MacDougall, who was Bureau Chief in Ottawa in 1968, said he came to appreciate women's talents when a couple of them worked at CP during the war. He also believed women and men were paid equally. Freeman interviews with Stewart and MacDougall.

26 Copy boys were the "go-fers" of the newsroom. Her Master's degree apparently meant little; she had no experience as a journalist when she was hired. Freeman interview with Reading.

27 Freeman interview with Arnopoulos. (No byline), "Star Women's Pages: They're for Every One," *En Ville*, Montreal, 29 Apr. 1968. Arnopoulos' pre-hearing stories included "Royal Commission on Status of Women: Mrs. Bird

Appeals for More Briefs from Canadian Women," *The Montreal Star*, 10 Jan. 1968; "Women Given a Real Chance to Air 'Beefs'," *The Montreal Star*, 7 Feb. 1968; and "Commission Suggests Topics to Use in Preparing Briefs," *The Montreal Star*, 8 Feb. 1968.

28 Freeman interview with Weiers. The Commission's Public Relations Officer, Angela Burke, thought the survey idea came from the *Star's* city editor, the late Martin Goodman, but archival documents suggest that it came from Burke herself. NAC RCSW, Vol. 1, SW -1-5-2-3, Burke to Martin Goodman, 15 Feb. 1968 and Burke to Weiers, who sent her a copy of it, 6 Mar. 1968. Freeman interview with Burke Kerrigan. See Margaret Weiers, "Here's Your Chance Men! Where Is a Woman's Place?" *Toronto Daily Star*, 4 Mar. 1968, 47; Weiers, "The Status of Women: What the Men Say," *Toronto Daily Star*, 26 Mar. 1968, section 4, p. 51 and, under headline "In 1968, Most Men Still Believe a Woman's Place Is in the Home," 52, with a photo of Weiers at her desk with the replies, which, the caption said, were sent on to the Commission. On Weier's pro-union stance, see NAC CWPC, Vol. 32, Margaret Weiers, "Unions and Equal Pay," *Newspacket*, Vol. 32, No. 1, October 1969, 4, 5.

29 Freeman interview with Crittenden.

30 Freeman interview with Siggins

31 Ibid. Others who commented on the educational division included Eleanor Dunn of The Ottawa Citizen and Gail Scott of CBC news. Freeman interviews with Dunn and Scott. See *Report of the Special Senate Committee on Mass Media*, Vol. 1, "The Uncertain Mirror," 125-30.

32 Freeman interview with Dunn. Eleanor S. Dunn, "Royal Commission Welcome," *The Ottawa Times Weekly*, 8 Feb. 1967, 1, 5.

33 Ibid. Eleanor Dunn, "Status Seekers Set to Make Case," *The Saturday Citizen*, 28 Sept. 1968, 35.

34 Ibid. Eleanor Dunn, curriculum vitae; NAC RCSW, Vol. 11, Brief No 55. Her brief, and comments made by the CWPC under questioning from the commissioners, were covered under Rosemary Speirs, "Women's Press Club Brief On Inequalities in Pay," *St. Catharines Standard*, 2 Oct. 1968. Dunn's newspaper covered her brief and that of the CWPC but did not include any comments made about the journalists' working conditions. Shirley Foley, "Status Is a Full Time Job," *The Ottawa Citizen*, 2 Oct. 1968, 32. Dunn also wrote as Louisa T. Katspaugh, "Hearings Over, Work Begins," *Southeaster Times*, Ottawa, 9 Oct. 1968. Freeman phone calls with Dunn, 11 and 12 June 1996.

35 NAC RCSW, audio tape #9998, Ottawa. On the Guild response to Dunn's brief, see CP (Toronto), "Union Denies Remarks," *The Ottawa Journal*, 3 Oct. 1968.

36 Special Senate Committee on the Mass Media, Brief No. 7. See (no byline), "Senate Committee Hears Newspaper Woman's Brief," *The Ottawa Journal*, 9 Apr. 1970.

37 Freeman interview with Dunn.

38 NAC CWPC, Vol. 18, Letters concerning 1964 CWPC survey from Jean Danard to Mrs. H. M. Roney of the RCSW, 15 Mar. 1967, offering the results of the 1964 survey; Mark McClung to Danard, 30 June 1967, saying the RCSW would pay $2,000 for the survey data to be analyzed; Vol. 3, File S-W-3, letter from Danard to Mark McClung, 5 July 1967, and the Press Club survey. Correspondence between Bird and various journalists are filed in NAC MacGill Papers, Vol. 3, Minutes of the Fourth Meeting of the Commissioners, 29 Aug. - 1 Sept. 1967, Appendix D, Report of the Chairman, 14 Aug. 1967. NAC RCSW, Vol. 1, File SW 1-5-2-3, letter from Marjorie McEnaney to Bird, 2 Nov 1967 and an acknowledgment from M. Coupal to McEnaney, 13 Dec 1967; Elva Fletcher of the national CWPC to Bird, 28 Apr. 1967, and Bird's reply, 7

May 1967; A. Burke to Fletcher, 26 Feb. 1968; Jenkins to Bird, 2 May 1967 and Bird to Jenkins, 12 May 1967. In 1969, the Economic Council of Canada placed the poverty line at $1,800 a year for a single person; $3,000 for a family of two; $3,600 for a family of three; $4,200 for a family of four, and $4,800 for a family of five. NAC RCSW Vol.34, Maynard File. For a discussion of women and the workforce see Armstrong and Armstrong, *The Double Ghetto,* Chapter 2; *Report of the Royal Commission,* Chapter 2; Kinnear, *In Subordination,* Chapter 1.

39 NAC CWPC, Vol. 18, File 18-14, "Royal Commission on the Status of Women: Correspondence Re: Brief 1967-73," Brief #328; RCSW audio tape #9998, Ottawa; CP, "Women Journalists Attack Pay Rates," *The Telegram,* Toronto, 2 Oct. 1968, 67; CP, "Women Reporters' Pay Rates Bring Collusion, Brief says," *Toronto Daily Star,* 2 Oct. 1968, 72. *Report of the Royal Commission,* 25-28.

40 *Report of the Special Senate Committee on Mass Media,* Vol. II, 212, 214-15, Table 71; broadcast statistics, 304-14. Freeman interviews with Crittenden and Weiers, among others. In 1970 in the United States, the average wage for any American male journalist was $11,955, which was $4,221 higher than the average salary for a woman journalist. The authors conclude that, even with other factors taken into consideration, the lower salaries for the women were due to gender discrimination, the gap between the sexes becoming worse, not better, as the woman aged. Johnstone et al., *The News People,* Chapter 8, especially 131-39, and Table 8.3, p. 236. The minimum yearly wage for a unionized journalist at the *New York Times* in 1946 was $3,200, about the same as the lowest paid female journalist was making in Canada almost 20 years later. (Annunziatio, "Collective Bargaining," 81.)

41 NAC, Marjorie McEnaney Papers, MG 30 E 342, Vols. 1-3. NAC Bird Papers, Vol. 5, File 5-21, Brief #94; Toronto Branch—Canadian Women's Press Club.

42 Rosemary Speirs, "Top Perch Out for Newshens," *The Province,* Vancouver, 8 June 1968.

43 Quotes from Freeman interview with Anderson; see also, Anderson, *Rebel Daughter;* Crean, *Newsworthy* 293-301. On *Chatelaine* and women's issues, see Wilson, "The Relationship between Mass Media Content and Social Change," Chapter 7. Friedan wrote, however, that American women's magazines were noting discontent among middle-class suburbanites as early as 1960. Friedan, *The Feminine Mystique,* 66. For a further discussion of Anderson's approach to Chatelaine and its content, see Korinek, "Roughing It in Suburbia," and Sutherland, *The Monthly Epic,* 243-55. Davey gave the magazine's circulation figures a mixed review. Davey, "The Uncertain Mirror," 156-58. Editorials include Doris Anderson, "Let's Find Out What's Happening to Women," *Chatelaine,* July 1966, 1, and "Can We Make This Royal Commission Count?" *Chatelaine,* Mar. 1968, 1.

44 NAC RCSW, Vol. 36, File marked "Relations with Participants— Miscellaneous—1, letter from F. Bird to Doris Anderson, 14 Dec. 1967 and Anderson's reply, 20 Dec. 1967; Jean Y. Wright, Managing Editor to Bird, 22 Dec. 1967 and 23 Jan. 1968, and Bird to Wright, 8 Dec. 1967. See also NAC MacGill Papers, Vol. 6, Third Meeting of the Commissioners, 24-26 May 1967, memo dated 11 May 1967 from Bird to the commissioners, suggesting that Anderson be among several people asked to meet privately with them. It is not clear if a meeting followed. NAC RCSW, Vol. 1, File SW 1-1-2: "Correspondence with Commissioners," and File SW 1-5-2-3- (#3), a note to the effect that Donna Hinchey, Personnel Manager of the Maclean Hunter Publishing Company, *Chatelaine*'s parent company, was one of those women who took part in a Commission-sponsored seminar on women and work.

45 Freeman interview with Gillen and a letter to Freeman from Gillen, 26 Oct. 1995. See Gillen, "The Royal Commission on the Status of Women: Will It Do

Any Good?" *Chatelaine*, Jan. 1968, 21-23, 60-62 which includes the survey questions. Gillen, "Report: What You Think of Women's Status," *Chatelaine*, June 1968, 30, 76, 80, 82. The Chatelaine survey results were presented as Commission brief #346 and covered in the press. Rosemary Speirs, "Quebec Women Head List as Feminists," *The Ottawa Journal*, 3 June 1968, 19. Speirs also wrote an article about Bird and the Commission after the hearings. See Speirs, "Will This Woman Change Your Life?" *Chatelaine*, July 1969.

46 Freeman interview with Bird.

47 CWPC Toronto Branch, Brief #94.

48 Rutherford, *When Television Was Young* Chapter 11. Schudson, *Discovering the News*, Chapter 5. Freeman interview with Sarty.

49 NAC RCSW, Vol. 1, Script for Twenty Million Questions, CBC Program No. 151-5153-0137, 19 Jan. 1967. The continuity script, but not necessarily the dialogue, was written by Edmund Reid, the same Reid who later covered the Commission hearings for *Take 30* and *CBC Matinee*. According to the script, a "Bird animation," or cartoon, which was one of Reid's specialities, opened the program, along with a song concerning suffragettes. See also, Charles Lynch, "Les Girls on the March," *The Ottawa Citizen*, 4 Feb. 1967.

50 Taylor, "Window on the World," and Crean, Chapter 4. See also NAC RCSW, Vol. 34, file marked "Notes of Meetings with Mrs. Bird—Confidential," notes on a meeting with Mrs. Bird, dated 19 June 1967, Item #4. See also NAC MacGill Papers, Vol. 6, Third Meeting of the Commissioners, 24-26 May 1967, memo dated 11 May 1967 from Bird to the Commissioners. NAC RCSW, Vol. 1, File SW 1-1-2, "Correspondence with Commissioners." The meeting between Bird and the four unnamed, former CBC employees is mentioned in NAC MacGill Papers, Vol. 3, Minutes of the Fourth Meeting of the Commissioners, 29 Aug.—1 Sept. 1967, Appendix F, undated memorandum from the Chairman to the Commissioners. Also, NAC RCSW, Vol. 31, File 5, "Administration: Budget estimates for the Commission (2)." Draft of "Introduction to the Commission's Requisition for Budget 1968-69—Labour," a notation that read "promotion: a case study (C.B.C.)." Freeman interview with Bird. The CBC study was a response to the general recommendations made by the Royal Commission and was collated from May to September 1974. *See Women in the CBC: Report of The CBC Task Force on the Status of Women.*

51 Freeman interview with Higgins McIntosh.

52 Freeman interview with Robb, Toronto, May 17, 1993.

53 The CBC's *Journalistic Policy* of 1982 noted that the duty of all broadcasters to provide fair and balanced coverage was entrenched in the Broadcasting Act of 1968, and was a matter of policy within the CBC. *Journalistic Policy* and the *CBC News Style Book*, 24-25, 31.

54 Freeman interview with Sarty. Clarkson remembers that the co-hosts did not travel during the on-air season. Even today, Sarty and the show's male co-host, Paul Soles, remember the *Take 30* audience as almost equally male and female, whereas Robb and the female co-host, Clarkson perceive the audience primarily as intelligent women who worked in the home. Freeman interviews with Clarkson, Soles, Sarty and Robb. See also Crean, 183-85.

55 Freeman interview with Soles.

56 (No byline), "CBC Is Accused of Bias on Women Executives," *The Globe and Mail*, 7 June 1968, 13.

57 NAC RCSW, Vol. 2, File SW 1-7-1, Dodi Robb to Florence Bird, 14 Mar. 1968; Freeman interviews with Robb and Soles.

58 Ed Reid's resumé is in the Reid Private Collection. Reid was the son of a church minister and a nephew of Escott Reid, the "radical mandarin" of the federal civil service. He died after being struck by a bus in Honduras, where he was

working as a volunteer helping poor street children. See the tribute to him on *Take 30* Master Tape #16655, 14 Mar. 1977. Freeman interviews with Soles, Sarty, Robb, Patterson, Clarkson, Bird and Speirs. I also spoke to his two brothers and sisters-in-law in Toronto and to Jean Bruce, a friend and colleague. The family and Bruce interviews were not taped at the request of the participants.

59 The Reid cartoon first aired on *Take 30*, 22 Apr. 1968, RCSW hearings in BC

60 Reid Private Collection, Jim Millican interview with Ed Reid, CFWH Whitehorse, Yukon, 7 Aug. 1968. I am indebted to Reid's family for lending me this tape.

61 *CBC Matinee*, RCSW hearings in Montreal and Quebec City.

62 *CBC Matinee*, RCSW hearings in Ottawa.

63 Freeman interview with Bird and telephone conversation with her, 14 July 1994.

64 We did not discuss racial prejudice, except in general terms. Robb recalls seeing a few racist letters from viewers directed at Clarkson, which she locked in her office drawer, rather than show to her. Clarkson, who was considered a glamorous figure, was also occasionally described as "inscrutable" in the media (Freeman interviews with Robb; Crean: on Clarkson, *Newsworthy*, Chapter 5, 178-92; and a younger colleague's recollections of her support, 216. Freeman interview with Clarkson. *Take 30*, 12 Mar. 1968, Clarkson interview with Bird; 22 Oct. 1970 with Friedan.

65 Freeman interview with Patterson.

66 NAC RCSW, Vol. 35, "Public Relations—Press Radio, TV, etc." file. NAC RCSW, Vol. 1, File 1-5-2-3, Letters from Burke to two of the commentators, 22 Feb. 1968. See also NAC MacGill Papers Vol. 3, Minutes of the Fourth Meeting of the Commissioners, 29 Aug. - 1 Sept. 1967, Appendix "G," memo from Bird to the Commissioners, 26 June 1967; Appendix "D," Report of the Chairman, 14 Aug. 1967. Robb has only a vague memory of such a meeting Freeman interview with Robb. Robb later confirmed that she received budget approval for the western hearings and the national ones in Ottawa while the rest were still tentative. In the end, they were all covered. NAC RCSW, Vol. 2, File SW 1-7-1, Robb to Bird, 14 Mar. 1968. In the North, Kay Vaydik, a CBC broadcaster in Yellowknife, spoke to them about local conditions and also showed them around and introduced them to people, NAC RCSW, Vol. 35, Notes from Kay Vaydik; Burke to Kay Vaydik, 16 July 1968 and undated note from Bird to Vaydik. Bird was hoping other reporters would present briefs, a suggestion from Burke, although it was unusual. NAC RCSW Vol. 35, Bird to Bégin, 3 July 1968. The session with Lange was taped but the record does not appear to have survived. NAC RCSW, Vol. 35, Minutes of the Seventh Meeting of the Commissioners, 15-16 Feb. 1967, Lola Lange, Report on Activity, Feb. 1968. NAC RCSW Vol. 1, File SW 1-5-2-3- (#3), thank-you letter from Dorothy Cadwell, Research Co-Ordinator to Miss Betty Zimmerman, Director of Overseas and Foreign Relations, CBC, Ottawa, 25 Mar. 1968.

67 My emphases. *CBC Matinee*, 2 May 1968, RCSW hearings in Saskatoon. The other reporters who spoke with Bird were not named. NAC RCSW, Vol. 35, Bird to Bégin, 3 July 1968.

68 Freeman interview with Bird.

69 *CBC Matinee*, 7 June 1968, RCSW hearings in Toronto.

70 *CBC Matinee*, 20 Sept. 1968, RCSW hearings from the Atlantic provinces; *Take 30*, RCSW hearings in the Atlantic provinces. The entire exchange was recorded on NAC RCSW audio tape #9991, Charlottetown hearing; Freeman interview with Patterson.

71 Freeman interview with Earle, Ottawa, 8 May 1996. Earle's comments match the CBC's policy on news analysis, which was discussed in its brief to the

Special Senate Committee on the Mass Media, 1970, and reproduced in the *CBC News Style Book*, 28-29. Commentary by Frank Tumpane, CBC Radio News, *The World at Six*, 3 Feb. 1967. See also Frank Tumpane, Toronto Telegram News Service, "Equality's Great—Er, I Think It Is," *The Yukon News*, 10 Feb. 1967.

72 Freeman interview with Scott. Crean, *Newsworthy*, 208-210, 229. Journalist Frank Daley interviewed, for the inquiry, other women in local TV in Ottawa, who complained that they were expected to be "kooks" and "sex bombs," but also admitted they were biased against women bosses. NAC RCSW, Vol. 19, Daley report. It was critiqued in "Report of the Commission Editorial Staff—Sandra Gwynn" in NAC RCSW, Vol. 37.

73 The response rate was 25% for newspapers, 30% for broadcast outlets and just under 50% for periodicals. Frederick Elkin, "Family Life Education in the Media of Mass Communication;" NAC Vanier Institute of the Family, MG 28 I Vol. 117, Box 20, "Learning for Family Living Project." See also Hilda Kearns, "Media Survey Takes Conservative Stand on Family Life," *The Montreal Star*, 19 Feb. 1971. Supportive comments from male journalists on equal rights for women included Marshall Wilson, "Our Women Fight for Sex Equality," *The Vancouver Sun*, 20 Apr. 1968, 11.

74 Freeman interview with Burke Kerrigan. NAC RCSW, Vol. 1, File SW 1-5-1-2 Press Conference, Angela Burke to John Morgan, editor of *The Montrealer*, 3 Jan 1968 and John Scott, Editor, *Time* magazine, Montreal office, 4 Jan. 1968.

75 Freeman interviews with Burke Kerrigan and Westell.

76 George Bain, "The Battle of the Sexes," *The Globe and Mail*, 6 Feb. 1967. Tim Creery, "Quebec Not Expected to Cede Hemline of Rights over Women," *The Ottawa Citizen*, 6 Feb. 1967, 19. The script of the commentary, dated 5 Feb. 1967, was sent to the Commission by Fran Cutler, a CBC producer and colleague of Bird. Letter of thanks from Bird to Cutler, 13 Mar. 1967. Both letter and script are in NAC RCSW, Vol. 1, File SW 1-5-2-3. On the omnibus bill, see Kinsman, *The Regulation of Desire*, Chapter 9.

77 Editorial, "Women in Bunches," *The Ottawa Journal*, 4 Feb. 1967. Eric Nicol, "Committee for Birds," *Kingston Whig-Standard*, 21 Feb. 1967, and his "Design for Living" column, *The Province*, Vancouver, 20 Apr. 1968, 27.

78 (No byline), "Hearings on Status of Women to Begin on April 15 in BC," *The Globe and Mail*, 21 Oct. 1967, 15. George Bain, "The Ladies, Bless 'Em," *The Globe and Mail*, 3 May 1968, 6. The brief was covered under CP, "Status of Women: Ban on Child Marriages Advocated," *The Ottawa Citizen*, 1 May 1968.

79 Freeman interviews with Becker and Speirs.

80 Freeman interview with Westell.

81 Freeman interview with Earle.

82 CBC Kine Collection, *Weekend*, 24 Jan. 1970. At the time, these men were colleagues of the author.

83 United Press International (UPI), "Ladies Win at National Press Club," *Toronto Daily Star*, 4 May 1970, 23. See also (no byline), "Press Club Condemned by Guild," *The Ottawa Citizen*, 26 Jan. 1970, 2; George Bain, "Four Nasty Notes," *The Globe and Mail*, 27 Jan. 1970, 6; Editorial, "On the Status of Canadian Women," *St. Thomas Times Journal*, Ontario, 12 Feb. 1970, reprinted from *The Telegram*, Toronto; a comparative reference to the press club in Mary Bletcher, "Secretaries Beat Sex Discrimination," *The Tribune*, Winnipeg, 11 Feb. 1970; Gerald Waring, "Gerald Waring Reports," *Sault Ste. Marie Star*, 24 Feb. 1970. Freeman interviews with Dunn, Westell and Becker Davidson.

84 Alice [sic?] Carter, "Ottawa War Report on the Battle of the Sexes," CWPC *Newspacket*, April 1970, 5,6. Copy in NAC CWPC Vol. 32, File 5. Judging by her writing style, I believe the author was Alixe Carter of *The Ottawa Journal*.

85 Freeman interviews with Scott and Westell.
86 NAC CWPC, Vols. 32 and 33, *Newspackets* record some of the name change debate.
87 Ericson et al., *Representing Order*, Conclusion; Hackett and Zhao, *Sustaining Democracy?*, Chapter 1.

Chapter 3

1 NAC RCSW, Vol. 17, Bonnie Kreps, Brief #373, 4.
2 Media coverage included a few paragraphs in a summary of the day's proceedings by Margaret Weiers, "Urge Dental Care in Medicare," *Toronto Daily Star*, 7 June 1968, 61; Leone Kirkwood, "Social disgrace to be single, commission told: Woman 'Expected to Act like Cinderella Waiting for Prince,'" *The Globe and Mail*, 7 June 1968, 13; and (no byline), "Cinderella May Not Dig Her Role," *The Telegram*, Toronto, 7 June 1968.
3 On the WLM, see Adamson, "Feminists, Libbers, Lefties and Radicals"; also Maggie Siggins, "The Feminists," *The Telegram*, Toronto, 5 Sept. 1969; Margaret Penman, "The Feminists Go Marching On," *The Montreal Star*, 8 May 1970, 23-24.
4 Bonnie Kreps, Brief #373.
5 The focus of the article shifted to the husband as Kirkwood wanted to know what it was like to live with a woman who believed in sexual equality. The answer was in the headline. Leone Kirkwood, "Attitude Changed after Marriage: Physics Professor Believes in Equality in the Kitchen," *The Globe and Mail*, 10 June 1968.
6 Tuchman, "The Symbolic Annihilation of Women" in Tuchman et al. (eds.), *Health and Home* and *Making News*, Chapter 7; Douglas, *Where the Girls Are*, 10.
7 Collette Charisse, "Portrayal of Women by the Mass Media" as cited in *Report of the Royal Commission*, 15.
8 (No byline), photos by Bruce Moss, "They Laugh When I Talk about My Seaweed," *Weekend*, No. 16, 1968, 68-70.
9 NAC RCSW, Vol. 9, "Letters of Opinion—Ontario," letter from Mrs. M.L. Boddy, n.d.
10 *Report of the Royal Commission*, 14-15; There are several examples in NAC RCSW, Vol. 7, "Letters of Opinion—B.C.—Folder 2"; Vol. 8, "Letters of Opinion—Sask."; "Letters of Opinion—Ontario, Folder 1"; Vol. 9, "Letters of Opinion—Quebec"; Vol. 36, File marked "Relations with Participants—Miscellaneous 2." Rutherford, *When Television Was Young*, Chapter 9. Macdonald, *Representing Women*, Chapter 3.
11 *Ibid.*, 3.
12 Ericson et al., *Visualizing Deviance*, 356. Also, Bird and Dardenne, "Myth, Chronicle and Story," 81; van Dijk, *News as Discourse*, 86, 122-23.
13 Macdonald, *Representing Women*, 4. Molotch, "The News of Women and the Work of Men."
14 Brownmiller, *Femininity*, 16. On the media construction of Canada's female politicians, which illustrates some of these points, see Robinson and Saint-Jean, "The Portrait of Women Politicians in One Media."
15 Examples include Marilyn Argue (CP), "Inquiry Head Anne Francis Never Met Discrimination," *Winnipeg Free Press*, 3 Feb. 1967, 22. Rosemary Speirs, "Girl Power: The Hand That Rocks the Cradle Would Prefer to Rule the World," *Toronto Life*, Aug. 1968, 42. CP (no byline), "Status Probe Set," *Winnipeg Free Press*, 3 Feb. 1967, 1.
16 Alan Edmonds, "Equality: Are Women Winning It?—Cheer Up, Girls, Help Is on the Way," *Maclean's*, Jan. 1968, 9-11, 52, 56.

17 For example, Clarkson interview with Bird, *Take 30*, 12 Mar., 1968.

18 For example, flattering photos of Bird, one by Malak, appeared in the *Toronto Daily Star*, 21 June and 4 Dec. 1967, and 10 July 1970.

19 For example, a photo by R. Olsen, *Toronto Daily Star*, 19 Dec. 1967 and 20 Jan. 1971. See also the photos with Edna Hampton, "Feeling of Hope Outweighs Anger, Commission Chairman Tells Press, "*The Globe and Mail*, 8 Dec. 1970, 10; Ben Tierney, "'Report on Women Vital to Both Sexes,'" *The Edmonton Journal*, 8 Dec. 1970, 1, and several CP versions including CP, "Inquiry Chairman Says Report Marks Career High Point," *The London Free Press*, 8 Dec. 1970, 48.

20 Alixe Carter, "Meet the Status of Women Commissioners," series, all in *The Ottawa Journal*: "Jeanne Lapointe," 28 Feb. 1968, 48; "Jacques Henripin," 6 Mar. 1968, 34; "Doris Ogilvie," 1 Mar. 1968, 26; "Elsie Gregory MacGill," 8 Mar. 1968, 23; "Lola Mary Smith Lange," 26 Feb. 1968, 18; "John P. Humphrey," 11 Mar. 1968, 18.

21 Speirs, "Girl Power," *Toronto Life*, Aug. 1968, 43.

22 Ashley and Olson, "Constructing Reality," 264.

23 Barker-Plummer, "News As a Political Resource."

24 Code, "The Tyranny of Stereotypes," 196.

25 Ibid., 197.

26 van Dijk, *News as Discourse*, 110. Graham Murdock discusses labelling in another context in "Political Deviance: the Press Presentation of a Militant Mass Demonstration," in Cohen and Young, *The Manufacture of News*, 156-75.

27 Barry Craig, "Women's March May Back Call for Rights Probe," *Globe and Mail*, 5 Jan. 1967, 1; CP ON, "Biological Beat of Bed, Board, Babies Attacked by Vocal Canadian Feminist," *The Montreal Star*, 14 Mar. 1967. Sabia twice ran for public office in 1968. See "Sabia Blames Religion for 'Passive Women,'" *Telegram*, Toronto, 11 June 1968; Margaret Weiers, "Next House Could Boast Even Fewer Women than Last," *Toronto Daily Star*, 21 Feb. 1968; John Sharp, "Feminist Will Need Male Help to Win Mayoralty," *The Telegram*, Toronto, 7 Nov. 1968, 58; Mary Jane Charters, "Laura Sabia Wants 'a Mass Injection' of Women into Public Life, Social Structure of Canada," *London Free Press*, Ontario, 6 Nov. 1968, 38.

28 See the chapter on "Voice" in Brownmiller, *Femininity*, especially 124. For example, a photo of Sabia with her mouth open and the caption which reads "Feminist, Laura Sabia. She's putting money where mouth is." (No byline), "Equality Champion Laura Sabia Seeks Seat in Parliament," *Toronto Daily Star*, 7 May 1968.

29 Freeman interview with Weiers.

30 Ken Clark (CP), "Watchdogs Ready to Pounce on Investigation Commission," *The Ottawa Journal*, 17 Feb. 1967, 24. Published as "Watchdogs All over the Place: Militant Group to Keep Track of Status of Women Study," *The Globe and Mail*, 17 Feb. 1967, 11.

31 Lorraine Shore, "Probe into Status of Women Hears UBC Co-ed Complain of Sex Barrier," *The Vancouver Sun*, 19 Apr. 1968.

32 CP (no byline), "War between Sexes Goes Public: Men Main Target of Commission on Women," *The Calgary Herald*, 22 Apr. 1968, 11.

33 The older woman figure may have represented an Iron Maiden, which was a medieval instrument of torture. Certainly, it signalled an outdated image of women. Another version which suggested that it represented the Commission itself was reproduced in *CBC Times*, Toronto, 25-31 Mar. 1967, 3.

34 CBC *Newsmagazine*, 28 Mar. 1967 is in the CBC TV Archives in Toronto. Stills of the woman cartoon were used to advertise the program. See *CBC Times*,

Toronto, 25-31 Mar. 1967, 3. Some newspapers ran it with their TV listings, for example, the *Moose Jaw Times-Herald*, Saskatchewan, 25 Mar. 1967.

35 NAC RCSW, Vol. 1, File SW 1-1-1: "Miscellaneous," Florence Bird to Helen Tucker of Toronto, 19 Apr. 1967 and to Mrs. A. Peltier of Edmonton, 14 April 1967; Maggie Magee of Toronto to *Newsmagazine* and copied to Bird, 28 Mar. 1967; George W. Cadbury of Toronto to *Newsmagazine* and copied to Bird, 6 Apr. 1967. See also the letters to the editor from (Mrs.) D. Chalmers, Owen Sound, Ont., and Cecelia Wallace, Toronto, under "Status of Women," *The Globe and Mail*, 10 Apr. 1967. Wallace, who was a member of the CEWC, castigated the CBC for its snide approach. Nancy Millar, "a woman's whirl," *The Advocate*, Red Deer, Alberta, 1 Apr. 1967. Other editorials, pro and con, appeared in (untitled comment), *The Albertan*, Calgary, 1 Apr. 1967 and (no byline), "Contemporary Women," *Elora Express*, Ontario, 6 April 1967. Later Don Newnham of *The Montreal Star* praised Bird's adept handling of Pierre Berton, who asked her frivolous questions on his program on CTV that Newnham said he would never have asked of a man. Don Newnham, "Baffled Berton Meets His Match," *The Montreal Star*, 12 Apr. 1967. In another article, the writer quoted Bird as saying, "I think that some of the people who have written rather stupid editorials are just born old." Bruce Phillips, Southam News Service, "Love is Great but It Isn't Enough, Says New Commissioner," *The Ottawa Citizen*, 29 Mar. 1967, 49.

36 "The Way It Is," 21 Apr. 1968. NAC RCSW, Vol. 1, File SW 1-5-2-3- (#3), Angela Burke to Ted Kotcheff, story editor for "The Way It Is," 30 Apr. 1968.

37 Mackenzie Porter, "Women Shall Remain Women, and That's That," *The Telegram*, Toronto, 2 Oct. 1968.

38 Speirs, "Girl Power," *Toronto Life*, Aug. 1968, 42-44.

39 Speirs (CP), "Ladies Reminded They're Women," *The Vancouver Sun*, 25 Apr. 1968, 47. This article appeared as "Femininity Plea," *The Leader-Post*, Regina, 25 Apr. 1968; and as "Married Women Told to 'Rely on Female Instincts,'" *The Ottawa Journal*, 25 Apr. 1968, among others. Anderson sounded as if she was talking down to her audience. RCSW audio tape #9915, Edmonton, 25 Apr. 1968.

40 *CBC Matinee*, 25 Apr., 1968.

41 *CBC Matinee*, 26 Apr., 1968.

42 Lorna Wright, "She's a 'Man's Woman'," *The Edmonton Journal*, 25 Apr. 1968, 1.

43 (No byline), "Officer Looked Chic," *The Ottawa Journal*, 2 Oct. 1968, 41. The fashion item and photo were on the same page as several, more detailed articles about other briefs presented at the hearings.

44 CP (no byline), "Forceful Law to End Sex Bias in Employment Urged by CLC," *The Globe and Mail*, 2 Oct. 1968, 9; Staff (no byline), "CLC Asks Fair Deal for Women," *The Telegram*, Toronto, 1 Oct. 1968. The *Citizen* took a different angle on the CLC brief. Eleanor Dunn, "Status of Women: Working Mother May Aid Child," *The Ottawa Citizen*, 2 Oct. 1968, 39. *Take 30*, 8 Oct. 1968 and *Matinee*, 4 Oct. 1968, RCSW hearings in Ottawa.

45 Rosemary Speirs, "'Stop Hiding Behind Skirts': Women Must Adjust Status Views, Commission Is Told," *Globe and Mail*, 23 Apr. 1968, 11. The photo accompanied Speirs, "Girl Power," *Toronto Life*, August 1968, 44. The same photo, but with captions that did not refer to her physical appearance, was published in some newspapers when the hearings began in April. See, for example, the *Charlottetown Guardian*, Prince Edward Island, 15 Apr. 1968, and the *Daily Gleaner*, Fredericton, 18 Apr. 1968.

46 Freeman interview with Reading.

47 Carrie M. Best, "Human Rights: Status of Women," *Pictou Advocate*, 19 Sept. 1968. McKim was castigating herself for not speaking out at a similar forum,

the Hellyer inquiry on housing. Eleanor McKim, "Frankly Speaking" column, *Evening Telegram*, St. John's, 29 Nov. 1968. It was her daughter Mary McKim, also a journalist, who covered the Status of Women hearings in St. John's for the *Telegram* in September 1968. It was Mary's first news assignment, which she says she was told to do because, in the words of her male editor, "you're a woman." Conversation, which was not taped, between the author and Mary McKim at the Women in the Media conference, Canadian Association of Journalists, Halifax, NS, 12 Nov. 1994.

48 CP (no byline), "Women Must Adjust Views, Hearing Told," *The Globe and Mail*, 23 Apr. 1968, 11. Speirs, "Girl Power," *Toronto Life*, August 68, 44.

49 (No byline), "Women Charge College Discrimination," *The Ottawa Citizen*, 4 Oct. 1968. CP (no byline) "Negro Journalist Lectures Women's Commission In N.S.," *Telegraph-Journal*, St. John, 13 Sept. 1968. *The Ottawa Journal* mentioned her intervention from the floor in Ottawa but gave no details of what she said. "Carrie Best's Moving Tribute," *The Ottawa Journal*, 4 Oct. 1968. It was not covered in the *Citizen* or by the CBC. Although she was usually outspoken she wrote in one column that she sometimes used the soft-spoken, philosophical approach strategically against intolerance. Best, *That Lonesome Road*, 71-72, and her columns in the *Pictou Advocate*, 19 Sept. 1968, section 1, p. 8; 12 Dec. 1968, 5 and 28 Dec. 1968, 7. She stated her case on race relations strongly in one interview I have heard. Public Archives of Nova Scotia, Ar. 2265-2268, 2279, interview with Carrie M. Best recorded c.1970. On depictions of Black women in the media, see Houston, "The Politics of Difference," 49.

50 CP "Sterilize 'Unready' Males at 16, Woman Doctor Urges," *Toronto Daily Star*, 18 Apr. 1968, 1.

51 (No byline), "Woman's Plea to Women's Probe: Sterilize All Young Men," *The Vancouver Sun*, 18 Apr. 1968, 1; CP, "Compulsory Vasectomies at 16 Advocated by Feminist Sociologist," *The Globe and Mail*, 19 Apr. 1968, 9.

52 RCSW audio tape #9908, Brief #113.

53 (No byline), "Teaching Nuns Seek Govt Aid for Feminist Groups," *Quebec Chronicle Telegraph*, 11 June 1968.

54 Gorham, "English Militancy and the Canadian Suffrage Movement"; Freeman, *Kit's Kingdom*, Chapter 5; Errington, "Pioneers and Suffragists." On journalists and "timeliness," see Schudson, "Deadlines, Datelines and History."

55 Marilyn Anderson, "The Fight for Women's Rights," *Niagara Falls Review*, 19 Oct. 1968.

56 Elizabeth Thompson's column, "Ashamed of Briefs to Commission," *The Globe and Mail*, 12 June 1968, 10; "Ignore Smokescreen and Fight for Rights, Woman Says," *The Globe and Mail*, 24 June 13; and "Women Unequal as Long as They Are Pampered Household Pets, Reader Says," *The Globe and Mail*, 2 July 1968, 11.

57 Elizabeth Thompson's column, "Women Unequal as Long as They Are Pampered Household Pets, Reader Says," *The Globe and Mail*, 2 July 1968, 11.

58 Letter from Cathy Scaife of Burlington, Ontario under the heading "Status of Women" in the letters feature "The Last Word Is Yours," *Chatelaine*, Mar. 1968, 95.

59 Yvonne Crittenden, "Students Think 'Feminists' Are Old Hat," *The Telegram*, Toronto, 19 Mar. 1968. See also (no byline), "Youth Suspicious of Probe," *The Tribune*, Winnipeg, 24 Feb. 1968; Bletcher, "Call for Women in Politics," *The Tribune*; CP (no byline), "Feminine Image Not Too Bright," *The Vancouver Sun*, 23 Mar. 1968, 32; Joyce Douglas, "Attitudes Are Most to Blame, Says McGill Undergraduate," *The Montreal Star*, 12 June 1968, 59, 63.

60 Lorraine Shore, "Probe into Status of Women Hears UBC Co-ed Complain of Sex Barrier," *The Vancouver Sun*, 19 Apr. 1968, 13. CP, "Mothers and Magazines

Force Phony Ideals on Girls," *The Ottawa Journal*, 20 Apr. 1968; also published as CP, "'Phony Womanhood Forced by Media'," *The Tribune,* Winnipeg 19 Apr. 1968, 14; CP, "'Phoney' Ideals for Girls: Varsity Co-Ed Complaints," *The Calgary Herald*, 19 Apr. 1968; CP, "Single Girl States Her Views in Brief," *The Montreal Star* 20 Apr. 1968; CP, "Against Glamor Image," *The Gazette*, Montreal, 20 Apr. 1968. RCSW audio Tape #9910, Vancouver hearings, Brief #100. Neither *The Province* nor the CBC covered Keate's brief.

61 Editorial, "'So I Said to Her'," *The Vancouver Sun*, 17 Apr. 1968. This editorial might have been written by any one of several editorial writers. Keate Hazel does not believe her father wrote it because "he was a much better writer than that," and, "he was not that kind of person." Freeman interview with Keate Hazel. One woman was so angry she insisted on reading out the editorial and her reply at a Commission hearing, a segment that was used out of context in the W-O-M-A-N montage on "The Way It Is" RCSW audio tape #9909; "The Way It Is".

62 Norris cartoon, *The Vancouver Sun*, 20, Apr. 1968. Freeman interview with Norris.

63 Keate Hazel interviewed on "The *Day* It Is," 6 June 1968.

64 Freeman interview with (Keate) Hazel. Kathryn Keate, "'Out from Under, Women Unite!" Subheaded: "Personal Notes of An Activist in the Women's Liberation Movement," *Saturday Night*, July 1970, 15-20. Newspaper coverage included Greg Connolley, "Pro-abortion Protest: House Screams to a Halt," *The Ottawa Citizen*, 12 May 1970, 1; (no byline), "Parliament Aborted: NDP Blamed for Women in House," *The Ottawa Citizen*, 12 May 1970, 33; and Greg Connolley, "RCMP Probing case of the Forged Passes," *The Ottawa Citizen*, 13 May 1970, 1. See also editorial, "How to Lose a Cause," *The Ottawa Citizen*, 13 May 1970, 6.

65 *CBC Matinee*, 3 May 1968, RCSW Hearings in Regina. Craig Oliver of CBC News and Speirs of CP focused on her comments that such stereotypes lead to unrealistic expectations in marriage. CBC News Direct Reports, 30 Apr. 1968; Speirs, "Mother Speaks Out: Marriage Shrouded in Myth," *The Herald*, Calgary, 30 Apr. 1968. *The Leader-Post* took a more general angle: Ruth Willson, "Sense of Worth Said Lacking: Women Denied Dignity, Status Commission Told," *The Leader-Post*, Regina, 30 Apr. 1968, 13 and, in a later edition, "Today's Women Said Struggling Against Self-Image, Brief Claims," 24. It is not clear if the VoW speaker was including men here. *Take 30*, 6 May 1968, RCSW hearings in Regina and Saskatoon.

66 RCSW audio tape #9960. RCSW hearings in Toronto. It was mentioned in (no byline), "Mass Media Rapped for Ignoring Women," *The Montreal Star*, 7 June 1968, 10. A week later, the *Star* also reported that a Quebec group, L'Association Féminine d'Education et d'Action, wanted censorship of advertising which took a limited view of women's role, but the story did not explain the group's stand. Sheila Arnopoulos, "Brief from Women Demands Censorship of Advertising," *The Montreal Star*, 14 June 1968, 41. On the conflicts between CBC management and current affairs staff, particularly "This Hour Has Seven Days," see Raboy, *Missed Opportunities,* Chapter 4.

67 Ericson et al., *Negotiating Control*, 2.

68 According to the names on the program credits, it was not the same crew who presented a brief to Bird; this one appeared to be based in Montreal as several were francophones. *Take 30*, 17 June 1968, RCSW hearings in Toronto, Montreal and Quebec City. On the Saskatchewan program, the cameraman, who occasionally panned the audience, shot a close-up of a row of women's legs. The "cutaway," a common film-editing technique, was use to disguise jumpy edits on the main reel, in this case, in the minister's presentation. The

content of the main reel and the shot of the women's legs bore no apparent relation to each other. *Take 30*, 6 May 1968, RCSW hearings in Saskatchewan.

69 Freeman interview with Sarty.

70 Freeman interview with Soles.

71 Dennis Braithwaite, "Subsidy to Women Who Stay at Home," *The Telegram*, Toronto, 6 Sept. 1968.

72 Yvonne Crittenden, "One Report Ottawa Can't Ignore," *The Telegram*, Toronto, 1 Oct. 1968, 1, 3, 9, and via the newspaper's own news service, as "Status of Women—One Report Ottawa Cannot Ignore," *The Star-Phoenix*, Saskatoon, 7 Oct. 1968, 7. This article won Crittenden the annual award for the best news story from the national Canadian Women's Press Club. CP (no byline) "Telegram's Yvonne Crittenden Wins News Award," unmarked clipping in NAC RCSW, Vol. 43, Binder 8. On Bird's preferred approach, see NAC RCSW, Vol. 38, 14th meeting of the Commissioners: minutes, reports and submissions, 30-31 Oct. 1968, Appendix "K," Report of the Chairman, items 4-7.

73 Brownmiller, *Femininity*, 235-237.

Chapter 4

1 Joyce Donovan, "Random Notes," *The Sunday Reporter*, Aylmer, Quebec, 3 Nov. 1968.

2 On cultural meanings in the rhetoric of news, see van Dijk, *News as Discourse*, Chapters 2 and 3; Hackett and Zhao, "Sustaining Democracy?" Chapter 1.

3 *Report of the Royal Commission*, 172-75; Chalus, "From Friedan to Feminism"; Prentice et al., *Canadian Women*, 394-98.

4 Doris Anderson, "How We Stack the Cards against Both Sexes," *Chatelaine*, February 1968, 1; a different argument from Sonja Sinclair, "Can Canada Afford Educated Housewives?" *Chatelaine*, November 1966, 20, 106-109. Monique Bégin believed there were fewer female graduate students than there had been in 1930. (No byline), "Fewer Woman [*sic*] in Post-Grad Schools Today," *The Montreal Star*, 4 Mar. 1968.

5 NAC RCSW, Vol. 9, File Marked "Trips to Quebec—1," Bégin to the Commissioners, 11 July 1969. NAC RCSW Vol. 9, File marked—"Letters of Opinion—Nova Scotia," letter from D.C.B. Stewart, Dean of Medicine at Dalhousie University, April 1, 1968. File marked "Letters of Opinion—Ontario," letter from Sharon A. King, a physical education instructor and guidance counsellor in a local high school, London Ontario, 3 Apr. 1968.

6 NAC RCSW, Vol. 36, File marked "Relations with Participants—Miscellaneous—1. Letter to Florence Bird from D.F. Dadson, Dean of the College of Education, University of Toronto, 10 Dec. 1969. See also, *Report of the Royal Commission*, 165 and Ford, *A Path Not Strewn with Roses*, 60-77. See also Jacqueline Stalker and Susan Prentice, eds., *The Illusion of Inclusion*, Introduction, 19.

7 Nancy Millar, "A Woman's Whirl," *Red Deer Advocate*, 27 Apr. 1968, 8. Education received second billing in CP (Montreal), "Abortion Topic at Status Inquiry," *Toronto Daily Star*, 13 June 1968, 76; and "For Those Who Choose: Pill, Abortion Recommended," *The Gazette*, Montreal, 13 June 1968, 18; (no byline, dateline Toronto), "To Aid the New Canadian: Free Language Courses for Immigrants," *The Montreal Star*, 5 June 1968, 60. There was no mention of language courses in another reporter's version of the story, which emphasized the harm done by sex-role stereotyping in the media. (No byline), "Would End the 'Hard Sell,'" *Toronto Daily Star*, 4 June 1968, 51-52. Exceptions include: (no byline), "'More Education Needed'—University Women Urge Wider

Opportunities," *The Edmonton Journal*, 25 Apr. 1968; (no byline), "Commission Briefs: Provide Measure of Social Progress," *The Montreal Star*, 12 June 1968.

8 Lorraine Shore, "Probe into Status of Women Hears UBC Co-ed Complain of Sex Barrier," *The Vancouver Sun*, 19 Apr. 1968, 13. Leone Kirkwood, "Status Commission Urged to Probe Discrimination in Law, Medicine," *The Globe and Mail*, 8 June 1968, 31.

9 Since there were two men on the Commission, it appears that one of them was absent that day. Nicole Tremblay, "Says Men Affected by Commission," *The Ottawa Journal*, 4 Oct. 1968 and (no byline), "She's Different," *The Ottawa Citizen*, 4 Oct. 1968. The women in this journalism class included the writer of this book. We attended the Commission hearing for a class assignment, and I also interviewed Florence Bird for a student TV production.

10 The abrupt transitions between points suggest that the original story was subjected to heavy editing. (No byline), "Female Deans 'Ineffectual'," *The Ottawa Citizen*, 8 Oct. 1968, 20. Rosemary Speirs, "'Flowery' Types Losing Appeal: Woman Student," *Winnipeg Free Press*, 8 Oct. 1968, 20. It appears that *The Ottawa Journal* did not cover this story.

11 CP, "All-Girl Universities a Thing of the Past," *Evening Times-Globe*, St. John, 14 Sept. 1968; as CP, "College President against Separate Life for Females," *The Moncton Daily Times*, 16 Sept. 1968, 3. Judy Reyno, "Women Cannot Stay in Isolation," *Halifax Mail-Star*, 13 Sept. 1968, 6. Later, her own Sisters of Charity shortened their habits and reverted to their original names. Alixe Carter, "A Modern Nun: They Talk to Her," *The Ottawa Journal*, 6 Nov. 1968. Counter-arguments included (no byline), "Housewife Would Abolish Co-educational Schools," *Toronto Daily Star*, 25 Apr. 1968, and Donna Flint, "Schoolgirl Calls for Woman Power," *The Gazette*, Montreal, 13 June 1968, 16. *CBC Matinee*, 20 Sept. 1968, and *Take 30*, 17 Sept. 1968, RCSW hearings in the Atlantic provinces.

12 Prentice et al., *Canadian Women*, 420-24; Adamson, "Feminists, Libbers, Lefties and Radicals"; Kostash, *Long Way from Home*; Gitlin, *The Whole World Is Watching*. Jasen, "In Pursuit of Human Values (Or Laugh When You Say That...)."

13 (No byline), "Liberal Women 'Welcome' Commission," *The Calgary Herald*, 23 Apr. 1968, 25.

14 (No byline), "Girls Protest That Sex Is Used to Sell Everything," *The Telegram*, Toronto, 7 June 1968, 27.

15 (No byline), "Commission Keeps Cool under Young Socialists' Fire," *The Globe and Mail*, 7 June 1968, 13.

16 Lillian Newberry (CP), "Student Power Group Protest Sex-Roles as Dictated by 'Profit-Oriented Society'" *London Evening Free Press*, 7 June 1968.

17 Margaret Weiers, "Bar socialists from criticizing Viet Nam policy," *Toronto Daily Star*, 7 June 1968, 61.

18 (No byline), "Canadian women play 'second fiddle'," *The Montreal Star*, 8 June 1968.

19 RCSW audiotape #9962, Toronto, 6 June 1968.

20 Newberry (CP), "Student power group protest sex-roles as dictated by 'profit-oriented society,'" *London Evening Free Press*, 7 June 1968. The Henderson quote was later removed from the middle of the story, which suggests that the editor did not consider it an important point. The shorter version appeared in a composite report from that day's hearings. CP, "Briefs Charge Discrimination in News Media and Education," *The Gazette*, Montreal, 8 June 1968, 7.

21 On media and deviance, see van Dijk, *News as Discourse*, 121-23.

22 McKenzie, *Pauline Jewett*, Chapters 2 and 3. On the brief to the RCSW, see Chapter 10, 168.

23 (No byline), "Professors Air Problems with Academic Peers," *The Ottawa Journal*, 4 Oct. 1968, 26.

24 Susan Becker (CP), "Universities Asked to Give Women Break," *Kitchener-Waterloo Record*, 4 Oct. 1968. See also CP, "Universities Discriminate," *Red Deer Advocate*, 4 Oct. 1968.

25 Betty Swimmings, "Status of Women: Ability Should Rule," and (no byline), "Women Charge College Discrimination," *The Ottawa Citizen*, 4 Oct. 1968. (No byline), "Professors Air Problems with Academic Peers," *The Ottawa Journal*, 4 Oct. 1968, 26.

26 *CBC Matinee*, 4 Oct. 1968, RCSW hearings in Ottawa.

27 Val Werier, "Do Women Not Like Women?" *The Tribune*, Winnipeg, 25 Apr. 1968. On women educators, see Kinnear, *In Subordination*, Chapter 2; Gillett, *We Walked Very Warily*, Chapter 9.

28 Maggie Siggins, "2nd-Class Citizen Tag Irks Female Teachers," *The Telegram*, Toronto, 4 June 1968, 25.

29 CP, "Brief Looks at Teaching," *The Gazette*, Montreal, 5 June 1968, 22.

30 The teachers accused Ottawa of "arrogance," and "bad taste" because it did not specifically include women when it prepared statistics about re-education. It also refused to hire women over 40 for National Defence schools overseas, whereas the cutoff age for men was 65. (No byline), "Ottawa Refuses to Hire Women Teachers over 40, Commission Told," *The Globe and Mail*, 4 June 1968, 13. CBC radio news took much the same angle. CBC Radio Reports, 4 June 1968, Tom Watt reporting for "The World at 8," and Direct Reports, CBC Radio, 4 June 1968, "Metro Extra."

31 CP (Toronto), "Girls, You're Second-Class Citizens: That's What Women Teachers Say," *Owen Sound Sun-Times*, 4 June 1968. The editorial writer referred to CP as its source. "Housewife-Mothers Not Second-Class Citizens," *Owen Sound Sun-Times*, 5 June 1968.

32 On the Ontario Federation and its battles, see Staton and Light, *Speak with Their Own Voices*, Chapters 5 and 6. Manitoba teachers did win equal pay, but its effects were questionable, since the men held most of the senior positions. See Kinnear, *In Subordination*, Chapter 6.

33 (No byline), "Female Teachers' Beefs in Brief," *Toronto Daily Star*, 4 June 1968, 51. For similar stories, see Michele Veilleux, "School System Fails Girls," *Winnipeg Free Press*, 31 May 1968, 10, which contrasts with the much more flippant (no byline), "Why No Mary Mahovlich?" *The Tribune*, Winnipeg, 31 May 1968, 17.

34 (No byline), "Defence Dept. Under Fire," *The Ottawa Citizen*, 3 Oct. 1968, 45; (no byline), "Teacher Status Problem," *The Telegram*, Toronto, 2 Oct. 1968, 65 and (no byline), "Equal Pay with Few Promotions," *The Ottawa Journal*, 3 Oct. 1968, 38. On discrimination against women in the federal civil service, see Morgan, "The Equality Game."

35 Joyce Douglas, "Labor and Women's Leaders Quoted: Supreme Court Judgement Said 'Shocking,'" *The Montreal Star*, 26 Jan. 1968, 10. Doris Anderson, "The Strange Case of Policewoman Beckett," *Chatelaine*, Apr. 1968, 1.

36 Morgan, "The Equality Game," 13.

37 *Take 30*, RCSW hearings in Victoria and Vancouver. The forestry researcher's story was included in Rosemary Speirs, "Status of Women: Plight of the Poor Hard to Visualize, Panel Told," 17 Apr. 1968, 41; Iain Hunter, "'Bosses Shun Equality,'" *The Vancouver Sun*, 17 Apr. 1968, 28.

38 (No byline), "Cite Wasted Women Power," *The Ottawa Journal*, 3 Oct. 1968; also Eleanor Dunn, "Women Denied Top CS Jobs, Commission Told," *The Ottawa Citizen*, 3 Oct. 1968, 45; Staff, "Ottawa 'Ignores' Women," *The Telegram*, Toronto, 2 Oct. 1968, 65.

39 Coverage of the nurses included: (no bylines), "Nurses' Group Calls for Wage Parity," *Edmonton Journal*, Family Section, Apr. 25, 1968, 19; "Low Wages Tempt Nurses to Quit Job," *Calgary Herald*, Apr. 25, 1968, and "Economic Factors Responsible for Canadian Nursing Problems," Fredericton *Gleaner*, 11 Sept. 1968, 5. Some nurses were diffident about their pay rates, unless they were supporting their families, however. See Kinnear, *In Subordination*, Chapter 5. Wage differentials are in Appendices, Table 25, 185. Armstrong and Armstrong, *The Double Ghetto*, 28-41. See also Armstrong, Choinière and Day, *Vital Signs*.

40 Kessler-Harris, *A Woman's Wage*, Blazer Lectures 1 and 4.

41 Ursel, *Private Lives, Public Policy*, 244-48; Burt, "Changing Patterns of Public Policy," 215-19.; Sangster, "Women Workers, Employment Policy and the State."

42 On the UN Declaration, see *Report of the Royal Commission*, 66-77. The FBPW's efforts to get the laws changed to specify "equivalent work" dated from 1956.

43 Margaret Weiers, "Women Seek Boards to Protect Rights," *Toronto Daily Star*, 3 June 1968, 49.

44 Sheila Arnopoulos, "Women Bitterly Protest Current Status Imbalance," *The Montreal Star*, 4 June 1968, 20.

45 Mollie Gillen, "The Royal Commission on the Status of Women. Will It Do Any Good?" *Chatelaine*, Jan. 1968, 61.

46 (No byline), "Businesswomen Present Brief Asking for Equality for Women," *Daily Times and Conservator*, Brampton, ON, 5 June 1968. The old 1952 Convention, which Canada eventually signed in 1964, specified only "equal pay for equal work." See Ursel, *Private Lives, Public Policy*, 241; Boyd, "Canadian Attitudes towards Women," 21; and Morgan, "The Equality Game," 21, n6. Canada ratified the new ILO convention in 1972 and amended its federal legislation in 1977. Prentice et al., *Canadian Women*, 353-55, 363-65.

47 (No byline), "Claims Canada Lagging in Promoting Women," *The Globe and Mail*, 4 June 1968, 13; (no byline), "Royal Commission Hearing: Ombudswoman Wanted," *The Telegram*, Toronto, 3 June 1968, 41. The same pattern was repeated with media coverage of a brief from the Congress of Canadian Women. (No byline), "Brief Asks Equal Job Opportunity for Women," *The Telegram*, Toronto, 5 June 1968, 62. In contrast, *The Montreal Star* took a different angle on the brief and did not mention the ILO convention. (No byline), "Careers in Politics for Women Urged," *The Montreal Star*, 6 June 1968, 67.

48 For an overview of this union and the industry, and its struggles over gender and race issues, see Muszynski, *Cheap Wage Labour*.

49 Beagle's emphasis. *CBC Matinee*, 19 Apr. 19, 1968 and *Take 30*, 22 April 1968, RCSW hearings in Victoria and Vancouver.

50 Direct Reports, CBC Radio, 17 April 1968, Brian Kelleher reporting for the 8 p.m. edition of *The World at Six*.

51 Rosemary Speirs, "Birth Control Appeal Heard," *Victoria Daily Times*, British Columbia, 17 April 1968, 20. See also Muszynski, *Cheap Wage Labour*, 215-216.

52 Terry French, "The fight for Status....on Day Two: Challenge to men on equal pay for women," *The Province*, Vancouver, 18 April 1968, 28; Ann Barling, "More Birth Control Aid Asked: Unwanted Children Increase," *The Vancouver Sun*, 17 April 1968, 1, 2.

53 Eleanor Dunn, "Status of women: Bureau 'sop to women,' *The Ottawa Citizen*, 1 Oct. 1968, 31; CP, Unions Discriminate, President Charges," *Winnipeg Free Press*, 1 Oct. 1968, 14; CP, "Women's labor bureau inadequate, ex-director says," and CP, "CUPE chief admits discrimination," *The Globe and Mail*, 1 Oct. 1968, 13; CP, "Labor bureau target as status briefs end," *Toronto Daily Star*, 5

Oct. 1968. *The Ottawa Journal* and the *Toronto Daily Star*, which may have written the story in advance of CUPE's appearance at the hearing, initially took different angles. (No byline,) "CUPE Discounts Myths About Women As Workers," *The Ottawa Journal*, 30 Sept. 1968 and "Day nursery aid stressed," *Toronto Daily Star*, 30 Sept. 1968. CBC News, 30 Sept. 1968 (on reel for 1 Oct 1968), Gail Scott reporting for *The World at Six*.

54 CP (no byline), "Forceful law to end sex bias in employment urged by CLC," *The Globe and Mail*, 2 Oct. 1968, 9; Staff (no byline), "CLC Asks Fair Deal For Women," *The Telegram*, Toronto, 1 Oct. 1968. *Take 30*, 8 Oct. 1968, RCSW hearings in Ottawa.

55 Freeman interview with Dunn. Rosemary Speirs, "Women's Press Club Brief On Inequalities In Pay," *St. Catharines Standard*, 2 October 1968. CP (Toronto), "Union Denies Remarks," *The Ottawa Journal*, 3 October 1968.

56 Sugiman, *Labour's Dilemma*, 137; Prentice et al., 2nd Edition, 369; Ursel, 239 - 252; *Report of the Royal Commission*, 61-65.

57 CP, "Status of women: Unions charged with ignoring women," *The Ottawa Citizen*, 6 June 1968, 41; Leone Kirkwood, "Discrimination study urged: Laid-off women say unions won't aid them," *The Globe and Mail*, 6 June 1968, p. W2; Sheila Arnopoulos, "Jobless women protest practice of discrimination," *The Montreal Star*, 6 June 1968, 61, 65; Margaret Weiers, "Factories don't need us—women," *Toronto Daily Star*, 5 June 1968, 71; Mary Jane Charters, "Kennedy shooting doesn't slow down status commission," *London Evening Free Press*, 6 June 1968.

58 (No byline), "Says Bill Of Rights Don't [sic] Mean a Thing," *Toronto Daily Star*, 8 June 1968, 42; (no byline), "Christine, The Solderer, Is Burned Up," *The Telegram*, Toronto, 7 June 1968, 27. It appears that the CBC did not cover these briefs.

59 For example, NAC RCSW, Vol. 7, "Letters of Opinion—B.C." File, letter from Mrs. G.A. Holm of Vancouver, 6 June 1968. Bird was quoted in (no byline) "'Our Turn to Speak Out,'" *The Telegram*, Toronto, 3 June 1968, 41.

60 The secretary was on *Take 30*, 22 Apr. 1968, RCSW hearings in Victoria and Vancouver.

61 See *Report of the Royal Commission*, 28-30. Beth Waters, "Women Now Organizing: Corporation Meetings 'to Be Invaded'," *The Calgary Herald*, 9 May 1967; and "Mrs. Sabia All Set: Gunning for Business." *The Telegram*, Toronto, 25 October 1967. Doris Anderson, "Women 1967: Gains and Misses of 1966"; and UPI, "Curator Shows the Sky's the Limit tor Career Women," *The Gazette*, Montreal, 16 Apr. 1968.

62 One notable exception was a Conservative MP who served several terms under Prime Minister John Diefenbaker. See Conrad, "'Not A Feminist, But...', 5-28.

63 Whitton is quoted in CP, "Women's Status Study Inexcusable: Whitton," *The Ottawa Citizen*, 4 Feb. 1967, 18. See also Kathy Hassard. "'Status' Commission Not Needed: Fighting Feminist Claims Battle Won," *The Vancouver Sun*, 11 Mar. 1967.

64 Robinson and Saint-Jean, The Portrayal of Women Politicians in the Media."

65 LaMarsh, *Memoirs of a Bird in a Gilded Cage*; McKenzie, *Pauline Jewett*, Chapters 4 and 7.

66 Bashevkin, *Toeing the Lines*, 74, 87-88, and Chapter 5; Myers, "'A Noble Effort.'" For specific examples of news stories about women's place in politics, see Lewis Seale, "Group Urges Provincial Inquiries on Status of Women" and Lotta Dempsey, "Sports, Politics Add up to Party," *Toronto Daily Star*, 4 May 1966, 79; Helen Bateson, "Men Promise Assistance to Stop Discrimination," *The Tribune*, Winnipeg, 17 Feb. 1968, 14; (no bylines), "Women Unready for

Politics Farm Wife Tells Committee," *The Tribune*, Winnipeg, 16 Feb. 1968; and "Her Sought-After Prize Is Political Equality," *The Tribune*, Winnipeg, 17 Feb. 1968, 14; Alixe Carter, "Human Rights Conference: Lonely Life in High Places," *The Ottawa Journal*, 3 Dec. 1968.

67 Doris Anderson, editorial, "Justice: 1 Woman to 263 Men?" Sept. 1968, 1. At the time, the media were playing up the sex appeal of Pierre Trudeau, the bachelor leader of the Liberals who was often photographed being chased and kissed by young women.

68 Yvonne Crittenden, "20 Women in the Race but Chances Look Slim," *The Telegram*, Toronto, 24 May 1968, 41; CP, "Lowest Number of Women Since '62 to Run in Election," Montreal *Gazette*, 12 June 1968, 25; Margaret Weiers, "Next House Could Boast Even Fewer Women than Last," *Toronto Daily Star*, 11 June 1968.

69 Jean Sharp, "Status of Women Top Newsmaker," *Toronto Daily Star*, 24 Dec. 1968.

70 CBC News, 29 May 1968, RCSW hearings in Winnipeg, Colin Hoath reporting for *The World at Six*; CP, "Political Women Sidelined, Brief Says," *Toronto Daily Star*, 30 May 1968; Shirley Foley, "Status Is a Full Time Job," *The Ottawa Citizen*, Ottawa, 2 Oct. 1968, 39. On the Alberta Liberal women, see (no byline), "Liberal Women 'Welcome' Commission, Criticize Provincial Human Rights Act," *The Calgary Herald*, 23 Apr. 1968, 25. Bashevkin, *Toeing the Lines*, 93-95.

71 Bruce Yemen, "Third of Gov't Jobs Requested for Women," *Victoria Times*, 16 Apr. 1968, 1 and 8. Their brief was included in (no byline), "Downgrading Charged by Women," *Victoria Colonist*, 17 Apr. 1968, 1, 2 and in CP, "Phones Ring for Hearings," *The Telegram*, Toronto, 16 April 1968. CBC Radio News, 16 Apr. 1968, Brian Kelleher reporting for *The World at Six*.

72 It was included in Rosemary Speirs, "Boys Showing Interest in Taking Home Economics," *Brockville Recorder and Times*, Ontario, 18 Sept, 1968. Much of Prowse's exchange with Humphrey was deleted from another version of the story: CP, "Status Hearings Open in Halifax," *Evening Times-Globe*, Saint John, 12 Sept. 1968, 3. For the national NDP position, see Betty Swimmings, "Ability Should Rule," *The Ottawa Citizen*, 4 Oct. 1968. A similar discussion took place in Winnipeg, but this time Commissioner Lange challenged a brief from the Manitoba Committee on the Status of Women, which opposed affirmative action. CBC News, 29 May 1968, RCSW hearings in Winnipeg, Colin Hoath reporting for *The World at Six*.

73 Rosemary Speirs, "Fuzzy Presentations Galore at Women's Status Hearings," *The Vancouver Sun*, 23 Apr. 1968, 25.

74 No byline, "Commission Study Said 'Like Holding up Mirror,'" *The Leader-Post*, Regina, 29 Apr. 1968, 18.

75 John Bird was commenting on the CP copy he had seen in the Ottawa papers. NAC Bird Papers, Vol. 1, John Bird to Florence Bird, undated, c. April 1968.

76 (No byline), "Liberal Women 'Welcome' Commission, Criticize Provincial Human Rights Act," *The Calgary Herald*, 23 Apr. 1968, 25.

77 CP, "Women Told to Stop Hiding Behind Own Skirts," *The Montreal Star*, 24 Apr. 1968 and "Women Must Adjust Views, Hearing Told," *The Globe and Mail*, 23 Apr. 1968, 11.

78 *CBC Matinee*, 26 Apr. 1968, RCSW hearings from Edmonton and Calgary.

79 (No byline), "'Accept Us as Individuals in Our Own Right,' Women Petition," *The Edmonton Journal*, 27 Apr. 1968, 21.

80 *The World at Six*, CBC Radio News, 29 May 1968, RCSW hearings in Winnipeg.

81 (No byline), "Thelma Tells the Girls to Stop Complaining," *The Tribune*, 30 May 1968, 1. Other coverage included Michele Veilleux, "Status of Women—Need Choice: Forbes," *Winnipeg Free Press*, 30 May 1968, 1, 4; CP, "Must Blame

Ourselves for Status Inequality—Woman Politician," *Toronto Daily Star*, 30 May 1968.

82 Mollie Gillen, "Women at Work," *Chatelaine*, Jan. 1969, 38, 58-59.

83 Margaret Butters, "Weekend Digest," *Welland-Port Colborne Tribune*, 8 June 1968.

84 See Speirs, "Girl Power," *Toronto Life*, Aug. 1968; CP, "'Women still slaves'," *The Ottawa Citizen*, 5 June 1968, 43; Yvonne Crittenden, "A Zombie Label for Canada's Men," *The Telegram*, Toronto, 5 June 1968, 62. See also Mary Jane Charters, "Status Of Women Hearings: Women Are Human, Not 'Blue-Eyed Protestant Virgin Images,'" the *London Free Press*, June 1968, 32. Mickleburgh also appeared on CBC Toronto's *The Day It Is*, with Kathryn Keate (Hazel).

85 Other examples using the same language included (no byline), "Plight like U.S. Negro's," *The Edmonton Journal*, 26 Apr. 1968. In one case, a woman cited the situations of both American Blacks and Canada's aboriginal people as comparisons. See Ruth Willson, "Sense of Worth Said Lacking: Women Denied Dignity, Status Commission Told," *The Leader-Post*, Regina, 30 Apr. 1968, 13.

86 On the experiences of Canada's Black people, see, for example, Glenda Simms, "Beyond the White Veil"; Bristow, et al., eds., *"We're Rooted Here and They Can't Pull Us Up."* On the American experience, see Jones, *Labor of Love, Labor of Sorrow*. On white women and the civil rights movement, see Evans, *Personal Politics*; Cohen, "The Canadian Women's Movement," 4.

87 Only *The Ottawa Journal* briefly mentioned her intervention from the floor in Ottawa. "Carrie Best's Moving Tribute," *The Ottawa Journal*, 4 Oct. 1968.

88 Gillen's emphases. "Report: What You Think of Women's Status," *Chatelaine*, July 1969, 30-31, 76, 80, 82-83.

89 Linda Curtis, "If the Tables Were Turned," *The Albertan*, 25 Apr. 1968, 6.

90 Shirley Hunter, "Why Must Women Have to Protest to Be Treated as Persons by Men?" *Western Catholic Reporter*, 2 May 1968.

91 Pat Dufour, "A Woman's Viewpoint," *Victoria Times*, 17 Apr. 1968.

92 Sheila H. Kieran, "Who's Downgrading Women? Women," *Maclean's*, August 1968, 18-19, 40-42. She may have been referring to Valliäres, *White Niggers of America*, among other examples.

93 Harry Bruce, "Are Women Better Than People?" *The Star Weekly*, 6 July 1968, 43.

94 Macpherson, *Toronto Daily Star*, 7 June 1968.

95 Gillen, "Report: What You Think of Women's Status," *Chatelaine*, July 1969, 30-31, 76, 80, 82-83. In addition, slightly over half of the respondents did not know if unions went after "equal pay" for female members, possibly because most of the respondents themselves were not unionized. On politics and public life, one-third of the respondents blamed what the magazine termed "women's inadequate representation in important posts" on lack of support for female candidates among both men and women, rather than among just men (9%) or just women (6%). Most of the other respondents blamed it on women's family responsibilities (20%), lack of interest (14%) or knowledge (9%), or said they were unsuitable by "emotion or character" (6%). In answer to the next question, 83% of the respondents agreed that women were underrepresented on the governing boards of companies, of unions, and of universities, and on government commissions and in the senior civil service.

96 Margaret Weiers, "The Status of Women: What the Men Say," *Toronto Daily Star*, 26 Mar. 1968, 51; continued as "In 1968, Most Men Still Believe a Woman's Place Is in the Home," 52.

97 Patricia Young, "Waste of Money," *The Vancouver Sun*, 19 Apr. 1968.

98 Miss Joel Hargan, who worked in a bank in Ottawa, had the opposite opinion. (No byline), "Status of Women," *Evening Telegram*, St. John's, 13 Sept. 1968;

Alixe Carter, "Whither the Status of Women?" *The Ottawa Journal*, 28 Sept. 1968.

99 R.W. Haynes, "Status of Women," and B. Smith, "Out of the Kitchen," *Kitchener-Waterloo Record*, Ontario, 14 and 20 Sept. 1968.

100 (No byline), "Attitudes Are Most to Blame, Says McGill Undergraduate," *The Montreal Star*, 12 June 1968, 59.

101 Percy Maddux, "Men Take Second Place in Today's Working World," *The Calgary Herald*, 24 Apr. 1968, 5.

102 "Old Man Who Knows," in Elizabeth Thompson's column under the heading, "The Way One Man Sees It, the Women Started the Fight," *The Globe and Mail*, 17 Sept. 1968, 10.

103 Mrs. Alixe Dobby, "Hobby," *The Ottawa Journal*, 26 Oct. 1968.

104 Mrs. Deirdre Graham, "What the Ladies Want Is Equality in Plumbing," *The Ottawa Citizen*, 17 Oct. 1968.

105 Boyd, "Canadian Attitudes towards Women," 14-22.

106 Freeman interview with Crittenden.

Chapter 5

1 Jeann Beattie, "A Single Woman Looks at Wives," *Chatelaine*, July 1968, 63.

2 Schudson, "The Sociology of News Production Revisited," 154.

3 For example, see (several authors), "The New Woman," *Star Weekly*, 6 Jan. 1968, 18-29; and "New Woman? What New Woman?" *Star Weekly*, 30 Mar. 1968, 12-15.

4 See MacDougal, *Newsroom Problems and Policies*, 395-96.

5 The separation of women's work from that done by the rest of the family, which left her dependent on her husband's wages, began during the industrialization of the workforce. Armstrong and Armstrong, *The Double Ghetto*, 86.

6 Eunice Gardiner, "CFUW Brief: New Concept of Taxation Sought," *The Ottawa Journal*, 4 Oct. 1968.

7 Carter recommendations cited in *Report of the Royal Commission on the Status of Women*, 296. For example, the Committee for the Equality of Women, led by Laura Sabia, the Manitoba Status of Women Committee and the National Council of Women all rejected the Carter proposal on the same grounds. Margaret Weiers, "Women Get No Reassurance at Tax Reports," *Toronto Daily Star*, 26 Feb. 1968, 43, 44; Jean Sharp (CP), "Tax Discrimination Charged as Carter Report Discussed," *The Tribune*, Winnipeg, 27 Feb. 1968, 12; Elinor Reading (CP), "National Council: Rejects Family Unit for Taxes," the *London Free Press*, 7 June 1968, 26. The New Democratic Party favoured it, however, which was one of the reasons Laura Sabia ran for the Conservatives in the federal election. (No byline), "Equality Champion Laura Sabia Seeks Seat in Parliament," *Toronto Daily Star*, 7 May 1968.

8 RCSW testimony included (no byline), "Income Tax Act Regards Wives as Chattels: Brief," *The Tribune*, Winnipeg, 30 May 1968, 23; and (no byline), "Recognize Labor in Home, Status Commission Told," *Winnipeg Free Press*, 29 May 1968, 21; Staff, "Financial Equality of Wives Spotlighted," *The Telegram*, Toronto, 1 Oct. 1968; (no byline), "Status Committee Gets Turn," *Toronto Daily Star*, 1 Oct. 1968.

9 Staff, "Credit Laws Discriminate, Probe Told," *The Albertan*, 23 Apr. 1968, 7.

10 *CBC Matinee*, 3 May 1968, RCSW Hearings in Regina, SK.

11 Maggie Siggins, "Pay for Wives Heartily Applauded," *The Telegram*, Toronto, 5 June 1968, 62.

12 See, for example, the studies cited in Cebotarev, "From Domesticity to the Public Sphere," 208-209; Taylor, "Should I Drown Myself Now or Later?"

13 NAC RCSW, Vol. 8, "Letters of Opinion – Sask.," letter from Mrs. A. MacDonald of Moose Jaw, 21 Feb. 1967.

14 Murdoch was eventually awarded a lump sum maintenance payment. The case mobilized women's groups to successfully demand legal changes, culminating in a favourable Supreme Court decision in 1993. Prentice et al., *Canadian Women*, 439-40; Armstrong and Armstrong, *The Double Ghetto*, 78-79; 86-87.

15 (No byline,) "Make Us Equal, Say the Girls from the Farms," *The Albertan*, Calgary, 23 Apr. 1968, 5. This brief was included in other coverage in Gwynn Pickett, "Pre-Marital Waiting Period Suggested," *The Calgary Herald*, 23 Apr. 1968, 25.

16 Sheila Arnopoulos, "Women Bitterly Protest Current Status Imbalance," *The Montreal Star*, 4 June 1968, 20; (no byline), "Downgrading Charged by Women," *Victoria Colonist*, BC, 17 Apr. 1968, 1, 2; Judi Freeman, "Marriage Should Be a 'Partnership' Rather than Maintenance Institution," *The Calgary Herald*, 23 Apr. 1968, 25. See also Margaret Weiers, "Women Seek Boards to Protect Rights," *Toronto Daily Star*, 3 June 1968, 49; Anne Bond, "Two Briefs Are Presented to Women's Commission," *Charlottetown Guardian*, 14 Sept. 1968, 1, 3.

17 On Mitchell, see (staff), "Agriculture 'Closed Shop' for Women," *The Albertan*, Calgary, 23 Apr. 1968, 7; CP, "Ranching a Closed Shop: Widow," *The Tribune*, Winnipeg, 20 Apr. 1968. See also CP (no byline), "Woman MLA Hopes for High Calibre Hearing," *The Edmonton Journal*, 24 Apr. 1968, 23; (no byline,) "Skill, Not Sex Should Dictate Job Qualification," *The Calgary Herald*, 24 Apr. 1968, 7; Judi Freeman, "Unmarried Persons Treated 'Inferior,'" *The Calgary Herald*, 24 Apr. 1968.

18 Quebec's Civil Code statutes concerning marital property were partly based on those of France. Under this system, all property owned by the spouses became their communal property upon marriage, but was nevertheless controlled by the husband. The wife was supposed to receive a half share in the assets acquired during the marriage should it dissolve, but this was difficult to enforce. By the 1960's, almost three-quarters of the couples in Quebec were signing marriage contracts allowing each spouse control over his or her own separate property. In 1964, Bill 16 gave the wife relatively more legal control over her own assets and actions, but did not help those who had no financial resources or property of their own. Neither did the new Quebec law, passed in 1970, which allowed separate assets, but considered those acquired during marriage as joint property to be settled as such after death, separation or divorce. Nicholas and Brisson, *"The Married Woman in Ascendance"*; Clio Collective, *Quebec Women*, 1987), 321-24.

19 *Take 30*, 17 June 1968, RCSW hearings in Toronto, Quebec City and Montreal; *CBC Matinee*, 14 June 1968, RCSW hearings in Quebec City and Montreal.

20 Sheila Arnopoulos, "Women in the Workforce Must Have Same Rights as Men, Is French-Canadian Women's View," *The Montreal Star*, 12 June 1968, 59, 71. CBC Radio News, Direct Reports, 11 June 1968, Doreen Kayes reporting for *The World at Six*; CP, "Notaries Urge Change in Marriage Control," *The Ottawa Citizen*, 12 June 1968, 40.

21 The new law was passed in February 1968 and came into effect the following July. "Marriage breakdown" referred to alcohol addiction, separation, desertion, and a "other" problems. The new grounds for divorce already included physical and mental cruelty, sodomy, bestiality, rape, homosexuality and bigamy. CP, "Divorce Widening Date Set," *The Leader-Post*, 1 May 1968, 22;

Allan Fotheringham's column, (no title), *The Vancouver Sun*, 27 Mar. 1969. Sev'er, *Women and Divorce*, 110-11. Women's groups put pressure on legislators to change the law. See Marsden and Busby, "Feminist Influence through the Senate." In 1968, there were 124.3 divorces per 100,000 married persons; by 1970, the rate had jumped to 311.5. Prentice et al., *Canadian Women*, 381-82; Armstrong and Armstrong, *The Double Ghetto*, Table 15, 78-79. Under the old law, adultery had to be proven, which often involved hiring a private detective. This was embarrassing and upsetting for many people. See Nancy Tayler White, "How Our Divorce Law Degrades Us," *Chatelaine*, Sept. 1966, 29, 30, 32, 146; Doris Anderson, "Does Our Proposed Divorce Law Go Far Enough?" *Chatelaine*, Sept. 1967, 1.

22 Gillen, "The Royal Commission on the Status of Women. Will It Do Any good?" *Chatelaine*, Jan. 1968, 21-23; 60-62, citation on p. 62.

23 RCSW audio tape #9905, Victoria hearings.

24 According to the *Sun*, she said, "I can't understand why he can be located when he has committed a traffic offence but not when it is a question of his moral obligation to support his children." Iain Hunter (Victoria Bureau), "Women's Beef to Commission: 'Bosses Shun Equality,'" *The Vancouver Sun* 17 Apr. 1968, 28. It is not clear who covered the story in her own newspaper. See (no byline), "Downgrading Charged by Women," *Daily Colonist*, 17 Apr. 1968, 1 and 2; also, Bruce Yemen, "Royal Commission in 'Dream World,'" *Victoria Times*, 17 Apr. 1968. Brown was also mentioned in Rosemary Speirs, "Plight of the Poor Hard to Visualize, Panel Told," *The Ottawa Citizen*, 17 Apr. 1968, 41. On mothers and divorce, see Sev'er, *Women and Divorce*, 228-31.

25 van Dijk, *News as Discourse*, 76.

26 *Take 30*, 6 May 1968, RCSW hearings in Regina and Saskatoon.

27 CP, "Appeal to Commission: Judge Cites 'Terrible Flaws' in Divorce, Separation Acts," *The Globe and Mail*, 3 May 1968, 10. See also (no byline), "Status of Women Enquiry Begins Sessions in Saskatoon," *The Star-Phoenix*, 2 May 1968, 12.

28 *Take 30*, 3 June 1968; and *CBC Matinee*, RCSW hearings in Winnipeg.

29 Margaret Weiers, "Women Asked to Give Views on Status," *Toronto Daily Star*, 20 Dec., 1967.

30 RCSW audio tape #9917.

31 Harding's brief, but no mention of violence, was covered in Rosemary Speirs, "Status of Women: Political Life Splits Responsibility," *The Ottawa Citizen*, 22 Apr. 1968, 40; (no byline), "Women Raising Families Alone Tell Status Probe of Problems," *The Edmonton Journal*, 26 Apr. 1968, 21. In this case, Harding's own newspaper covered the story but did not identify her as a *Journal* writer.

32 Ericson et al., *Negotiating Control*, 2-7.

33 There were several complaints to the RCSW from women who asked that their letters remain confidential. Some wrote citing the experiences of other women they knew, however. See, for example, NAC RCSW, Vol. 8, Letters of Opinion—Alberta", letter from Mrs. D. Ollenberger of Edmonton, 23 July 1969. See also, Bégin, "The Royal Commission," 31. The earliest research references to spousal abuse include Handleman, "Battered women," and MacLeod, "Wife Battering in Canada."

34 Colin Hoath, CBC Radio News, Direct Reports, for *The World at Eight* (on at 8, 9, 10, 11 a.m.), 30 May 1968, RCSW hearings in Winnipeg; see also (no byline), "Domestic Police Need Is Stressed," *The Tribune*, Winnipeg, 30 May 1968, 23; Lyn Schankerman, "Lack Time for Questioning," *Winnipeg Free Press*, 30 May 1968, 17. See also (no bylines), "Protection Wanted for Separated Wife," *Winnipeg Free Press*, 31 May 1968, 10; and "Women Raising Families Alone Tell Status Probe of Problems," *The Edmonton Journal*, 26 Apr. 1968, 21.

35 CP, "Feared Drunken Husband: Brief Tells of Wife Who Slept in Field,"
    Evening Times-Globe, Saint John, 14 Sept. 1968, 1; Ann Bond, "Two Briefs Are
    Presented to Women's Commission," *Charlottetown Guardian*, 14 Sept. 1968, 1,
    2.
36 *CBC Matinee*, 10 Sept. 1968, RCSW hearings in Fredericton, NB.
37 "*CBC Matinee*," 20 Sept. 1968, RCSW Hearings from the Atlantic provinces.
38 (No byline), "Unscheduled Brief Presented: 'Alcoholism Is a Weakness,'"
    Telegraph-Journal, 11 Sept. 1968, 3, corrected to "'Alcoholism Is An Illness,'"
    Evening Times-Globe, 11 Sept. 1968, 31; "Brief Submitted for Families," *Evening
    Times-Globe*, Saint John, 2 Sept. 1968, 2, and in the *Telegraph-Journal*, Saint John,
    12 Sept. 1968, 2. The lead spokeswoman was named in "Royal Commission
    Told: Economic Factors Responsible for Canadian Nursing Problems," *Daily
    Gleaner*, Fredericton, 11 Sept. 1968, 5. Notes on the Commission's procedures
    regarding confidentiality are in NAC RCSW, Vol. 35, file marked Public
    Hearings—Preparation; also, Freeman interview with Bird. NAC MacGill
    Papers, Vol. 4, Minutes of the Eighth Meeting of the Commissioners, 13-15
    Mar. 1968. Item 88 on press releases.
39 The single women also felt shut out from male professional groups, and some
    said their male friends felt lonely, too. Rowe's marital status is unclear. *The
    Albertan* referred to her as "Mrs." Rowe but the other two reporters called her
    "Miss." Linda Curtis, "Calgary Survey Reveals a Problem: Female, Single—
    and Isolated," *The Albertan*, Calgary, 24 Apr. 1968; Judi Freeman, "Unmarried
    Persons Treated as 'Inferior,' Hearing Told," *The Calgary Herald*, 23 Apr. 1968,
    23; Rosemary Speirs, "Single People Suffer Loneliness," *The Ottawa Citizen*, 24
    Apr. 1968, 46.
40 Margaret Weiers, "Equal Rights for Women Gets Its Foot in the Door of
    Masculinity's Last Bastion," *Toronto Daily Star*, 3 May 1968.
41 *Take 30*, 17 June 1968, and *CBC Matinee*, 14 June 1968, RCSW hearings in
    Quebec City and Montreal. It was one of several briefs covered by Sheila
    Arnopoulos, "Status of Women Hearings: Wider Cross Section Needed for
    Volunteer Work, Commission Told," *The Montreal Star*, 11 June 1968, 52. See
    also Andrea Goeb, "Brief Blasts Women as Own Worst Enemies," *The Gazette*,
    Montreal, 12 June 1968, 22.
42 Reid's emphasis. *CBC Matinee*, 25 Apr. 1968, RCSW hearings in Edmonton.
43 Rosemary Speirs, "Commission Ends Western Tour: Demands from Women
    May Result in Overhaul of Laws, Chairman Says," *The Globe and Mail*, 6 May
    1968; and an earlier version, "Women's Groups Missing Real Problems of
    Many," *Charlottetown Guardian*, 30 Apr. 1968. See also (no byline), "In 14 Years,
    Five Complaints: "Equal Pay for Women Discussed at Hearing," *The Leader-
    Post*, Regina, SK, 29 Apr. 1968, 1.
44 Sheila Arnopoulos, "Women's Brief Urges Break for Housewife," *The Montreal
    Star*, 6 June 1968, 49, 61 and (no byline), East York Wife Hits Commission," *The
    Telegram*, Toronto, 6 June 1968, 6.
45 (No byline), "Housewife Called an Anachronism," *The Telegram*, Toronto, 6
    June 1968, 58.
46 *CBC Matinee*, 20 Sept. 1968, RCSW hearings in the Atlantic provinces.
47 (No byline), "Voters' Lists Tell 'Rotten Lie,' Women Told," *Toronto Daily Star*, 5
    June 1968, 5. CP, "'Women Still Slaves'," *The Ottawa Citizen*, 5 June 1968, 43
48 *CBC Matinee*, 19 Apr. 1968, RCSW hearings in Victoria and Vancouver.
49 Terry French, "The Fight for Status...on Day Two: Challenge to Men on Equal
    Pay for Women—Would You Strike for Their Rights?" *The Province*,
    Vancouver, 18 Apr, 1968, 28; Ann Barling, "Royal Commission Ponders:
    'Mistress? Respectable?" *The Vancouver Sun*, 18 Apr. 1968, 42; CP, "Who Gives
    This Man in Marriage?" *The Telegram*, Toronto, 18 Apr. 1968, 51.

50 (No byline), "Dog Food, Divorcees...a Matter of Women's Status," *The Tribune*, Winnipeg, 31 May 1968, 17.
51 (No byline), "Royal Commission on Status of Women Gets a Day of Brickbats and Bouquets," *The Globe and Mail*, 6 June 1968, W2. Margaret Weiers, "Marriage a 'Career?' Nonsense, She Says," *Toronto Daily Star*, 3 June 1968, 1, 4 (late edition).
52 *CP Style Book*, 1974, ed., 94.
53 *Take 30*, 22 Apr. 1968, RCSW hearings in Victoria and Vancouver.
54 (No byline), "Credit Policy Attacked," *The Edmonton Journal*, 25 Apr. 1968, 19; and an unmarked clipping (no byline), "Plight like U.S. Negro's," in NAC RCSW, Vol. 41, Binder 3.
55 CP, "Immigrant Finds Forms Insulting," *The Montreal Star*, 27 Apr. 1968. The *CP* story might have been edited that way. See "Titles," *CP Style Book*, 1968 ed., 95.
56 CBC Radio News, Direct Reports, 26 Apr. 1968, RCSW hearings in Edmonton, Ron Smith reporting for *The World at Eight*, 10 a.m. edition.
57 For example, Rosemary Speirs, CP, "Short-Term Marriages Advocated by Bachelor Saskatchewan Farmer," *The Calgary Herald*, 4 May 1968, 29. This story appeared as "Short-Term Marriage System Suggested to Women's Probe," *The Tribune*, Winnipeg, 4 May 1968; as "Short-Term, Renewable Marriages Suggested by Bachelor in Saskatchewan," *The Globe and Mail*, 4 May 1968, 27; as "Status of Women: Farmer Suggests 5-Year Marriages," *The Ottawa Citizen*, 6 May 1968, 24; as "Marry Now!...and Reconsider Later Is Farmer's Proposal," *The Ottawa Journal*, 4 May 1968; as "In Status Brief: Renewable Marriage Urged," *The Gazette*, Montreal, 6 May 1968; as "Short-Term Contracts: Bachelor Suggests Renewable Vows, *The Montreal Star*, 6 May 1968.
58 *Take 30*, 6 May 1968, RCSW hearings in Regina and Saskatoon.
59 Michael Cope, "Canadian Commission Listens: Women Air Their Gripes," *The Sunday Bulletin*, Philadelphia, 16 Feb. 1969, Section 4, 10.
60 (No byline) "Equal Opportunity Recommendations," *The Star-Phoenix*, Saskatoon, 3 May 1968.
61 CP, "Widows Seeking Bachelor Tax," *The Telegram*, Toronto, 31 May 1968. See also, Lyn Schankerman, "Tax on Single Bliss? Housewife Asks Widow-Aid Levy On Bachelors," *Winnipeg Free Press*, 31 May 1968; (no byline), "Bachelor Tax, Too: Retain Names, Women Urged," *The Tribune*, Winnipeg, 31 May 1968. The bachelor tax idea was not a new one. See Lewis, (ed.), *Dear Editor and Friends*, 129.
62 *Take 30*, 3 June 1968 and *CBC Matinee*, 3 June 1968, RCSW hearings in Winnipeg. It was also covered by the radio news service, which treated it lightly as well. Colin Hoath, CBC Radio News, Direct Reports for 1 p.m., 31 May 1968.
63 The cartoon appeared with Donna Anderson, "Aimed at Bachelors: Tax Levy on Single Bliss," *The Vancouver Sun*, 7 June 1968. The signature on the cartoon is not clear.
64 Len Norris, "...and I say you'll go with me to hear our side of the story," *The Vancouver Sun*, 8 Apr. 1968. Freeman interview with Norris. Cartoon by Dow Nieuwenhuis for Alixe Carter, "Shape of Things to Come? First 'Status' Survey Shows Mothers Prefer Home to Work," *The Ottawa Journal*, 15 Feb. 1968, 35. The heading on the Toronto *Star* version appears to be misplaced under the circumstances, or was perhaps meant to be ironic: Margaret Weiers, "Canada's women shout for their rights." *Toronto Daily Star*, 12 Feb. 1968, Section 4, 43. A contrasting story about a married woman who opened her own personnel agency ran on the same page: (no byline), "Mixing marriage

and motherhood for success." See also, (no byline), "Survey results surprising," *The Tribune,* Winnipeg, 17 Feb. 1968.

65 Don Cayo, "Below the Newsline," *Western Star,* Corner Brook, 19 Sept. 1968.

66 Editorial, "Husband's Role," *Prince Rupert Daily News,* BC, 11 Sept. 1968, reprinted from *The Sudbury Star,* Ontario. Editorial, "The Status of Status."

67 *Portage Leader,* Manitoba, 6 June 1968.

68 Robertson backed down somewhat a bit in his column the following week, but still insisted that marriage breakdown and the resulting financial problems were a two-way street. John Robertson, "Another View," *Winnipeg Free Press,* 30 May 1968, 3; and 4 June 1968, 3. For similar sentiments, expressed more briefly, see Allan Fotheringham's column (no title), *The Vancouver Sun,* 27 Mar. 1969.

69 James K. Nesbitt (untitled), *The Vancouver Sun,* 3 June 1968.

70 Editorial, "Tax Proposal for Bachelors," *Brantford Expositor,* Ontario, 1 June 1968.

71 Editorial, "Pity the Bachelor," *The Belleville Daily Intelligencer,* Ontario 7 June 1968.

72 Bill Trebilcoe, "Coffee Break" column, *Winnipeg Free Press,* 3 June 1968.

73 Val Werier, "Behind the news: Do Women Not Like Women?" *The Tribune,* Winnipeg, 25 Apr. 1968.

74 Harriet Hill column, "Facts and Fancies," *The Gazette,* Montreal, 24 Oct. 1968. The young man concerned actually said women over 21, according to another report. (No byline), "Single Man Faces Commission," *The Ottawa Journal,* 4 Oct. 1968.

75 Val Werier, "Widows Supposed to Half Live," *The Tribune,* Winnipeg, 29 May 1968, 6.

76 Editorial, "Ballots and Billets," *Brantford Expositor,* Ontario, 8 June 1968.

77 Editorial, "Now We Are Experiencing New Kind Of Segregation," *Kamloops Daily Sentinel,* BC, 31 May 1968.

78 Weiers, "The Status of Women: What the Men Say," *Toronto Daily Star,* 26 Mar. 1968, 51.

79 Gillen, "Report: What You Think of Women's Status," *Chatelaine,* June 1968, 30, 76, 80, 82.

80 Letter from Mrs. J.B. Dodds of Sorrento, BC, in "The Last Word Is Yours," *Chatelaine,* Mar. 1968, 96.

81 In a (no byline) column in the *Brooks Bulletin,* Alberta, 19 Sept. 1968, reprinted from the *Elrose Review* in Saskatchewan.

82 Letter from Henry R. Rosenberg, "Women Aren't Men's Equal; It's Nonsense to Say They Are," *Toronto Daily Star,* 7 June 1968.

83 Ruby McIlwain of Wells, BC, under the heading, "The Status of Women," *The Quesnel Cariboo Observer,* 15 Aug. 1968.

84 Letter from Lillian Austin, under the heading "Dopey Dames," *The Telegram,* Toronto, 19 June 1968.

85 Letter from (Mrs.) R. Ditchfield, "Is It Equality?" *The Vancouver Sun,* 7 June 1968; see also an unsigned letter to the editor, "Taxing Bachelors," *Brantford Expositor,* Ontario, 3 June 1968.

Chapter 6

1 Janice Tyrwhitt, "Why the Hell *Can't* We Provide Daycare for Working Mothers' Kids?" *Star Weekly,* 27 July 1968, 13-17.

2 CP, "War between Sexes Goes Public: Men Main Target of Commission on Women," *The Calgary Herald,* 22 Apr. 1968, 22. (No byline), "Women Get That Hotline A-Sizzling," *The Province,* Vancouver, 17 Apr. 1968, 30; CP, "Pay for

Mothers Argued by Women," *The Ottawa Citizen*, 16 Apr. 1968, 22. Bruce Yemen, "Women Get Burned up on Hotline; Heat Turned on Working Mothers," *Victoria Daily Colonist*, 15 Apr. 1968.

3 Twenty-four percent of the female labour force were mothers. Just over one-third of them worked less than 35 hours a week. Canadian Department of Labour, Women's Bureau, "Working Mothers and Their Childcare Arrangements (Ottawa: Queen's Printer, 1970), 5-7, and Table 23, p. 41. Cited in *Report of the Royal Commission*, 263-64.

4 Arnup, *Education for Motherhood*, quote from p. 4; also 8-11, 49-56, 150-54. The influence of Freudian thought was still strong in the 1960s. Sev'er, *Women and Divorce*, 229-30. For an example of the media's use of "experts" in this debate, see the interview with the anthropologist Margaret Mead. Jock Carroll, "The Feminine Revolution: Who's to Look after The Children," *Weekend Magazine*, 30 Mar. 1968, 2-6.

5 Strong-Boag, "Canada's Wage-Earning Wives" and "Their Side of the Story"; Sangster, "Doing Two Jobs"; Prentice, "Workers, Mothers, Reds: Toronto's Postwar Daycare Fight."

6 Timpson, "Royal Commissions as Sites of Resistance," 126-27. Boyd, "*Canadian Attitudes toward Women*," 11-13 and Table 5, 44-47; Strong-Boag, "Discovering the Home." For an overview of the historiography of women and their work, see Kobayashi et al., "Introduction: Placing Women and Work"; Armstrong and Armstrong, *The Double Ghetto*, Chapter 3.

7 Znaimer co-hosted the program between 1967 and early 1968 with Clarkson and Soles. *Take 30*, 22 Apr. 1968, RCSW hearings in Victoria and Vancouver.

8 Newspaper stories included: CP, "Career Girl a Girl No More," *The Gazette*, Montreal, 10 June 1968, 14; (no byline), "64 Percent Increase: More Women Work—But Many Part-Time," *The Montreal Star*, 13 June 1968, 15; Susan Becker (CP), "Statistics Study Shows Fairly Sizable Pay Gaps," *The Ottawa Citizen*, 2 Oct. 1968, 41.

9 The statistical data on poverty is from a brief from the Economic Council of Canada to the Special Senate Committee on Poverty, April 1969. On page 6, it defines poverty as delineated by income: $1,800 a year for a single person; $3,000 for a family of two; $3,600 for a family of three; $4,200 for a family of four, and $4,800 for a family of five. Copy in NAC RCSW, Vol. 34, "Maynard" File. See also *Report of the Royal Commission*, Chapter 2 and p. 263; Finkel, "Even the Little Children Cooperated," 112. The vulnerability of these women to poverty has not changed. Armstrong and Armstrong, *The Double Ghetto*, 80.

10 Cited in Schull's obituary: Donn Downey, "Journalist Had the Gourmet Touch," *The Globe and Mail*, 17 May 2000, R8.

11 My emphasis. David Quinter (CP), "Retreat to Cave Flayed," *The Ottawa Citizen*, 13 June 1968, 45, published as CP, "Backlash at Women," *The Telegram*, Toronto, 12 June 1968.

12 Andrea Goeb, "Brief Blasts Women As Own Worst Enemies," *The Gazette*, Montreal, 12 June 1968, 22. Actually, according to the CBC's coverage, they applauded after, not as, Schull read her brief and again later when she declared that women were jealous of each other and did not support each other. It was only under questioning from Commissioner Lange that her co-presenter Lou Connor acknowledged that the women's husbands also held them back (see Chapter 5). *Take 30*, 17 June 1968, and *CBC Matinee*, 14 June 1968, RCSW hearings in Quebec City and Montreal. The Rosemere brief was included but not headlined in a round-up of the day's briefs in Sheila Arnopoulos, "Status of Women Hearings: Wider Cross Section Needed for Volunteer Work, Commission Told," *The Montreal Star*, 11 June 1968, 52.

13 Calnek's emphasis. *Take 30*, 6 May 1968; and *CBC Matinee*, 3 May 1968, RCSW Hearings in Regina and Saskatoon; Rosemary Speirs, "Mother Speaks Out: Marriage Shrouded in Myth," *The Calgary Herald*, 30 Apr. 1968.

14 On women's rights internationally, see Doris Anderson, "Progress in the World of Women," and "Rights: U.S. Women Have More," *Chatelaine*, May and Sept. 1969, 1. Monique Bégin and Dorothy Cadwell of the Commission staff planned a three-week research trip to Europe and Sweden early in March 1968. It was postponed indefinitely for budgetary reasons. E. Kaplansky, Information officer to Mrs. Elizabeth Johnstone of the International Labour Office, Geneva, dated 5 Apr. 1968. NAC RCSW, Vol. 38, Files marked Trips—Europe—1 and 2.

15 van Dijk, *News as Discourse*, 11.

16 Margaret Weiers, "Marriage a 'career?' Nonsense, she says," *Toronto Daily Star*, 3 June 1968, 1, 4.

17 *The Ottawa Citizen*, 4 June 1968, 33; Leone Kirkwood, "Housewife's Role 'Must Be Abolished': Father Must Share Responsibility for Raising Children, Royal Commission Told," *The Globe and Mail*, 4 June 1968, 13.

18 The historian Franca Iacovetta particularly challenges the idea that immigrant women had little agency. Iacovetta, "Remaking Their Lives," "From Contadina to Worker," and *Such Hardworking People*.

19 In the *Gazette* version of the CP copy, there was a banner headline, "Young Women Speak Up on Status," over separate headlines for the Kathryn Keate story about media images of young women and this one. See CP, "Against Glamor Image" and "On Behalf of Mothers," *The Gazette*, 20 Apr. 1968. The immigrant daughters' story was published as "Many New Canadian Mothers Scared to Look for Jobs They Might Want," *The Montreal Star*, 20 Apr. 1968.

20 Ann Barling, "Claim Students in Brief: Mothers Belong at Home," *The Vancouver Sun*, 19 Apr. 1968, 26. Personal description from Terry French, "Call for Equality in Birth Control, Too." *The Province*, Vancouver, 19 Apr. 1968, 28.

21 RCSW audio tape #9909, Vancouver, 18 Apr. 1968. Arscott, "Twenty-Five Years," 41.

22 Rosemary Speirs, "Commission Ends Western Tour: Demands from Women May Result in Re-Examination of Laws, Chairman Says," *The Globe and Mail*, Toronto, 6 May 1968, 13.

23 (No byline), "She'd Raise Motherhood's Stature," *Toronto Daily Star*, 4 June 1968, 52; Sheila Arnopoulos, "Women's Brief Urges Break for Housewife," *The Montreal Star*, 6 June 1968, 49, 61. (no byline), "She's Supporting Stay-Home Moms," *Waterloo Chronicle*, 12 June 1968, which notes that her husband "spoke briefly" at the hearing.

24 Rosemary Speirs (CP), "More Women than Men Have Emotional Ills," *Evening Times-Globe*, Saint John, 10 Sept. 1968, 1; "Working Mothers Have Problems," *Telegraph-Journal*, Saint John, 11 Sept. 1968, 7, 9; CP, "Non-Working Mother's Frustration Factor in Mental Health Problems," *Evening Times-Globe*, 11 Sept. 1968, 7. See also, Rosemary Speirs (CP), "Running a Home 'Deadens' Women," *Winnipeg Free Press*, 13 June 1968, 22.

25 *Take 30* 23 Sept. 1968; *CBC Matinee*, 20 Sept. 1968, RCSW hearings in the Atlantic provinces. Finkel, "Even the Little Children Cooperated," 96, 108-14.

26 (No byline), "Housewife Called an Anachronism," *The Telegram*, Toronto, 4 June 1968, 58.

27 *Take 30*, 3 June 1968, RCSW hearings from Winnipeg.

28 Their financial status is evident from data in the *Chatelaine* survey. Respondents were almost evenly divided between full-time homemakers and women who worked outside the home, 23 percent of them full-time. Most of these women indicated that they were "in moderately-comfortable" financial

circumstances, with only 17 percent making less than $5,000 a year. Just over half were between the ages of 30 and 50, while about 30% were younger. Gillen, "Report: What You Think of Women's Status," *Chatelaine*, June 1968, 30, 76, 80, 82. Street surveys include Aune Carelius and Murray Carter, "Enquiring Reporter," *Port Arthur News Chronicle*, Ontario, 25 May 1968; Joyce Douglas, "Attitudes Are Most to Blame, Says McGill Undergraduate," *The Montreal Star*, 12 June 1968, 59; "Status of Women: Local Women Are Interested but None Are Militant," *Evening Telegram*, St. John's, 13 Sept. 1968, 12.

29 Alixe Carter, "Whither the Status of Women?" *The Journal*, Ottawa, 28 Sept. 1968.

30 Bill Bantey, "Women's Slavery Days Are Gone, and Ibel Webb Is Happy About It," *The Gazette*, Montreal, 11 June 1968, 5.

31 Ericson et al., *Negotiating Control*, 15.

32 Little, "'No Car, No Radio, No Liquor Permit,'" 145.

33 *Take 30* and *CBC Matinee*, 3 June 1968, RCSW hearings in Winnipeg.

34 See (no bylines), "Sole-Support Mothers Seek Guaranteed Income," "Recognize Labor in Home, Status Commission Told," and "Man. Brief 'Impresses' Status Study Chairman," *Winnipeg Free Press*, 29 May 1968, 21, 23; Marilyn Dill, "Women's Probe to Study Plight of Single Parent," *The Tribune*, 29 May 1968; Rosemary Speirs, "70 Percent Supplement Incomes: Mothers Work out of Need," *The Calgary Herald*, 29 Apr. 1968, 26.

35 Ruth Willson, "Day Care Centre: Sask. Would Share Program," *The Leader-Post*, Regina, 1 May 1968, 1 and 4. Rosemary Speirs, "Saskatchewan to Share Setting-Up Cost of Federal Day Care Scheme," *The Calgary Herald*, 1 May 1968, 37. *CBC Matinee*, 3 May, and *Take 30*, 6 May 1968, RCSW hearings in Saskatchewan.

36 (No byline), "The Realm: Woman Power," *Time* magazine (Canadian edition), 10 May 1968, 14. The federal government stopped funding daycare in Quebec and Ontario after World War II. Finkel, "Even the Little Children Cooperated," 94-95.

37 *Take 30*, 22 Apr. 1968, RCSW hearings in Victoria and Vancouver. *Chatelaine* followed the issue closely. See, for example, Margaret Kesslering (Weiers), "Canada's Backward Thinking on Day Nurseries," *Chatelaine*, Apr. 1966, 41, 68, 70, 72, 74-76; Mollie Gillen, "Why You Still Can't Get Daycare," *Chatelaine*, Mar. 1970, 28-29, 70-72, 74-75, 78; Doris Anderson, "Yes, Dear Governments, We Can Afford Day Care," *Chatelaine*, Mar. 1971, 1. The Prime Minister shrugged it off, saying it was not a federal responsibility. Hélène Pilotte (trans. Jean Wright), "Prime Minister Trudeau Talks to Chatelaine," *Chatelaine*, June 1969, 27, 65-66; 68-69. See also, Finkel, "Even the Little Children Cooperated," 116-118.

38 *CBC Matinee*, 6 June 1968, RCSW hearing in Toronto. *Take 30*, 22 Apr. 1968, RCSW hearings in Victoria and Vancouver; Sheila Arnopoulos, "Child Day Care Setup Bitterly Criticized," *The Montreal Star*, 7 June 1968, 10. See also, "Day Care Prevented Mother Hitting Child," *The Telegram*, 6 June 1968. On the "maternal deprivation" theories of John Bowlby and others, see Finkel, "Even the Little Children Cooperated," 109, n81, 114-16. Other briefs included Eleanor Dunn, "Working Mother May Aid Child," *The Ottawa Citizen*, 2 Oct. 1968, 39.

39 (No byline), "Want Govt. Funds for Day Nurseries," *Winnipeg Free Press*, 30 May 1968, 30.

40 See Timpson, "Royal Commissions as Sites of Resistance." The various recommendations on kinds of childcare are contained in most of the references cited in this chapter. For other examples, see, on daycare: Rosemary Speirs,

"Saskatchewan to Share Setting-Up Cost of Federal Day Care Schemes," *The Calgary Herald*, 1 May 1968, 37; on flexible hours: Alixe Carter, "Married Women Doctors Have Problems Too," *The Ottawa Journal*, 5 Oct. 1968; on education: Lorraine Shore, "Probe Into Status of Women Hears UBC Co-ed Complain of Sex Barrier," *The Vancouver Sun*, 19 Apr. 1968, 13; on guaranteed incomes: (no byline), "Sole-Support Mothers Seek Guaranteed Income," *Winnipeg Free Press*, 29 May 1968, 23; on wages for housework: (no byline), "VoW See Pay for Housewife," *The Edmonton Journal*, 26 Apr. 1968, 21; and (no byline), "Is Wage Break for Motherhood Coming Thing?" *The Tribune*, Winnipeg, 3 May 1968.

41 Anthony Westell, "3-Month Notice of Ouster by Technology Proposed: Liberals Promise Labor Code Overhaul," *The Globe and Mail*, 13 June 1968. Unions, which had been slow to take up this cause, did ask the Commission for it. Terry French, "Challenge to Men on Equal Pay for Women—Would You Strike for Their Rights?" *The Province*, Vancouver, Apr. 18, 1968, 28; (no byline), "Prepare for Status Inquiry: Women Trade Unionists Make Plea for Maternity Leave," *The Globe and Mail*, June 26, 1967; (no byline), "Maternity Leave Law Proposed," *The Leader-Post*, Regina, 1 May 1968, 1, 4; Sheila Arnopoulos, "Status of Women Hearings: Women in the Workforce Must Have Same Rights as Men, Is French-Canadian Women's View," *The Montreal Star*, 12 June 1968, 59, 71; Jean Sharp, "Teatime Topics," *Vankleek Hill East Ontario Review*, 5 Sept. 1968. *Take 30*, RCSW hearings in British Columbia; *CBC Matinee*, RCSW hearings in Ottawa. The Commission recommended it be covered by unemployment insurance and this suggestion was accepted. Paid maternity leave became part of the Canada Labour (Standards) Code in 1970. *Report of the Royal Commission*, 84-88; Burt, "Changing Patterns of Public Policy," 222.

42 Rosemary Speirs, "Suggestions Would Wipe Out Social Ills: Housewives' Salary Plan Outlined for Commission," *The Leader Post*, Regina, 3 May 1968, and "Status of Women: Political Life Splits Responsibility," and (no byline), "VoW Seeks Pay for Housewife," *The Edmonton Journal*, 26 Apr. 1968, 21. (No byline), "Briefs Presented to Commission on the Status of Women," "Aid for One-Parent Homes Suggested by Farm Women," and "Farm Wife Wage Urged," all in *The Star-Phoenix*, Saskatoon, 3 May 1968, 6; Speirs, "Demands from Women May Result in Re-examination of Laws, Chairman Says," *The Globe and Mail*, 6 May 1968, 13.

43 Freeman interviews with Crittenden, Creighton, Sharp Cochrane, Weiers and Dunn. Data on women journalists from CWPC 1964 survey, and brief from the Toronto branch of the CWPC (see Chapter 2). Data on male opinion is in Elkin, "Family Life Education in the Media of Mass Communication."

44 Eleanor McKim, "Frankly Speaking," *Evening Telegram*, St. John's, 23 Aug. 1968, 10, and 13 Sept. 1968, 12.

45 Thelma Cartwright: "Equality a 'Myth': 20th Century Trying Time for Women," *Canadian Labour*, February 1967; and on *Matinee*, RCSW hearings in Ottawa.

46 Dorothy Dearborn, "In My Opinion: Canada Shouldn't Pay Mothers to Have Children," *Telegraph-Journal*, Saint John, 16 Sept. 1968, 5.

47 Linda Curtis, "Royal Commission Ends," The *Albertan*, Calgary, 26 Oct. 1968.

48 According to the press, the idea was to give sons a manly role model, because the Swedish researchers thought that boys became too aggressive when dominated by their mothers at home. *Washington Post/LA Times* News Service, "Equality of the Sexes: Changes Urged in Family Structure," *The Telegram*, Toronto, 7 Oct.1968.

49 Editorial, "Ponder This while Washing Dishes," *Financial Post*, Toronto, 16 Nov. 1968, republished in several other newspapers.

50 Dennis Braithwaite, "Subsidy to Women Who Stay at Home," *The Telegram*, Toronto, 6 Sept. 1968.
51 Eric Nicol, "Design for Living," *The Province*, Vancouver, 20 Apr. 1968, 27; Jack Hutton (Toronto *Telegram* News Service), "Husband-Housekeeper Has All the Answers," *Daily Gleaner*, Fredericton, 22 May 1968. Other examples of male opinion include, "Working Women 'Off Base' in Claims for Special Aid," *The Sudbury Star*, Ontario, 5 June 1968; "Housewife-Mothers Not Second-Class Citizens," *Owen Sound Sun-Times*, 5 June 1968; (no heading) comment reprinted from the *Kingsbury Reporter* in "Weekly Views of the News," *The London Free Press*, 25 Apr. 1968, 6; "Women Deserve a Fairer Deal," *Toronto Daily Star*, 8 June 1968; "The Women Have a Point," *Star Weekly*, 2 July 1968, which appeared in the same edition as the Tyrwhitt article on daycare; "A Grim Conclusion," (on poverty among women), Winnipeg *Tribune*, 9 Nov. 1968; editorial, "A Woman's Place," *Evening Telegram*, 18 Sept. 1968, 8.
52 Freeman interview with Barron.
53 Sid Barron, *Toronto Daily Star*, 2 Mar. 1968, 6.
54 Rusins (Kaufmanis), *The Ottawa Citizen*, 1 Oct. 1968, 6.
55 Gillen, "Report: What You Think of Women's Status," *Chatelaine*, June 1968, 30-31, 76, 80, 82-83. An Office Overload survey of its part-time female office help received a low response, but what there was suggested that these "unsophisticated" women would rather stay home. The headline was quite misleading. Margaret Weiers, "Canada's Women Shout for Their Rights," *Toronto Daily Star*, 12 Feb. 1968, 43.
56 Letter from Mrs. R. Heider, Toronto, under the heading "Status of Mothers," in magazine's regular letters feature, "The Last Word Is Yours," *Chatelaine*, Sept. 1968, 132.
57 Weiers, "The Status of Women: What the Men Say," *Toronto Daily Star*, 26 Mar. 1968, 51; continued as "In 1968, most men still believe a woman's place is in the home," 52.
58 This is evident from the financial data in the *Chatelaine* survey. The sociologist who later evaluated the *Toronto Star* survey for the Commission concluded that two-thirds of the respondents were middle to upper class and therefore not typical of male opinion in Toronto. Margaret Weiers, "Traditional Man No Mate for 'New Woman,' Sociologist Finds," *Toronto Daily Star*, 19 July 1969.

Chapter 7

1 Gillen's emphasis. Mollie Gillen, "Our New Abortion Law: Already Outdated? *Chatelaine*, Nov. 1969, 29, 102, 104-107, citation on p. 102.
2 CP, "Abortion Choice Is Woman's, Group Argues," *The Globe and Mail*, 18 Apr. 1968. There were many battles to be fought before abortion was removed from the Criminal Code. See Pierson, "The Politics of the Body"; and Bourne, "Women, Law and the Justice System."
3 Schudson, "The Sociology of News Production Revisited"; Ericson et al., *Negotiating Control*; van Dijk, *News as Discourse*, Chapters 2 and 3.
4 Examples of news stories include, Nikki Moir, "Cost of Unwanted Children Soaring," *The Province*, Vancouver, 20 Apr. 1967; Staff, "Women Liberals Want Inquiry into Abortion," *The Globe and Mail*, 4 Apr. 1967, 10; Yvonne Crittenden, "These Women Want Abortion Laws Changed," *The Telegram*, Toronto, 30 Oct. 1967, 41; CP, "Women Politicians Make News during Centennial Year," *The Gazette*, Montreal, 27 Dec. 1967, 10; Margaret Weiers, "'Let Women Pay Taxes!' Declare Women Liberals," *Toronto Daily Star*, 9 Feb. 1968, 53; Michele Veilleux, "Compulsory Sterilization Is Suggested," *Winnipeg Free Press*, 15 Feb. 1968, 18; Helen Bateson, "Pre-marital Counselling Proposed," *The Tribune*, Winnipeg,

19 Feb. 1968, 10; and CP, "Abortion Inquiry Needed," *Winnipeg Free Press*, 30 May 1968, 4.

5 One brief, from the Corrections Association of Canada, referred to lesbianism in prison as a threat to the inmates, which was noted by the local media but not sensationalized. (No byline) "Crime Report: Improved Care for Female Offenders Urged in Brief," *The Ottawa Citizen*, 2 Oct. 1968, 74; Alixe Carter, "Commissioners Get Facts in Corrections Association Brief," *The Ottawa Journal*, 3 Oct. 1968, 38. One CP version does not mention this angle at all. It's possible it was edited out. Rosemary Speirs, "Are Courts Pushing Our Youngsters?" *Nelson Daily News*, BC, 3 Oct. 1968. *Chatelaine* articles at the time suggested that lesbians were maladjusted. See Valerie Korinek."'Don't Let Your Girlfriend Ruin Your Marriage': Lesbian Imagery in *Chatelaine* Magazine, 1950-1969," 83-109.

6 Adams, *The Trouble with Normal*, 166-67.

7 McLaren and McLaren, *The Bedroom and The State*, 131-36. For positive editorial references, and a detailed analysis of the process by which the laws were changed, see de Valk, *Morality and Law in Canadian Politics*, 90-98. Medical breakthroughs also received some coverage. See Earle Damude, "The Medical Discovery That Could Legalize Abortion," *Chatelaine*, Sept. 1966, 35; 60-63. Lorna R. Marsden, "Family Planning and Women's Rights in Canada."

8 The Federation released its brief in advance and appeared before the Commission in October 1968. CP, "Birth Control Essential Part of Equality of Sexes: Brief," *Winnipeg Free Press*, 12 Feb. 1968, 10; Eleanor Dunn, "Working Mother May Aid Child," *The Ottawa Citizen*, 2 Oct. 1968, 39; *Take 30*, 8 Oct. 1968, RCSW hearings in Ottawa.

9 de Valk, *Morality and Law in Canadian Politics*, 90-98; McLaren and McLaren, *The Bedroom and the State*, 132; Jean Sharp, CP, "Status of Women Top Newsmaker," *Toronto Daily Star*, 24 Dec. 1968.

10 Powell, "Female Sterilization"; Carl F. Grindstaff and G. Edward Ebanks, "Vasectomy: Canada's Newest Family Planning Method." *Report of the Royal Commission*, 280-81.

11 de Valk cites legislative changes in Britain, the shock still being felt over the thalidomide affair, and the media's success at shaping public opinion as important elements in the debate over changing the law. His media analysis is limited, however de Valk, *Morality and Law in Canadian Politics*, 29-45, Gallup poll cited on p. 44. For a specifically feminist approach to the question, see Pelrine, *Abortion in Canada*. Articles which expressed concern about the plight of the unmarried girl or woman forced to seek out a dangerous, illegal abortion include Marilyn Dill, "Criminal Abortion," *The Tribune*, Winnipeg, 30 Nov. 1968. For a sympathetic profile of a willing doctor, see Alexander Ross, "Your Friendly, Local Abortionist," *Maclean's*, May 1968, 30.

12 *Take 30*, 22 Apr. 1968, RCSW hearings in Victoria and Vancouver; *CBC Matinee*, 19 Apr. 1968, RCSW hearings in Victoria and Vancouver.

13 CP, "Abortion Choice Is Woman's, Group Argues," *The Globe and Mail*, 18 Apr. 1968.

14 Rosemary Speirs, "Birth Control Appeal Heard," *Victoria Daily Times*, 17 Apr. 1968, 20. Ann Barling, "More Birth Control Aid Asked: Unwanted Children Increase," *The Vancouver Sun*, 17 Apr. 1968, 1. *The Province*, in a much briefer treatment, noted that the CAS was asking for "freedom of choice" on abortion. Terry French, "Challenge to Men on Equal Pay for Women," *The Province*, Vancouver, 18 Apr. 1968, 28. This was not an unusual argument among social services professionals. On the American case, see Luker, *Dubious Conceptions*, Chapter 2.

15 Rosemary Speirs, "Permissiveness with One Pill Invites Extremes with Another," *The Globe and Mail*, 26 Apr. 1968; (no byline), "Moral Code Strengthening Asked," *The Edmonton Journal*, 26 Apr. 1968, 21. Speirs story also ran as "Sees Serious Consequence in Society's Use of Pill," *The Ottawa Journal*, 27 Apr. 1968; "Fears Birth Control May Lead to Control of Death," *Charlottetown Guardian*, 30 Apr. 1968; "One Pill Leads to Another, Says Woman," in *The Calgary Herald*, 26 Apr. 1968; "Commission Told: After the Pill: Legalized Murder," *The Vancouver Sun*, 27 Apr. 1968; "Status Women Told 'Ban the Pill'," *Toronto Daily Star*, 26 Apr. 1968: "Commission Brief Hits Pill, Divorce," *The Ottawa Citizen*, 26 Apr. 1968, 40.

16 Sheila Arnopoulos, "Women's Brief Urges Break for Housewife," *The Montreal Star*, 5 June 1968, 49, 61.

17 Staff, "Abortion on Request Vetoed by Calgary Women's Brief," *The Calgary Herald*, 22 Apr. 1968, 22. See also (no byline), "Make Pay Fair for All, Say Jaycettes," *The Albertan*, Calgary, 23 Apr. 1968, 5. John Fogan, "National President: CWL Modernizing Its Role," *Evening Times-Globe*, Saint John, NB, 8 June 1968; and Mollie Bouchard, "Status of Women Commission: CWL Brief Presented in Toronto," *The B.C. Catholic*, Vancouver, 6 June 1968. CP, "Abortion Inquiry Urged," *Winnipeg Free Press*, 30 May 1968, 4.

18 Maggie Siggins, "Pay for Wives Bid Heartily Applauded," *The Telegram*, 5 June 1968, 62; see also (no byline), "Problem of the Deserting Father," *Toronto Daily Star*, 5 June 1968. De Valk, *Morality and Law in Canadian Politics*, 62, 85-90.

19 Rosemary Speirs, "Women Can't Agree on Role in Society," *Winnipeg Free Press*, 6 June 1968, 18. The Catholics were recorded on RCSW audio tape #9954. They were followed by the Visiting Homemakers Association. That brief and the subsequent one from the Socialists were recorded on RCSW audio tape #9955. All three were presented during the evening session of 4 June in Toronto. Judi Freeman, "Abortion Decisions Should Be Private," *The Calgary Herald*, 24 Apr. 1968, 61.

20 (No byline), "Cecelia Wallace: She Challenges R.C. Hierarchy," *The Telegram*, Toronto, 27 Apr. 1967; (no byline), "Says CWL Supports Commission which Studies Status of Women," *The Windsor Star*, Ont., 26 May 1967. The story mistakenly calls her group the St. John's Alliance.

21 Margaret Weiers, "Hot Weather Cools Status of Women," *Toronto Daily Star*, 8 June 1968, 42. *The Telegram* publicized the Alliance's brief when it was first released to the media, and did only a short, two-paragraph version from the hearings. See Yvonne Crittenden, "Catholic Brief Seeks Justice for Women," *The Telegram*, Toronto, 21 Mar. 1968, 73; and (no byline), "Catholic Critics of Abortion Hit," *The Telegram*, Toronto, 7 June 1968. Wallace's name appears on the CEWC minutes from 1966.

22 Rosemary Speirs, "Fuzzy Presentations Galore at Women's Status Hearings," *The Vancouver Sun*, 23 Apr. 1968, 25.

23 My emphasis. CBC Radio News, Direct Reports, 3 June 1968, Harry Nuttall reporting from the RCSW hearings in Toronto. See also, Margaret Weiers, "Nobody's Going to Tell Me Whether I'll Have a Baby, Status Commission told," *Toronto Daily Star*, 4 June 1968, 51.

24 Elsie Gregory MacGill, "Separate Statement," *Report of the Royal Commission on the Status of Women*.

25 *Take 30*, 23 Sept. 1968 and CBC Matinee, 20 Sept. 1968, RCSW hearings from the Atlantic provinces.

26 (No byline), "Halifax Mother of Ten Opposes Legal Abortion," *Halifax Mail-Star*, 13 Sept. 1968.

27 Galtung and Ruge, "Structuring and Selecting News," in Cohen and Young, eds., *The Manufacture of News*, 68-71.

28 CBC Radio News Direct Reports, 3 June 1968, Harry Nuttall reporting from the RCSW hearings in Toronto.

29 Margaret Weiers, "Nobody's Going to Tell Me Whether I'll Have a Baby, Status Commission told," *Toronto Daily Star*, 4 June 1968, 51.

30 (No byline), "Briefs Presented to Commission on Status of Women," *The Star-Phoenix*, Saskatoon, 3 May 1968, 6. Similar sentiments were expressed in Vancouver from Jean Rand, a former candidate for mayor. See Ann Barling, "Mistress? Respectable?" *The Vancouver Sun*, 18 Apr. 1968, 42.

31 Louisa T. Katspaugh (Eleanor Dunn), "Hearings Over, Work Begins," *The Southeaster Times*, Ottawa, 9 Oct. 1968.

32 On farm women and their longstanding concerns about birth control, see McLaren, "'Keep Your Seats and Face Facts.'" Catherine Carson, "Commission Lends Ear to Everyone's Brief," *The Edmonton Journal*, 25 Apr. 1968, 19. CBC Radio Direct Reports, John Warren reporting for the 8 and 9 p.m. versions of *The World at Six*, 22 Apr. 1968. Judi Freeman, "Retraining Proves Major Problem: Women Speak Out at Hearings," *The Calgary Herald*, 22 April 1968, 22. The headline was somewhat misleading since the outspokenness angle actually referred to birth control and abortion, not retraining. Bird made the same basic point at other news conferences later, for example, in Regina and Toronto. (No byline), "Commission Study Said 'Like Holding Up Mirror,'" *The Leader-Post*, Regina, 29 Apr. 1968, 18; (no byline), "Abortion, poverty the chief issues," *The Telegram*, Toronto, 8 June 1968, 12. See also, Sheila Arnopoulos, "Cross-Country Hearings Reveal Public Opinion Appears to Be Away Ahead of Present Government Views," *The Montreal Star*, 10 June 1968, 10, 14.

33 Reid's question with his emphasis is on CBC *Matinee*, 26 Apr. 1968, RCSW hearings in Edmonton and Calgary. The film coverage of the Calgary hearing is the only one missing from the *Take 30* programs on the Commission in the National Archives of Canada. This audio excerpt of the Institute's brief is from the Reid Private Collection, RCSW hearing in Calgary, 22 Apr. 1968, morning session, audio tape #2.

34 Rosemary Speirs, "Plea Issued to Free 'Worn Out' Mothers," *The Tribune*, Winnipeg, 22 Apr. 1968, 2, and "Marriage Waiting Period Urged in Brief," *The Ottawa Citizen*, 23 Apr. 1968.

35 On Quebec attitudes, see Maroney, "'Who Has the Baby?'" The Clio Collective, *Quebec Women*, 306; Prentice et al., *Canadian Women*, 380-81.

36 Reid's résumé gave his personal background. *Take 30*, 17 June 1968, RCSW hearings in Toronto, Quebec City and Montreal. CBC *Matinee*, 14 June 1968, RCSW hearings in Quebec City and Montreal.

37 Gillen, "Report: What You Think of Women's Status," *Chatelaine*, June 1968, 30, 76, 80, 82.

38 Ibid.

39 *Take 30*, 17 June 1968; and CBC *Matinee*, 14 June 1968, RCSW hearings from Quebec City and Montreal.

40 The boys in the schoolgirls' survey thought married women should stay home. Both sexes said they believed in premarital chastity. Since the newspaper did not attribute CP stories, it is not clear if they were written by Rosemary Speirs or a local reporter. The somewhat stilted writing style suggests the latter. (No byline), "Job Inequities Stressed Today in Commission Brief," *Quebec Chronicle Telegraph*, 10 June 1968; (no byline), "Quebec Women Interested in Life as Career Women and Mother," *Quebec Chronicle Telegraph*, 11 June 1968. For example, one suggesting trial marriages, birth control and sex education from Dr. Serge Mongeau of Montreal, who had opened Quebec's first family planning clinic, despite the law, in 1960. Linde Howe Beck, "Doctor Recommends Trial Marriages, Sex Education," *The Gazette*, Montreal, 15 June 1968, 13; (no byline,)

Royal Commission hearings: "Trial Marriages Suggested for Couples," *The Montreal Star*, 15 June 1968, 62. On Mongeau, see The Clio Collective, *Quebec Women*, 306; Sheila Arnopoulos, "Brief from Women Demands Censorship of Advertising," *The Montreal Star*, 14 June 1968, 41. It was not the only group that was divided on the issue. CP, "'Don't Rock the Boat, Women Plead,'" *Toronto Daily Star*, 14 June 1968, 54; See also (no byline), "Prohibition of Abortion, Withdrawal of Homosexuality Law Urged," *The Gazette*, Montreal, 14 June 1968, 11.(No byline), "Local Briefs 'Typical," *The Gazette*, Montreal, 15 June 1968, 13.

41 CP, "Magazine Brief Says: Quebec Leads in Feminism," *The Gazette*, Montreal, 4 June 1968, 17; Rosemary Speirs, "Quebec Women Head List as Feminists," *The Ottawa Journal*, 3 June 1968, 19.

42 CBC Radio News, Direct Reports, 11 June 1968, Doreen Kayes reporting for *The World at Six*. Local coverage was included in the following stories: (no byline), "Questionnaire Uncovers Distaff Discontent," *The Montreal Star*, 4 June 1968, 20; Sheila Arnopoulos, "Status of Women Hearings: Wider Cross Section Needed for Volunteer Work, Commission Told," *The Montreal Star*, 11 June 1968, 52; Donna Flint, "Men and Women Can Never Be Equal Woman Doctor Tells Commission," *The Gazette*, 12 June 1968, 22.

43 *CBC Matinee*, 3 May 1968, RCSW hearings in Regina; *Take 30*, 6 May 1968, RCSW hearings in Regina and Saskatoon.

44 Ruth Willson, "Slow Changes Predicted," with the subheading, "Women Sandwiched between Etiquette and Folklore," *The Leader-Post*, Regina, 1 May 1968, 13; Rosemary Speirs, "Demands from Women May Result in Overhaul of Laws, Chairman Says," *The Globe and Mail*, 6 May 1968.

45 Sally Barnes, "Ottawa Refuses to Test Abortion Pills—Women," *Toronto Daily Star*, 3 Oct. 1968. A story from Parliament Hill, which appeared several weeks after the Commission hearings were over, suggests that the government turned down her request on the grounds that the pills contained substances that were legal under the federal Food and Drug Act. The minister maintained that unless the police were involved, the directorate concerned could not follow up on her complaint. CP, "Grosart Gets Abortion Report," *The Gazette*, Montreal, 29 Nov. 1968, 68.

46 Petrie, *Gone to an Aunt's*, 2. This social history, written in journalistic style, is still one of the few accounts of life in Canadian homes for unwed mothers between the 1940s and 1960s. The parents of these pregnant young women kept this "disgrace" a secret, and often told friends that their daughters had simply gone to visit an aunt in another city.

47 In Toronto, a group of social workers said that unmarried mothers were often stigmatized and ignored by government officials and others when they needed housing and other services. Donna Mason, "Aid Minus Bias Asked for Unwed Mothers," *Toronto Daily Star*, 3 June 1968, 69. Ruth Willson, "Marriage Age under Fire," *The Leader-Post*, Regina, 30 Apr. 1968, 1, 4. It was the only aspect of female sexuality discussed in St. John's: Eleanor McKim, "Frankly Speaking," *Evening Telegram*, St. John's, 17 Sept. 1968, 12. In Calgary, one mother whose daughter had eloped said the laws should enforce a waiting period of a month in order to ensure a couple's medical suitability for marriage, even when the woman was pregnant. See (no byline), "News from the Commission: Make 'Em Wait, Says an Angry Mother," *The Albertan*, Calgary, 23 Apr. 1968, 5; Rosemary Speirs, "Marriage Waiting Period Urged in Briefs," *The Ottawa Citizen*, 23 Apr. 1968. Canadian Press, "Financial Aid Needed for Unwed Mothers," *The Calgary Herald*, 1 May, 1968, 37. See also, Doris Anderson, "Should Unwed Mothers Keep Their Babies?" *Chatelaine*, Sept. 1965, 1. Statistics from *Vital Statistics, Preliminary Annual Reports*, Statistics Canada, Cat. #84-201, Ottawa 1967-71.

48 Tutt's emphasis. *CBC Matinee,* 3 May 1968, RCSW hearings in Regina. She did not appear on *Take 30,* nor were there photographs of her in the newspapers.

49 Rosemary Speirs, "Commission Told: A Better Deal Needed for Unmarried Mothers," *The Ottawa Journal,* 1 May 1968; and CP, "Financial Aid Needed for Unwed Mothers," *The Calgary Herald,* 1 May 1968, 37;

50 Ruth Willson, "Problems of Single Parents Are Outlined—Before Royal Commission," *The Leader-Post,* Regina, 1 May 1968, 9. Speirs, "Commission Told: A Better Deal Needed for Unmarried Mothers.

51 *Take 30,* 6 May 1968, RCSW hearings from Regina and Saskatoon.

52 (Staff), "Maritime Women More Conservative," *Western Star,* Corner Brook, 17 Sept. 1968; and (no byline), "Maritime Women 'Homebodies' Says Commissioner," *Evening Telegram,* St. John's, 16 Sept. 1968, 1.

53 Ann Bond, "Two Briefs Are Presented to Women's Commission," *The Charlottetown Guardian,* 14 Sept.1968, 1, 3. A local columnist noted the reticence of Newfoundland women but did not explain it. Eleanor McKim, "Frankly Speaking," *Evening Telegram,* 17 Sept, 1968, 12. Rosemary Speirs, "Commission Ends Western Tour: Demands from Women May Result in Overhaul of Laws, Chairman Says," *The Globe and Mail,* 6 May 1968.

54 Huband was interviewed by Gail Scott, CBC *Radio News,* Direct Reports, 4 Oct. 1968, RCSW hearings in Ottawa.

55 Rosemary Speirs, "Couples Should Marry Themselves, Young Men Tell Status Commission," unmarked clipping which also notes that the CP version was published by 29 other papers listed, most of them on 4 Oct. 1968. See NAC RCSW, Vol. 42, Binder 7. Speirs, "Couples Should Marry Themselves"; (no byline), "Single Man Faces Commission," *The Ottawa Journal,* 4 Oct. 1968; (staff), "Sterilize Males at Puberty, Suggests Bachelor," *The Telegram,* Toronto, 4 Oct. 1968. See also, (no byline), "Commission Hears Some Novel Ideas," *The Ottawa Citizen,* 4 Oct. 1968, 31.

56 Sheila Arnopoulos, "MP's Views Outdated: McGill Medical Students Demand Abortion Reform," *The Montreal Star,* 15 June 1968, 62. Rosemary Speirs, "Virginity for Wedding Dress Obsolete Swap, Hearing Told," *The Vancouver Sun,* 27 Apr. 1968; and (no byline), "Girls Protest That Sex Is Used to Sell Everything," *The Telegram,* Toronto, 7 June 1968, 27.

57 Doris Anderson, "The Pope and the Pill," *Chatelaine,* Nov. 1968, 1. Joan O'Donnell, "A Catholic Mother Answers the Pope," *Chatelaine,* Nov. 1968, 26.

58 NAC, 1996-473-23 Clark Davey Collection, creation date 20 September, 1968.

59 Jan Kamienski, "Women Are Here to Stay," *The Tribune,* Winnipeg, 31 May 1968, 6.

60 Val Sears, "Brief to the Royal Commission on the Status of Men?" *Toronto Daily Star,* 8 June 1968, 31.

61 On Verwey's proposal, there was a letter from (Mrs). R. J. Lumsden of North Surrey, "Woman's Place," *The Vancouver Sun,* 25 Apr. 1968, and a letter from Rabbi Nathan Kop of Montreal, under the heading "Compulsory Temporary Vasectomy Would Break Down Moral Values," *Montreal Star,*29 Apr. 1968, 8. Concern about suicide was expressed by Mrs. Olive Heron, under the heading, "Out of Touch?" *The Telegram,* Toronto, 8 June 1968, 6.

62 Yvonne Crittenden, "These Women Want Abortion Laws Changed," *The Telegram,* Toronto, 30 Oct. 1967, 41.

Chapter 8

1 Elinor Reading, "Indian Girl Uneducated, Has Problems," *Pembroke Observer,* Ontario, 24 Aug. 24, 1968; and CP, "Story of Indian's Woe Heard by Commission," *Winnipeg Free Press,* 10 Aug. 1968, 22.

2 Schudson, "The Sociology of News Production Revisited"; Ericson et al., *Negotiating Control*; van Dijk, *News as Discourse*; Weston, *Native Americans in the News*. See also Burgess and Valaskakis, *Indian Princesses and Cowgirls*.

3 Pierson, "Experience, Difference, Dominance and Voice." See also, Houston, "The Politics of Difference." For a discussion of how minorities in general are treated in the media, see Fleras, "Beyond the Mosaic."

4 Weston's research does not concentrate on aboriginal women, however. Weston, *Native Americans in the News*, Introduction and Chapter 6.

5 For a broader discussion of stereotyped images of aboriginal women in relation to white women, see Burgess and Valaskakis, *Indian Princesses and Cowgirls*. During Canada's centennial, the Native Council of Canada held "Indian Princess" pageants at Expo '67 in Montreal, which suggests that some aboriginals had internalized this image, or exploited it for their own reasons. Patterson, *The Canadian Indian*, 177.

6 The shorter Canadian study is Harris, "Colonizing Mohawk Women."

7 Daniel Francis, *The Imaginary Indian*, 121-22.

8 The old terms for native people are used here in historical context, that is, as they were described in the mainstream media at the time. Today, the nomenclature has changed. First Nations refers mainly to those bands who have treaty or registered status with the federal government. The Métis have mixed "Indian" and white heritage, and may or may not be registered, while Inuit has generally replaced the disparaging term "Eskimo." In Canada, all these peoples, and those who do not fall neatly into any of these categories, refer to themselves generally as aboriginal people and sometimes as "native." See McNab, "From the Bush to the Village to the City," 131, n3. For scholarly alternatives used mainly in the US, see Dickason, *Canada's First Nations*, 15-17.

9 Michelle Brant Castellano and Janice Hill, "First Nations Women." Maria Campbell, *Halfbreed*.

10 While the birthrate was twice as high as that for whites, namely four percent versus two percent a year, the mortality rate ranged from eight times the white rate for pre-school children to three-and-a-half times for adults. The maternal mortality rate was five times greater than that of white women. Very few of the people lived above the poverty line, the unemployment rate was ten times the national average, and the high school dropout rate was 90 percent. Barbara Frum, "Canadian Indians 1968: How Ottawa (and We) Slept," *Chatelaine*, Nov. 1968, 48-55, 109-11; Marvin D. Lipton, "Current Events," *The Leader-Post*, Regina, 2 May 1968, 20. (No byline), "Annual Health Report for N.W.T. Published," *News of the North*, Yellowknife, 25 July 1968, 13. Similar statistics also appeared in *The Report of the Royal Commission*, 329-31. For an overview, see Frideres, *Native Peoples in Canada*, Chapter 5, "Demographic and Social Characteristics." Also, Jean Bruce, "A Study of Eskimo Women in the Keewatin Region of the Northwest Territories," Mar. 1968. unpublished study, NAC RCSW, Vol. 25, Microfilm C-6798.

11 Tobias, "Protection, Civilization, Assimilation"; Frideres, *Native Peoples in Canada*; Miller, *Skyscrapers Hide the Heavens*, 211-35; Patterson, *The Canadian Indian*, 176-91; Dickason, *Canada's First Nation*, 328-39, 352-65, 380-411. Jamieson, *Indian Women and the Law*, 75-81. For the view of a native man, see Cardinal, *The Unjust Society*.

12 On the Northwest Territories, see Bruce, "A Study of Eskimo Women." Castellano and Hill, "First Nations Women." See McNab, "From the Bush to the Village to the City." On women in the north, see Cruikshank, *Life Lived like a Story* and Crnkovich, ed., *"Gossip."*

13 Jamieson, *Indian Women and the Law,* Chapter 14. Krosenbrink-Gelissen, "The Native Women's Association of Canada," Chapter 9, in Frideres, *Native Peoples in Canada.*

14 Weston, *Native Americans in the News,* 129-30.

15 It appears that this emphasis reflected the concerns of social services workers. "Illegitimate" births among native women in Canada were regarded in the same light as those among Black teenagers in the United States. Luker argues that they were really indicative of deeper conflicts over gender and sexuality, race and poverty. Luker, *Dubious Conceptions,* 12-13.

16 Weston, *Native Americans in the News,* 127-32.

17 RCSW audio tape #9918, Edmonton, 26 Apr. 1968. CP, "Violence among Metis Feared," *The Ottawa Citizen,* 26 Apr. 1968, 40; Rosemary Speirs, "Violence Forecast at Hearings: Metis Problems Serious, Says Edmonton Manager," in *The Leader-Post,* Regina, 27 Apr. 1968; CP, "'Metis Will Explode,'—They Can't Take Much More Degredation [*sic*]", *The Albertan,* Calgary, 25 Apr. 1968, 7; CP, "Help Metis Now or Face a Watts Riot in 10 Years, He Warns," *Toronto Daily Star,* 27 Apr. 1968.

18 (No byline), "First-Hand Probe Urged for Metis," *The Edmonton Journal,* 27 Apr. 1968, 21. *CBC Matinee,* 26 Apr. 1968, RCSW hearings from Edmonton and Calgary. The only surviving TV clip of Thorpe shows him telling the Commissioners that the federal government didn't "give a damn" about the Métis, and that the women were the worst off. It was shown during a retrospective sequence about the hearings two years later. *Take 30,* 8 Dec. 1970, RCSW recommendations.

19 Jamieson, *Indian Women and the Law,* 80. CP, "Commission Hears Tragic Story of Destitute Métis Women," *Daily Gleaner,* Fredericton, 27 Apr. 1968, 2; CP, "Recorded in Brief: Metis Girl's Life," *The Montreal Star,* 29 Apr. 1968, 12.

20 See Sangster, "Criminalizing the Colonized." This harsher treatment had been written into the Indian Act and was commonly applied against non-Status natives as well. The Saskatchewan government brief was included in an overview story of that day's hearings. Willson, "Day Care Centre: Sask. Would Share Program." *The Leader-Post,* Regina, 27 Apr. 1968. See CP, "But Treatment Needed: Offenders Jailed," *The Montreal Star,* 4 May 1968; (no byline), "Status of Women Enquiry Begins Session in Saskatoon," *The Star-Phoenix,* Saskatoon, 2 May 1968, 12; Michele Veilleux, "Status Commission Asked to Aid Women in Jail," *Winnipeg Free Press,* 1 June 1968, 21; Rosemary Speirs, "Says Former Inmate: Jails Promote More Troubles," *The Montreal Star,* 3 June 1968, 12 and (no byline), "Jail Breeds Crime, Ex-Inmate Claims," *The Tribune,* Winnipeg, 1 June 1968, 13. The CBC apparently did not report on these briefs but it and the press covered several other hearings where the problems with the laws were aired, although they did not focus on native women specifically. CP, "Branding Prostitutes Criticized," *The Ottawa Citizen,* 31 May 1968, 33; Margaret Weiers, "Status Probers Told of Discrimination," *Toronto Daily Star,* 6 June 1968, 78; Yvonne Crittenden, "The Female Offender's Plight," *The Telegram,* Toronto, 2 Oct. 1968, 65; Rosemary Speirs, "Are Our Courts Pushing Youngsters?" *Nelson Daily News,* BC, 3 Oct. 1968; CBC Radio News, 1 and 2 Oct. 1968, Gail Scott reporting for *The World At Six.*

21 Editorial, "Our Colored Problem," *Red Deer Advocate,* Alberta, 29 Apr. 1968, 4.

22 (No byline), "1-Way Street Leads to Common Law," *The Edmonton Journal,* 27 Apr. 1968, 21. See the first person accounts of four aboriginal women in Castellano and Hill, "First Nations Women."

23 *Take 30,* 8 Dec. 1970. Also, CP, "Metis Seeking Home Schools," *The Calgary Herald,* 27 Apr. 1968, 32. Her brief was not covered on *CBC Matinee.*

24 (No byline), "1-Way Street Leads to Common Law"; AP(CP), "Women Ask for Schools on Reserves to Protect Language, Customs," *The Globe and Mail*, 27 April 1968; CP, "Metis Seeking Home Schools," *The Calgary Herald*, 27 Apr. 1968, 32.

25 Griesbach said he was there as Emily's chauffeur and moral support. Their exchange was recorded on RCSW audio tape #9918, Edmonton, 26 Apr. 1968.

26 Direct Reports, CBC Radio News, 22 Apr. 1968, Wayne Erickson reporting for *Canadian Roundup*.

27 AP(CP), "Women Ask for Schools on Reserves to Protect Language, Customs," *The Globe and Mail*, 27 Apr. 1968; CP, "Metis Seeking Home Schools," *The Calgary Herald*, 27 Apr. 1968, 32; (no byline), "1-Way Street Leads to Common Law," *The Edmonton Journal*, 27 Apr. 1968, 21. One CP analysis drew a parallel between the isolation they felt to that of the white farm women living in remote areas whose children also left for the city. Rosemary Speirs, "Women Ask Help to Overcome Isolation, "*The Leader-Post*, Regina, 29 Apr. 1968, 18. Most stories reflected the native women's concern for their own autonomy. RCSW audio tapes #9918 and #9919, Edmonton, 26 Apr. 1968.

28 RCSW audio tape #9926, Regina, Sask. 2 May 1968. *Take 30*, 6 May 1968; *CBC Matinee*, 2 and 3 May, 1968, RCSW hearings in Regina and Saskatoon. On the Alberta conference: CP, "Indian Women Silent Too Long—Speaker": and "Indian Women Send Second Telegram to PM," *The Leader-Post*, Regina, 18 Mar. 1968. Later, Lavallee spoke to the provincial Council of Women, saying the conditions under which natives lived were similar to Watts in Detroit. CP (Swift Current, SK), "Indians Suffer from Callous Indifference of White Man," *The Montreal Star*, 29 Apr. 1968, 13.

29 Ruth Willson, "Plea Made for Status for Indian Men," and "Indian Women's Brief Asks Status for Men," in two different editions of *The Leader-Post*, Regina, 2 May 1968, 11, 16.

30 CP, "Indian Women Just Doormats Status Commissioners Told," *Toronto Daily Star*, 2 May 1968; published as CP, "Society Uses Indian Women as Doormats, Commission on Women's Status is Told," *The Globe and Mail*, 2 May 1968. CP, "Indian Appeals for Understanding," *The Gazette*, Montreal, 3 May 1968, 15.

31 Rosemary Speirs, "Indian Woman Has Plea for Sympathetic Attitude," *Charlottetown Guardian*, 2 May 1968; and "Society Uses Indian Women as Doormats, Commission on Women's Status is Told," *The Globe and Mail*, 2 May 1968.

32 *Take 30*, and *CBC Matinee*, RCSW hearings in Saskatchewan.

33 Mary Two Axe Earley first approached the Commission in 1967, after reading about it in *The Montreal Star*, saying Mohawk women would like to present a brief. NAC RCSW, Vol. 1, File SW 1-5-2-1, "Requests for Information from Private Individuals," letter to the RCSW from Mary Two Axe Earley, Caughnawaga, Quebec, 19 Sept. 1967. It was brief #245, listed as one of those which "seem to be of very doubtful value and I would hope that special care will be brought to the organization of the National and the Ottawa hearings. We should be less permissive in allowing people to present briefs in this last part of our national tour because of the fact we will be holding these hearings in the National Capital." NAC RCSW, Vol. 36, M. Coupal to John Stewart, 16 July 1968. See also, Vol. 35, "Public Hearings Ottawa" file, a note from Bird, saying, "The Ottawa hearings should be conducted with particular dignity and care for obvious reasons." Bird to Bégin, 5 July 1968.

34 On Horn, a news brief column in the *Telegraph-Journal*, Saint John, 20 Sept. 1968, 2; see also, CP, "Miss Horn Has Many Opponents: 'Indians Your Landlords—Pay Up,'" *The Evening Times-Globe*, Saint John, 16 Sept. 1968, 10.

35 This was only a partial list of their grievances. See Weaver, *First Nations Women*, 94.

36 Earley had been allowed to live in the house left to her by her parents until 1967, when the band council told her that, according to the Act, she was no longer entitled to property on the reserve. Krossenbrink-Gelissen, "The Native Women's Association of Canada," in Friders, *Native Peoples in Canada,* 337.

37 (No byline), "Indian Women Want to Be Indians," *Toronto Daily Star,* 3 Oct. 1968; Wendy Dey, "Status of Women: Indians Tell of Fears," *The Ottawa Citizen,* 3 Oct. 1968, 43; CP, "'Discrimination' in Indian Act Aired by Women," *The Montreal Star,* 4 Oct. 1968.

38 The relevant statements from Bourque were: "I want my Indian rights. Why? Because I am 50 percent Indian. It is my right, it is my privilege and it is my HERITAGE. As a child I believed I was Indian, then I was separated from my friends and my relatives. Why? Because they told me I wasn't Indian." She described some of the privileges she could not enjoy on the reserve because of her status. Then she added: "I don't know where I stand. I don't know what I am. Am I Indian? Am I not Indian? I mean, it creates a problem...all of us children are being deprived of our childhood joys and our childhood rights. Again I ask, is it right? No. Because we ARE Indian, each and every single one of us. Please, I BEG of you, give me back my heritage." RCSW audio tape #10001, Ottawa, 4 Oct. 1968.

39 (No byline), "Indian Women Want to Be Indians," *Toronto Daily Star,* 3 Oct. 1968. Wendy Dey, "Status of Women: Indians Tell of Fears," *The Ottawa Citizen,* 3 Oct. 1968, 43; Sheila Arnopoulos, "Status of Women Roundup: Hearings Are Over, But Public Support Is Still Needed," *The Montreal Star,* 5 Oct. 1968. (No byline), "By Indians: Rights of Women Debated at Meet," *Standard-Freeholder,* Cornwall, 4 Oct. 1968.

40 CP, "'Discrimination' in Indian Act Aired by Women," *The Montreal Star,* 4 Oct. 1968.

41 Editorial, "Discrimination in Canada Not Always 'White' Failing," *The Sudbury Star,* Ontario, 4 Oct. 1968.

42 Jamieson, *Indian Women and the Law,* Chapter 14; Jeannette Lavell's account in Castellano and Hill, "First Nation's Women," 236, 240; Weaver, "First Nations Women," 93-100. NAC RCSW, Vol. 36, File marked "Relations with Participants—Miscellaneous—2," letter to Monique Bégin of the RCSW from Mary Two Axe Earley, 26 Nov. 1968. Sheila Arnopoulos, "Indian Blood Loses Status when Women Marry Whites," *The Montreal Star,* 4 June 1969, 83. See also NAC RCSW, Vol. 36, File marked "Relations with Participants—Miscellaneous—1, an unsigned letter to Commissioner John Humphrey from an aboriginal woman, 15 Apr. 1970 asking the Commission for its support on the issue. See also Krossenbrink-Gelissen, *"The Native Women's Association of Canada,"* in Frideres, *Native Peoples in Canada,* 336-38; The women finally won the right to retain their Indian status when the Act was changed in 1985.

43 A brief note in *The Yukon News,* 11 July 1968; and in Susan Johnson's column, "Ex-School Report," *The Yukon News,* 15 July 1968; (no byline), "Woman Member Wires Request," *The Whitehorse Star,* 18 Apr. 1968, 1; and "Commission Coming," *The Whitehorse Star,* 22 Apr. 1968; (no byline), "Women in the Labour Force, 1967," *The Whitehorse Star,* 2 May 1968, included a letter from Monique Bégin asking the editor, Flo Whyard, to get local people to submit briefs. See also (no byline), "Never Mind a Written Brief—Come and Speak Your Piece to Royal Commission on Tuesday," *The Whitehorse Star,* 1 Aug. 1968, 17. *The Yukon News* is not available on microfilm. For the Northwest Territories, see (no bylines), "Sufferagettes [sic] Hit Town," *News of the North,* 25 July 1968, 17; "Mrs. Bird Flies North Next Week," *News of the North,* 1 Aug. 1968. 7; and "Women!" *News of the North,* 8 Aug. 1968, 1. Don

Harvey (CP), "No Longer a Bush Town: Whitehorse Swings with Fun, Adventure," *Evening Times-Globe*, Saint John, 9 Sept.1968, 20. CP, "Yukon Women Are Different," *Evening Telegram*, St. John's, 9 Aug. 1968, 10; CP, "Women of the North Claim Special Problem," *Winnipeg Free Press*, 8 Aug. 1968, 22.

44 In the Yukon, the "Indian" population was matrilineally and linguistically Tlingit and Athapaskan and was further divided into separate clans. In NWT, the "Indians" were predominantly Dene and Métis, who also had their own separate groups and customs. There were several recognized sub-groups among the Inuit, but, linguistically, they spoke similar Inuktitut dialects. Crnkovich, *"Gossip"*, Introduction. See also an unpublished study done for the Royal Commission: Jim Lotz, "The Changing Role of Canadian Indian Women," Vol. 28, Reel C-6801. This report was written with research associate Julie Cruikshank, and focuses on the "Indian" women of the Yukon.

45 *CBC Matinee*, RCSW hearings in Whitehorse and Yellowknife. Dodds background from "Profile of the Week: Dedie Dodds," *News of the North*, 5 Dec. 1968, 16.

46 *CBC Matinee*, RCSW hearings in Whitehorse and Yellowknife. Whyard is mentioned in Don Harvey (CP), "No Longer a Bush Town: Whitehorse Swings with Fun, Adventure," *Evening Times-Globe*, Saint John, NB, 9 Sept. 1968, 20. Editorial under the subheading, "Some Weren't There," *Whitehorse Star*, 8 Aug. 1968, 4. (No byline), "Women at YK!" *News of the North*, 15 Aug. 1968, 4.

47 *CBC Matinee*, 9 Sept. 1968, the RCSW in the North. CP, "Non-Status Women Considered Fair Game for Respectable Males," *Oshawa Times*, Ont. 13 Aug. 1968; "Non-Status Women Claimed 'Fair Game,'" *The Star-Phoenix*, 12 Aug. 1968; "'Non-Status' Women Make Fair Game, Commission Told," *Winnipeg Free Press*, 10 Aug. 1968, 19.

48 Freeman interview with Reading.

49 Thrasher appeared on *CBC Matinee*, 9 Sept. 1968, RCSW hearings in the North. Other stories included (no byline), "Women at YK!" *News of the North*, 15 Aug. 1968, 4.

50 CP, "Status Commission Hears Plea for Better Housing," *Winnipeg Free Press*, 12 Aug. 1968, 14. Bird made it clear during the hearing that Lahache sent a personal letter meant for her. It contained some personal details of her situation, including the fact that she had epilepsy, which also appeared in the published version. It is possible that Elinor Reading was given permission by either Bird or Lahache to use the letter as long as she left out certain details; in fact, her original copy read that it was "part of" what Lahache had to say. "Part of" was edited out, perhaps as superfluous. RCSW Transcript of the Yellowknife hearings. Original copy of the CP story in Reading Private Collection. See also NAC RCSW, Vol. 35, Transcript of the hearing at Yellowknife. I use it here as it was widely distributed by CP and became part of the public media record.

51 Reid Private Collection, Millican interview with Reid.

52 On local coverage of the meetings concerning the amendments to the Indian Act, see, for example (no bylines), "Government Men Thrice Ejected by Indians," "Editorial: No Special Status for Indians Or Anyone Else," and "Ottawa's Idea of a Pow-Wow?" *News of the North*, Yellowknife, 1 Aug. 1968, 1, 2 and 9.

53 *CBC Matinee*, 9 Sept. 1968, RCSW hearings in the North.

54 Her conversation with Reid are from Reading's notes of that trip. She can't remember the entire context. Freeman interview with Reading.

55 Reid said he read a book by "Judge Sissons," probably John Howard Sissons who first ruled that custom adoptions should be considered legal. See Sissons,

Judge of the Far North. Millican interview with Reid. Freeman interview with Reading; she was featured in Sue Hudspeth's column, *The Calgary Herald*, c. 1967. Unmarked clipping, Reading Private Collection. There were nine media people on the tour in all. (No byline), "Keewatin Eskimos Adopted," *News of the North*, 22 Aug. 1968, 11. Williamson and his wife fostered three Inuit boys at their Saskatoon home, one of whom was about to go to medical school. See (no byline), "Rankin Boy Studies Pre-Med," *News of the North*, 26 Sept. 1968, 21, with a photograph of the boys with the Williamsons.

56 NAC MacGill Papers, Vol. 4, File 2, Minutes of the Ninth Commissioners' Meeting, April 1968. Several documents referring to these arrangements are in NAC RCSW, Vol. 35, "Public Hearings—Yukon and Northwest Territories" file, including two memos from Bird to Bégin, and Bird to Burke, 31 July 1968. Bird had told the Commissioners, "What I am very anxious is that we should not be criticized for not doing what seems to be our duty. ...I only hope that it is not too strenuous a trip....We will at least be able to say that we took the trouble to look for ourselves. I have an idea that looking for ourselves will be a valuable experience." Confidential memo from Bird to the Commissioners, 24 June 1968. Freeman interview with Sarty; *Take 30*, 17 Sept. 1968, the RCSW in the north.

57 *Take 30*, 17 Sept. 1968, the RCSW in the north. Reading agrees that the reporters were in closer contact with the Commissioners on this trip than they were at formal hearings. Freeman interview with Reading. Mr. Justice Morrow had told Bird that she should feel free to insist on private meetings with the local people. NAC RCSW, Vol. 35, "Public Hearings—Yukon and Northwest Territories" file, Bird to Bégin, 31 July 1968. As someone who worked as a journalist in Ottawa in the late 1960s and the mid-'70s, I remember the unwritten rule about not quoting civil servants because it might put their jobs at risk.

58 *Take 30*, RCSW hearings in the north.

59 (No byline), "Rankin Inlet Develops Arctic Industries," *News of the North*, 22 Aug. 1968, 10, 11. See Bruce, "A Study of Eskimo Women," 9, 12, 22-38. (No byline), "Building Lots on Sea: Ottawa Defeats Coral Harbour Land Speculators," *News of the North*, 22 Aug. 1968, 1-2.

60 Lange's report is in NAC RCSW, Vol. 35, file marked Public Hearings Yukon and NWT

61 *Take 30*, 17 Sept. 1968, the RCSW in the north.

62 Elinor Reading, "There's Always a Happy Ending to Adoption Court in the Arctic Villages," *The Ottawa Citizen*, 3 Oct. 1968, 46.

63 Freeman interview with Reading.

64 *Take 30*, 17 Sept. 1968, the RCSW in the north.

65 Elinor Reading, "Royal Commission in N.W.T.: Eskimo Women Boss in the Home," *Telegraph-Journal*, Saint John, 21 Aug. 1968 and CP, "Women Rule Roost in the North Too," *The Edmonton Journal*, 17 Aug. 1968.

66 Freeman interview with Reading.

67 CP, "Northern Trip Gives Insight to Eskimo Life," *Simcoe Reformer*, 5 Sept. 1968. Gary Bannerman, "Status Hearings across Canada: 300 Briefs Submitted So Far," *Evening Times-Globe*, Saint John, 10 Sept. 1968, 26. Speirs, "Women Ask Help to Overcome Isolation" and "Confident Recommendations Will Not Be Put Aside," *Halifax Chronicle Herald*, 10 Sept. 1968, 3; (no byline), "Royal Commission Faces Basically Same Problems," *Halifax Chronicle Herald*, 12 Sept. 1968, 10; Diane Grell, "Metis Problems Are Subject Discussed by Royal Commission, *Daily Times and Conservator*, Brampton, Ont., 4 June 1968. *Take 30*, 8 Dec. 1970, RCSW recommendations. Elinor Reading, "Eskimos Want Co-Ops," *The Calgary Herald*, 16 Aug. 1968; a shorter version was published as CP, "Co-Operative Store Idea for Eskimos," *Kelowna Daily Courier*, 20 Aug. 1968.

68 *Take 30*, 17 Sept. 1968, the RCSW hearings in the north.
69 (No byline), "Status of Keewatin Women," *News of the North*, Yellowknife, 29 Aug. 1968.
70 *Take 30*, 17 Sept. 1968, the RCSW in the north.
71 (No byline or headline), staff photo, *News of the North*, 25 Sept. 1968, 7. CP, "Eskimo Girl Link between Cultures," *Prince Albert Herald*, 18 Oct. 1968, 6. Bruce, "A Study of Eskimo Women," 5, 17-18. These programs and articles were aimed at southern audiences. CBC programs and CP copy did reach the urban north in limited ways. Both *CBC Matinee* and *Take 30* were aired in Yellowknife and the surrounding areas. Radio and TV schedules, *News of the North*, 15 Aug. 1968.
72 *Take 30*, 17 Sept. 1968, the RCSW in the north.
73 Letter from Ethel Brant Monture under the heading, "Is Skid Row All?" in the letters feature "The Last Word is Yours," *Chatelaine*, Apr. 1968, 126. Other objections came from Mrs. W.O. Betts of Port McNeill, BC, and Pearl Willows of the BC Conference Indian Subcommittee of the United Church of Canada in Vancouver. The original story appeared in *Chatelaine*, Feb. 1968.
74 Letter from M. Assheton-Smith, "Letters to the Editor," *News of the North*, Yellowknife, NWT, 15 Aug. 1968, 11.

Chapter 9

1 Editorial, "God Bless 'em," *The Tribune*, Winnipeg, 9 Dec. 1970, 6.
2 van Dijk, *News as Discourse*; Hackett and Zhao, *Sustaining Democracy?*, Chapter 1.
3 Schudson's culturalist approach in "The Sociology of News Production Revisited"; Macdonald, *Representing Women*. Various studies of the media coverage of the women's movement in the US and Canada, including Tuchman, "The Symbolic Annihilation of Women," in Tuchman et al., (eds.), *Hearth and Home*, and *Making News*, Chapter 7; Barker-Plummer, "News as a Political Resource"; Ashley and Olson, "Constructing Reality"; Sharon D. Stone, "Getting the Message Out."
4 Edna Hampton, "Feeling of Hope Outweighs Anger, Commission Chairman Tells Press, "*The Globe and Mail*, 8 Dec. 1970, 10. See photo in that story and in Ben Tierney, "Report on Women Vital to Both Sexes," *The Edmonton Journal*, 8 Dec. 1970, 1, and several CP versions including CP, "Inquiry Chairman Says Report Marks Career High Point," *The London Free Press*, 8 Dec. 1970, 48.
5 John Humphrey, "Minority Report," 433-51: Jacques Henripin, "Separate Statement," 421-28; Doris Ogilvie, "Separate Statement," 431; and Elsie Gregory MacGill, "Separate Statement," 429 *Report of the Royal Commission*.
6 Edna Hampton, "One Male Member Issues Minority Report: Commissioners Divided by Their Sex on Recommendations on Woman's Roles," *The Globe and Mail*, 8 Dec. 1970, 10. CP, "Male Member Presents A Dissenting View in Minority Report," *The Calgary Herald*, 8 Dec. 1970, 61; CP," Man Writes Minority Report," *Winnipeg Free Press*, 8 Dec. 1970, 59.
7 Humphrey, "Minority Report"; Henripin, MacGill and Ogilvie, "Separate Statement(s)," *Report of the Royal Commission*.
8 Humphrey, "Minority Report"; *Report of the Royal Commission*, 324-25. See also, CP, "Income Guarantees: One-Parent Aid Paramount Need," *The Gazette*, Montreal. 8 Dec. 1970, 48.
9 Patrick O'Callaghan, Southam News Services (SNS), "A Dissenting Voice: Women: Never Be Wards of Society," *The Gazette*, Montreal, 8 Dec. 1970, 4. Marjorie Nichols, "Commission's Prescription: For Women: 'Special Treatment,'" *The Ottawa Journal*, 8 Dec. 1970, 1, 5. Elizabeth Dingman,

(Telegram Women's Editor), "Commissioner Feels Report Discriminatory to Both Sexes," *The Telegram*, Toronto, 8 Dec. 41. Humphrey, "Minority Report," *Report of the Royal Commission*, 433-35; 437-41.

10 Zoe Bieler, "Status of Women Chairman Attacks Equal Opportunity Myth," *The Montreal Star*. 8 Dec. 1970, 65; Eleanor Dunn, "Attitudes Blasted," *The Ottawa Citizen*, 8 Dec.1970, 45; Ben Tierney, "'Report on Women Vital to Both Sexes,'" *The Edmonton Journal*, 8 Dec. 1970, 1; Yvonne Crittenden, "Status Chairman: Women 'Treated like Children,'" *The Telegram*, Toronto, 8 Dec. 1970, 41; Ben Tierney, "'Not for Female Eyes Only,' Says Mrs. Bird," *The Province*, Vancouver 8 Dec. 1970, 9. See also, CP, "Special Status Proposed Only as Temporary Thing for Women," *The Edmonton Journal*, 28 Dec. 1970, 14; Kay Alsop, "Reporting on the Report: 'Most Critics Haven't Even Read the Book,'" *The Province*, Vancouver, 29 Jan. 1971, 22, and Leslie Peterson, "The Status Report Gains High Status," *The Vancouver Sun*, 29 Jan. 1971, 26; Leone Kirkwood, "Satellite Sex Called Good Title for Report on Status of Women," *The Globe and Mail*, 24 Mar. 1971.

11 Leone Kirkwood, "Commission Asks Easier Abortions and Paid Leaves for Childbearing," *The Globe and Mail*, 8 Dec. 1970, 1, 2. "Criteria and Principles," *Report of the Royal Commission*, xi-xii. On the "equality" and "difference" discussion among feminists, see Code, "Feminist Theory," 48-52. Arscott, "Canadian Women and 'Second-Class Citizenship.'" Scott, *Gender and the Politics of History*, Part IV.

12 Rosemary Speirs, "Equal Pay Laws Are Often Ignored, Report Says." With subhead: Governments Must Ensure That Women Get Same Wages for Jobs of Comparable Skill," *Toronto Daily Star*, 8 Dec. 1970, 12. *Report of the Royal Commission*, 66-80.

13 (No byline), "Minority Report for 'Forgotten' Woman," *The Montreal Star*, 9 Dec. 1970, 58; CP (Montreal), "Minority Report Given for 'Forgotten Women,'" *Winnipeg Free Press*, 10 Dec. 1970, 21 and "'Unfair to Housewives': Male Commissioner Doesn't Like Report," *The Ottawa Journal*, 8 Dec. 1970, 33.

14 For example, Patrick O'Callaghan (SNS), "A Dissenting Voice: Women: Never Be Wards of Society," *The Gazette*, Montreal, 8 Dec. 1970, 4. See Humphrey, "Minority Report," paragraph 4, 434, *Report of the Royal Commission*.

15 Yvonne Crittenden, "Status Chairman: Women 'Treated like Children,'" *The Telegram*, Toronto, 8 Dec. 1970, 41. *Take 30*, 8 Dec. 1970, Report of the Royal Commission.

16 Socialist perspective can be found in Rosemary Speirs, "Women Can't Agree on Role in Society," *Winnipeg Free Press*, 6 June 1968, 18; and Prentice et al., *Canadian Women*, 426-28. On the RCSW recommendation, see John Gray, "Another Chants 'Abortion on Demand'," *The Montreal Star*, 8 Dec. 1970, 65; Zoe Bieler, "Report Asks Abortion on Demand," continued as "Abortion on Demand Urged," *The Montreal Star*, 7 Dec. 1970, 1, 6. Richard Mackie (Ottawa Bureau), "Abortions Should Be 'Available on Demand,'" *The Telegram*, Toronto, 8 Dec. 1970, 41; and Yvonne Crittenden, "Women Second-Class Citizens—Report," *The Telegram*, Toronto, 7 Dec. 1970. Marjorie Nichols, "'Status of Women' Proposal: Report May Ask Abortions on Demand," *The Ottawa Journal*, 7 Dec. 1970, 1. Several newspapers which used CP's version headlined the term, "on demand"; for example, Susan Becker, "Abortion on Demand Should Be Allowed," *Winnipeg Free Press*, 8 Dec. 1970, 57. The *Toronto Daily Star* used the same phrase but its emphasis was different: Ottawa Bureau, "Abortion Law Benefits Doctors Most," *Toronto Daily Star*, 8 Dec. 1970, 12. (no byline), "Commission Backs Demand Abortions," *The Gazette*, Montreal, 7 Dec. 1970, 9; and Gail Scott, "167 Requirements Listed to Give Women Par Status," with subhead: "Every Aspect of Life Covered by Report"

and continued on next page under "Abortion Rights, Day-Care in Top Issues," *The Gazette*, Montreal, 8 Dec. 1970, 1, 2. (This is a different Gail Scott from the one who worked at the CBC.) Patrick O'Callaghan (SNS), "Abortion Most Critical Area," *The Ottawa Citizen*, 8 Dec. 1970, 45; Ottawa Bureau of the Globe and Mail, "Abortion on Request Suggested for Pregnancies of 12 Weeks," *The Globe and Mail*, 8 Dec. 1970, 10. Jean Sharp, "Long Wait Noted," *Winnipeg Free Press*, 8 Dec. 1970, 5. My emphases, *Report of the Royal Commission*, 286-87. MacGill, "Separate Statement."

17 Susan Becker (CP), "Moncton Judge Doesn't Support Relaxed Abortion Laws," *Daily Gleaner*, Fredericton, 8 Dec. 1970, 23. *Report of the Royal Commission*, 231; 275-81. CP, "Teaching in Sexual Behavior Urged in Primary and Secondary Schools," *Toronto Daily Star*, 8 Dec. 1970, 13, published as "Report Favors Contraceptives for Young Girls," *The Gazette*, Montreal, 8 Dec. 1970, 7; and "Sterilization for Birth Control Should Be 'Available to All,'" *The Ottawa Journal*, 8 Dec. 1970, 34. On the marriage age, see United Press International (UPI), "Age 18 Urged Earliest to Wed," *The Gazette*, Montreal, 8 Dec. 1970, 1; (no byline), "Minimum Age 18 Seen for Marriage," *The Telegram*, Toronto, 8 Dec. 1970, 41; and Star Ottawa Bureau, "18 Urged as Marriage Minimum," *Toronto Daily Star*, 8 Dec. 1970, 12.

18 Gail Scott, "Abortion Rights, Day-Care in Top Issues," *The Gazette*, Montreal, 8 Dec. 1970, 2. Globe Ottawa Bureau, "Government Financing Urged for Daycare Centres," *The Globe and Mail*, 8 Dec. 1970, 10; CP, "Not Just the Working Mother: Day-Care Centres for All Who Need Them Suggested," *The Ottawa Journal*, 8 Dec. 1970, 33. Star Ottawa Bureau, "Ottawa Urged to Pay Half of Day Care Centres' Costs," *Toronto Daily Star*, 8 Dec. 1970, 13. Nick Hills (SNS), "And $500 a Year Per Child: Maternity Benefits Recommended," *The Ottawa Citizen*, 8 Dec. 1970, 70, published as "Holiday—With Pay—Proposed for Pregnant Workers," *The Tribune*, Winnipeg, 8 Dec. 1970, 32. Maternity leave was covered in CP, "Public Service Should Set Example, Says Commission On Status Of Women," *The Calgary Herald*, 9 Dec. 1970, 74; and in Peter Thomson (Ottawa Bureau) "Female Labor Said Greatest Untapped Manpower Source," *The Telegram*, Toronto, 8 Dec. 1970, 41. Leone Kirkwood, "Commission Asks Easier Abortions and Paid Leaves for Childbearing," *The Globe and Mail*, 8 Dec. 1970, 1, 2. Lewis Seale, "Allowance of $500 Proposed: Report Suggests Guaranteed Annual Income for One-Parent Family Heads," *The Globe and Mail*, 8 Dec. 1970, 11; CP, "Income Guarantees: One-Parent Aid Paramount Need," *The Gazette*, Montreal. 8 Dec. 1970, 48. Humphrey, "Minority Report," 444-46; Henripin, "Separate Statement," 424-28, *Report of the Royal Commission*.

19 Yvonne Crittenden, "Look, Ma! No Prejudice!" *The Telegram*, Toronto, 11 Dec. 1970. Ironically, a few days before, Crittenden had written in a column that the "wildfire" spread of women's liberation across North America in recent years "means women no longer face the same ridicule when they talk about women's rights." See Crittenden, "Catching Up with Women," in "Pulse" column, *The Telegram*, 3 Dec. 1970. Zoe Bieler, "The Question: Will Anything Be Done?" *The Montreal Star*, 9 Dec. 1970, 56.

20 Bieler, "Status of Women Chairman Attacks Equal Opportunity Myth," *The Montreal Star*, 8 Dec. 1970, 65; Anthony Westell, "Report is More Explosive than Any Terrorist's Time Bomb," *Toronto Daily Star*, 8 Dec. 1970, 13.

21 Yvonne Crittenden, "Status Chairman: Women 'Treated like Children'", *The Telegram*, Toronto, 8 Dec. 1970, 41; Lillian Newberry (CP), "Report Reflects List of Women's Grievances," *Winnipeg Free Press*, 8 Dec. 1970, 1, 10; CP, "Proposals 'Just a Step,'" *The London Free Press*, 8 Dec. 1970, 28; and a profile of Bird CP, "'High Point of My Career,'" *The Telegraph-Journal*, Saint John, 10 Dec. 1970, 9.

22 Lillian Newberry, "Women Losing Out on Privileges, Responsibilities of Public Life," *The Ottawa Citizen*, 8 Dec.1970, 48. For a similar approach, see Jim Tost, "More Female Participation in Public Life Sought: Women Senators from Each Province Wanted," *The Ottawa Journal*, 8 Dec. 1970, 33. Eleanor Dunn, "Commissioners Concerned with Men's Status, Too," *The Ottawa Citizen*, 8 Dec. 1970, 47. See also, Ottawa bureau, "Income Tax Bias Urged Changed," *Toronto Daily Star*, 8 Dec. 1970, 13. Divorce and separation were covered in (no byline), "Minimum Age 18 Seen for Marriage," *The Telegram*, Toronto, 8 Dec. 1970, 41. *Report of the Royal Commission*, 410-11. Sev'er, *Women and Divorce*, 110-11.

23 CBC Radio News, 7 Dec. 1970, Tom Earle Reporting for "The World At Six."

24 (No byline), "The Realm: Call to Arms," *Time* (Canadian edition), 21 Dec. 1970, 5, 6. Ben Tierney, "Women Would Get Equality at Home, Work," *The Edmonton Journal*, 7 Dec. 1970, 1, 2. See also, Tierney, "'Not for Female Eyes Only,' says Mrs. Bird," *The Province*, Vancouver 8 Dec. 1970, 9.The story was the same; only the headline changed. Wayne MacDonald, "Status of Women Report Urges: 'End Discrimination; Give Equality,'" *The Vancouver Sun*, 7 Dec. 1970, 1. Final edition: "Commission on Women Urges: Paid Vacation for Housewives," *The Vancouver Sun*, 7 Dec. 1970, 1, 2. On page 2, the headline was "Status Report Urges Total Equality" both editions. *Report of the Royal Commission*, 36-40, especially paragraph 86.

25 *Report of the Royal Commission*, 369-85. Nick Hills, "Criminal Code Unfair to Men—Commission," *The Edmonton Journal*, 7 Dec. 1970, 2: Star Ottawa Bureau (no byline), "Sex Laws Said Unfair to Men," *Toronto Daily Star*, 8 Dec. 1970, 12. CP, "Report Opposes Prison for Women," *The London Free Press*, 8 Dec. 1970, 48. (No byline), "Closing of Kingston Women's Prison Sought; Maximum-Security Setting Said Unnecessary," *The Globe and Mail*, 8 Dec. 1970, 11; (no byline), "Flexible Rehabilitation Plan Wanted: Status of Women Commission Urges Women's Prison in Kingston Be Closed," *The Ottawa Journal*, 8 Dec. 1970, 34.

26 *Take 30*, 8 Dec. 1970.

27 *Report of the Royal Commission*, Chapter 1, quote on p. 12.

28 Rosemary Speirs, "'We Recommend Simple Justice' commission says," *Toronto Daily Star*, 8 Dec. 1970, 12.

29 (No byline), "Who Needs It? Sugar 'n' Spice," *The Ottawa Citizen*, 8 Dec. 1970, 45; Ottawa Bureau, "Use of 'Sex-Typed' Schoolbooks Discourages Girls, Report Says," *The Globe and Mail*, 8 Dec. 1970, 11; Terence Moore, "Family Life Programs Suggested to Overcome Traditional Roles," "continued as "Family Life Programs Stressed," *Toronto Daily Star*, 8 Dec. 1970, 65, 66. Most were similar to CP, "Entry to Military Colleges is Urged for Women," *The Globe and Mail*, 8 Dec. 1970, 10; and "Military 'Cadettes' Urged for Canada," *The Gazette*, Montreal, 8 Dec. 1970, 4. An exception was CP "'Sex-Typing' Prevalent in Educational System," *The Telegram*, Toronto, 8 Dec 1970, 41.

30 CP, "Ugly Air Hostesses?—Insistence on Youth, Beauty Called Unfair," *The London Free Press*, 8 Dec. 1970, 48; published as "Drop Bunny Club Philosophy," *Daily Gleaner*, Fredericton, 8 Dec. 1970, 28. See also Patrick O'Callaghan (SNS) "Sex-Object Image Slammed," *The Calgary Herald*, 7 Dec. 1970, 1. *Report of the Royal Commission*, 89-90. Apparently, the only story published when their brief had been presented had been done by CP, which led with, "Canadian Air Lines Adopt a 'Bunny Club' Attitude towards Their Stewardesses." CP, "'Bunny club' Attitude—Brief," *The Ottawa Citizen*, 4 Oct. 1968, 50. Certain details were inserted into Eleanor Dunn, "Status of Women: Doctors Favor Abortions," the following day. On the same page was a close-up photo of two attractive members of the Air Line Flight Attendants Association presenting their brief with the caption, "'Bunny girl' image." The camera angle positioned the micro-

phone suspiciously close to one of their mouths, in what could be seen as a crude sexual double-entendre, *The Ottawa Citizen*, 5 Oct. 1968, 39.

31 Ericson et al., *Negotiating Control*, 5.

32 *Report of the Royal Commission*, on education, 210-18; on marital status, 237-38. Ottawa Bureau, "Report Sympathetic to Indians, Eskimos," *The Globe and Mail*," 8 Dec. 1970, 11. Henripin said they did not focus on women specifically, but most of them did. Henripin, "Separate Statement," *Report of the Royal Commission*, 425-26. It is not clear if CP's story originally included these additional paragraphs and they were dropped by other newspapers, or if the *Tribune* simply added them. CP, "Textbooks Blamed for Choice of Life," *Winnipeg Free Press*, 8 Dec. 1970, 59. Other newspapers mentioned these issues in other articles, for example, in Lewis Seale, "Allowance of $500 Proposed: Report Suggests Guaranteed Annual Income for One-Parent Family Heads," *The Globe and Mail*, 8 Dec. 1970, 11; (no byline), "Minimum Age 18 Seen for Marriage," *The Telegram*, Toronto, 18 Dec. 1970, 41; CP, "Guaranteed Wage for Single Parents?" *The Ottawa Journal*, 8 Dec. 1970, 33.

33 Ottawa Bureau, "Woman MP Fears 'Hen Pen,'" *Toronto Daily Star*, 8 Dec. 1970, 13. CP, "Grace Asks You to Goad Pierre," with the subhead: "Letters Can Force Action to Better Women Status," *The Vancouver Sun*, 11 Dec. 1970, 31; CP, "Status of Women Report: Women's Groups Support 'Flood the Mail' Tactic," *The Gazette* Montreal, 15 Dec. 1970, 33. For other reactions from female politicians, see CP (Nanaimo, BC), 'Senate Seat Should Be Based on Abilities,'" *The Edmonton Journal*, 9 Dec. 15. CP (Ottawa), "Senator Opposes Council Idea," *Toronto Daily Star*, 4 Feb. 1971; (no byline), "Says Report Has Encouraging Implications," *Daily Gleaner*, 9 Dec. 1970, 15. *Report of the Royal Commission*, 341. The Minister of Health and Welfare promised "urgent consideration," but this was not reflected in one headline. Ottawa Bureau, "Munro Promises 'Urgent' Action," *Toronto Daily Star*, 8 Dec. 1970, 1. See also, CP, "Women Must Wait for Cabinet Study," *The Ottawa Citizen*, 8 Dec. 1970, 1; Ben Tierney (SNS), "Parliamentary Debate Next: Govt. Is in No Hurry to Act on Abortion Change," *The Ottawa Citizen*, 10 Dec. 1970, 54. CP, "Maternity Leave under Govt. Study," *The Ottawa Citizen*, 10 Dec. 1970, 62. CP, "Status of Women Portfolio: PM Hints at Appointment," *The Ottawa Citizen*, 10 Dec. 1970, 49. Anthony Westell, "Parliament Groans under Load of Reports," in his "Ottawa in Perspective" column, *The Ottawa Journal*, 12 Dec. 1970, 7.

34 CP, "Recommendations Draw Mixed Canadian Reaction," *Quebec Chronicle Telegraph*, 8 Dec. 1970, 1. CP and staff, "Step Forward for Women Reaction to Commission Report," *The Ottawa Journal*, 8 Dec. 1970, 41, published as CP, "Status of Women: 'Only First Step towards Full Equality,'" *The Ottawa Citizen*, 8 Dec. 1970, 5; and CP, "First Step toward Equality," *Evening Telegram*, St. John's, 8 Dec. 1970, 1. The same story was published as "No Pigeon-Hole' for This Report—Women Vow," *The Chronicle-Herald*, Halifax, 8 Dec. 1970, 1; as CP, "Women Urged to Press Cause," *The Telegraph-Journal*, Saint John, 8 Dec. 1970, 1. See also, (no byline), "Women Urged to Keep Report from Stalling," *The Globe and Mail*, 8 Dec. 1970, 11.

35 Second versions of this story were published as CP, "Report Outdated Say Women," *The Calgary Herald*, 8 Dec. 1970, 1, 2; CP, "'Waste of Time,'" (Kreps), and "'Outstripped, Late and Also Outdated,'" (Sabia), *Daily Gleaner*, Fredericton, 8 Dec. 1970, 1; see also "Woman Who Began It Says Report Outdated," *The Tribune*, Winnipeg, 8 Dec. 1970, 1, 2; "Project Termed Outdated," *Winnipeg Free Press*, 8 Dec. 1970, 1, 11 and "Report on Women 'Already Outdated,'" *The Edmonton Journal*, 8 Dec. 1970, 10. The Kreps story in the *Star* ran as Jo Carson, "Feminists Criticize Report on Status of Women as

Upholding Status Quo," *The Globe and Mail*, 8 Dec. 1970, 15. There was one headline reference to the recommendation concerning a status of women council, which was mentioned in the first CP overview story. Susan Becker, CP, "Status of Women Report Urges Special Council," *The Leader-Post*, Regina, 7 Dec. 1970, 1, 4. See also editorial, "Women's Status" Needed Boost for 'Liberation,' *The Ottawa Citizen*, 8 Dec. 1970, 6.

36 (No byline), "Other Women's Groups Praise It: Militants Scoff at 'Crumbs' in 'Half-Hearted' Report," *Toronto Daily Star*, 8 Dec. 1970, 13. On MacGill, Margaret Weiers, "Women's Status Report 'Better than Expected,'" *Toronto Daily Star*, 18 Dec. 1970.

37 CP (Ottawa), "Union to Support Women's White Paper [sic] Recommendations," *The Gazette*, Montreal, 11 Dec. 1970, 31. See also, CP (Ottawa), "Women Get CLC Support," *The Edmonton Journal*, 9 Dec. 15.

38 CP, "Status of Women: 'Only First Step Towards Full Equality,'" *The Ottawa Citizen*, 8 Dec. 1970, 65, includes Stan Daniels. Others versions, such as *The Gazette* in Montreal, did not include Daniels' comments. CP, "Women's Groups Welcome Report, Press for Implementation," *The Gazette*, Montreal, 8 Dec. 1970, 7. CBC *Cross Country Checkup*, 13 Dec. 1970. *Report of the Royal Commission*, Recommendation #193, 215-16.

39 Kathy Hassard (editor), Ann Barling and Leslie Peterson, with banner headline, "Jeers, Cheers, Doubts Greet Status" and "Some Hopes Soar, Some Are Dashed," *The Vancouver Sun*, 8 Dec. 1970, 48 and 49. The competing *Province* played its reaction stories in a similar way. See "That Royal Commission Report Rates Cheers to Downright Ridicule," *The Province*, Vancouver, 9 Dec. 1970, 26. For other reactions, see Susan Purcell, "Marlene Dixon Says Report Not Complete," *The Montreal Star*, 9 Dec. 1970, 9; and Adrian Waller, "Action Unlikely on Women's Rights," *The Gazette*, 9 Dec. 1970, 3. Eleanor Dunn, "Women Assess Status Recommendations," *The Ottawa Citizen*, 9 Dec. 1970, 41; and (no byline), "Two Sides Heard as Status Report Simmers," *The Ottawa Citizen*, 11 Dec. 1970, 37. Alixe Carter, "Status of Women News to Them," *The Ottawa Journal*, 8 Dec. 1970, 41. (No bylines) "Divorce Group Leader Says: Counsel, Too," and "Local Women Comment," *Winnipeg Free Press*, 8 Dec. 1970, 57. No bylines "Family Welfare Head Backs Day Care," "Not Far Enough—Women's Lib," and "Women's Views: Report Immediate," *The Star-Phoenix*, Saskatoon, 8 Dec. 1970, 3; and "Regina Women React to Report," *The Star-Phoenix*, Saskatoon, 9 Dec. 1970, 50; (no byline), "Women's Rights Upheld," *The Star-Phoenix*, Saskatoon, 11 Dec. 1970, 15. CP and staff, "Women Urged to Push for Equality," *The Albertan*, 8 Dec. 1970, 1, 2. Banner headline, "Miss N.B. Likes the Report," and two others (mistakenly transposed) Betty Anne Colp, "Women's Feelings," and Dave Gibbs, "Men: Good Points," *The Daily Gleaner*, Fredericton, 9 Dec. 1970, 15. Mary McKim, "Status of Women Report: Province's Briefs Stressed Points in Recommendations," *Evening Telegram*, St. John's, 9 Dec. 1970, 3.

40 (No byline), "In Calgary, the Report Is Just 'Ho-Hum,'" *The Calgary Herald*, 8 Dec. 1970, 61. See also, (no bylines), "Edmontonians Surveyed Support Many of Commission's Proposals," "Abortion Still Contentious," and "Maternity Leave Termed Excellent Idea," *The Edmonton Journal*, 8 Dec. 1970, 16; (no byline), "Guaranteed Annual Income, Not More Family Allowance," *The Edmonton Journal*, 8 Dec. 1970, 17; 9no byline), " Sex Education Seems like a Good Idea," *The Edmonton Journal*, 8 Dec. 1970, 18 and (no byline), "Labor Minister Reierson Endorses Many Commission Recommendations," *The Edmonton Journal*, 9 Dec. 1970, 5.

41 The women who married these men next were welcome to join its affiliate, "The Other Woman Organization." Jeff Carruthers, "Mini-Men's Lib Fights

Sex-Based Discrimination," *The Ottawa Journal*, 14 Dec. 1970, 3. See also Helen Worthington and Wendy Dey, "What Five Men Think about the Status of Women Report," *Toronto Daily Star*, 12 Dec. 1970, 77

42 CBC *Cross Country Checkup*, 13 Dec. 1970.

43 van Dijk sees novelty as the "tip of the iceberg of presupposition," meaning that certain cultural understandings must supersede any attempt to introduce new ideas. van Dijk, 121.

44 Editorial: "Not News, but a Blueprint for Action," *The Albertan*, Calgary. 9 Dec. 1970, 4. Editorial: "More Discrimination No Solution." 10 Dec. 1970, 6. See also editorial: "Discrimination in the Law," *The Globe and Mail*, 10 Dec. 1970.

45 My emphases. Editorial, "More Discrimination No Solution," The *London Free Press*, 10 Dec. 1970, 6.

46 Editorial, "Status of Women," *The Edmonton Journal*, 9 Dec. 1970, 4. Arthur Blakely, "Status Question: Women in Politics—Do They Really Want It?" *The Gazette*, 14 Dec. 1970, 7. See also, George Bain, "Box of Mixed Notes," *The Globe and Mail*, 29 Dec. 1970.

47 Betty Shapiro, "Status of Women: Pros and Cons of Report," *The Gazette*, 11 Dec. 1970, 28. See also Shapiro, "'Hooker's' Claim: Spurred by the Pill, Prostitution Flourishes," *The Gazette*, Moncton, 14 Dec. 1970, 28; and Leon Harris, "Panel Discusses Women's Lib: Stiffer Court Sentences Said Part of Women's Lot," *The Gazette*, Moncton, 14 Dec. 1970, 31. Editorial: "They'll Be Heard From," *The Telegraph-Journal*, Saint John, 12 Dec. 1970, 4. Editorial, "Equality of Opportunity," *The Gazette*, Montreal, 9 Dec. 1970, and Editorial: "A Moderate Plea for Women's Rights," *The Montreal Star*, 8 Dec. 1970, 8. On daycare, see editorial: "Female Equality," *The Calgary Herald*, 8 Dec. 1970, 4. For similar views, see editorial: "Vive la difference—with a Difference," *The Province*, Vancouver, 9 Dec. 1970, 4, and editorial: "The Status of Women," *Evening Telegram*, St. John's, 9 Dec. 1970, 6. On pensions, see W.A. Wilson, "Details Hobble Report," *The Montreal Star*, 8 Dec. 1970, 9, and Zoe Bieler, "The Question: Will Anything Be Done?" *The Montreal Star*, 9 Dec. 1970, 56.

48 Editorial: "It's a man's—and women's—world," *The Telegram*, Toronto, 8 Dec. 1970, 24. Editorial: "Women in Our Time," *The Ottawa Journal*, 8 Dec. 1970, 6.

49 Editorial, "Are They Serious?" *Daily Gleaner*, Fredericton, 8 Dec. 1970, 4. For a similar traditional view of women, see Elsie Ann Bullen, "This Was the Woman that Was—and Not Bad!" *The London Free Press*, 10 Dec. 1970, 6.

50 The Dominion Bureau of Statistics was the precursor of Statistics Canada. Doris Anderson, editorial, "The Report: Making Women More Equal," *Chatelaine*, Feb. 1971, 1.

51 Marney Roe, "Women Must Be Relentless in Pushing Implementation," *The London Free Press*, 9 Dec. 1970, 37, and "Report Clearly Shows Needs of Women," *The London Free Press*, 10 Dec. 1970, 1.

52 Leone Kirkwood, "Loud Echoes of Women's Lib in the Status Report?" *The Globe and Mail*, 11 Dec. 1970, 7. Margaret Weiers, "One Woman's View: Too Little...Too Late," *Toronto Daily Star*, 12 Dec. 1970, 77. *Report of the Royal Commission*, 328-31.

53 Margaret Weiers, "Too Little...Too Late," *Toronto Daily Star*, 12 Dec. 1970. (Ottawa bureau), "Status of Women Report Costs $4.50," *Toronto Daily Star*, 8 Dec. 1970, 13.

54 Dingman agreed with Humphrey, however, that a $500 child allowance might encourage overpopulation. Elizabeth Dingman, women's editor, "Revolutionary: Women Report Realistic." *The Telegram*, Toronto, 8 Dec. 1970, 58.

55 Anthony Westell, "Report More Explosive Than Any Terrorist's Time-Bomb," *Toronto Daily Star*, 8 Dec. 13; Freeman interview with Westell. See also Victor

Mackie (staff), "Report On Women 'Political Bomb,'" *Winnipeg Free Press*, 9 Dec. 1970, 63, and Don Peacock, "Don't Pooh-Pooh Report" in his "On the Other Hand," *The Albertan*, Calgary, 14 Dec. 1970, 10.

56 Douglas Fisher, "PM Key to Women's Status," *The Telegram*, Toronto, 8 Dec. 1970. James Eayrs, "Mothers of Confederation Arise!" *Toronto Daily Star*, 15 Dec. 1970.

57 Ray Guy's column, *Evening Telegram*, St. John's, 8 Dec. 1970, 2; see also negative comments of Dennis Braithwaite, "Flash! Women Are Dissatisfied," just below Fisher column, *The Telegram*, Toronto, 8 Dec. 1970; Fred Kennedy, "Women of Canada, Arise!" in his "I Write as I Please," column, *The Albertan*, Calgary, 9 Dec. 1970, 9; and James K. Nesbitt, untitled column, *The Vancouver Sun*, 9 Dec. 1970, 20; a quirkier approach from Eric Nicol, "We'll Overcome," *The Province*, Vancouver, 12 Dec. 1970, 31.

58 Norm Ibsen, "A Stamp of Approval for First-Class Males: How Come All the Great Linebackers Are Men?" *The London Free Press*, 11 Dec. 1970, 6; and Christopher Dafoe, untitled column, *The Vancouver Sun*, 9 Dec. 1970, 41.

59 Ting (Merle Tingley), *The London Free Press*, 10 Dec. 1970, 6.

60 Edd Uluschak, *The Edmonton Journal*, 9 Dec. 1970, 4. See also Tom Innes, "Royal Commission on the Status of Women Recommends RCMP Be Open to Women—News Item." *The Calgary Herald*, 8 Dec. 1970, 4.

61 John Collins, *The Gazette*, Montreal, 9 Dec. 9, 1970.

62 Robert Chambers, *The Chronicle Herald*, Halifax, 9 Dec. 1970, 6; Kuch, *Winnipeg Free Press*, 9 Dec. 1970, 45.

63 Freeman interview with Earle. Part of Earle's report was an interview with Grace MacInnis which might have been done by another colleague and inserted. CBC Radio News, 7 Dec. 1970, Tom Earle reporting for "The World at Six." Archival references suggest he filed another report for "From the Capitals," but it does not appear to be available. Susan Becker Davidson of CP remembers working at home half the night on the *Report* summary with her CP colleague, Lillian Newberry, while her journalist husband kept them fed and edited their copy. Freeman interviews with Becker Davidson. The Davey report was released the same week and received extensive coverage.

64 See, for example, *The Vancouver Sun*, starting 9 Dec. 1970 and continuing for several days.

65 Trudeau quote in Canada, House of Commons, *Debates*, 3rd Session, 28th Parliament, Vol. II, 13 Nov.–18 Dec., 1970, 1840. Hansard recorded Trudeau's earlier refusal to deal with the issue on pages 1787 and 1795 of the same volume. Trudeau's comment was recalled two years later in an article that surveyed Canada's MPs on the issue of women's rights. Erna Paris, "Women's Status—How the MPs Rate You," in *Chatelaine*, May 1972. Republished in Fraser, ed., *A Woman's Place*, 212.

66 Canada, House of Commons, *Debates*, 3rd Session, 28th Parliament, Vol. II, 7 Dec. 1970, 1787 and 1795; 8 Dec. 1970, 1840. Vol III, 3rd Session, 28th Parliament, 11 Jan. 1971, 2267.

67 See Barbara Frum's critique of the male political structure in Frum, "Why There Are So Few Women in Ottawa," *Chatelaine*, Oct. 1971, republished in Fraser ed., *A Woman's Place*, 208-11.

68 Yardley Jones, *The Telegram*, Toronto, 24 Feb., 1971.

69 *The Telegram*, Toronto, 8 Dec. 1970, 40.

Conclusion

1 Hardt and Brennan, "Communication and the Question of History." See also Ehrlich, "Using 'Ritual' to Study Journalism."

2 Ericson, Baranek and Chan, *Negotiating Control: A Study of News Sources* and *Visualizing Deviance: A Study of News Organization*; also, *Representing Order*.
3 van Dijk, *News as Discourse*.
4 Jansen, "'The Future Is Not What It Used to Be.'" van Zoonen, "Feminist Perspectives on the Media." Henry, "Changing Media History through Women's History," in Creedon, (ed.), *Women in Mass Communication*. Robinson, "Monopolies of Knowledge in Canadian Communications Studies."
5 Meyers, "Fracturing Women."
6 Meyers, "Fracturing Women"; Tuchman, "The Symbolic Annihilation of Women" in Tuchman et al., (eds.), *Hearth and Home*; Barker-Plummer, "News as a Political Resource"; and Ashley and Olson, "Constructing Reality." For a Canadian comparison, see Stone, "Getting the Message Out."
7 Douglas, *Where the Girls Are*; and Korinek, *Roughing It in Suburbia*.
8 Byerly, "News, Feminism and the Dialectics of Gender Relations."
9 Gill, "REAL Women and the Press"; Goddu, "Powerless, Public-Spirited Women."
10 Tuchman, "Making News," Chapter 7; Cantor, "Where are the Women in Public Broadcasting?" in Tuchman et al., *Hearth and Home*, 78-89; Morris, "Newspapers and the New Feminists: Black Out as Social Control?" and "The Public Definition of a Social Movement. Douglas, *Where the Girls Are*, Chapters 7 and 8.
11 Meyerowitz, "Beyond the Feminine Mystique." She cites Friedan, *The Feminine Mystique*. Korinek, "Roughing It in Suburbia"; Freeman interview with Anderson. Anderson, *Rebel Daughter*, Chapters 10 and 11.
12 Hackett and Zhao, *Sustaining Democracy?*, 7. MacDougall, *Newsroom Problems and Policies*, Chapters 1, 2 and 6; Tuchman, *Making News*, Chapter 8; CBC, *Journalistic Policy*.
13 Mindich, *Just the Facts*, 5-6.
14 For a current example of scholarly inquiry, see Durham, "On the Relevance of Standpoint Epistemology to the Practice of Journalism."
15 Hall, "The Determination of News Photographs," in Cohen and Young (eds.), *The Manufacture of News*; Langer, "The Structure and Ideology of the 'Other News' on Television." Barthes, "Myth Today."
16 Canadian Corrections Association, Brief #398. Emerging research was apparent in papers presented at the annual meeting of the Canadian Historical Association, Ottawa, June 1998. They included Korinek, "'Don't Let Your Girlfriends Ruin Your Marriage': Lesbian Imagery in *Chatelaine* Magazine 1950-1969"; Brownlie, "Crimes of Passion: Lesbians and Lesbianism in Canadian Prisons, 1960-1995"; and Gary Kinsman with Patrizia Gentile, "Gay Community Formation and Non-Cooperation with the National Security Campaigns in Ottawa, 1955-1970." Freeman interview with Bird.
17 Strutt and Hissey, "Feminisms and Balance," 61-74.
18 Durham, "On the Relevance of Standpoint Epistemology to the Practice of Journalism."
19 Benedict, *Virgin or Vamp*.
20 Michele Landsberg, "Investing in Young Kids Its Own Reward," *The Toronto Star*, 13 June 1998, L1.
21 Julia S. O'Connor, "Employment Equality Strategies," in Tremblay and Andrew, (eds.), *Women and Political Representation in Canada*. Armstrong and Armstrong, *The Double Ghetto*, 86-90. Governments are restoring spending to some programs, but politicians and businesses still focus on deficit reduction as desirable.
22 Stalker and Prentice, (eds.), *The Illusion of Inclusion*.

Bibliography

Archival Sources

National Archives of Canada (NAC)

Aitken, Kate Papers. MG 30 D 206.
Bird, Florence Bayard Papers. MG 31 D 63.
Flaherty, Dorothy Eva and John F. Papers. MG 31 K 25.
Long, Elizabeth Papers, MG 30 E 366.
MacGill, Elsie Gregory Papers. MG 31 K7.
McEnaney, Marjorie Papers. MG 30 E 342.
Media Club of Canada Papers (Canadian Women's Press Club). MG 28, I 232.
Royal Commission on the Status of Women in Canada. RG 33/89.
Vanier Institute of the Family Papers. MG 28 I Vol. 117, Box 20, "Learning for Family Living Project."

Public Archives of Nova Scotia (PANS)

Family Papers, Lane Collection. MG 1 Vols. 535 - 539.

Audio Visual Material

National Archives of Canada

Bird, Florence, audio interviews by Jean Bruce. NAC ISN #163393, Oct. 1980; and by Peter Stursberg, NAC ISN #163396. 23 June 1976.
Clark Davey Collection, NAC 1996-473-23.
CBC TV, National News audio recordings
- 68041600 (A/C 2300 25895). 16 Apr. 1968.
- 680417-00 (A/C 2300 25946). 17 Apr. 1968.
- 680422-00 (2300A/C 26110). 22 Apr. 1968.
- 680503-00 Access 0120 on Reel #26578. 3 May 1968.
- 680603-00 on Reel #27850. 3 June 1968.
CBC TV News Filmpacks (miscellaneous clips)
- Master 8208-1089 Aired 1968-04-18. ISN 178817.
- Master 8208-1000 Aired 1968-06-05. ISN 178303.

- Master 8208-0999 Aired 1968-06-06. ISN 178299.
- CAN #108 V4 8401 064 AND V1 8401 0129. 17 Apr. 1968.
- CAN #268 V1 8502 001. 2 June 1968.
- CAN #271 V1 8502 002. 3 June 1968.
- CAN #277 V1 8502 0025. 4 June 1968.
- CAN #280 and #281 V1 8502 0039. 5 June 1968.
- CAN #282 V1 8502 0039. 6 and 7 June 1968.
- CAN #284 V1 8502 0040. 7 June 1968.

Take 30
- 680312, Print Master 765, 12 Mar. 1968.
- 680422, Print Master 751, 22 Apr. 1968.
- 680506, Print Master 751, 6 May 1968.
- 680603, Print Master 717, 3 June 1968.
- 680617, Print Master 716, 17 June 1968.
- 680917, Print Master 778, 17 Sept. 1968.
- 680923, Print Master 775, 23 Sept. 1968.
- 681008, Print Master 945, 8 Oct. 1968.
- 681205, Print Master 725, 12 Dec. 1968.
- IDCISN: 100222, 1970-12-08, 8 Dec. 1970.
- 701006, Print Master 726, 6 Oct. 1970.
- 701022, Print Master 771, 22 Oct. 1970.
- 71012, Print Master 511, 12 Oct. 1970.
- 710122, Print Master 771, 22 Jan. 1971.

The Day It Is. CBLT Toronto, VI-8401-016, 1968-06-06 (6 June 1968).
The Way It Is. CBC VI 8402-0044, ISN #9183, 1968-04-21 (21 Apr. 1968).
Update. CBC VI-8412-072(2). ISN 98323. Aired 70-12-12.
Weekend. CBC Kine Collection, Kine Prt #23356, accession #84-74, 24 Jan. 1970.

Royal Commission on the Status of Women in Canada: audio tape recordings of public hearings, numbers C9902 to C10009.

Canadian Broadcasting Corporation, Radio Archives, Toronto

CBC Matinee
- 680419-8 on 681216-2. 19 Apr. 1968.
- 680425-6 on #680425-3. 25 Apr. 1968.
- 680426-7 on #681216-3. 26 Apr. 1968.
- 680502-6. 2 May 1968.
- 680503-8 on # 81216-4. 3 May 1968.
- 680603-10 on #681216-5. 3 June 1968.
- 680607-12 on #681216-6. 7 June 1968.
- 680614-10 on #681216-7. 14 June 1968.
- 680909-7. 9 Sept. 1968.
- 680910-10. 10 Sept. 1968.
- 680920-3 on #680920-2. 20 Sept. 1968.
- 681004-10 and 681004-11. 4 Oct. 1968.

CBC Radio News, Direct Reports
- 670509-0. May 9, 1967.
- 680417-0(2). 17 Apr. 1968.

- 680422-0(2). 22 Apr. 1968.
- 680423-0(2). 23 Apr. 1968.
- 680426-0(2). 26 Apr. 1968.
- 680430-0(2). 30 Apr. 1968.
- 680501-0(2). 1 May 1968.
- 680529-0(2). 29 May 1968.
- 680530-0(2). 30 May 1968.
- 680531-0(2). 31 May 1968.
- 680603-0(2). 3 June 1968.
- 680604-0(2). 4 June 1968.
- 680611-0(2). 11 June 1968.
- 680910-0(2). 10 Sept. 1968.
- 680912-0(2). 12 Sept. 1968.
- 681001-0(2). 1 Oct. 1968.
- 6810040(2). 4 Oct. 1968.
- 7012070(1). 7 Dec. 1970.
- 701208-0(2). 8 Dec. 1970.

CBC Radio News, The World at Six
- 670130-0(1) on Digital Tape #890915-11(12). 30 Jan. 1967.
- 670203-0(1). 3 Feb. 1967.
- 6705090(2). 9 May 1967.
- 680416-0(1). 16 Apr. 1968.
- 680502-0(1). 2 May 1968.
- 680503-0(1). 3 May 1968.
- 680529-0(1). 29 May 1968.
- 680611-0(1). 11 June 1968.
- 681001-0(1). 30 Sept. and 1 Oct. 1968.
- 681002(1) on #681002-4. 2 Oct. 1968.
- 70-1207-0(1). 7 Dec. 1970.

Cross Country Checkup, #701213-4. 13 Dec. 1970.

Canadian Broadcasting Corporation, Television Archives, Toronto Newsmagazine, 670328, 28 Mar. 1967.

Public Archives of Nova Scotia (PANS)

Film and Sound Division, Ar. 2265-2268, 2279, Carrie M. Best interviewed by unidentified man, recorded c.1970.

Film and Sound Division, FSG1 CBHT Film Collection, S 2126, *Around Town with Abbie Lane*, Monday 27 Oct. 1958.

Reading Private Collection

Original stories by Elinor Reading.

Reid Private Collection

Cartoons by Ed Reid.

Ed Reid interviewed by Jim Millican, CFWH Whitehorse, Yukon, 7 Aug. 1968.

RCSW hearing in Calgary, 22 Apr. 1968, morning session, audio tape #2, recorded as a sound track for *Take 30*.

Daily Newspapers 1966-1971

The Albertan, Calgary, AB.
The Calgary Herald, AB.
Charlottetown Guardian/Patriot, PEI.
Chronicle-Herald/Mail Star, Halifax, NS.
Chronicle Telegraph, Quebec City, QC.
Daily Gleaner, Fredericton, NB.
Daily Times/Colonist, Victoria, BC.
The Edmonton Journal, AB.
Evening Telegram, St. John's, NF.
The Gazette, Montreal, QC.
The Globe and Mail, Toronto, ON.
The Leader-Post, Regina, SK.
Lethbridge Herald, AB.
The London/Evening Free Press, ON.
Moncton Daily Times/Transcript, NB.
The Montreal Star, QC.
The Ottawa Citizen, ON.
The Ottawa Journal, ON.
The Province, Vancouver, BC.
Red Deer Advocate, AB.
The Star-Phoenix, Saskatoon, SK.
The Telegram, Toronto, ON.
Telegraph-Journal/Evening Times-Globe, St. John, NB.
Toronto Daily Star, ON.
The Tribune, Winnipeg, MB.
The Vancouver Sun, BC.
Winnipeg Free Press, MB.

Weekly Newspapers

News of the North, Yellowknife, NWT, 1968.

Magazines 1966-1971

Chatelaine
Maclean's
Saturday Night
Star Weekly
Weekend Magazine

Selected Articles from NAC RCSW, Vols. 40-45, 1967-1970

Newspapers

Aurora Banner, ON.
Belleville Daily Intelligencer, ON.
Brandon Sun, MB.
Brantford Expositor, ON.

The BC Catholic.
Brockville Recorder and Times, ON.
Brooks Bulletin, AB.
Calgary North Hill News, AB.
Chatham Daily News, ON.
Claresholm Local Press, AB.
Daily News, St. John's, NF.
Daily Times and Conservator, Brampton, ON.
Dauphin Herald, MB.
Elora Express, ON.
The Financial Post, Toronto, ON.
Guelph Daily Mercury, ON.
Kamloops Daily Sentinel, BC.
Kelowna Daily Courier, BC.
Kitchener-Waterloo Record, ON.
Medicine Hat News, AB.
Moose Jaw Times-Herald, SK.
Nelson Daily News, BC.
Niagara Falls Review, ON.
The Ottawa Times Weekly, ON.
Owen Sound Sun-Times, ON.
Pembroke Observer, ON.
Penticton Herald, BC.
Pictou Advocate, NS.
Portage Leader, Portage La Prairie, MB.
Port Arthur News Chronicle, ON.
Prince Albert Herald, SK.
Prince George Citizen, BC.
Prince Rupert Daily News, BC.
Recorder and Times, Brockville, ON.
St. Catharines Standard, ON.
St. Thomas Times-Journal, ON.
Sarnia Observer, ON.
Sault Ste. Marie Star, ON.
The Sherbrooke Record, QC.
Simcoe Reformer, ON.
Southeaster Times, Ottawa, ON.
The Spectator, Hamilton, ON.
The Standard-Freeholder, Cornwall, ON.
The Sudbury Star, Sudbury, ON.
The Sunday Bulletin, Philadelphia, PA.
The Sunday Reporter, Aylmer, QC.
Sussex Kings County Record, NB.
Vankleek Hill East Ontario Review, ON.
The Waterloo Chronicle, ON.
Welland-Port Colborne Tribune, ON.
Western Star, Corner Brook, NF.
The Whig-Standard, Kingston, ON.
The Windsor Star, ON.

The Whitehorse Star, YT.
The Yukon News, Whitehorse, YT.

Periodicals

The Canadian Magazine.
CBC Times, Toronto.
The Family Herald.
Time Magazine (Canadian edition).
Toronto Life, August 1968.
Canadian Labour, February 1967.
The Labour Statesman.
New Democrat.
The Register, Kingston, ON.
The Ryersonian. Toronto, ON.
The United Church Observer.
Western Catholic Reporter.

Interviews

Conducted by Barbara M. Freeman

Anderson, Doris. Toronto, ON. 21 Dec. 1992.
Arnopoulos, Sheila. Montreal, QC. 4 Apr. 1996.
Barron, Sid. Coombs, BC. 20 Feb. 1995.
Bégin, Monique Ottawa, ON. 21 June 1995.
Bird, Florence. Ottawa, ON. 18 Nov. 1992; subsequent telephone communica-
     tions on 21 Apr. 1994; 18 and 20 July 1994.
Bruce, Jean. 19 Jan. 1996.
Clarkson, Adrienne. Toronto, ON. 1 Mar. 1993.
Cochrane, Jean Sharp. Toronto, ON. 17 Aug. 1995.
Creighton, Judy. Toronto, ON. 17 Aug. 1995.
Crittenden, Yvonne. Toronto, ON. 25 Sept. 1995.
Davidson, Susan Becker. Ottawa, ON. By telephone, 15 Dec. 1995.
Dunn, Eleanor. Ottawa, ON. 8 July 1994.
Earle, Tom. Ottawa, ON. 8 May 1996.
Forbes, Sandy (aka Sandra Came). Chatsworth, NSW Australia, by electronic
     mail. 17 and 18 June 1996.
Gillen, Mollie. Toronto, ON. By telephone, and a letter from Gillen the same
     date. 26 Oct. 1995.
Gordon, Donald, Jr. Waterloo, ON. By telephone. 27 June 1996.
Hazel, Kathryn Keate. London, ON. 27 July 1995.
Henripin, Jacques. Montreal, QC. 5 June 1995.
Kerrigan, Angela Burke. Knowlton, QC. 27 Aug. 1995.
Lange, Lola. White Rock, BC. 25 Feb. 1995.
Lapointe, Jeanne. Quebec City, QC. Aug. 1995.
MacDougall, Fraser. Ottawa, ON. By telephone, 17 July 1996.
McIntosh, Lynne Higgins. Toronto, ON. 25 Sept. 1995.
McKim, Mary. Halifax, NS. 12 Nov. 1994.
Norris, Len. Langley, BC. 25 Feb. 1995.
Ogilvie, Doris. Fredericton, NB. By telephone, 26 Nov. 1995.

Patterson, Pat. Toronto, ON. 15 Oct. 1993.
Reading, Elinor. Toronto, ON. 17 Aug. 1995.
Reid Family. Toronto, ON. 9 Nov. 1995.
Robb, Dodi. Toronto, ON. 17 May 1993.
Sabia, Laura. Toronto, ON. 17 May 1993.
Sarty, Glenn. Ottawa, ON. 18 Oct. 1994.
Scott, Gail. Ottawa, ON. 8 May 1996.
Siggins, Maggie. Montreal, QC. 26 Aug. 1995.
Soles, Paul. Toronto, ON. 17 Oct. 1993.
Speirs, Rosemary. Ottawa, ON. 15 Dec. 1992.
Stewart, William. Montreal, QC. 27 Aug. 1995.
Weiers, Margaret. Toronto, ON. 18 Aug. 1995.
Westell, Anthony. Toronto, ON. 9 Nov. 1995.

Print Sources

Adams, Mary Louise. *The Trouble with Normal: Postwar Youth and the Making of Heterosexuality*. Toronto: University of Toronto Press 1997.

Adamson, Nancy. "Feminists, Libbers, Lefties and Radicals: The Emergence of the Women's Liberation Movement." In Parr, ed. *A Diversity of Women*.

_____, Linda Briskin, and Margaret McPhail. *Feminists Organizing for Change: The Contemporary Women's Movement in Canada*. Toronto: Oxford University Press, 1988.

Albota, Robert. "Dan McArthur's Concept of Objectivity and His Struggle to Defend the Integrity of the CBC News Service 1940-1945." MA thesis, Carleton University, Ottawa, 1988.

Allan, Stuart. "(En)gendering the Truth: Politics of News Discourse." In Carter, Brandston and Allan, eds. *News, Gender and Power*.

Anderson, Doris. *Rebel Daughter: An Autobiography*, Toronto: Key Porter Books, 1996.

Anderson, Kathryn et al. "Beginning Where We Are: Feminist Methodology in Oral History." *Oral History Review*: 15 (Sept. 1989), 103-27.

Andrew, Caroline and Sandra Rodgers, eds. *Women and the Canadian State/Les Femmes et l'État canadien*. Montreal and Kingston: McGill-Queen's University Press, 1997.

Andrews, Margaret W. "Attitudes in Canadian Women's History." *Journal of Canadian Studies* 12, 4 (Summer 1977): 69-78.

Annunziato, Frank R. "Collective Bargaining: A Foundation for Workers' Rights." In Brasch, ed, *With Just Cause*.

Armstrong, Pat, and Hugh Armstrong. *The Double Ghetto: Canadian Women and Their Segregated Work*, 3rd ed., Toronto: McClelland and Stewart, 1994.

Armstrong, Pat, Jacqueline Choinière, and Elaine Day. *Vital Signs: Canadian Nursing in Transition*. Toronto: Garamond Press, 1993.

Arnold, Gladys. *One Woman's War: A Canadian Reporter with the Free French*. Toronto: Lorimer, 1987.

Arnup, Katherine. *Education for Motherhood: Advice for Mothers in Twentieth Century Canada*. Toronto: University of Toronto Press, 1994.

Arnup, Katherine, Andrée Lévèsque, and Ruth Roach Pierson, eds. *Delivering Motherhood: Maternal Ideologies and Practices in the 19th and 20th Centuries*. London and New York: Routledge, 1989.

Arscott, Jane. "Twenty-Five Years and Sixty-Five Minutes after the Royal Commission on the Status of Women." *International Journal of Canadian Studies/Revue internationale d'etudes canadiennes* 11 (Spring/Printemps 1995): 33-58.

_____. "'More Women.' The RCSW and Political Representation, 1970." In Tremblay and Andrew, eds. *Women and Political Representation in Canada.*

_____. "'A Job Well Begun'...Representation, Electoral Reform and Women." In Gingras, ed. *Gender and Politics in Contemporary Canada.*

_____. "Canadian Women and 'Second-Class' Citizenship, 1970." A paper presented at the annual meeting of the Canadian Political Science Association, Brock University, St. Catharines, Ontario, 4 June 1996.

Ashley, Laura, and Beth Olson. "Constructing Reality: Print Media's Framing of the Women's Movement, 1966-1986. *Journalism and Mass Communication Quarterly* 75, 2 (Summer 1998): 263-77.

Axelrod, Paul, and John G. Reid, eds. *Youth, University and Canadian Society: Essays in the Social History of Higher Education.* Montreal and Kingston: McGill-Queen's University Press, 1989.

Backhouse, Constance, and David H. Flaherty, eds. *Challenging Times: The Women's Movement in Canada and the United States.* Montreal and Kingston: McGill-Queen's University Press, 1992.

Bagdikian, Ben H. *The Media Monopoly.* 3rd ed. Boston: Beacon Press, 1990.

Baker, Maureen, et al. *Families: Changing Trends in Canada.* Toronto: McGraw Hill Ryerson, 1990.

Bakker, Isabella. "The Political Economy of Gender." In Clement and Williams, eds. *The New Canadian Political Economy.*

Barker-Plummer, Bernadette. "News as a Political Resource: Media Strategies and Political Identity in the U.S. Women's Movement, 1966-1975." *Critical Studies in Mass Communication* 12 (1995): 306-24.

Barnouw, Erik. *Tube of Plenty: The Evolution of American Television.* 2nd rev. ed. New York: Oxford University Press, 1990.

Barthes, Roland. "Myth Today," In Sontag, ed. *A Barthes Reader.*

Bashevkin, Sylvia. *Toeing the Lines: Women and Party Politics in English Canada.* Toronto: Oxford University Press, 1993.

Beaujot, Roderic P. and Kevin McQuillan. "The Social Effects of Demographic Change: Canada 1851-1981." *Journal of Canadian Studies* 21, 1 (Spring 1989): 57-69.

Bégin, Monique. "The Royal Commission on the Status of Women in Canada: Twenty Years Later." In Backhouse and Flaherty, eds. *Challenging Times.*

Benedict, Helen. *Virgin or Vamp: How the Press Covers Sex Crimes.* London: Oxford University Press, 1992.

Beniger, James R. *The Control Revolution: Technological and Economic Origins of the Information Society.* Cambridge, MA: Harvard University Press, 1986.

Bennett, James R. *Control of the Media in the United States: An Annotated Bibliography.* New York: Garland, 1992.

Bennett, Judith M. "Feminism and History." *Gender and History* 1, 3 (Autumn 1989): 251-72.

Berkhofer, Jr., Robert F. "A New Context for a New American Studies?" *American Quarterly* 41 (1989): 588-613.

Best, Carrie M. *That Lonesome Road.* Halifax: Clarion, 1977.

Beynon, Francis Marion. *Aleta Dey*, Introduction by Anne Hicks. London: Virago, 1988.

Bird, Florence. *Anne Francis: An Autobiography*. Toronto: Clark, Irwin, 1974.

_____. Introduction, *Ottawa Law Review* 22 (1990).

Bird, Roger. *The End of News*. Toronto: Irwin Publishing, 1997.

Bird, S. Elizabeth, and Robert W. Dardenne. "Myth, Chronicle and Story. Exploring the Narrative Qualities of News." In Carey, ed., *Media, Myths and Narratives*.

Black, Naomi. "The Canadian Women's Movement: The Second Wave," in Burt et al., eds. *Changing Patterns*.

Blake, Raymond B., and Jeff Keshen, eds. *Social Welfare Policy in Canada: Historical Readings*. Toronto: Copp Clark, 1995.

Bland, M. Susan. "Henriettta the Homemaker and Rosie the Riveter: Images of Women in Advertising in *Maclean's* Magazine, 1939-1950." *Atlantis* 8, 2 (Spring 1983).

Boyd, Monica. "Canadian Attitudes towards Women: Thirty Years of Change." Ottawa: Labour Canada Women's Bureau, 1984.

Bothwell, Robert, Ian Drummond, and John English. *Canada since 1945*. 2nd ed., Toronto: University of Toronto Press, 1989.

Bourne, Paula, ed. *Women's Paid and Unpaid Work: Historical and Contemporary Perspectives*. Toronto: New Hogtown Press, 1985.

_____. "Women, Law and the Justice System." In Pierson et al. *Canadian Women's Issues*.

Bradbury, Bettina. "Women's History and Working Class History." *Labour/le travail* 19 (Spring 1987): 23-43.

Bradley, Patricia. "Media Leaders and Personal Ideology: Margaret Cousins and the Women's Service Magazines." *Journalism History* 21, 2 (Summer 1995): 79-87.

_____. "Mass Communication and the Shaping of US Feminism." In Carter, Brandston and Allan, eds. *News, Gender and Power*.

Brandt, Gail Cuthbert. "'Pigeon-Holed and Forgotten': The Work of the Subcommittee on the Post-War Problems of Women, 1943." *Histoire Sociale/Social History* 15, 29 (March-May 1982): 239-59.

_____. "Postmodern Patchwork: Some Recent Trends in the Writing of Women's History in Canada." *Canadian Historical Review*, Special Issue on Women's History 72, 4 (December 1991): 441-70.

Brantlinger, Patrick. *Crusoe's Footprints: Cultural Studies in Britain and America*. New York and London: Routledge, 1990.

Brasch, Walter M. *With Just Cause: Unionization of the American Journalist*. Lanham, MD.: University Press of America, 1991.

Bristow, Peggy et al., eds. *"We're Rooted Here and They Can't Pull Us Up": Essays in African Canadian Women's History*. Toronto: University of Toronto Press, 1994.

Brownlie, Robin. "Crimes of Passion: Lesbians and Lesbianism in Canadian Prisons." A paper presented at the annual meeting of the Canadian Historical Association, Ottawa, June 1998.

Brownmiller, Susan. *Femininity*. New York: Fawcett Columbine, 1984.

Bruce, Jean. "Women in CBC Radio Talks and Current Affairs." Canadian Oral History Association *Journal* 5, 1 (1981-82): 7-18.

_____. "A Study of Eskimo Women in the Keewatin Region of the Northwest Territories," March 1968. Unpublished study, RCSW, Vol. 25, Microfilm C-6798.

Burgess, Marilyn, and Gail Guthrie Valaskakis. *Indian Princesses and Cowgirls: Stereotypes from the Frontier.* Montréal: OBORO 1992.

Burnet, Jean, ed. *Looking into My Sister's Eyes: An Exploration in Women's History.* Toronto: Multicultural History Society of Ontario, 1986.

Burr, Christina. *Spreading the Light: Work and Labour Reform in Late-Nineteenth Century Canada.* Toronto: University of Toronto Press, 1999.

Burt, Sandra, Lorraine Code and Lindsay Dorney, eds. *Changing Patterns: Women in Canada.* Toronto: McClelland and Stewart, 1990.

Burt, Sandra B. "Changing Patterns of Public Policy," In Burt et al., eds. *Changing Patterns.*

_____. "Gender and Public Policy. Making Some Differences in Ottawa." In Gingras, ed. *Gender and Politics in Contemporary Canada.*

Butler M., and W. Paisley. *Women and the Mass Media.* New York: Human Sciences Press, 1980.

Byerly, Carolyn M. "News, Feminism and the Dialectics of Gender Relations." In Meyers, ed. *Mediated Women.*

Campbell, D'Ann. *Women at War with America: Private Lives in a Patriotic Era.* Cambridge, Mass.: Harvard University Press, 1984.

Campbell, Maria. *Halfbreed.* Toronto: McClelland and Stewart, 1973.

Canada. House of Commons, 3rd Session, 28th Parliament. *Debates.* vols. II and III.

Canadian Broadcasting Corporation (CBC). *Journalistic Policy.* Ottawa: Canadian Broadcasting Corporation, 1982.

_____. *CBC News Style Book.* Ottawa: Canadian Broadcasting Corporation, 1971.

Canadian Women's Studies (Summer/Fall 1986). Two issues on women's history.

Cancian, Francesca M., and Bonnie L. Ross. "Mass Media and the Women's Movement: 1900-1977." *The Journal of Applied Behavioral Science* 17, 1 (1981): 9-25.

Cardinal, Harold. *The Unjust Society: The Tragedy of Canada's Indians.* Edmonton: Hurtig Publishers, 1969.

Carey, James. *Communication as Culture.* Boston: Unwin Hyman, 1989.

_____. ed. *Media, Myths and Narratives. Television and the Press.* Sage Annual Reviews of Communication Research, vol. 15. Newbury Park: Sage, 1988.

Carriere, Gabrielle. *Careers For Women in Canada.* Toronto: J.M. Dent and Sons, 1946.

Carter, Alice. "Ottawa War Report on the Battle of the Sexes." CWPC *Newspacket,* April 1970, 5, 6.

Carter, Cynthia, Gill Brandston, and Stuart Allan, eds. *News, Gender and Power.* London: Routledge 1998.

Castellano, Michelle Brant, and Janice Hill. "First Nations Women: Reclaiming Our Responsibilities." In Parr, ed., *A Diversity of Women.*

Castro, Ginette. *American Feminism: A Contemporary History.* Trans. Elizabeth Loverde-Bagwell. Introduction by Kathleen Barry. New York and London: New York University Press, 1990.

Cavanaugh, Catherine Anne, and R. R. Warne. *Standing on New Ground: Women in Alberta.* Edmonton: University of Alberta Press, 1993.

Cebotarev, E.A. (Nora). "From Domesticity to the Public Sphere: Farm Women, 1945-86." In Parr, ed. *A Diversity of Women.*

Chafe, William. *The Unfinished Journey: America Since World War II.* New York and Oxford: Oxford University Press, 1986.

Chalus, Elaine H. "From Friedan to Feminism: Gender and Change at the University of Alberta, 1960-1970." In Cavanaugh and Warne, eds. *Standing on New Ground.*

Clement, Wallace. *The Canadian Corporate Elite: An Analysis of Economic Power.* The Carleton Library Series, no. 89, Toronto: McClelland and Stewart, 1975.

Clio Collective. *Quebec Women: A History.* Trans. Roger Gannon and Rosalind Gill. Toronto: The Women's Press, 1987.

Code, Lorraine. "Feminist Theory." In Burt et al., eds., *Changing Patterns.*

_____. "The Tyranny of Stereotypes." In Storrie, ed. *Women, Isolation and Bonding.*

Cohen, Marjorie Griffin. "The Canadian Women's Movement." In Pierson, Bourne and Masters, *Canadian Women's Issues,* vol. 1.

Cohen, S., and J. Young, eds. *The Manufacture of News: Social Problems, Deviance and the Mass Media.* London: Constable, 1981.

Coleman, William D. *The Independence Movement in Quebec, 1945-1980.* Toronto: University of Toronto Press, 1984.

Connelly, M. Patricia, and Pat Armstrong, eds. *Feminism in Action: Studies in Political Economy.* Toronto: Canadian Scholars' Press, 1992.

Conrad, Margaret. "'Not a Feminist, But...': The Political Career of Ellen Louks Fairclough, Canada's First Female Federal Cabinet Minister." *Journal of Canadian Studies* 31, 2 (Été 1996 Summer): 5-28.

Cook, Ramsay. *The Maple Leaf Forever: Essays on Nationalism and Politics in Canada.* Toronto: Macmillan, 1970.

Costain, Anne N. *Inviting Women's Rebellion: A Political Process Interpretation of the Women's Movement.* Baltimore and London: Johns Hopkins University Press, 1992.

Cott, Nancy F. *The Grounding of Modern Feminism.* New Haven and London: Yale University Press, 1987.

Cowan, Ruth Schwartz. *More Work for Mother: The Ironies of Household Tech- nology from the Open Hearth to the Microwave.* New York: Basic Books, 1983.

CP Style Book: A Guide for Writers and Filing Editors. Toronto: Canadian Press, 1968; 1974.

Crean, Susan. *Newsworthy: The Lives of Media Women.* Toronto: Stoddart, 1985.

Creedon, Pamela, ed. *Women in Mass Communication.* 2nd ed. Newbury Park: Sage, 1992.

_____. "The Challenge of Revisioning Gender Values." In P. Creedon, ed. *Women in Mass Communication.*

Crowley, Terry. "Did Canada Miss the Enlightenment? Women and Human Rights Before World War II." A paper presented at the annual meeting of the Canadian Historical Association, Congress of the Social Sciences and Humanities, Sherbrooke, Québec, June 1999.

Crittenden, Danielle. *What Our Mothers Didn't Tell Us: Why Happiness Eludes the Modern Woman.* New York: Simon and Schuster, 1999.

Crnkovich, Mary, ed. *"Gossip": A Spoken History of Women in the North.* Ottawa: Canadian Arctic Resources Committee, 1990.

Cruikshank, Julie. *Life Lived like a Story: Life Stories of Three Native Yukon Elders*. Lincoln: University of Nebraska Press, 1990.

Cumming, Carman. *Sketches fron a Young Country: The Images of Grip Magazine*. Toronto: University of Toronto Press, 1997.

Cumming, Judith. "The Report of the Royal Commission on the Status of Women: A Liberal Feminist Analysis." MA thesis, Carleton University, Ottawa, 1991.

Curran, James, and Michael Gurevitch, eds. *Mass Media and Society*. London: Edward Arnold, 1991.

Czitrom, Daniel J. *Media and the American Mind from Morse to McLuhan*. Chapel Hill: University of North Carolina Press, 1982.

Dahlgren, Peter and Colin Sparks, eds. *Communication and Citizenship: Journalism and the Public Sphere in the New Media Age*. London and New York: Routledge, 1991.

Daumier, Honoré. *Intellectuelles (Bas Bleus) et Femmes Socialistes*. Paris: Editions Vilo Paris, 1974.

Dauphin, Cecile et al. "Women's Culture and Women's Power: An Attempt at Historiography." *Journal of Women's History* 1, 1 (Spring 1989).

Davis, Natalie Zemon. *Society and Culture in Early Modern France*. Stanford, CA: Stanford University Press, 1975.

De Beauvoir, Simone. *The Second Sex*. Trans. and ed. by H.M. Parsley. Vintage Books, New York: Random House, 1974.

DeBrou, David, and Aileen Moffatt, eds. *"Other" Voices: Historical Essays on Saskatchewan Women*. Regina: Canadian Plains Research Centre, University of Regina, 1995.

Degler, Carl N. *At Odds: Women and the Family in America from the Revolution to the Present*. New York and Oxford: Oxford University Press, 1980.

D'Emilio, John, and Estelle B. Freedman. *Intimate Matters: A History of Sexuality in America*. New York: Harper & Row, 1988.

Dempsey, Lotta. *No Life for a Lady*. Markham, ON: Paperjacks, 1977.

Denning, Michael. "'The Special American Conditions': Marxism and American Studies." *American Quarterly* 38 (1986): 356-80.

Desbarats, Peter, and Terry Mosher (Aislin). *The Hecklers*. Toronto: McClelland and Stewart, 1979.

Descarries-Belanger, Francine, and Shirley Roy. "The Women's Movement and Its Currents of Thought." Trans. Jennifer Beeman. The CRIAW Papers, No. 26. Ottawa: Canadian Research Institute for the Advancement of Women, 1991.

De Valk, Alphonse. *Morality and Law in Canadian Politics: The Abortion Controversy*. Dorval, Montreal: Palm, 1974.

Dickason, Olive Patricia. *Canada's First Nations: A History of Founding Peoples from Earliest Times*. Norman: University of Oklahoma Press, 1992.

Donovan, Josephine. *Feminist Theory: The Intellectual Traditions of American Feminism*. New York: Continuum, 1991.

Douglas, Susan J. *Where the Girls Are: Growing Up Female with the Mass Media*. New York: Random House-Times Books, 1994, 1995.

Downie, Jill. *A Passionate Pen: The Life and Times of Faith Fenton*. Toronto: HarperCollins, 1996.

Dubinsky, Karen, and Lynne Marks. "Beyond Purity. A Response to Sangster." *left history* 3, 2 (Fall 1995), 4, 1 (Spring 1996): 205-20.

DuBois, Ellen Carol and Vicki L. Ruiz, eds. *Unequal Sisters: A Multicultural Reader in US Women's History*. New York, Routledge, 1990.

Dumont, Micheline. "The Origins of the Women's Movement in Quebec." In Backhouse and Flaherty, eds. *Challenging Times*.

Durham, Meenakshi Gigi. "On the Relevance of Standpoint Epistemology to the Practice of Journalism: The Case for 'Strong Objectivity.'" *Communication Theory* 8, 2 (May 1998): 117-40.

Eaman, Ross. *Channels of Influence: CBC Audience Research and the Canadian Public*. Toronto: University of Toronto Press, 1994.

Echols, Alice. *Daring to Be Bad: Radical Feminism in America, 1967-1975*. Minneappolis: University of Minnesota Press, 1989.

Edwards, Julia. *Women of the World: The Great Foreign Correspondents*. New York: Ballantine-Ivy Books, 1988.

Ehrlich, Matthew C. "Using 'Ritual' to Study Journalism." *Journal of Communication Inquiry* 20, 2 (Fall 1996): 3-17.

Elkin, Frederick. "Family Life Education in the Media of Mass Communication." The Vanier Institute of the Family (Sept. 1970).

Epstein, Laurily Keir. *Women and the News*. New York: Hastings House, 1978.

Ericson, Richard V., Patricia M. Baranek and Janet B. L. Chan. *Visualizing Deviance: A Study of News Organization*. Toronto: University of Toronto Press, 1987.

_____. *Negotiating Control: A Study of News Sources*. Toronto: University of Toronto Press, 1989.

_____. *Representing Order: Crime, Law and Justice in the News Media*. Toronto: University of Toronto Press, 1991.

Errington, Jane. "Pioneers and Suffragists." In Burt et al., eds. *Changing Patterns*.

Evans, Sara M. *Born for Liberty: A History of Women in America*. New York: Free Press, 1989.

_____. *Personal Politics: The Roots of Women's Liberation in the Civil Rights Movement and the New Left*. New York: Alfred A. Knopf, 1979.

_____. "The Women's Movement in the United States in the 1960s." In Backhouse and Flaherty, eds. *Challenging Times*.

Faderman, Lillian. *Odd Girls and Twighlight Lovers: Lesbianism in Twentieth Century America*. New York: Columbia University Press, 1991.

Fedler, Fred, Arlen Carey, and Jim Counts. "Journalism's Status in Academia: A Candidate for Elimination?" *Journalism and Mass Communication Educator* 53, 2 (Summer 1998).

Ferguson, M. *Forever Feminine. Women's Magazines and the Cult of Femininity*. London: Heineman 1983.

Fetherling, Douglas. *The Rise of the Canadian Newspaper*. Toronto: Oxford University Press, 1990.

Findlay, Sue. "Facing the State: The Politics of the Women's Movement Reconsidered:" In Maroney and Luxton, eds. *Feminism and Political Economy*.

Finkel, Alvin. "'Even the Little Children Cooperated: Family Strategies, Childcare Discourse and Social Welfare Debates, 1945-1975." *Labour/le travail* 36 (Fall 1995): 91-118.

Fishman, Mark. *Manufacturing the News*. Austin: University of Texas Press, 1980.

Fleras, Augie. "Beyond the Mosaic, Minorities and the Media in a Multi-racial/Multicultural Society." In Singer, ed., *Communications in Canadian Society.*

Ford, Anne Rochon. *A Path Not Strewn with Roses: 100 Years of Women at the University of Toronto, 1884-1984.* Toronto: University of Toronto Press, 1985.

Forestell, Diane G. "The Necessity of Sacrifice for the Nation at War: Women's Labour Force Participation 1939-1946." *Histoire Sociale/Social History* 22, 44 (November 1989): 333-48.

Frances, David. *The Imaginary Indian: The Image of the Indian in Canadian Culture.* Vancouver: Arsenal Pulp Press, 1992.

Franzen, Monika and Nancy Ethiel, comps. *Make Way! 200 Years of American Women in Cartoons.* Chicago: Chicago Review Press, 1988.

Fraser, Sylvia, ed. *A Woman's Place: Seventy Years of* Chatelaine *Magazine.* Introduction by Rona Maynard. Toronto: Key Porter Books, 1997.

Freeman, Barbara M. *Kit's Kingdom: The Journalism of Kathleen Blake Coleman.* Women's Experience Series, No. 1, Ottawa: Carleton University Press, 1989.

_____. "Mother and Son: Gender, Class and War Propaganda in Canada, 1939-1945." *American Journalism,* Special issue: The Media and World War II, 12, 3 (Summer 1995): 260-75.

Frideres, James S. *Native Peoples In Canada: Contemporary Conflicts.* 4th ed. Scarborough, ON: Prentice Hall, 1993.

_____. "The Royal Commission on Aboriginal Peoples: The Route to Self-Government." *Canadian Journal of Native Studies* 16, 2: 247-66.

Friedan, Betty. *The Feminine Mystique.* Laurel Books, New York: Dell Publishing. 1984.

Frontiers (Spring and Fall 1983). Special issues on Oral History.

Galtung, John, and Mari Ruge. "Structuring and Selecting News." In Cohen and Young, eds. *The Manufacture of News.*

Gans, Herbert J. *Deciding What's News.* New York: Vintage Books, 1979.

Gatlin, Rochelle. *American Women Since 1945.* Jackson and London: University Press of Mississippi, 1987.

Geiger, Susan. "What's So Feminist about Women's Oral History?" *Journal of Women's History* 2, 1 (Spring 1990): 169-82.

Gill, Donna. "REAL Women and the Press: An Ideological Alliance of Convenience." *Canadian Journal of Communication* 14, 3 (1989): 1-16.

Gillett, Margaret. *We Walked Very Warily: A History of Women at McGill.* Montreal: Eden Press Women's Publications, 1981.

Gingras, Francois-Pierre, ed. *Gender and Politics in Contemporary Canada.* Toronto: Oxford University Press.

_____. "Daily Male Delivery: Women and Politics in the Daily Newspapers." In Gingras, ed. *Gender and Politics in Contemporary Canada.*

Gitlin, Todd. *The Sixties: Years of Hope, Days of Rage.* New York: Bantam Books, 1987.

_____. *The Whole World Is Watching.* Berkeley, CA: University of California Press, 1980.

Gluck, Sherna Berger, and Daphne Patai, eds. *Women's Words: The Feminist Practice of Oral History.* New York and London: Routledge, 1991.

Goddu, Jennu. "'Powerless, Public-Spirited Women,' 'Angry Feminists,' and 'The Muffin Lobby': Newspaper and Magazine Coverage of Three National

Women's Groups from 1980 to 1995." *Canadian Journal of Communication*, 24 (1999): 105-26.

Gordon, Linda. *Heroes of Their Own Lives: The Politics and History of Family Violence*. New York: Viking, 1988.

Gorham, Deborah. "Flora MacDonald Denison, Canadian Feminist." In L. Kealey, ed. *A Not Unreasonable Claim: Women and Reform in Canada, 1880s-1920s*. Toronto: Canadian Women's Educational Press, 1979.

_____. "English Militancy and the Canadian Suffrage Movement." *Atlantis*, 1, 1 (Fall 1975): 83-112.

Grant, George. *Lament for A Nation: The Defeat of Canadian Nationalism*. Toronto: McClelland and Stewart 1965. Carleton Library Series #50. Ottawa: Carleton University Press, 1989.

Grewe-Partsch, M., and Gertude Joch Robinson. *Women, Communication and Careers*. New York: K. G. Saur, 1980.

Griffiths, N.E.S. *The Splendid Vision: Centennial History of the National Council of Women of Canada*. Ottawa: Carleton University Press, 1993.

Grindstaff, Carl F., and G. Edward Ebanks. "Vasectomy: Canada's Newest Family Planning Method." In Schlesinger, ed. *Family Planning in Canada*.

Hackett, Robert A., and Yuezhi Zhao. *Sustaining Democracy? Journalism and the Politics of Objectivity*. Toronto: Garamond, 1998.

_____, and Richard Gruneau. With Donald Gutstein, Timothy A. Gibson and NewsWatch Canada. *The Missing News: Filters and Blind Spots in Canada's Press*. Ottawa and Aurora, ON: Canadian Centre for Policy Alternatives/Garamond Press, 1999.

Haig, Kennethe M. *Brave Harvest: The Life Story of E. Cora Hind*. Toronto: Thomas Allen, 1945.

Hall, Stuart. "The Determination of News Photographs." In Cohen and Young, eds. *The Manufacture of News*.

Hamilton, John David. *Arctic Revolution: Social Change in the Northwest Territories, 1935-1994*. Toronto and Oxford: Dundurn Press, 1994.

Handleman, Mark. "Battered Women: Emergency Shelter and the Law." Windsor, ON: Community Law Program, University of Windsor, 1976.

Hardt, Hanno, and Bonnie Brennan. "Communication and the Question of History." *Communication Theory* 3, 2 (May 1993): 130-35.

Harris, Debbie Wise. "Colonizing Mohawk Women: Representations of Women in Mainstream Media." *Resources for Feminist Research* 20, 1 & 2 (1991): 15-20.

Hartmann, Susan M. *The Home Front and Beyond: American Women in the 1940s*. Boston: Twayne Publishers, 1982.

_____. *From Margin to Mainstream: American Women and Politics Since 1960*. New York: Alfred A. Knopf, 1989.

Heilbrun, Carolyn. "Non-Autobiographies of 'Privileged' Women: England and America." In *Life/Lines: Theorizing Women's Auto-biography*. Ed. Bella Brodzki and Celeste Schench. Ithaca and London: Cornell University Press, 1988.

Henry, Susan. "Changing Media History Through Women's History." In Creedon, ed. *Women in Mass Communication*.

Herman, Edward S., and Noam Chomsky. *Manufacturing Consent: The Political Economy of the Mass Media*. New York: Pantheon Books, 1988.

Holmes, Helen, and David Taras. *Seeing Ourselves: Media Power and Policy in Canada*. 1st ed. Toronto: Harcourt Brace Canada, 1992; 2nd ed., 1996.

Honey, Maureen. *Creating Rosie the Riveter: Class, Gender and Propaganda during World War II*. Amherst: University of Massachusetts Press, 1984.

hooks, bell. *Yearning: Race, Gender and Cultural Politics*. Toronto: Between the Lines, 1990.

Hosley, David H., and Gayle K. Yamada. *Hard News: Women in Broadcast Journalism*. New York and Westport, CT: Greenwood Press, 1987.

Hou, Charles, and Cynthia Hou. *Great Canadian Political Cartoons, 1820-1914*. Vancouver: Moody's Lookout Press, 1997.

Houston, Marsha. "The Politics of Difference: Race, Class and Women's Communication." In Rakow, ed. *Women Making Meaning*.

Humphreys, Nancy K. *American Women's Magazines: An Annotated Historical Guide*. New York: Garland, 1989.

Iacovetta, Franca. *Such Hardworking People: Italian Immigrants in Postwar Toronto*. Montreal and Kingston: McGill-Queen's University Press, 1992.

_____. "Remaking Their Lives: Women Immigrants, Survivors and Refugees." In Parr, ed., *A Diversity of Women*.

_____. "From Contadina to Worker: Southern Italian Immigrant Working Women in Toronto, 1947-62." In Burnet, ed. *Looking into My Sister's Eyes*.

Iacovetta, Franca, and Mariana Valverde, eds. *Gender Conflicts*. Toronto: University of Toronto Press, 1992.

_____, and Wendy Mitchinson, eds. *On the Case: Explorations in Social History*. Toronto: University of Toronto Press, 1998.

_____, and Linda Kealey. "Women's History, Gender History and Debating Dichotomies." *left history* 3, 2 (Fall 1995), 4, 1 (Spring 1996): 221-37.

Jackel, Susan. "Canadian Prairie Women's History: A Bibliographic Survey." CRIAW Papers, No. 14. Ottawa: Canadian Research Institute for the Advancement of Women, 1985.

Jamieson, Kathleen. *Indian Women and the Law in Canada: Citizens Minus*. Ottawa: Minister of Supply and Services Canada, 1978.

Jansen, Sue Curry. "'The Future Is Not What It Used to Be": Gender, History and Communication Studies." *Communication Theory* 3, 2 (May 1993): 136-47.

Jasen, Patricia. "In Pursuit of Human Values (Or Laugh When You Say That...): The Student Critique of the Arts Curriculum in the 1960s." In Axelrod and Reid, eds. *Youth, University and Canadian Society*.

Johnstone, J.W.C., Edward J. Slawski, and William W. Bowman. *The News People: A Sociological Portrait of American Journalists and Their Work*. Chicago: University of Illinois Press, 1976.

Jones, Jacqueline. *Labor of Love, Labor of Sorrow: Black Women, Work, and the Family from Slavery to the Present*. New York: Vantage, 1985.

Journal of Newspaper and Periodical History. 6, 2 (1990). Special Issue on Women and the Press.

Kaledin, Eugenia. *Mothers and More: American Women in the 1950s*. Boston: Twayne Publishers, 1987.

Kasirer, Nicholas, and Jean-Maurice Brisson. "The Married Woman in Ascendance, the Mother Country in Retreat: From Legal Colonialism to Legal Nationalism in Quebec Matrimonial Law Reform, 1886-1991." No.

93-5 in the *Canadian Legal History Project Working Paper Series*. Faculty of Law, University of Manitoba, 1993.

Kealey, Gregory S., ed. *Class, Gender, and Region: Essays in Canadian Historical Sociology*. St. John's Canadian Committee on Labour History, Memorial University of Newfoundland, 1988.

Kealey, Linda, and Joan Sangster, eds. *Beyond the Vote: Canadian Women and Politics*. Toronto: University of Toronto Press, 1989.

Keate, Stuart. *Paper Boy: The Memoirs of Stuart Keate*. Toronto: Clarke, Irwin, 1980.

Kelly, Joan. *Women, History and Theory: the Essays of Joan Kelly*. Chicago: University of Chicago Press, 1984.

Kerber, Linda K., Alice Kessler-Harris, and Kathryn Kish Sklar, eds. *US History as Women's History: New Feminist Essays*. Chapel Hill and London: University of North Carolina Press, 1995.

Kessler-Harris, Alice. *A Woman's Wage: Historical Meanings and Social Consequences*. Lexington: University Press of Kentucky, 1990.

Kimmel, Michael. *Manhood in America: A Cultural History*. New York: Free Press, 1996.

Kinnear, Mary. *In Subordination: Professional Women 1870-1970*. Montreal and Kingston: McGill-Queen's University Press, 1995.

Kinsman, Gary. *The Regulation of Desire: Sexuality in Canada*. Montreal: Black Rose Books, 1987.

Kinsman, Gary, with Patrizia Gentile, "Gay Community Formation and Non-Cooperation with the National Security Camaigns in Ottawa." Paper presented at the annual meeting of the Canadian Historical Association, Ottawa, June 1998.

Kobayashi, Audrey K., ed. *Women, Work and Place*. Montreal and Kingston: McGill-Queen's University Press, 1994.

Kobayashi, Audrey, Linda Peake, Hal Benenson, and Katie Pickles. "Introduction: Placing Women and Work." In *Women, Work and Place*.

Korinek, Valerie. "Roughing It in Suburbia: Reading *Chatelaine* Magazine 1950-1969." PhD dissertation, University of Toronto, 1996.

_____. "'Don't Let Your Girlfriend Ruin Your Marriage': Lesbian Imagery in *Chatelaine* Magazine, 1950-1969." *Journal of Canadian Studies* 33, 3 (automne 1998 fall): 83-109.

Kostash, Myrna. *Long Way from Home: The Story of the Sixties Generation in Canada*. Toronto: James Lorimer and Company, 1980.

Laframboise, Donna. *The Princess at the Window: A New Gender Morality*. Toronto: Penguin Books, 1996.

LaMarsh, Judy. *Memoirs of a Bird in a Gilded Cage*. Toronto: McClelland and Stewart, 1969.

Lamoureux, Diane. "Nationalism and Feminism in Quebec: An Impossible Attraction." In Maroney and Luxton, eds. *Feminism and Political Economy*.

Landes, Joan B. "The Public and the Private Sphere: A Feminist Reconsideration." In Johanna Meehan, ed. *Feminists Read Habermas*.

Lang, Marjory. *Women Who Made the News: Female Journalists in Canada, 1880-1945*. Montreal and Kingston: McGill-Queens University Press 1999.

_____. "Separate Entrances: The First Generation of Canadian Women Journalists." In *Re(Dis)covering Our Foremothers: Nineteenth Century Canadian*

Women Writers. Edited and with an introduction by Lorraine McMullen. Ottawa: University of Ottawa Press, 1989.

_____, and Linda Hale. "Women of the *World* and Other Dailies: The Lives and Times of Vancouver Newspaperwomen in the First Quarter of the Twentieth Century." *BC Studies* 85 (Spring 1990).

Langer, John. "The Structure and Ideology of the 'Other News' on Television." In Patricia Edgar, ed. *The News in Focus: The Journalism of Exception.* South Melbourne, Australia: Macmillan, 1980.

Laxer, James. "The Americanization of the Canadian Student Movement." In Lumsden, ed. *Close the 49th Parallel.*

Leavitt, Judith Walzer. *Brought to Bed: Childbearing in America 1750-1950.* New York: Oxford University Press, 1986.

Lerner, Gerda. "Reconceptualizing Differences among Women." *Journal of Women's History* 1, 3 (Winter 1990): 106-22.

_____. *The Creation of Patriarchy.* Vol. 1, *Women and History.* New York: Oxford University Press, 1986.

Lévèsque, Andrée. *Making and Breaking the Rules: Women in Quebec, 1919-1939.* Trans. of *La Norme et Les Deviantes* by Yvonne M. Klein. Toronto: McClelland and Stewart, 1994.

Lewis, Norah L., ed. *Dear Editor and Friends: Letters from Rural Women of the Northwest,* 1900-1920. Waterloo, ON: Wilfrid Laurier University Press, 1998.

Light, Beth, and Ruth Pierson, eds. *No Easy Road: Women in Canada, 1920s to 1960s.* Toronto: New Hogtown Press, 1988.

Linden-Ward, Blanche, and Carol Hurd Green. *Changing the Future: American Women in the 1960s.* New York: Twayne Publishers, 1993.

Lipsitz, George. *Class and Culture in Cold War America: "A Rainbow at Midnight."* New York: Prager, 1981.

_____. "Listening to Learn and Learning to Listen: Popular Culture, Cultural Theory and American Studies." *American Quarterly* 42 (1990): 615-36.

_____. "'This Ain't No Sideshow': Historians and Media Studies." *Critical Studies in Mass Communication,* 5 (1988): 147-61.

Little, Margaret Jane Hillyard. *"'No Car, No Radio, No Liquor Permit': The Moral Regulation of Single Mothers in Ontario, 1920-1997.* Toronto: Oxford University Press 1998.

Loo, Tina, and Lorna R. McLean, eds. *Historical Perspectives on Law and Society in Canada.* Toronto: Copp Clark Longman, 1994.

Lowe, Graham. *Women in the Administrative Revolution.* Toronto: University of Toronto Press, 1987.

Luker, Kristin. *Dubious Conceptions: The Politics of Teenage Pregnancy.* Cambridge, MA: Harvard University Press, 1996.

Lumsden, Ian, ed. *Close the 49th Parallel: The Americanization of Canada.* Toronto: University of Toronto Press, 1979.

Luxton, Meg. *More Than a Labour of Love: Three Generations of Women's Work in the Home.* Toronto: Women's Press, 1980.

Macdonald, Myra. *Representing Women: Myths of Femininity in the Popular Media.* London: Edward Arnold, 1995.

MacDougall, Curtis D. *Newsroom Problems and Policies.* New York: Dover Publications, 1963.

MacGill, Elsie Gregory. *My Mother the Judge*. Introduction by Naomi Black. Toronto: Peter Martin Associates, 1981.

MacLeod, Linda. "Wife Battering in Canada: The Vicious Circle." Ottawa: Canadian Advisory Council on the Status of Women, 1980.

Macpherson, Kay. *When in Doubt, Do Both: The Times of My Life*. Toronto: University of Toronto Press, 1994.

Mandell, Nancy, and Ann Duffy. *Reconstructing the Canadian Family: Feminist Perspectives*. Toronto and Vancouver: Butterworths, 1988.

Manji, Irshad. *Risking Utopia: On the Edge of a New Democracy*. Vancouver: Douglas & McIntyre, 1997.

Manoff, Karl, and Michael Schudson, eds. *Reading the News: A Pantheon Guide to Popular Culture*. New York: Pantheon, 1987.

Maroney, Heather Jon, and Meg Luxton, eds. *Feminism and Political Economy: Women's Work, Women's Struggles*. Toronto: Methuen, 1987.

Maroney, Heather Jon. "'Who Has the Baby?' Nationalism, Pronatalism and the Construction of a 'Demographic Crisis' in Quebec 1960-1988." In Connelly and Armstrong, eds. *Feminism in Action*.

Marsden, Lorna R. "Family Planning and Women's Rights in Canada." In Schlesinger, ed. *Family Planning in Canada*.

Marsden, Lorna R. and Joan E. Busby. "Feminist Influence through the Senate: The Case of Divorce, 1967." *Atlantis* 14, 2 (Spring, 1989): 72-80.

Marshall, Barbara L. "Communication as Politics: Feminist Print Media in English Canada." *Women's Studies International Forum* 18, 4 (1995): 463-74.

Martin, Michèle. With contributions by Graham Knight. *Communication and Mass Media: Culture, Domination, and Opposition*. Trans. by Benoît Ouellette. Scarborough: Prentice Hall, 1997.

Martineau, Barbara Halpern. "Before the Guerillières: Women's Films at the NFB during World War II." In Seth Feldman and Joyce Nelson eds., *Canadian Film Reader*. Toronto: Peter Martin, 1977.

Marzolf, Marion. *Up From the Footnote: A History of Women Journalists*. New York: Hastings House, 1977.

Matthews, Glenna. *"Just A Housewife": The Rise and Fall of Domesticity in America*. New York: Oxford University Press, 1987.

Matthews-Klein, Yvonne. "How They Saw Us: Images of Women in National Film Board Films of the 1940s and 1950s." *Atlantis* 4, 2 (Spring 1979): 20-33.

May, Elaine Tyler. *Homeward Bound: American Families in the Cold War Era*. New York: Basic Books, 1988.

McCormack, Thelma. "Politics and the Hidden Injuries of Gender: Feminism and the Making of the Welfare State." CRIAW Papers, No. 28. Ottawa: Canadian Research Institute for the Advancement of Women, 1991.

McEnaney, Marjorie Winspear. *Who Stole The Cakes?* Erin, ON: Boston Mills Press, 1981.

McKenzie, Judith. *Pauline Jewett: A Passion for Canada*. Montreal and Kingston: McGill-Queen's University Press, 1999.

McLaren, Angus and Arlene Tigar McLaren. *The Bedroom and the State: The Changing Practices and Politics of Contraception and Abortion in Canada, 1880-1980*. Toronto: McClelland and Stewart, 1986.

McLaren, Angus. "'Keep Your Seats and Face Facts': Western Canadian Women's Discussions of Birth Control in the 1920s." *Canadian Bulletin of Medical History* 8, 2 (1991).

McLaughlin, Lisa. "Gender, Privacy and Publicity in 'Media Event Space.'" In Carter, Brandston and Allan, eds. *News, Gender and Power.*

McNab, Miriam. "From the Bush to the Village to the City." In DeBrou and Moffatt, eds. *"Other" Voices.*

McQuail, Denis. *Mass Communication Theory: An Introduction.* 3rd ed. Sage: London, 1994.

McRoberts, Kenneth. *Quebec: Social Change and Political Crisis.* 3rd ed. Toronto: McClelland and Stewart, 1989.

Mead, Margaret. *A Way of Seeing.* New York: McCall, 1970.

_____. *Male and Female: A Study of the Sexes in a Changing World.* New York: Morrow, 1967.

Mead, Margaret, and Frances Bagley Kaplan, eds. *American Women: Report of the President's Commission on the Status of Women.* New York: Scribner's, 1965.

Meehan, Johanna, ed. *Feminists Read Habermas: Gendering the Subject of Discourse.* New York: Routledge 1995.

Meyer, J. et al. "Women in July Fourth Cartoons." *Journal of Communication* 30, 1: 21-30.

Meyerowitz, Joanne, ed. *Not June Cleaver: Women and Gender in Postwar America, 1945-60.* Philadelphia: University of Pennsylvania Press, 1994.

_____. "Beyond the Feminine Mystique: A Reassessment of Postwar Mass Culture, 1946-1958." *Journal of American History* (March 1993): 1455-82.

Meyers, Marian. "Reporters and Beats: The Making of Oppositional News." Critical Studies in Mass Communication 9 (1992): 75-90.

_____, ed. *Mediated Women. Representations in Popular Culture.* Cresshill, New Jersey: Hampton Press 1999.

_____. "Fracturing Women." In Meyers, ed. *Mediated Women.*

Milkman, Ruth. *Gender at Work: The Dynamics of Job Segregation by Sex during World War II.* Chicago: University of Chicago Press, 1987.

Miller, J.R. *Skyscrapers Hide the Heavens: A History of Indian-White Relations in Canada.* Rev. edition. Toronto: University of Toronto Press, 1991.

Millet, Kate. *Sexual Politics.* New York: Ballantine Books, 1970.

Mills, Kay. *A Place in the News: From the Women's Pages to the Front Page.* New York: University of Columbia Press, 1990.

Mindich, David T. Z. *Just the Facts: How "Objectivity" Came to Define American Journalism.* New York: New York University Press, 1998.

Molotch, Harvey L. "The News of Women and the Work of Men." In Tuchman et al., eds. *Hearth and Home.*

Morgan, Nicole. "The Equality Game: Women in the Federal Public Service, 1908-1987." Ottawa: Canadian Advisory Council on the Status of Women, 1988.

Morris, Cerise. "'Determination and Thoroughness': The Movement for a Royal Commission on the Status of Women in Canada." *Atlantis* (1981): 1-21.

_____. "'A Matter of Simple Justice': The Royal Commission on the Status of Women and Social Change in Canada." PhD dissertation, McGill University, Montreal, 1982.

Morris, Monica B. "Newspapers and the New Feminists: Black Out as Social Control?" *Journalism Quarterly* 50 (1973): 37-42.

_____. "The Public Definition of a Social Movement: Women's Liberation." *Sociology and Social Research* 57 (1974): 526-43.

Morris, Raymond N. *Behind the Jester's Mask: Canadian Editorial Cartoons about Dominant and Minority Groups, 1960-79.* Toronto: University of Toronto Press, 1989.

_____. *The Carnivalization of Politics: Quebec Cartoons on Relations with Canada, England, and France, 1960-1979.* Montreal, PQ: McGill-Queen's University Press, 1995.

Morton, Patricia. *Disfigured Images: The Historical Assault on Afro-American Women.* Westport, CT: Greenwood Press, 1991.

Moscovitch, Allan and Jim Albert, eds. *The "Benevolent" State: the Growth of Welfare in Canada.* Toronto: Garamond Press, 1987.

Mott, George Fox, and Others. *New Survey of Journalism.* College Outline Series. New York: Barnes and Noble College Outline Series, 1968.

Munson, Eve Stryker, and Catherine A. Warren, eds. *James Carey: A Critical Reader.* Minneapolis: University of Minnesota Press, 1997.

Muszynski, Alicja. *Cheap Wage Labour: Race and Gender in the Fisheries of British Columbia.* Montreal and Kingston: McGill-Queen's University Press, 1996.

Myers, Patricia A. "'A Noble Effort': The National Federation of Liberal Women of Canada, 1928-1973." In Kealey and Sangster, eds. *Beyond the Vote.*

Nett, Emily. *Canadian Families: Past and Present.* Toronto and Vancouver: Butterworths, 1988.

New Directions for Women, 13 (Mar-April 1984).

Nichols, Marjorie with Jane O'Hara. *Mark My Words: The Memoirs of a Very Political Reporter.* New York: Bantam Books, 1994.

Nielson, Doris. *New Worlds for Women.* Toronto: Progress Books, 1944.

O'Connor, Julia. "Employment Equality Strategies and Their Representation in the Political Process in Canada, 1970-1994." In Tremblay and Andrews, eds. *Women and Political Representation in Canada.*

Offen, Karen, Ruth Roach Pierson, and Jane Rendall, eds. *Writing Women's History: International Perspectives.* London: Macmillan, 1991.

Ohmer, Susan. "Female Spectatorship and Women's Magazines: Hollywood, Good Housekeeping and World War II." *Velvet Light Trap* 25, (1990): 53-68.

Osler, Andrew. *News: The Evolution of Journalism in Canada.* Toronto: Copp Clark Pitman, 1993.

Owram, Douglas. *Born at the Right Time: A History of the Baby Boom in Canada.* Toronto: University of Toronto Press, 1996.

Palmer, Bryan D., *Working Class Experience: The Rise and Reconstitution of Canadian Labour, 1800-1980.* Toronto and Vancouver: Butterworths, 1983.

Parr, Joy, ed. *A Diversity of Women: Ontario, 1945-1980.* Toronto: University of Toronto Press 1995.

_____. *The Gender of Breadwinners: Women, Men and Change in Two Industrial Towns, 1880-1950.* Toronto: University of Toronto Press, 1990.

Parr, Joy, and Gunilla Ekberg. "Mrs. Consumer and Mr. Keynes in Postwar Canada and Sweden." *Gender and History* 8, 2 (August 1996): 212-30.

Patterson, E. Palmer II. *The Canadian Indian: A History Since 1500.* Toronto: Collier Macmillan Canada, 1972.

Pedersen, Diana. *Changing Women, Changing History: a Bibliography of the History of Women in Canada*. Toronto: Green Dragon Press, 1992; 2nd ed. Ottawa: Carleton University Press, 1996.

Personal Narratives Group. *Interpreting Women's Lives: Feminist Theory and Personal Narratives*. Bloomington: Indiana University Press, 1989.

Pelrine, Eleanor Wright. *Abortion in Canada*. New Women Series. Toronto: New Press, 1971.

Petrie, Anne. *Gone to an Aunt's: Remembering Canada's Homes for Unwed Mothers*. Toronto: McClelland and Stewart, 1998.

Phelan, E.C., ed. *The Globe and Mail Style Book*, 3rd ed. Toronto: *The Globe and Mail*, 1963.

Pierson, Ruth Roach. *"They're Still Women after All": The Second World War and Canadian Womanhood*. Toronto: McClelland and Stewart, 1986.

Pierson, Ruth Roach, Marjorie Griffin Cohen, Paula Bourne, and Philinda Masters. *Canadian Women's Issues*, vol. 1. Toronto: Lorimer 1993; vol. 2, 1995.

_____. "Experience, Difference, Dominance and Voice in the Writing of Canadian Women's History." In Offen et al., *Writing Women's History*.

_____. "The Politics of the Body." In Pierson et al., *Canadian Women's Issues*.

Porter, John. *The Vertical Mosaic*. Toronto: University of Toronto Press, 1965.

Powell, Marion G. "Female Sterilization." In Schlesinger, ed. *Family Planning in Canada*.

Prentice, Alison. "Bluestockings, Feminists, or Women Workers? A Preliminary Look at Women's Early Employment at the University of Toronto." *Journal of the Canadian Historical Association*, New Series, 2 (1991): 231-61.

Prentice, Alison, Paula Bourne, Gail Cuthbert Brandt, Beth Light, Wendy Mitchinson and Naomi Black. *Canadian Women: A History*. 2nd ed. Toronto: Harcourt Brace Canada, 1996.

Prentice, Susan. "Workers, Mothers, Reds: Toronto's Postwar Daycare Fight." In Blake and Keshen, eds. *Social Welfare Policy in Canada*.

Raboy, Marc. *Missed Opportunities: The Story of Canada's Broadcasting Policy*. Montreal and Kingston: McGill-Queen's University Press, 1990.

Rakow, Lana, ed. *Women Making Meaning*. London and New York: Routledge, 1992.

Real, Michael. "Media Theory Contributions to an Understanding of American Mass Communications." In *American Quarterly* 32 (1980): 238-58.

Reid, Escott. *Radical Mandarin: The Memoirs of Escott Reid*. Toronto: University of Toronto Press, 1989.

Report of the Royal Commission on the Status of Women in Canada. Ottawa: Information Canada, 1970.

Report of the Special Senate Committee on Mass Media, vols. 1-3. Ottawa: Queen's Printer, 1970.

Report of the CBC Task Force on the Status of Women. Toronto: Canadian Broadcasting Corporation, 1975.

Resources for Feminist Research. 8, 2 (1979). Canadian Women's History Issue.

Rex, Kay. *No Daughter of Mine: The Women and History of the Canadian Women's Press Club, 1904-1971*. Toronto: Cedar Cave Books, 1995.

Riley, Denise. *"Am I That Name?" Feminism and Category of "Women" in History*. Minneapolis: University of Minnesota Press, 1988.

Roberts, Barbara. "'Why Do Women Do Nothing to End the War?': Canadian Feminist-Pacifists and the Great War." CRIAW Papers, No. 13, Ottawa: Canadian Research Institute for the Advancement of Women, 1985.

_____. "Women's Peace Activism in Canada." In Kealey and Sangster, *Beyond the Vote*.

Robinson, Gertrude J. "Monopolies of Knowledge in Canadian Communication Studies: The Case of Feminist Approaches." *Canadian Journal of Communication* 23 (1998): 65-72.

_____. "The Portrayal of Women Politicians in the Media: Political Implications." In Gingras, ed., *Gender and Politics in Contemporary Canada*.

_____. "Women Journalists in Canadian Dailies: A Social and Professional Minority Profile." Working Papers in Communications, Montreal: Program in Communications. McGill University, 1981.

_____. "The Future of Women in the Canadian Media." *McGill Journal of Education* XII, 1 (Spring 1977).

Robinson, Gertrude J., and Armande Saint-Jean. "Women's Participation in the Canadian News Media: Progress since the 1970s." Montreal: McGill University, Graduate Program in Communication, May 1997.

Roiphe, Katie. *The Morning After: Sex, Fear and Feminism on Campus.* Boston: Little Brown and Company 1993.

Rooke, Patricia T., and R.L. Schnell. "'An Idiot's Flowerbed': A Study of Charlotte Whitton's Feminist Thought, 1940-1951." In *Rethinking Canada: The Promise of Women's History.* Veronica Strong-Boag and Anita Claire Fellman, eds. Toronto: Copp Clark Pitman, 1986.

Rosen, Ruth. "The Feminist Generation Gap: Daughters of the Fifties and the Origins of Contemporary American Feminism." In Kerber et al. (eds.), *U.S. History as Women's History: New Feminist Essays.* Chapel Hill and London: University of North Carolina Press, 1995.

Rosenberg, Rosalind. *Beyond Separate Spheres: Intellectual Roots of Modern Feminism.* Yale University Press, 1982.

Ross, Andrew, ed. *No Respect: Intellectuals and Popular Culture.* New York: Routledge, 1989.

Ross, Ishbel. *Ladies of the Press: The Story of Women in Journalism by an Outsider.* New York and London: Harper and Brothers, 1936.

Rothman, Sheila. *Woman's Proper Place: A History of Changing Ideals and Practices 1870 to the Present.* New York: Basic Books, 1978.

Royce, Marion V. *The Effects of the War on the Life of Women.* Washington, DC: World's YWCA, 1945.

Rupp, Leila J. *Mobilizing Women for the War: German and American Propaganda, 1939-1945.* Princeton: Princeton University Press, 1978.

Rupp, Leila, and Verta Taylor. *Survival in the Doldrums: The American Womens' Rights Movement, 1945 to the 1960s.* New York: Oxford University Press, 1987.

Rutherford, Paul. *A Victorian Authority: The Daily Press in Late Nineteenth Century Canada.* Toronto: University of Toronto Press, 1982.

_____. *When Television Was Young: Prime Time Canada, 1952-1967.* Toronto: University of Toronto Press, 1990.

Ryan, Mary P. *Womanhood in American: From Colonial Times to the Present.* New York: New Viewpoints, 1975.

Sangster, Joan. *Dreams of Equality: Women on the Canadian Left, 1920-1950.* Toronto: McClelland and Stewart, 1989.

_____. "Beyond Dichotomies: Re-assessing Gender History and Women's History in Canada." *left history* 3, 1 (Spring/Summer 1995): 109-21.

_____. "Telling Our Stories: Feminist Debates and the Use of Oral History." *Women's History Review* 3, 1 (1994): 5-28.

_____. "Women Workers, Employment Policy and the State: The Establishment of the Ontario Women's Bureau, 1963-1970." *Labour/le travail* 36 (Fall 1995): 119-45.

_____. "Criminalizing the Colonized: Ontario Native Women Confront the Criminal Justice System, 1920-60. *The Canadian Historical Review* 80, 1 (March 1999): 32-60.

_____. "Doing Two Jobs." In Parr, ed. *A Diversity of Women.*

Schiller, D. *Objectivity and the News.* Philadelphia: University of Pennsylvania Press, 1981.

Schiller, Herbert. *Culture, Inc.: The Corporate Takeover of Public Expression.* Oxford and New York: Oxford University Press, 1989.

Schlesinger, Benjamin, ed. *Family Planning in Canada: A Source Book.* Toronto: University of Toronto Press, 1974.

Schudson, Michael. *Discovering the News: A Social History of American Newspapers.* New York: Basic Books, 1978.

_____. "Deadlines, Datelines and History." In Manoff and Schudson, eds. *Reading the News.*

_____. "The Sociology of News Production Revisited." In Curran and Gurevitch, eds. *Mass Media and Society.*

_____. "In All Fairness." *Media Studies Journal* (Spring/Summer 1998): 34-41.

Scott, Joan Wallach. *Gender and the Politics of History.* New York: Columbia University Press, 1988.

Sev'er, Aysan. *Women and Divorce in Canada: A Sociological Analysis.* Toronto: Canadian Scholars Press, 1992.

Sheppard, Alice. *Cartooning for Suffrage.* Introduced by Elizabeth Israels Perry. Albuquerque: University of New Mexico Press, 1994.

Silverman, Elaine Leslau. "Writing Canadian Women's History, 1970-1982: An Historiographical Analysis." *Canadian Historical Review* 63, 4 (December 19-82).

Simms, Glenda. "Beyond the White Veil." In Backhouse and Flaherty, eds. *Challenging Times.*

Singer, Benjamin, ed. *Communications in Canadian Society*, 3rd and 4th ed. Scarborough: Nelson Canada, 1991, 1995.

Sissons, John Howard. *Judge of the Far North.* Toronto: McClelland and Stewart, 1968.

Sklar, Kathryn Kish, and Thomas Dublin, eds. *Women and Power in American History.* Vol. II from 1870. New Jersey: Prentice Hall, 1991.

Smith-Rosenberg, Carroll. *Disorderly Conduct: Visions of Gender in Victorian America.* New York: Knopf 1985.

Snell, James. *In the Shadow of the Law: Divorce In Canada, 1900-1939.* Toronto: University of Toronto Press, 1991.

Sochen, June. *Enduring Values: Women in Popular Culture.* New York: Praeger, 1987.

Solomon, William S., and Robert W. McChesney, eds. *Ruthless Criticism: New Perspectives in U.S. Communication History*. Minneapolis and London: University of Minnesota Press, 1993.

Susan Sontag, ed. *A Barthes Reader*. New York: Hill and Wang, 1982.

Speers, Kimberly Marie. "The Royal Commission on the Status of Women: A Study of the Contradictions and Limitations of Liberalism and Liberal Feminism." MA thesis, Queen's University, Kingston, 1994.

Spigel, Lynn. *Make Room for TV: Television and the Family Ideal in Postwar America*. Chicago: University of Chicago Press, 1992.

Spigel, Lynn and Denise Mann, eds. *Private Screenings: Television and the Female Consumer*. Minneapolis: University of Minnesota Press, 1992.

Stalker, Jacqueline, and Susan Prentice, eds. *The Illusion of Inclusion: Women In Post-Secondary Education*. Halifax: Fernwood Publishing, 1998.

Stanley, Della. "The 1960s: The Illusions and Realities of Progress." In E. R. Forbes and D.A. Muise, *The Atlantic Provinces in Confederation*. Toronto and Fredericton, NB: University of Toronto Press/Acadiensis Press, 1993.

Stanley, Liz. "Recovering *Women* in History from Feminist Deconstruction- is- m." *Women's Studies International Forum* 13, 1/2 (1990): 151-57.

Staton, Pat, and Beth Light. *Speak with Their Own Voices: A Documentary History of the Federation of Women Teachers of Ontario and the Women Elementary Public School Teachers of Ontario*. Toronto: Federation of Women Teachers of Ontario, 1987.

Steinem, Gloria. *Outrageous Acts and Everyday Rebellions*. New York: Holt, 1983.

Steiner, Linda. "Body Language,: Gender in Journalism Textbooks." In Creedon, (ed.), *Women in Mass Communication*.

_____. "Newsroom Accounts of Power at Work." In Carter, Brandston and Allan, eds. *News, Gender and Power*.

Stewart, Lee. *Women Volunteer to Go to Prison: A History of the Elizabeth Fry Society of BC*. Victoria, BC: Orca Book Publishers, 1993.

Stone, Sharon D. "Getting the Message Out: Feminists, the Press and Violence against Women." *Canadian Review of Sociology and Anthropology* 30, 3 (1993): 377-400.

Storrie, Kathleen, ed. *Women, Isolation and Bonding*. Toronto: Methuen, 1987.

Strong-Boag, Veronica. *The New Day Recalled: Lives of Girls and Women in English-Canada, 1919-1939*. Markham, ON: Penguin Books, 1988.

_____. "Independent Women, Problematic Men: First and Second Wave Anti-Feminism in Canada from Goldwin Smith to Betty Steele." Histoire Sociale/Social History, 29, 57 (May 1996): 1-22.

_____. "Canada's Wage-Earning Wives and the Construction of the Middle Class, 1945-60." *Journal of Canadian Studies* 29, 2 (Autumn 1994): 5-25.

_____. "Home Dreams: Women and the Suburban Experiment in Canada, 1945-60." *Canadian Historical Review*, Special Issue on Women's History, 72, 4 (December 1991): 472-504.

_____. "Their Side of the Story." In Parr, ed. *A Diversity of Women*.

_____. "Discovering the Home: The Last 150 Years of Domestic Work in Canada." In Bourne, ed. *Women's Paid and Unpaid Work*.

Struthers, James. *The Limits of Affluence: Welfare in Ontario, 1920-1970*. Toronto: University of Toronto Press, 1994.

Strutt, Suzanne, and Lynne Hissey. "Feminisms and Balance." *Canadian Journal of Communication* 17 (1992): 61-74.

Sugiman, Pamela. *Labour's Dilemma: The Gender Politics of Auto Workers in Canada.* Toronto: University of Toronto Press, 1994.

Susman, Warren I., ed. *Culture as History.* New York: Pantheon, 1984.

Sutherland, Fraser. *The Monthly Epic: A History of Canadian Magazines, 1789 1989.* Toronto: Fitzhenry and Whiteside, 1988.

Taylor, Alison. "Window on the World: A History of Women in CBC Radio Talks and Public Affairs, 1936-1966." MA thesis, Carleton University, Ottawa, 1985.

Taylor, Georgina M. "'Should I Drown Myself Now or Later?' The Isolation of Rural Women in Saskatchewan and Their Participation in the Homemakers Clubs, the Farm Movement and the Co-operative Commonwealth Federation, 1910-1967." In Storrie, ed. *Women, Isolation and Bonding.*

Tilly, Louise, and Joan Wallach Scott. *Women, Work and Family.* New York: Holt, Rhinehart and Winston 1978; Methuen, 1987.

Timpson, Annis May. "Royal Commissions as Sites of Resistance: Women's Challenges on Child Care in the Royal Commission on the Status of Women." *International Journal of Canadian Studies/Revue internationale d'etudes canadiennes* 20 (Fall/automne 1999): 123-48.

Tippett, Maria. *Making Culture: English-Canadian Institutions and the Arts before the Massey Commission.* Toronto: University of Toronto Press, 1990.

Tobias, John L. "Protection, Civilization, Assimilation: An Outline History of Canada's Indian Policy." In Loo and McLean, eds. *Historical Perspectives on Law and Society in Canada.*

Tremblay, Manon and Caroline Andrew, eds. *Women and Political Representation in Canada.* Ottawa: University of Ottawa Press, 1998.

Trofimenkoff, Susan Mann. *The Dream of Nation: A Social and Intellectual History of Quebec.* Toronto: Gage, 1983.

_____. "Feminist Biography." *Atlantis* 10, 2 (Spring 1985): 1-9.

Tuchman, Gaye. *Making News: A Study in the Construction of Reality.* New York: Free Press, 1978.

_____. "The Symbolic Annihilation of Women." In Tuchman et al., eds., *Hearth and Home.*

Tuchman, Gaye, Arlene Kaplan Daniels, and James Benet, eds. *Hearth and Home: Images of Women in the Mass Media.* New York: Oxford University Press, 1978.

Ursel, Jane. *Private Lives, Public Policy: 100 Years of State Intervention in the Family.* Toronto: Women's Press, 1992.

Vallières, Pierre. *White Niggers of America.* Toronto: McClelland and Stewart, 1971.

Valverde, Mariana. "Poststructuralist Gender Historians: Are We Those Names?" *Labour/le Travail* 25 (Spring 1990): 227-36.

Vance, Carol S., ed. *Pleasure and Danger: Exploring Female Sexuality.* Routledge and Kegan Paul, 1984.

van Dijk, Teun A. *News as Discourse.* Hillsdale, NJ: Lawrence Erlbaum Associates, 1988.

Van Kirk, Sylvia. "What Has the Feminist Perspective Done for Canadian History?" In Ursula M. Franklin et al., eds. *Knowledge Reconsidered: A Feminist*

Overview. Ottawa: Canadian Research Institute for the Advancement of Women, 1984.

Van Steen, Marcus. "Freelance Writing in Canada." *Newspacket* 31, 2 (January 1969): 6.

Van Zoonen, Liesbet. *Feminist Media Studies*. London: Sage, 1994.

_____. "Feminist Perspectives on the Media." In Curran and Gurevitch, eds. *Mass Media and Society*.

_____. "'One of the Girls': The Changing Gender of Journalism." In Carter, Brandston and Allan, eds. *News, Gender and Power*.

Vickers, Jill. "The Intellectual Origins of the Women's Movement in Canada." In Backhouse and Flaherty, eds. *Challenging Times*.

Vipond, Mary. *Listening In: The First Decade of Canadian Broadcasting, 1922-1932*. Montreal and Kingston: McGill-Queen's University Press, 1992.

_____. *The Mass Media in Canada*. Toronto: Lorimer, 1989, 2000.

_____. "The Image of Women in Canadian Mass Circulating Magazines in the 1920's." In S. Trofimenkoff and A. Prentice, eds. *The Neglected Majority*, vol. 1. Toronto: McClelland and Stewart, 1981.

Vital Statistics, Preliminary Annual Reports, Statistics Canada, Cat. #84-0201, Ottawa, 1967-71.

Von Heyking, Amy. "Red Deer Women and the Roots of Feminism." *Alberta History* (Winter 1994): 14-27.

Wagner, Lilya. *Women War Correspondents of World War Two*. Westport, Conn: Greenwood Press, 1989.

Waller, Jane, and Michael Vaughan-Rees. *Women in Wartime: The Role of Women's Magazines, 1939-1945*. London: Macdonald and Co., 1987.

Walsh, Andrea S. *Women's Film and Female Experience, 1940-1950*. New York: Praeger, 1984.

Wandersee, Winnifred D. *On the Move: American Women in the 1970s*. Boston: Twayne Publishers, 1988.

Warner, Marina. *Monuments and Maidens*. London: Weidenfeld and Nicolson, 1985.

Wartella, Ellen, and D. Charles Whitney, eds. *Mass Communication Review Yearbook*, vol. 4, 1983.

Weaver, Sally. "First Nations Women and Government Policy, 1978-92: Discrimination and Conflict." In Burt et al., eds., *Changing Patterns*.

Weiers, Margaret. "Unions and Equal Pay." *Newspacket* 32, 1 (October 1969): 4, 5.

Weston, Mary Ann. *Native Americans in the News: Images of Indians in the Twentieth Century Press*. Westport, CT: Greenwood Press, 1996.

Williams, Alison M. "Canadian Urban Aboriginals: A Focus on Aboriginal Women in Toronto." *Canadian Journal of Native Studies* 17, 1 (1997): 75-101.

Williams, Toni. "Re-forming Women's Truth: A Critique of the Report of the Royal Commission on the Status of Women in Canada." *Ottawa Law Review* 22 (1990).

Williamson, Janice and Deborah Gorham, eds. *Up and Doing: Canadian Women and Peace*. Toronto: The Women's Press, 1989.

Wilson, S. J. *Women, Families and Work*. 3rd ed. Toronto: McGraw-Hill Ryerson, 1991.

_____. "The Changing Image of Women in Canadian Mass Circulating Magazines, 1930-1970. *Atlantis* 2, 2, Part 2 (Spring 1977): 33-44.

_____. "The Relationship between Mass Media Content and Social Change in Canada: An Examination of the Image of Women in Mass Circulating Canadian Magazines, 1930-1970. PhD dissertation, University of Toronto, 1977.

Wine, Jeri Dawn, and Janice L. Ristock, eds. *Women and Social Change: Feminist Activism in Canada*. Toronto: James Lorimer and Company 1991.

Winter, James. *Common Cents: Media Portrayal of the Gulf War and Other Events*. Montreal and New York: Black Rose Books, 1992.

Women's Studies International Forum 13, 1/2 (1990). Special Issue on British Feminine Histories.

Wright, Gwendolyn. *Building the Dream: A Social History of Housing in America*. Cambridge: MIT Press, 1983.

Index

aboriginal women, 2; conflict model and, 190, 199; economic concerns of, 4; education and, 193-94; lives of, 187, 189-90; media and, 87-88, 187-209, 222-23; in north, 199-208; representation of at RCSW hearings, 87-88; stereotypes of, 208, 246

aboriginals, in Canada, 189; compared with US Blacks and other minorities, 208; in prison, 192

abortion, 2, 165, 167, 168, 215-18

academic studies, of women's issues, 4

affirmative action, 111

alcohol, journalism and, 66-67, 70

analytical reporting, 46

anthropology, news and, 7-8

appearance, sexual double standard on women's, 2. *See also* femininity

Arnopoulos, Sheila, 50-51

bachelor tax, 136, 139-40

backlash against women's rights, 17-18

battered women. *See* spousal abuse

bias, editorial, media images and, 11; unconscious, 46

Bird, Florence, 3; bio of, 27; CBC and, 59; media images of, 77-78; role in coverage of RCSW, 27-28, 32-38

birth control 166, 167. *See also under* reproductive freedom

British Columbia, legislation on dis-

crimination against women, 106

broadcasting, women's programs in, 43

business, and economic barriers to married women, 124

camera crews, images of women and, 94

Canadian Women's Press Club, 42-43, 55-57

cartoons. *See* editorial cartoons

CBC, coverage of RCSW, 14-15; current affairs, 58-65; Florence Bird and, 59; *News*, 66-68; objectivity at, 65, 156; women in, 42, 59

censorship 93-94. *See also* objectivity

Chatelaine magazine, 57-58, 175-76. *See also* Speirs, Rosemary

childcare. *See* daycare

choice, meaning of 185-86. *See also under* reproductive freedom

church, reproductive freedom and, 168, 183-85; sexuality and, 168

Clarkson, Adrienne, 60, 62-63

class, mass communication studies and, 6

cognitive psychology, news and, 7-8

commercial press, 8

Commission. *See* Royal Commission on the Status of Women

Commissioners, 3, 27-28, 32-38, 59, 77-83, 213

Committee for the Equality of Women in Canada (CEWC), 25-27, 28